THE WORKS OF JONATHAN EDWARDS

VOLUME 3

John E. Smith, General Editor

PREVIOUSLY PUBLISHED

PAUL RAMSEY, ed., *Freedom of the Will*
JOHN E. SMITH, ed., *Religious Affectations*

JONATHAN EDWARDS

Original Sin

EDITED BY CLYDE A. HOLBROOK

PROFESSOR OF RELIGION, OBERLIN COLLEGE

New Haven and London

YALE UNIVERSITY PRESS, 1970

Library of Congress catalog card number: 57-2336

ISBN 0-300-01198-9

Designed by John O. C. McCrillis, set in Baskerville type, and printed in the United States of America by Vail-Ballou Press, Inc., Binghamton, N.Y. Distributed in Great Britain, Europe, Asia, and Africa by Yale University Press Ltd., London; in Canada by McGill University Press, Montreal; and in Latin America by Centro Interamericano de Libros Académicos, Mexico City.

THE

Great Chriſtian Doctrine

OF

ORIGINAL SIN

defended;

Evidences of it's *Truth* produced,

AND

Arguments to the *Contrary* anſwered.

Containing, in particular,

A Reply to the Objections and Arguings of Dr. JOHN TAYLOR, in his Book, Intitled, "The Scripture-Doctrine of *Original Sin* pro-"poſed to free and candid Examination, &c.

By the late Reverend and Learned

JONATHAN EDWARDS, A.M.

Preſident of the College of *New-Jerſey*.

MATTH. IX. 12. *They that be whole, need not a Phyſician; but they that are ſick.*

---Et hæc non tantum ad Peccatores referenda eſt; quia in omnibus Maledictionibus primi Hominis, omnes ejus Generationes conveniunt.--- R. SAL. JARCHI.

Propter Concupiſcentiam, innatam Cordi humano, dicitur, In Iniquitate genitus ſum; atque Senſus eſt, quod à Nativitate implantatum ſit Cordi humano *Jètzer harang*, Figmentum malum.--- ABEN-EZRA.

---- Ad Mores Natura recurrit
damnatos, fixa et mutari neſcia.---
---- Dociles imitandis
turpibus et pravis omnes ſumus.--- JUV.

BOSTON, NEW-ENGLAND:

Printed and Sold by S. KNEELAND, oppoſite to the Probate-Office in Queen-ſtreet. 1758.

CONTENTS

EDITOR'S INTRODUCTION

THE controversy over human depravity in the eighteenth century was no mere intramural squabble among theologians. It was an important phase of a revolution that was occurring in Western man's estimate of his nature and potentialities. Literature, philosophy, economic and political theory, as well as theology, were to feel the decisive impact of this revolution. The notion of man as a fundamentally rational, benevolently inclined individual was emerging as the unquestionable postulate for the expansionist mood of Western culture. But the doctrine of original sin marred this flattering image. It stood for everything the spirit of the Enlightenment detested. Theologians and philosophers, busy developing their systems in the clear light of reason, were convinced that "the idea of an original sin which is visited upon succeeding generations" was absolutely absurd and "an insult to the first laws of logic and ethics." [1]

Thus, when Edwards entered the lists as champion of the hated doctrine, he saw himself as not only defending a particular dogma, but also combating an increasingly dominant drift of opinion that had engulfed much of Europe and England and now, he felt, was encroaching dangerously upon America. The situation abroad had alarmed him for some time. As early as 1739, when he laid out the beginnings of his *History of the Work of Redemption,* he noted that Satan had been busy on the Continent opposing the Protestant Reformation. Socinianism, which held that "Christ was a mere man, and denied Christ's satisfactions, and most of the fundamental doctrines of the Christian religion," had gained a foothold in Poland, Germany, and Holland. Arminianism, although condemned at the Synod of Dort, had "spread and prevailed." [2] Worst of all, England, "the principal kingdom of the Reformation," was sliding into hetero-

1. E. Cassirer, *The Philosophy of the Enlightenment,* trans. F. C. A. Koelln and J. P. Pettigrove (Princeton, Princeton University Press, 1951), pp. 141, 159.
2. *The Works of President Edwards* (8 vols. Worcester, 1808–09, cited below as Worcester ed.), *2,* 304–5.

dox opinions, to the great detriment of evangelical interests. Since the reign of Charles I, the Church of England had largely succumbed to loose opinions, until its divines "are become almost universally Arminians." Deism also prevailed in many quarters, a movement not of heretics but of "professed infidels," who "deny that Christ was the Son of God and say that he was a mere cheat . . . and say that God has given mankind no other light to walk by but their own reason." Reading the news from England, Edwards felt that never had there been such an apostacy, such a scoffing and ridiculing of the Gospel. "The principles on which the power of godliness depends, are in great measure exploded." Not only had vital piety decayed, but those who support it are "commonly looked upon to be crack brained and beside their right mind." [3] However, ever hopeful that more heartening news might be forthcoming from Britain, Edwards asked his Scottish correspondent Reverend John Erskine in a letter of August 1748, to confirm some encouraging reports he had received on the religious life of the mother country. "I should be glad if you would inform me more particularly in your next, concerning this affair and what the present state of Infidelity in Great Britain is." [4]

One piece of news which Edwards already had received was enough to convince him further, if that were necessary, that evangelical Christianity in Britain was in an extremely parlous state. In the same letter to Erskine, he thanked his friend for the gift of John Taylor's books, including that author's treatise on original sin. Here laid out boldly was one of the most impressive and destructive criticisms of that doctrine which more than any other contradicted the Enlightenment view of man.

Clearly, Taylor was a figure to be reckoned with seriously. *The Scripture-Doctrine of Original Sin, Proposed to Free and Candid Examination* was a substantial treatise.[5] It bore the marks of thorough

3. Ibid., pp. 304–6, 311–12.

4. *The Works of President Edwards* (10 vols. New York, 1829–30, cited below as Dwight ed.), *1*, 252.

5. Taylor's major book will be referred to as *Scripture-Doctrine;* JE's treatise, as *Original Sin*. H. S. Smith contends the date of Taylor's publication is 1740 (*Changing Conceptions of Original Sin,* New York, Charles Scribner's Sons, 1955, p. 13); Perry Miller and Faust and Johnson hold to the traditional date of 1738 (Miller, *Jonathan Edwards,* New York, William Sloane Associates, 1949, p. 110; Clarence H. Faust and Thomas H. Johnson, *Jonathan Edwards, Representative Selections, with Introduction, Bibliography, and Note,* New York, American Book Co., 1935, p. lxvi).

scholarship and breathed an air of amiable open-mindedness, with its talk of plain reason, commonsense morality, and unperverted meanings of Scripture. So telling was its impact abroad that a story circulated as to its complete invulnerability. A Calvinist pastor in Northern Ireland, it was said, warned his flock against its pernicious teachings, calling it a "bad book and a dangerous book and an heretical book," but woefully conceding that it was unanswerable.[6] Several divines in England did not capitulate so easily. Isaac Watts came forth with his *Ruin and Recovery of Mankind* (1740), while David Jennings, in the same year, published *The Vindication of the Scripture Doctrine of Original Sin.*[7] Taylor paid his respects to both books in a lengthy Supplement appended to the second edition of 1741. The major portion of the Supplement bore down heavily, but respectfully, on Watts, while Jennings was casually dismissed with a few sharp lines on his method of conducting the controversy and his inconsistent reasoning. Watts in fact fared little better in defending the doctrine, his treatise, in the estimation of a modern interpreter, being "a study of hesitant Calvinism." [8] John Wesley also tried his hand at answering Taylor, but although an Arminian himself, he could not fit his analysis with complete conviction between the extremes of Calvinistic predestination and original sin on the one hand, and the too easygoing moralism of ultra-Arminianism on the other. In the meantime, Taylor's book went into a third edition, printed at Belfast, Ireland, and this was the edition that Edwards received from Erskine.

The stir which Taylor had created in England was not destined to remain long confined to that country. His views survived a transatlantic crossing and became securely lodged among the clergy of eastern Massachusetts, to the delight of some and the distress of others. The revolution of which Taylor was both a reflection and an agent

6. The original story appeared in a note in Taylor's *History of the Octagon Church, Norwich* (London, 1848), p. 27. Dwight retells another tale in which Taylor is described as having indiscreetly boasted that his book would never be answered. However, JE's reply to it was so devastating that Taylor's days were shortened by mortification! (Dwight ed., *1*, 613).

7. JE had heard of Jenning's answer to Taylor but claims never to have seen it "nor heard of its being in these American parts: so that, however sufficient it may be, it has been of no service to that purpose here" (Author's Preface, 1st ed., below, p. 102).

8. Roland N. Stromberg, *Religious Liberalism in Eighteenth Century England* (New York, Oxford University Press, 1954), p. 116.

had arrived with a vengeance, as the spirited pamphlet war in colonial New England soon proved.

1. *The New England Controversy on Original Sin*

The American soil upon which Taylor's views were to fall and germinate had been prepared before Arminianism or Pelagianism in any technical sense had been imported from England.[9] The mischief

9. JE's use of the term "Arminianism" has evoked considerable discussion. Ramsey refers to it as "a loose term for all forms of the complaint of the aggrieved moral nature against the harsh tenets of Calvinism" (*The Works of Jonathan Edwards,* New Haven, Yale University Press, 1957——, cited below as Yale ed., *1,* 3). Thomas Shafer calls the Arminianism which JE met "a native American variety of human self-sufficiency which expressed itself still within the forms of the Covenant theology" ("Jonathan Edwards and Justification by Faith," *Church History, 20* [1951], 55). F. A. Christie ("The Beginnings of Arminianism in New England," *Papers of the American Society of Church History,* Ser. 2, *3* [1912], 153 ff.) argues that "what Edwards saw and feared was not a spread of Arminianism among the Congregationalists, a desertion of old orthodoxy. It was the rise of Episcopalianism." He also cites Ezra Stiles' observation that he could not find an Arminian in the Connecticut clergy in 1740 and doubted that there were any in New England. However, Christie admits that JE did not "deign to mention them [Episcopalians] in his controversial works" (p. 165). In a letter to Rev. William McCulloch (July 6, 1750), JE, to be sure, does speak of the "strange progress" which Arminianism and Pelagianism have made and then immediately states, "The Church of England, in New England, is, I suppose treble what it was seven years ago" (Dwight ed., *1,* 413). However, those inclined toward what JE called Arminianism did not turn to Episcopalianism in great numbers during or after the Great Awakening; rather they became Old Lights, Baptists, Methodists, or moved toward Unitarianism and Universalism (C. C. Goen, *Revivalism and Separatism, 1740–1800,* New Haven, Yale University Press, 1962). Perry Miller suggested, in partial agreement with Christie's judgment, that early New England identified Arminianism with Prelacy, but that by the mid-eighteenth century what alarmed JE was the fact that notable nonconformists, such as Taylor, who were not Prelatists, were moving into Arminian ranks (*Jonathan Edwards,* pp. 106, 110, 112). See also Conrad Wright, *The Beginnings of Unitarianism in America* (Boston, Beacon Press, 1955), p. 6, and Clifford K. Shipton, "The New England Clergy of the 'Glacial Age,'" *Publications of the Colonial Society of Massachusetts, 32* (1933–37), 25. The term "Arminianism" then must be left to stand for a complex of notions involving an elevated confidence in freedom of choice, a sharply upward revised estimate of human nature, and a form of commonsense moralism, all of which were related to an acute dissatisfaction with Calvinism. Mark H. Curtis, writing of the origin of the term in the British universities of the late sixteenth and early seventeenth centuries, calls Arminianism "an inaccurate but indispensable name" and finds its basic affirmations flourishing at Oxford and

had begun innocently enough with the teachings of such Covenant or Federal theologians as William Perkins, William Ames, Richard Sibbes, and John Preston. These tutors of the earliest Massachusetts clergy had developed a brand of orthodoxy by which the intolerable tension between sinful man and a righteous, sovereign God could be perceptibly alleviated.[1] There was great comfort in the notion that God had willingly bound himself in covenant with the Puritan venture in the New World. Man was a sinner, of course, but the fall of Adam had not totally deprived him of the proper use of reason or certain seminal inclinations to virtue. Therefore he was capable of taking some faltering steps toward his own salvation by "closing" with the Covenant of Grace, which God had mercifully extended to him. Adam's melancholy debacle was interpreted largely in contractual or legal terms. He had broken the bond and rightly received expulsion from the garden, but he had not received inherent pollution as his sentence. "It was just such a disability as a man would suffer who was under sentence for embezzlement or defalcation," Miller comments. His punishment was then passed on to his descendants "as a legal responsibility, not as an inherent disease." [2] As a debt inherited from their father's malfeasance, Adam's posterity would have been in difficult straits had not God provided a new Covenant, that of Grace, into which man could enter. This new arrangement was providentially ordered to appeal to those few faculties as yet untouched by the original disobedience of Adam. From such a doctrine the most hopeful prospects for human salvation could be anticipated. Thus, to those wavering souls unsure of their status before God, Samuel Willard could speak these reassuring words: "Your many weaknesses and infirmities cannot undermine or subvert your safety; they cannot destroy or breake the peace that is made in Christ between God and you: thy ways, if fallen into through neglect of duty, and remissness in your spiritual watch, procure you the dis-

---

Cambridge "before Arminius himself had formulated his propositions and doctrines" (*Oxford and Cambridge in Transition, 1558–1642,* Oxford, Clarendon Press, 1959, pp. 166, 226).

1. See Perry Miller, "The Marrow of Puritan Divinity," *Pub. of Col. Soc. Mass., 32* (1933–37), 247 ff.

2. Ibid., pp. 281–92. H. S. Smith takes exception to Miller's heavy emphasis on the notion of legal imputation and his minimizing of inherited corruption. Smith holds that the Federal doctrine of original sin retained the notion of natural generation as well as that of legal imputation as a means of passing on original sin to successive generations (*Changing Conceptions,* p. 34).

pleasure of a father, discovering itself in his chastising of you with affliction: but can never alienate his heart from you though your grace be faint and your corruption strong . . . yet still all shall be well at the last." [3]

The great God still loomed in the background. His might and justice were as unsearchable as his mercy, but a definite direction that narrowly skirted some form of Arminianism was set in New England thought. Men could do something about their salvation, at least by way of preparation, since God, with whom the ultimate initiative lay, had opened the way to them. Here was an interpretation of the human situation which cleared a path into realms where men could take a firmer grasp on their own destinies. Something was happening to New England religious life that would eventually shape the American mind. "A teleological universe, wherein men were expected to labor for the glory of God, wherein they were to seek not their own ends but solely those appointed by Him, was imperceptibly made over into a universe in which men could trust themselves even to the extent of commencing their own conversions, for the sake of their own well-being and God could be expected to reward them with eternal life." [4] Nor were celestial rewards sufficient for hardy and earthy New Englanders. The utilitarian spirit of Covenant theology joined neatly with a Yankee self-sufficiency that was burgeoning by the opening of the eighteenth century. Cotton Mather, himself no high Calvinist, lamented that an "insatiable desire after land and worldly accommodations" had seized many, whereas "we differ from other outgoings of our nation in that it was not any worldly considerations that brought our fathers into this medium but religion. . . . Now religion is made subservient unto worldly interests." [5] But what did Mather expect? God not only had bound himself to those who entered into Covenant with him, but had promised to undergird and bring to a good end the entire Puritan social enterprise in the New World. He had, it was understood, promised material rewards to its Covenant faithful—security, prosperity, health, and success at arms. But as Cotton Mather and his distressed fellow divines realized, material rewards have a way of diverting men's minds from the giver and the conditions under which the

3. *A Brief Discourse of Justification* (Boston, 1686), pp. 163–4.

4. Perry Miller, "Preparation for Salvation in Seventeenth Century New England," *Journal of the History of Ideas, 4* (June 1943), 286.

5. *Magnalia Christi Americana* (Hartford, 1855), p. 324.

reward is given. Thus, a cruel dilemma remained for the clergy who had for a generation harnessed the Massachusetts and Connecticut foundings to covenantal interpretations. Obviously, material benefits seduced men from a due allegiance to God, yet material benefits were one part of the arrangement with God and visible signs of his faithfulness to his bound word.[6] The clergy could scarcely blame the Almighty for whatever signs of favor he bestowed, although these signs won men's hearts to increased worldliness rather than deeper piety. Nor did the person in the pew require a formal course in Arminian and Pelagian tenets to ease his way ever closer to those heresies for which Taylor was the spokesman.

The sense of divine sovereignty was by no means dead, nor was there any relaxation of emphasis upon the horrendous character of sin. But somehow, by the opening of the eighteenth century, the traditional doctrines had lost their vigor. It remained for Edwards and his fellow revivalists to breathe fresh vitality into the familiar Calvinistic formulas and to bring into question the very securities for which the Covenant theology had provided a palliative rationale. The seductively comforting image of a God conveniently bound to the interests of men had to be broken, and once more men were placed in all the inescapable wretchedness of their sinful state before the transcendent glory of God. Only by unmerited grace, not by legalistic devices, could salvation come. Charles Chauncy, of course, thought Edwards went about his preaching in a too fierce, emotional, and even inhumane fashion, but Edwards defiantly asked in return, "Why should we be afraid to let persons, that are in an infinitely miserable condition, know the truth or bring them into the light for fear it should terrify them?" [7]

This, however, was precisely the question to be debated. Are men in "an infinitely miserable condition"? And if so, is this low estate brought about by anything except their own individual efforts? As the incessant drumming upon human depravity of the Great Awakening began to die away, it was understandable that some critically minded individuals wished to give closer scrutiny to a doctrine that had helped drive distraught souls into a frenzy and cast obloquy upon human dignity. The sermons and tracts were soon flying about among clergymen in the vicinity of Boston. The Arminian battle

6. Perry Miller, *The New England Mind* (New York, Macmillan Company, 1939), pp. 422–81.

7. Worcester ed., *3*, 195–6.

over the doctrine of original sin was thus well launched when the full impact of Taylor's book was felt.[8]

The search for a mediating position between the extremes of strict Calvinistic and Arminian principles was represented by Experience Mayhew's *Grace Defended in a Modest Plea for an Important Truth*.[9] Mayhew professed that he did not want to upset Calvinism, but merely to remove some things which were in no way necessary to its principal articles. "I have not in this Essay had any Design against the Doctrine of Original Sin, God's eternal decrees . . . and the sovereignty of God in the affair of man's salvation" (p. v). He did not waver on the point of human depravity, but he continued to give a covenantal explanation of mankind's relation to Adam. Adam and Eve fell; God threatened them with death and immediately began to execute his sentence by removing his holy spirit from Adam and his descendants, "and without any positive act of God, infusing any sinful dispositions into him, [Adam] became a most vile miscreant" (pp. 7–8). Since the whole species of mankind was by covenant in Adam, all men come into the world as sinners. "All men are, by Nature, Servants of Sin, wholly under the Dominion of it" (p. 29). But at this point Mayhew began to veer toward the Arminian position, for he insisted that men also come into the world "in a salvable Condition" (p. 22). Men are encouraged to strive to put themselves in the way of salvation, though of course they cannot achieve it for themselves. He then clearly laid out the differences he saw between himself and those who opposed him.

> [The difference] does not lie in this, that I exalt the power of men in their natural state, more than they do; but in this rather, that I exalt the grace of God more: for whereas they affirm, that the faith and repentance which God requires as the condition of the Covenant of Grace, is such as none can exercise 'till they are become good and holy persons. . . . I on the contrary endeavour to maintain, that the faith and repentance, by God required as the condition of the new Covenant, is of a lower kind than those

8. A more detailed study of the controversy than is offered here may be found in Joseph Haroutunian, *Piety Versus Moralism: The Passing of the New England Theology* (New York, Henry Holt, 1932).

9. H. S. Smith believes that Mayhew was replying directly to Taylor, but I find no grounds for this assumption in the book. JE apparently owned a copy of the book, as his entry in the "Memo Book" for January 5, 1744, refers to the loan of it to a Mr. Billing [?] [illegible].

> who oppose me will allow of; and suppose it to be such as men, by divine assistance, can perform, before they are savingly renewed by the Spirit, and so become true saints. . . . I really think that God, in the Covenant of Grace, does not insist on such terms, as my opposers imagine and which can never be complied with by any sinner, while he is in his miserable and undone estate; but then only, when he has got into a state of safety, and has already obtained eternal life. (pp. 136–7)

Mayhew clearly wanted the best of two worlds. He sought a wider liberty in which man's will could be exercised, but he also wished to retain the doctrine of original sin. Men cannot save themselves, but let the opponents of Calvinistic doctrines understand that the doctrine of original sin is a great truth and that God designs to glorify his grace and mercy in the redemption of men by Jesus Christ through a new covenant, the terms of which men by divine help can accept, and then "I think many people would not be so averse to the doctrine of Original Sin as they now seem to be" (p. 196).

A much less conciliatory note was struck when young Lemuel Briant published in 1749 a hard-hitting sermon, whose title made clear his animus against the implications of human depravity: "The Absurdity and Blasphemy of deprecating Moral Virtue." From the point of view of the orthodox, this was a foully mistaken use of their favorite text, "All our righteousness are as filthy rags" (Is. 64:6). The Reverends John Porter and Thomas Foxcroft, using the same text in 1750 to bring the brash pastor to account, showed that human righteousness was no substitute for the righteousness of Christ and that Briant's position smacked of "Popery." At a council called to examine Briant's views, it developed that he had recommended Taylor's *Scripture-Doctrine* to others. For this misdemeanor he was soundly rebuked, but he pleaded innocent to the charge of advocating the doctrines found in the book.[1] The elderly Reverend Samuel Niles entered the squabble in 1752, roundly scoring Briant for delinquencies in his pastoral duties as well as for his disavowal of orthodox doctrine and his espousal of Arminian tendencies.[2] Two

1. Wright, *Beginnings of Unitarianism,* p. 71; see also Williston Walker, *A History of the Congregational Churches in the United States* (New York, Charles Scribner's Sons, 1900), pp. 271 ff.

2. Niles published *The True Scripture-Doctrine of Original Sin Stated and Defended* in 1757. JE wrote of it: "I had finished my defense of the doctrine of original sin, and prepared the copy (as here you have it) for the press, and had

years later the death of Briant cut off what promised to be one more front in the spreading battle over human depravity.

The same year in which Briant had published his upsetting sermon, Jonathan Mayhew went to press with a collection of sermons which, without explicitly attacking the doctrine of original sin, nevertheless placed it and other cherished Calvinistic doctrines in a context of critical rationalism which boded ill for orthodoxy.[3] The sermons were moralistic in tone and clearly showed signs of the new rationalism. In the course of the first three sermons, he stressed man's natural competence to judge between truth and falsity and praised reason, by which men most resemble God, for "to speak reproachfully of reason in general is nothing less than blasphemy against God" (p. 39). This was a thrust against the deluded enthusiasts caught up in the Great Awakening's frenzy, the best of whom were no more than "enlightened idiots" (p. 38). Mayhew urged that all propositions be open to calm and dispassionate examination, that evidence be set forth to substantiate the basic truths of Christianity, and that rational argument be followed wherever it led, "whatever notions it may contradict, whatever censures it may expose us to" (p. 44). Even "our Lord aimed at bringing men to believe in him, only by dint of argument" (p. 52), and the apostles encouraged "liberty and freedom of thought; never intimating, as most of their pretended successors have done, that this is hazardous to men's souls" (p. 53). If reason were thus unchained and men placed themselves in a "state of indifferency" or "aequi librio," Mayhew saw reason and evidence eliminating what he regarded as a pernicious aspect of the doctrine of original sin. "Hence it follows," he argued, "that the doctrine of a total ignorance, and incapacity to judge of moral and religious truth, brought upon mankind by the apostacy of our first parents, is without foundation." And, with a characteristic gibe at tradition, he continued, "How much brighter and more vigorous our intellectual faculties were in Adam, six thousand years before we had any existence, I leave others to determine. It is sufficient for my purpose to consider mankind as they are at present, without inquiring what they were before they had any being" (p. 38).

---

wrote the preceding part of this preface, before I had received the least intimation of anything written or intended to be written by the Rev. Mr. Niles, in answer to Dr. Taylor" (Author's Preface, below, p. 103).

3. Jonathan Mayhew, *Seven Sermons* (Boston, 1749).

In 1756, Mayhew again appeared in print.[4] In this collection of sermons, Calvinistic, Arminian, and Pelagian overtones are mingled in a confused manner. Accordingly, he could inform his congregation that the message of the Kingdom "is a dispensation of the grace of God to a guilty lost world: a revelation of his mercy to us by his Son, considered as sinful, perishing creatures, justly liable to wrath and destruction" (p. 37). Salvation was not man's due, but proceeded wholly from God's undeserved favor "as a gift" (p. 92). "We constantly disclaim the doctrine of merit," he firmly announced, "even after we have obeyed the gospel, we account it great grace in God to accept us and to bestow eternal life upon us" (p. 144). Conventional orthodoxy rings through his words when he attributes human morality to "the apostacy of our first parents" upon whom God wrought his "righteous displeasure" by subjecting Adam and his sons to death (p. 330). Consequently, "we have no demand upon his justice for a longer or happier life than that which he bestows upon us in this world, short and unhappy as it is" (p. 336). Men's hope for salvation and happiness in heaven depends solely upon divine revelation in Christ, as "mere reason, or the light of nature, suggests no arguments for a happy immortality, which are conclusive and satisfactory, so that we can rest upon them" (p. 337).

Mayhew may have paid his compliments to orthodoxy in these terms, but he also showed his deviation from Calvinism. "Be men; be Christians; be protestants. Use the understandings which God has given you, in seeking his will. . . . Exercise your reason, and the liberty you enjoy, in learning the truth, and your deity from it" (p. 27), he boldly challenged his hearers. Although he had denied the meritorious character of good works, he made a place for them as part of salvation in a disturbingly ambiguous fashion: "Our obedience and good works are really acceptable to God in some degree; otherwise he would not have required us to perform them, and promised to reward them" (p. 94).

How far he was willing to go in describing the unfortunate consequences of the fall is uncertain. Man is ruined in some degree by the fall, but his reason has not been corrupted, although "turbulent, disorderly, and uneasy passions" have been unleashed. But these, like the physical bodies we inhabit, expose men to temptation to such a

4. Jonathan Mayhew, *Sermons, upon the Following Subjects . . .* (Boston, 1756).

degree "that it is almost, if not altogether impossible for us, wholly to avoid sinning." Yet Mayhew will not have it that sinfulness arises directly from passions or affections; sin becomes sin only by willful or careless indulgence. A creature cannot, strictly speaking, be a sinner "'till he has violated some law of God, or of nature" (pp. 333–5). Statements like these go some distance toward denying the native corruption of man and pave the way for a moralistic definition of sin.[5]

If any grounds exist for believing that Mayhew wavered in his interpretation of original sin, certainly there could be none concerning a vigorous tract which appeared anonymously in 1757. It bore the engaging title, *A Winter Evening's Conversation upon the Doctrine of Original Sin . . . Wherein the Notion of Our Having Sinned in Adam and Being on That Account Only Liable to Eternal Damnation, Is Proved To Be Unscriptural, Emotional, and of Dangerous Tendency* (New Haven, 1757). The author, who turned out to be the Reverend Samuel Webster, had managed to bring the controversy to incandescent heat by virtually parroting the opinions of Taylor's *Scripture-Doctrine*.[6]

Webster's attack was direct and uncompromising, and he even dared to describe the doctrine as "a very little thing" (p. 4). He vigorously supported the notions of the benevolence of God, the immorality and inhumanity of consigning infants to hell, the illogicality of blaming guilt and evil on those who had no hand in Adam's sin, and the lack of scriptural evidence for the doctrine. He asked, "How can you reconcile it to the goodness, holiness, or justice of God, to make them [infants] heirs of hell?" (p. 5). The imputation of Adam's sin and guilt were complete nonsense. "Sin and guilt (so far as I can see) are personal matters, as much as knowledge, and I can as easily conceive of one man's knowledge being imputed to another as of his sins being so" (p. 6). If men were body and soul in the loins of Adam, they were not moral agents and so not accountable, and if

5. The collection of sermons shows Mayhew well on his way to "liberalism," but the shadow of orthodoxy clung to many of his statements. By the time of his death he was firmly in the camp of Charles Chauncy, Ebenezer Gay, and others of the liberal wing, and was counted a Unitarian by John Adams (Walker, *History*, pp. 276–8; E. M. Wilbur, *A History of Unitarianism*, 2 vols., Cambridge, Harvard University Press, 1952, 2, 387–90).

6. Ola E. Winslow, *Jonathan Edwards, 1703–1758* (New York, Macmillan Company, 1941), p. 307, refers to Webster's booklet as a "mere paraphrase" of Taylor. See also Faust and Johnson, *Edwards, Selections*, p. lxvii.

they did sin in Adam, imputation was unnecessary and impossible (p. 9). Moreover, the whole business of men being implicit in Adam or covenantally identified with him was not scriptural: "not one word about any such covenant made with Adam . . . nor one word about his being such a representative for his posterity, as that we should be charged with his sin! nor one word about damnation in another world! How infatuated must men be with prejudice to see all these things here, when none of them are to be seen" (p. 11). Of course, men suffer as a consequence of the sins of others, but "we are not guilty of others' sins" (p. 7). As he saw it, the doctrine was "gradually growing out of credit, especially of late years. . . . And I doubt not, in a short time, will be disown'd by every body" (p. 21).

The Reverend Peter Clark came forth as a champion of the "old way" in a treatise bearing the genial title, *Scripture-Doctrine of Original Sin Stated and Defended. A Summer Morning's Conversation between a Minister and a Neighbor, a Reply to a Winter Evening's Conversation* (Boston, 1758). Clark attempted to put the burden of proof on Webster by pointing out that the doctrine "is a doctrine evidently held forth in scripture, receiv'd by the Catholick Church in all ages, agreed to in all the confessions of the Reformed Churches, confirm'd by sad observation and experience, felt and lamented as the heaviest burden by the most enlightened pious souls . . . so to dispute against it, is to dispute against fact, and experience, as well as the plain dictates of sacred writ" (p. 2). Then Clark stooped to conquer by a personal gibe at Webster's spiritual estate; he quoted another divine who had remarked that "men's denying this doctrine is one argument to prove it; were not men blind and dead in sin they could not but be sensible of it" (p. 2).

But Clark found the going heavy as he attempted to distinguish between the actual corruption of human nature, which for him was a matter of plain experience, and the imputation of Adam's guilt, which he was moved to admit was known only by faith and Scripture. On the tender spot of the damnation of infants, Clark was forced to hedge: " 'Tis true, whilst we were in the womb, we were as innocent as the child unborn; But he [Webster] has not proved, that the child unborn is so pure and innocent, as he pretends" (p. 92). Yielding to Webster's insinuating humanitarian spirit, Clark affirmed that few or none maintain that infants suffer eternal torments; at worst, they receive "eternal privation of life" (p. 8). Having gone so far to ameliorate the condition of infants, Clark waded in further by maintaining, in spite of ignorance in such matters, that in the case of the children of Christian parents "there is no room to doubt, but when they die their souls are received to the society of the spirits in Paradise . . . and they may be taken by Jesus Christ to be partakers of his redeeming mercy" (pp. 96–7). By giving over in this respect, however, Clark had breached the doctrine at one of its strongest but most distasteful points. Christ died for all, including children and infants; therefore, infants and children must be as sinful as mature individuals.

Clark thrashed Webster for having misrepresented the whole doctrine, for having shamefully abused its defenders and "blackened our scheme," but the charge that stung Webster personally was that of Pelagianism. Webster whipped out another tract against Clark, *The Winter's Conversation Vindicated* (Boston, 1758), in which he professed to be deeply grieved at Clark's allegation. After citing five points held by Pelagians, from which he dissented, he roundly swore, "I despise Pelagius . . . as much as he, and am much more different from him, than Mr. Clark is from me. . . . I therefore demand Christian satisfaction for this gross abuse, which runs through his book" (p. 15). By this point in the debate, ad hominem arguments were being lavishly used, but Webster wanted to get the argument straight on stronger grounds in this round. He did not doubt that all mankind was "in actual degeneracy and apostacy" whether by Adam or by having corrupted themselves, since "the melancholy fact, is too plain to be doubted" (p. 14). "Who denies the real apostacy of human nature, the fall of Adam, or a real original corruption? I have not" (p. 113). But Clark had gone off the mark when he claimed that few if any Calvinists believed in infant damnation. He simply must have been out of touch with opinion on this point. Furthermore, Clark had not cleared up the notion of involuntary sin. "Is it not of the essence of sin, that it be voluntary? . . . Don't all mankind go upon this maxim that absolute force destroys the nature of sin?" asked Webster. If this point was not valid, all else in his argument, he admitted, was useless. On Clark's grounds, what an absurd conclusion would follow! "And so when we were all made in Adam, five thousand years before we were made at all, we had such a good nature, as was worthy of God: and such as we had reason to be thankful for; and therefore we ought to be very thankful for a nature now that is very evil. I must say this appears to me perfect jargon, or words without any meaning" (p. 27).

By this time Charles Chauncy took a hand in the fray by offering a pamphlet entitled *The Opinion of One Who Has Perused the Summer Morning's Conversation* (Boston, 1758). He criticized Clark's writing as being "in some places, at least, unintelligible" and too long-winded (p. 4), but more importantly, he fastened on Clark's surrender of the notion of infant damnation. "No one, who had not departed from the principles of Calvinism, can be mentioned that explains this eternal death, in any other sense, than including the torments of hell-fire," and since Webster's book was principally an attack on the liability of infants to such a damnation, Clark's whole effort to make exemption for infants was beside the point (pp. 14–16). "The supposing therefore that all that die in infancy are saved is no vindication of the Calvinistical doctrine upon the head under debate," concluded Chauncy.

The strife, however, was not yet over. Clark answered Chauncy in *Remarks on a Late Pamphlet, Entitled the Opinion* (1758) and turned on Webster again in two more tracts, *Answer to the Winter Evening's Conversation Vindicated* and *A Defence of the Principles of the Summer Morning's Conversation* (Boston, 1760). Clark obviously had run out of steam when he wrote the latter, since he admitted "the public has had enough of the controversy" (p. 4). Besides, by this time Edwards' *Original Sin* was on the market, and Clark was relieved to bow out and let Edwards hold the field. He noted that much had been lately written and printed on the subject "especially by the late Reverend and learned President Edwards . . . in which he [Webster] might have found all or most of his arguings and objections anticipated, and finally and for ever silenced" (p. 4). He also had smoked out the source of Webster's arguments when he pointedly, if not maliciously, suggested that Webster "is not altogether a stranger to a certain modern Latitudinarian writer, risen up in the English nation, who might more properly be stil'd his preceptor" (p. 29). If Webster wanted further to examine the scriptural evidences for original sin, Clark referred him to "President Edwards' late treatise on this subject, in which he has fully vindicated the said texts (against the exceptions of Dr. John Taylor whom this gentleman follows, in most things) to the general satisfaction" (p. 128).

Joseph Bellamy, Edwards' friend and former pupil, also interjected himself into the dispute in 1758 by bringing out *A Letter to the Reverend Author of the Winter-Evening's Conversation on Orig-*

inal Sin (Boston). He purported to be writing to the neighbor to whom Webster had addressed himself, and suggested some correlative reading: "I can heartily recommend to you two sermons, one on justification, and another on the justice of God in the damnation of sinners, published by the Rev. Mr. Edwards, late President of New Jersey College, above twenty years ago. And there is now in the press by the same author, a book on original sin, wherein all these points are fully considered, and every objection, of any moment, answered" (pp. 13–14).

With Edwards' book in the field, or soon to be, there remained little reason for the orthodox to continue the pamphlet war.[7] Edwards, however, seems to have paid no attention to the long-winded controversy, although it is possible that the publication of *Original Sin,* rather than other works he had in manuscript, was hastened by Webster's opening blast.[8] In any case, he published his treatise under the impression that Taylor's book had been "spread abroad in the land, without any answer to it, as an antidote" (Author's Preface, below, p. 102). Thus he implied that Clark's defense, if he knew of it, had failed, although the probability is that he had finished his own writing by the time Webster and Clark had burst into print.[9]

2. *Edwards' Life and Literary Sources*

Obviously, Taylor's publication proved popular as well as deeply disturbing in New England. Samuel Hopkins read it with profound uneasiness. Briant had recommended it "to the prayerful perusal of some of his brethren." John Bass was quoting from Taylor's *Key to the Apostolic Writings,* which occasionally circulated with the *Scripture-Doctrine.* Charles Chauncy was to pay tribute to Taylor's works in his *Mystery Hid from Ages and Generations . . . or the Salvation of All Men the Grand Thing Aimed At in the Scheme of God.* Sam-

7. Bellamy also published a large work on the subject in 1758, entitled *The Wisdom of God in the Permission of Sin (Works,* Dodge ed., 1811, 2).

8. Walker, *History,* p. 275.

9. Walker, *Ten New England Leaders* (Boston, Silver, Burdett and Co., 1901), p. 258. The lack of reference to Clark conceivably may be due to JE's animosity toward Clark's tenuous connection with the controversy which led to his expulsion from Northampton. The Ecclesiastical Council, having heard that Clark was working on an answer to JE's *Qualifications for Communion,* asked him "to expedite what he had undertaken." Apparently Clark declined to do so several months later, but JE did know that the Council expected assistance from Clark (Dwight ed., *1,* 369, 396).

uel Gookin's bookstore in Boston advertised Taylor's books at the head of a list which included such controversial authors as Tindal, Whitby, Emlyn, and Butler.[1] Unquestionably, Webster had helped himself liberally to the *Scripture-Doctrine,* and in 1760 Joseph Bellamy was still tracing out the evil effects of Taylor when he charged the liberal party of the New Hampshire churches with attempting to model the Shorter Catechism on Taylor's scheme by omitting the doctrines of the trinity, eternal decrees, and original sin.[2] Taylor assuredly was speaking to the condition of those persons who had had their fill of the extravagances of the Great Awakening and were rapidly becoming disenchanted with the yoke of Calvinistic principles. Moreover, his words carried the authority not of a freethinker or Anglican, of whom no better might be expected, but of that branch of nonconformist Presbyterianism which once in Britain had been a stronghold of Calvinism, but now had fallen off into Arminianism.[3] As its articulate spokesman, Taylor seemed to have succeeded in undermining not only the Calvinistic system, but the entire drama of salvation for which human depravity provided the first act. Little wonder then that Edwards remarked in the Preface to his own treatise, "No one book has done so much towards rooting out of these western parts of New England, the principles and scheme of religion maintained by our pious and excellent forefathers." And Samuel Niles proclaimed the same approaching disaster when he stated that the doctrine of original sin was "most eagerly struck at, and virulently opposed by many, in the present age." [4]

Even before he was acquainted with Taylor, Edwards had intended to publish on the subject of human depravity. In his youthful *Notes on the Mind,* he reminded himself to write "concerning the corruption of man's nature. How it comes to be corrupt. What is the positive cause of corruption." [5] And, of course, his sermons repeatedly dealt with the theme.[6] But it was Taylor who finally precipi-

1. Wright, *Beginnings of Unitarianism,* pp. 71, 73, 76, 78.
2. Walker, *History,* p. 279.
3. Norman Sykes refers to the Presbyterian declension as "a veritable landslide from orthodoxy into what later became known as Unitarianism" (*The English Religious Tradition,* London, S.C.M. Ltd., 1953, p. 62).
4. *The True Scripture-Doctrine,* p. 40.
5. No. 22; Dwight ed., *1,* 666.
6. See especially, two sermons still in manuscript, circa 1730, on Rom. 7:14, where he developed much of the argument employed in *Original Sin* (Yale Collection).

tated the writing of *The Great Christian Doctrine of Original Sin Defended.* It is not known exactly when Edwards became aware of Taylor's writings. In his Preface, Edwards claimed that the *Scripture-Doctrine* had been known for many years, but the earliest possible clue to be found seems to be a leaf from a narrow notebook made from the *Daily Gazette,* dated January 12, 1743. On this scrap there is a reference to Taylor's *Key,* and there is a heading marked *Original Sin,* with two paragraphs following, through which a line has been drawn.[7] In view of the date of the newspaper, it has been suggested that by that time Edwards was acquainted with Taylor. This is doubtful. Edwards hoarded paper and may have written these observations at a later date. Stronger grounds for doubt lie in his letter of August 31, 1748, to John Erskine. In this letter he thanked Erskine for the gift of two books, "Taylor's on Original Sin," and the "Key to the Apostolic Writings," with the "Paraphrase on the Epistle to the Romans." He continued, "I had before borrowed and read Taylor on Original Sin, but am very glad to have one of my own; if you had not sent it, I intended to have sought opportunity to buy it. The other book, his Paraphrase etc. I had not heard of; if I had, I should not have been easy till I had seen it, and been possessed of it." [8] Edwards here clearly refers to only two books and the reference to the *Paraphrase* includes the *Key.* He says explicitly that he had not heard of the *Paraphrase,* and consequently it must be concluded that he had not read the *Key* at the earlier date of 1743. The earliest date at which he became acquainted with the *Paraphrase* and *Key* was probably the summer of 1748, and at some indefinite time before that he had studied the *Scripture-Doctrine.*[9] Probably he began col-

7. A facsimile of the page is in the *Princeton University Library Chronicle, 15* (Winter 1954), 76–7, in an article on JE's materials by Howard C. Rice, Jr. I am obliged to Professor T. A. Shafer for this reference.

8. Dwight ed., *1,* 251.

9. His "Memo Book" shows that he loaned Taylor's *Scripture-Doctrine* to a Dr. van Horn (?) sometime between October and November 2, 1749, and that "my wife lent Mr. Billing Taylor on original sin, Feb. 1750/51." On the next to the last page, JE wrote "sent to him [Samuel Hopkins] Taylor orig & Key, May 6, 1757" (Yale Collection). In the "Catalogue," p. 15, col. 2, JE stated, "The latest books I hear of about Arminianism are Taylor against Original Sin and Jennings' Answer." His "Interleaved Bible" (Yale MS. VI) reveals that he was in the habit of checking Taylor's interpretations of Scripture in the *Paraphrase* and *Scripture-Doctrine.* The first reference to Taylor among the "Miscellanies" is to his *Key,* p. 163, in Miscell. No. 1101, followed by an extensive quotation from the Preface to *Paraphrase* in Miscell. No. 1111.

lecting notes for *Original Sin* at that time and continued to work them over until his actual writing began in the summer of 1756.[1] He undoubtedly realized with some apprehension the difficulties that lay before him in making the doctrine plausible. In the "Miscellanies," No. 654, *Mysteries of Religion, Absolute Decrees, Original Sin,* etc., he had meditated on certain problems which occurred to him to have the semblance of falsity. Such doctrines, he commented, "that have been most difficult to reconcile to God's justice and goodness will serve to give us a stronger and fuller persuasion and a higher sense of these perfections of God, when we see him to be perfectly just and holy in those things that have occasioned the blasphemies of multitudes against these perfections of God and that the whole world and we ourselves have been so much perplexed about." In the margin he scribbled, "written out under the head Original Sin." [2] Apparently Edwards himself had undergone some trials in coming to terms with the doctrine, although his completed treatise shows no indication of faltering. By May 26, 1757, he had completed the piece, and later in the same year it went to the printer. He reviewed a few of the printed pages, but he did not live to see the work in final form. He died at Princeton, March 22, 1758, the same year in which the book was published.

The figure of Taylor seems to have haunted the eventful years during which Edwards gathered his thoughts for the final assault. Even the controversy with his Northampton parish, which led to his expulsion on January 22, 1750, was marred by the Norwich divine. During the quarrel with his church, Edwards had attempted a careful defense of his position on the subject of qualifications for communion and was answered soon thereafter by the Reverend Solomon Williams.[3] Edwards might well have saved himself the trouble of a reply to Williams for all the good it would do his cause, but ever tenacious of what he considered an important doctrine, he published *Misrepresentations Corrected and Truth Vindicated* two years after

1. Dwight ed., *1,* 556.

2. Yale Collection, Miscell. 654 pp. 158–59.

3. JE's essay was entitled *An Humble Inquiry . . . Concerning the Qualifications Requisite to a Complete Standing and Full Communion* (Boston, 1749). Williams' attack was entitled *The True State of the Question Concerning the Qualifications Necessary to Lawful Communion in the Christian Sacraments* (Boston, 1751). According to Dwight, the church underwrote the cost of publishing Williams' pamphlet and distributed it to all the families in Northampton (Dwight ed., *1,* 495).

the irrevocable decision against him had been taken. He had detected in Williams' tract ideas, which at certain points coincided with those of Taylor, "the author who lately has been so famous for his corrupt doctrine" and whose scheme of religion "seems scarcely so agreeable to the Christian scheme, as the doctrine of many of the wiser heathen." In a letter to his former parishioners, appended to the *Misrepresentations Corrected,* he went on to warn his former flock that if the church fell in with Williams' views it would also have accepted "the strange opinion of Mr. Taylor," whose conception of Christianity "utterly explodes the doctrines you have been formerly taught, concerning eternal election, conversion, justification; and so, of a natural state of death in sin; and the whole doctrine of original sin." Before he had retired from the Northampton scene, Edwards recalled, "it was very evident, that Arminianism, and other loose notions of religion, and Mr. Taylor's in particular, began to get some footing among you." [4] In the meantime, he had received news of Taylor's success abroad from his friend Erskine and, in the light of this discouraging report, he observed disconsolately that "things are going down hill so fast, and truth and religion, both of heart and practice, are departing by such swift steps that I think it must needs be, that a crisis is not very far off." [5]

In this pessimistic mood he left Northampton in 1751. He was a tarnished figure, with little hope of winning an influential pulpit, and therefore had to be content to serve the little church of Stockbridge and act as missionary to the Indians gathered nearby. His salary was to be furnished jointly by the parish itself, the "Society in England, for Propagating the Gospel in New England, and the Parts Adjacent," and the Massachusetts legislature, which annually set aside funds for civilizing the Indians.[6] His Stockbridge days were described in the *Memoir* included in the Worcester edition as a period of relative calm, when studies were less interrupted by company and calls and "former anxieties were now removed." [7] However, Edwards' correspondence belies this comforting picture, for it reveals that he had by no means retired to an idyllic existence in the wilderness. His turmoil of mind and spirit were soon matched by the press of practical affairs and problems of health.

4. Worcester ed., *4,* 546, 601, 599.
5. Dwight ed., *1,* 497.
6. Ibid., p. 471.
7. Worcester ed., *1,* 84–5.

Even before he was settled, Edwards recognized that affairs in the Mission School for Indians had been sloppily managed, and it was not long before he was embroiled with difficulties on that score, not a few of which originated with the Williams family, the same clan that had so effectively helped to badger him out of Northampton. Squabbles over land speculation, the fleecing of both Indians and the commissioners of the Society, inadequate instruction and unjust treatment of the primitives, gossip zealously kept alive by the Williams faction, the hardships attendant upon settling his family in a frontier home, to say nothing of the necessity of adopting new modes of preaching for a congregation removed by centuries culturally and religiously from those to whom he was accustomed—all these placed severe strains upon his patience and health. But as time passed, Edwards won his way by just dealings and personal integrity. The successes of the whole enterprise were few and transient, although he had the satisfaction of defeating decisively the commercial machinations of his old enemies.

War came close to the village in 1754 when, after several inhabitants had been killed by a raiding party of French and Indians, the town was temporarily turned into a garrison. Every family had soldiers quartered with them, but Edwards politely asked the commanding officer to billet no more than four in his household, offering as one of his reasons that he was "in a low state as to my health, and not able to go much abroad, and upon that and other accounts, under much greater disadvantages, than others to get provisions." [8] It was neither lack of patriotism nor selfish interest that dictated his reluctance to lodge the soldiers. He had undergone a severe illness which, as he wrote Erskine, "exceedingly wasted my flesh and strength, so that I became like a skeleton," and which caused him to fear that he was going into "a dropsy." [9]

Edwards was disturbed not only by the immediate threats to the little outpost where he lived, but also by the discouraging news from other war fronts. He feared that the recent successes of French arms were ruining the British cause and at the same time threatening prospects for Protestantism in America. Accordingly, he took seriously his responsibility for the Indians at the mission, several of whom were chieftains of the powerful Mohawk tribe. He complained of the unfair treatment given to members of this tribe by

8. Dwight ed., *1*, 544.

9. Ibid., p. 546.

local authorities, which, if continued, would cause the whole Six Nations to go over to the cause of France. Religious and literary instruction of the Indians, he counseled the Speaker of the Massachusetts Assembly, was "the only means of securing their attachment to the British cause," for if the Six Nations broke with England, "almost all the nations of Indians in North America, will follow them." [1] The Stockbridge mission might not loom large in the minds of the London authorities, but for Edwards its role in holding the Iroquois as British allies was no contemptible contribution to British fortunes.

In the midst of pressing duties, personal difficulties, and threats of warfare, it is remarkable that Edwards produced anything of consequence during his Stockbridge days. Yet, by 1754 he had published *The Freedom of the Will* and shortly after his debilitating illness had worked out much of his *End for Which God Created the World* and *The Nature of True Virtue,* both of which were to be published posthumously. His "Book of Controversies" reveals how diligently he collected material for these works and how his mind moved back and forth among ideas intended for these treatises, as well as for *Original Sin* and his "Miscellaneous Notes on Efficacious Grace." At one point, for example, the thought struck him that the question of moral taste might be discussed in a treatise on original sin, but he wavered as to whether it might not be better treated in *The Nature of True Virtue.* He settled the perplexity for the moment by deciding that whichever work was published first should include the discussion of moral taste.[2] Apparently, he also contemplated producing one major treatise which would have included what we now know as *Original Sin, The Nature of True Virtue,* and the *End for Which God Created the World.* He refers to it as "a treatise the first part concerning the nature of true virtue and in this treat of God's end in creating the world. And in the next part concerning original sin an inquiry into the truth of the doctrine both as to corruption of nature and imputation and in the next place concerning the manner in which man's nature came to be corrupt and in total corruption and

1. Ibid., pp. 472, 547.

2. "Book of Controversies," Yale Collection, Folder 28, sec. 4. The two citations read: "Perhaps under the head of original sin treat of moral taste. see forward under the head of true virtue" (p. 97a); "Define how what our modern philosopher calls moral taste. treat of this either here or in the discourse on original sin according to which is published first" (p. 180a).

then concerning infused habits and concerning the saving grace's differing from common grace in nature and kind and concerning that moral taste that [sic] natural men to show that there is nothing of true virtue in it.[3] The "Book of Controversies" also shows that Taylor was to be the subject of attack not only in the treatise on original sin but also other projected works. The entries on perseverance, justification and predestination, and efficacious grace turn up Taylor's name repeatedly.[4] Edwards had promised to attend closely "to Taylor's piece in all its parts and that nothing that has the slightest resemblance to an argument should be left unanswered." His thorough workmanship on Taylor's writings, by which he redeemed that promise, is displayed by the three closely written pages of the "Book of Controversies" wherein he listed the words which Taylor had employed to describe "the state and privileges of professing Christians." [5] Certainly no misuse of terms by Taylor was to be allowed to mar the success of Edwards' defense, as further analyses of Taylor's "corruptness" in the "Miscellanies" make abundantly clear.

A careful inspection of the completed work reveals little of the voluminous reading and notetaking which had gone into its composition. Taylor and the Scriptures were extensively quoted, and George Turnbull is cited several times. Three other authors figure briefly in the text: John Locke, *An Essay Concerning Human Understanding;* Francis Hutcheson, *Inquiry Concerning Moral Good and Evil,* which is the second of two treatises in the *Essay on the Nature and Conduct of the Passions and Affections;* and Henry Winder, *A Critical and Chronological History of the Rise, Progress, Declension and Renewal of Knowledge, Chiefly Religious.* Sizeable extracts from other authors appear in the footnotes. Johannes Buxtorf's *Concordance* was used for the translation of Hebrew terms; Johann F. Stapfer's *Institutiones Theologicae, polemicae universae* was gladly seized upon as a theological authority, as was also Matthew Poole's *Synopsis criticorum aliorumque Sacrae Scripturae Interpretum.* Brief incidental references were made to Theophilus Gale's *The Court of the Gentiles,* Isaac Watts' *Ruin and Recovery,* and Henry Ainsworth's *Annotations upon the First Book of Moses Called Genesis.* The last lengthy footnote includes quotations from the pagan au-

3. Ibid., p. 102.
4. Ibid., pp. 120–3, 143–4, 261, 286. See also Worcester ed. *5*, 442–5, 447.
5. Ibid., pp. 121–3.

thors Seneca, Plutarch, and Juvenal, probably garnered from Gale or Watts.[6]

The "Book of Controversies" yields further indications of Edwards' sources, although conclusions as to the eventual impact of some of them on the finished treatise must remain highly conjectural. Of these, the following items may be identified with a fair degree of plausibility: Thomas Boston's *Human Nature in Its Fourfold State,* William Delaune's *Sermon on Original Sin,* William Dodwell's *Two Sermons on the Eternity of Future Punishments,* James Fraser's *Scripture Doctrine of Sanctification,* a sermon by John Hubbard in *Berry Street Sermons,* Alexander Moncrief's *Review and Examination of the Principles of Campbell,* Henry More's *Divine Dialogues,* Thomas Ridgley's *Doctrine of Original Sin,* and Thomas Sherlock's *Use and Intent of Prophecy.* There is not an author on this list whose writings proved of enduring value, although Boston's book has recently been republished.[7] Greater assurance may be felt concerning the references to Taylor, Locke, Poole, Watts, Hutcheson, and Turnbull. Of Turnbull, Edwards wrote, "Remember when I go about writing on original sin to borrow Trumbull's [Turnbull's] Moral Philosophy and with regard to what he says of there being vastly more virtue than vice in the world etc." [8] A quotation of peculiar interest from Hutcheson found its way into the text. However, much of it there was credited to Turnbull, who may have been quoting Hutcheson, but it is more likely that Edwards had forgotten the original source when he began to write.[9] Additional fugitive references to Chubb, Erasmus, Mandeville, Pelagius, and Whitby provide too ephemeral a connection with the *Original Sin* to be noted here.

Edwards' "Catalogue" of books also offers only tantalizing intimations of sources.[1] The references which stand out as potential candidates are noted as "Wigglesworth on Original Sin" and Anthony Burgess' *The Doctrine of Original Sin.* Both items were lined

6. Notes on Locke, Watts, and Gale may be found in Yale ed., *1,* 47 ff., 89 ff.; 2, 70–1. For other authors mentioned above, see below, Intro., Sec. 4. JE took comfort in the thought that non-Christian authors of antiquity held to the doctrine of original sin. In Gale, he found support from references to Plato's *Timaeus, Laws,* and *Gorgias* and in Watts' citations from Horace, Vergil, Seneca, Juvenal, Ovid, Pliny, and Manlius ("Miscellanies," No. 1162).

7. London, The Banner of Truth Trust, 1964.

8. Yale Collection, Folder 28, p. 96.

9. See below, Intro., Secs. 3 and 4.

1. The "Catalogue" is identified in the Yale Collection as No. ix, 1, A and B.

through by Edwards, suggesting that they had been read or used, but it is impossible to decide with accuracy the meaning of his marks.[2] The Burgess book was cited in the *Religious Affections,* but no reference to it appears in the "Book of Controversies," the *Original Sin,* or the "Miscellanies." [3] John Clark against Hutcheson, Hutcheson on the passions, Stapfer, and Winder are also mentioned, and each of them except Clark turns up in the *Original Sin.*

The "Miscellanies" offer the firmest clues to Edwards' preparation. In this collection he deposited what he considered to be choice quotations from the authors whom, with two exceptions, he cited in the completed work. Boston (No. 1078) and Manton (No. 1136) do not appear in the text, although Manton's argument on the infinite heinousness of sin closely parallels that of Edwards. Extensive citations occur from Buxtorf, Turnbull, Winder, Hutcheson, Poole, and most copiously from Stapfer. Strangely enough, the majority of these notes are found nowhere in the *Original Sin,* although other citations from the same authors do occur. At one point in the "Miscellanies," Edwards paid his compliments to Solomon Stoddard when he wrote, "The best philosophy that I have met with of original sin and all sinful inclinations, habits and principles is that of Mr. Stoddard of this town of Northampton" (No. 301). However, Stoddard is nowhere given credit in the final work.

Edwards read as widely as his restricted estate at Northampton and Stockbridge permitted, and in spite of his relative isolation, his literary acquaintance was phenomenal, as Johnson has pointed out.[4] The authors he read, with several outstanding exceptions, were not to be counted as theological and philosophical giants by later generations, but that century in the English-speaking world was not conducive to the emergence of theological eminence.

Edwards' literary sources may have been largely of mediocre status, but close at hand lay a kind of evidence to which Taylor had no access and of which he had no inkling. The American Indians and the brutalities of border warfare offered Edwards an opportunity to take advantage of his adversary when Taylor expounded the innate capacity for virtue which men untouched by the Gospel enjoyed. If man in his natural condition possesses light and sufficient means to

2. See T. H. Johnson, "Jonathan Edwards' Background of Reading," *Pub. of Col. Soc. Mass., 28* (1930–33), 206, 210.

3. Yale ed., *2,* 71.

4. "Background," p. 221.

obey the will of God, Edwards asked, why has so little progress been made in that direction by those savages who know nothing of Christ's saving grace? "What appearance was there, when the Europeans first came hither, of their being recovered, or recovering, in any degree from the grossest ignorance, delusions, and most stupid paganism?" [5] If Taylor persisted in counting the whole of humanity as capable of achieving virtue, Edwards reminded him that the phrase "all mankind" must include these same Indians along with the inhabitants of Africa and Australia. For all Taylor's expansive talk about the moral capacities of mankind, he had gone off the mark by taking his norm from the cultured society and acquired decencies of Englishmen and Europeans. But compared with these presumed paragons, Edwards charged, "the poor savage Americans are mere babes and fools (if I may so speak) as to proficiency in wickedness, in comparison of multitudes that the Christian world throngs with." [6] Here was evidence for original sin which put the inhabitants of Christendom and of uncivilized lands on the same footing, with a slight advantage given to the savage! Thus, from the solid foundation of personal experience no less than from the testimony of Scripture and learned authorities, Edwards set out with strict logic and appeals to "the intelligent and candid reader" to establish the doctrine which lay at the very foundation of the divine drama of salvation.

3. *Exposition of Arguments*

Edwards' defense of the doctrine of original sin rests upon three major interlocking contentions: first, that all men, in a wide diversity of circumstances, unfailingly and persistently do fall into heinous sin, which is justly punishable by God; second, that the only rational explanation for this deplorable state of affairs is mankind's vitiated and corrupt nature, brought about by the fall of Adam, in which all men participated by virtue of the principle of identity; and third, that God, although completely sovereign, cannot in the least be regarded as the active author of sin or as unjust in his arrangement of a world in which this continuing debacle takes place. To these lines of argument were added Edwards' rejoinders to a miscellaneous group of criticisms and a commentary on the tone of Taylor's writings.

5. Below, p. 151.
6. Below, p. 183.

THE FACT AND NATURE OF SIN

According to Edwards, there are two parts to the doctrine of original sin: the depravity of the human heart and the imputation of Adam's first sin to his posterity. He concentrates on the first of these by attempting to establish beyond any shadow of a doubt the actual sinfulness of mankind. To accomplish this end, a rudimentary operative principle was set forth, namely, "That is to be looked upon as the true tendency of the natural or innate disposition of man's heart, which appears to be its tendency when we consider things as they are in themselves, or in their own nature, without the *interposition of divine grace*" (pp. 109, 113). If grace were introduced into the picture, a false impression of man's nature would emerge, and this, of course, was what the Arminians had offered as a representation of man's fundamental decency. But to understand man as he actually is, he must be seen stripped of those ministrations of divine favor by which good is brought out of evil by the free pleasure of God. Having established this article of his strategy, Edwards proceeded to amass his evidence for the vile condition of humankind.[7]

To establish his case, Edwards waded into one of the touchiest subjects in the repertory of Arminian objections, that of the condition of infants and children. Since all mankind is sinful there can be no exceptions, and this is shown by the fact that no sooner are children born than they show their true nature by "immediately transgressing God's law." [8] Although Edwards wanted to prove beyond

7. Perry Miller insisted that *Original Sin* was "a strictly empirical investigation, an induction, in the manner of Bayle and Newton, of a law for phenomena" (*Jonathan Edwards,* p. 267). The term "empirical" is slippery in this context. It is true that JE drew upon human experience in a broad sense, but it is equally true that much of the evidence he offered in support of the doctrine of man's actual evil was drawn from Scripture. To validate Miller's use of the term "empirical," it is necessary to understand with JE that Scripture is a fairly full report of human history as well as the word of God. It should also be noted in support of the extended sense of "empirical" that JE approved of Turnbull's recommendation "That the experimental method of reasoning ought to be gone into in moral matters" (ibid., p. 110 n.) which to JE meant to look upon man with the utmost dispassion, as one would in the realm of natural objects.

8. JE agonized over the problem of the sinful nature and punishment of infants, as his extensive notes on the subject in the "Book of Controversies" show (Yale Collection, Folder 28, sec. 4–6, 10b, 11a, 15, pp. 33, 51, 56, 59–60, 63, 65–6, 69, 73, 87). In sec. 13, he wrote: "It is evident in fact that aversions to

peradventure that there was no escape from sin for a single individual, he was forced to waver on the question as to exactly when a youngster evinced his inherent depravity. In a footnote (p. 135), he moderated the force of the word "immediately" by admitting that at least "no considerable time passes" before the ugliness of one's nature breaks forth, but he proceeded to sweep this aside as inconsequential to the main drift of the argument. "If the time of freedom from sin be so small" that it plays no part in Scripture, "it is also so small, as not to be worthy of notice in the present argument." [9] However, it would seem that he had given away something in his case by this admission, for he was out to establish not only that all people sin, but that all of a man's nature is corrupted. He returned to the stern line on infant depravity in the development of his argument on death, where he argued "that infants are not looked upon by God as sinless, but that they are by nature children of wrath" and, as some passages of Scripture indicate, are justly exposed to divine punishment (p. 215). Edwards never satisfactorily resolved the problem of the exact time in a human life when sin declares itself. "Hard facts," Scripture, and logic drove him to insist that all Adam's posterity arrive in this world in such a state that they are "exposed, and justly so, to the sorrows of this life, to temporal death, and eternal ruin, unless saved by grace" (p. 395). Yet this lamentable state of affairs he greeted with no relish, as is shown by his persistent wrestlings with the issue of the damnation of infants in the "Book of Controversies" and his expressions of genuine sorrow over the whole sorry plight of mankind.[1] "We are by nature, *companions* in a

goodness and violent propensities to vice may early exist and show themselves in all born into our . . . world. Who does not see in others and has not felt in himself from the tenderest age from the first openings of the rational capacities . . . a strong disinclination and disaffection to what is spiritually good mixed with as strong an addictedness to vanity, pride, lying, stubbornness, revenge. . . . These evils we learn and practice of ourselves without a master and prompter."

9. He also slightly moderated this insistence upon the depravity of infants when he admitted that all who come into the world and act as moral agents are "in greater or lesser degree, guilty of sin" (below, p. 114).

1. Since death fell so heavily upon children three years of age and under, according to JE's reckoning, he was forced to conclude at one point in the "Book of Controversies" that there were "more influences of this fruit of sin on those that are in infancy than of any other age" (Yale Collection, Folder 28, p. 87). He also indulged himself with the idea that "the infant that has a disposition in his heart to believe in Christ if he had a capacity and opportunity

miserable helpless condition; which, under a revelation of the divine mercy, tends to promote mutual *compassion*" (p. 424).

Taylor, however, had to be put straight on the nature of children. If he wanted to palm off responsibility for children's wickedness on bad examples, Edwards points out that in the most eminently pious families children fall into sin as soon as they are capable of it, even as they did in the days of greatest purity in the primitive church (pp. 194, 283). Nor will he permit the idea of a partial imputation of Adam's sin and all worldly suffering to infants to pass muster as a way out of attributing a corrupt nature to them. "To think of poor little infants bearing such torments for Adam's sin, as they sometimes do in this world, and these torments ending in death and annihilation, may sit easier on the imagination, than to conceive of their suffering eternal misery for it. But it does not at all relieve one's *reason*" (p. 410). Such delicacy of feeling on behalf of infants does nothing to relieve the rigor of an argument built on the solid base of evidence and scriptural authority. Neither did Taylor's effort to draw from Scripture a picture of little children as models of virtue meet with any better reception at Edwards' hands. In the light of the texts, Edwards concludes that little children are recommended as patterns of "negative virtue," much as doves may be used as images of meekness and harmlessness. But they are not to be regarded as paragons of true virtue. "That little children have a *negative* virtue or innocence, in relation to the *positive* acts and hurtful effects of vice, is no argument that they have not corrupt nature within them . . . 'tis no wonder that they ben't guilty of positive wicked action, before they are capable of any moral action at all." After all, explained Edwards in a figure for which the world's softhearted can scarce forgive him, "a young viper has a malignant nature, though incapable of doing a malignant action, and at present appearing a harmless creature." To rise to a higher, if less striking, level of argument, Edwards turned against Taylor his own line of reasoning. If virtue springs from the free exercises of reason and choice, then Tay-

---

is looked upon and accepted as if he actually believed in Christ and so is entitled to eternal life through Christ," but he balanced the books by adding "so the infant that has a full disposition in his heart to seek an act of rebellion as Adam's is looked upon and treated as though he actually so rebelled and is actually condemned to eternal death through him" (ibid., p. 65). "Miscellanies," No. 849, offers the ameliorative opinion that "yet 'tis generally supposed to be a common thing that the infants of the godly that die in infancy are saved."

lor's showing that infants and children do not enjoy these capacities proves that they cannot be righteous (p. 423).

As Edwards reviewed human history and Scripture, it seemed to him overwhelmingly obvious not only that mankind sins immediately, but that it continues and flourishes in it. In spiritual matters, in affairs affecting one's eternal destiny, men have run off into idolatry and immorality and, even when all kinds of means have been used to prevent the headlong flight into perdition, they have persisted. Given the long span of centuries for experimentation, if men were as much inclined to virtue as to vice, would they not have found the true God and risen to high levels of moral conduct? Must it not be that failing that achievement, men are in fact held by "a dreadful stupidity of mind, occasioning a sottish insensibility" of the high importance of matters spiritual and ethical? (p. 157) Even the animal world contains no creature "so destructive of its own kind, as mankind are" (p. 168). Taylor himself had admitted that there was much wickedness in the world and that even Christians, as they gained in power and secular advantages, declined in piety and flourished in corruption and wickedness (p. 167). Must he not then face up to plain evidence and clear reasoning and conclude with Edwards that in spite of all efforts to steer mankind away from the brink of eternal disaster, it universally, totally, and persistently shows its true bent by behaving in a fashion which warrants divine punishment? (Pt. I, sec. 8)

Taylor had raised an acutely embarrassing question for those who, like Edwards, drew universal, affirmative judgments about mankind. He asked how one can know that all men are or have been vicious, and to what degree, if no thorough examination has ever taken place (p. 160). Even more pertinently, how can one delve into the invisible depths of each person, to say nothing of the hearts of infants, to pronounce so confidently on their essential character? The bite of Taylor's criticism lay not in the fact that relevant data had remained unexamined, but rather that such an examination was in principle as well as in fact impossible. On this nominalistic ground, all propositions with the enormous generality of scope which Edwards had labored to establish were doomed.

Edwards was not at his best in parrying this objection. He admitted, for example, that he had "never seen so much as the thousandth part of the Indians" of this country or looked into their minds, but that on the basis of the sample before him he could with reasonable confidence affirm of them as a whole that there were "not many good philosophers among them" (p. 160). But this weak retort did not stand by itself. Taylor had been guilty of the same fault with which he charged Calvinists. He had indulged in generalizing judgments about humanity on no sounder basis than had his opponents. He had asserted that "The greatest part of mankind have been, and still are, very corrupt, though not equally so in every age and place."[2] And he adjudged "the generality of Christians are the most wicked of all mankind." Edwards pounced on such expressions as flat contradictions to the method which Taylor wished to impose upon Calvinists (p. 49). But he was not satisfied with even this mutilated form of a tu quoque argument. The last court of appeal and the most decisive was Scripture, which Taylor himself accepted as authoritative.[3] Edwards laid the principle down flatly: "If men are not sufficient judges, whether there are few of the world of mankind but what are wicked, yet doubtless God is sufficient, and his judgment, often declared in his word, determines the matter" (p. 161). At this point, divine authority overrides "empiricism" and "nominalism."

Edwards' affirmation of the universality of sin was further buttressed by arguments drawn from the fact of universal mortality as the punishment for sin, and the nature of the redemption offered to men by Christ. To the first of these, Taylor's nominalistic charge could offer no threat if the word "dead" signified only physical demise. However, death for Edwards was not "merely a limiting of existence," but a "terrible calamity." God brought this dread eventuality on man not in his role of Creator, but of Judge, since death entered the world by sin (p. 206). Here Edwards echoed Paul and further elaborated his argument from Scripture, showing the horror and gloom associated with death as the supreme punishment of mankind. If men were guiltless, there would be no death as punishment, and for Edwards the Calvinistic system made clear that death was a punishment, not merely an accidental event or arbitrary act of God

2. *Scripture-Doctrine* (3rd ed., 1746), p. 168.

3. "The revelation of God alone is the rule of my judgment, not any schemes or opinions of men" (ibid., p. iii). "All truth necessary to salvation is revealed in the Holy Scriptures" (p. 2). Taylor, however, had hastened to add that in the interpretation of Scripture, "we ought not to admit any thing contradictory to the common sense and understanding of mankind. For the Scripture can be no rule to us, if the understanding God hath given us is not a rule in judging of their sense and meaning" (p. 3). Thereby he had allowed himself a test of Scripture that was sufficiently pliable to establish his own position.

in his original creation. It was a crucially meaningful event in the complex of divine–human relations.

Taylor, of course, could not blink at death, but his mind ran in a quite different direction from Edwards'. He complacently viewed death as a great benefit to mankind. By it, God had taken effectual steps to wean men from the vanity of this world, to excite in them sober reflections, and to induce in them moderation of appetite (pp. 209, 250). It is God's love, his fatherly concern for his children's welfare, his grace, that has brought about death (pp. 311, 319). Even the increasing brevity of life since Old Testament days bespeaks God's dispensation of mercy, since by bringing death closer in a shorter life, he has brought human sinning into "narrower bounds," thereby lessening the temptations and opportunities for fresh acts of transgression.[4] But Edwards would hear nothing of these shallow blandishments, this cheapening of the real evil of death.

With scriptural citation he firmly bound sin with death and went on with biting irony to raze Taylor's urbane analysis (p. 207). Afflictions and death may be means to bettering humanity, but, he asked, would these be necessary if man were not a depraved creature? When men need such "sharp medicine" and when the bounties of God's gifts are insufficient to bring them to love and obedience, then how can one conclude anything except that they are diseased of spirit? "If anything can be proof of a perverse and vile disposition, this must be a proof of it, that men should be most apt to forget and despise God, when his providence is most kind; and that they should need to have God chastise them with great severity, and even to kill them, to keep them in order" (p. 210). And if all the benefits Taylor found in death are accurately represented, then why is it that death should fall so heavily on infants who obviously are incapable of making any "improvement of it"?

Taylor was not so far gone from a conventional sense of Adam's parental connection with the human race as to deny the relationship, but whereas for him death and suffering were consequences of Adam's failure, Edwards maintained that they were punishments as well as consequences. Taylor would have it that men suffer by the sin

4. Ibid., pp. 67–8, 237. The pages JE wrote in answer to Taylor, Miller called some of his finest pages. "Edwards' realism is firmly planted upon an indomitable knowledge that pain is pain and he would not degrade mankind by pretending that for the living death is not evil" (*Jonathan Edwards,* pp. 272–3).

of their primitive forebears, "but we are not punished for their sin, because we are not guilty of it" (cf. p. 89).[5] But if Adam enjoyed a blessed and happy state in Eden, how could one possibly conceive that stripping him of these amenities was a benefit? (p. 210) After all, did not God threaten Adam, and in Adam all his posterity, with death, and how could this be if death were a benefit and not an evil? Only punishments are threatened; one does not threaten with benefits (p. 247). Edwards sees nothing here but silly reasoning, which denies at root the whole scriptural doctrine of salvation (pp. 367ff.).

For Taylor, as has been seen, death simply meant physical death, the cessation of the physical body's functioning, the common mortality of all men (pp. 237, 306).[6] But Edwards would have none of this. What Adam and his posterity were threatened with and what they have experienced is both a physical death and a spiritual death. Taylor wanted to argue that a proper understanding of the word "death" could be arrived at by contrasting it with the "life" God had given Adam at creation, which signified for him life in a biological sense. Edwards takes another tack. To understand what the Scriptures teach on death, one must regard it as it stands opposed to life in a deeper and fuller sense. "If it be so, that the death threatened to Adam can, with certainty, be opposed only to the life given to Adam, when God created him; I think, a state of perfect, perpetual and hopeless misery is properly opposed to that state Adam was in, when God created him" (p. 237). Clearly, Adam did have a happy life before the fall, and the opposite of that is misery. And to go beyond this, if Adam had proved obedient, he would have been rewarded with eternal life, not merely longevity. "Death" then means, by comparison with its opposite, eternal or spiritual death (p. 237). Hence the conclusion: "That life which the Scripture speaks of as the reward of righteousness, is a whole containing several parts, viz. the life of the body, union of soul and body, and the most perfect sensibility, activity and felicity of both, which is the chief thing. In like manner the death, which the Scripture speaks of as the punishment of sin, is a whole including the death of the body, and the death of the soul, and the eternal, sensible, perfect destruction and misery of both" (p. 308). Thereby, universal mortality in this inclusive sense

5. *Scripture-Doctrine,* p. 21.

6. "Here is not one word, or the least intimation of any other death, but that dissolution, which all mankind undergo when they cease to live in this world" (ibid., pp. 19–20).

provided Edwards with additional support for his major contention of universal sinfulness.[7]

The case for universal depravity was capped by the argument from the need for Christ's redemption. Only a desperately fallen mankind would require the kind of drastic remedy which God has offered in the scriptural plan. All whom Christ came to save are clearly counted as sinners, deserving of punishment (p. 354). They must be inwardly transformed to their depths, thus showing that their corruption is no superficial, transient defection from the path of righteousness. What need would there be for Christ's sacrifice and why would the gospel system be so full of the need for conversion if it were not true that mankind was far gone in its natural state? Only such a nature would call forth God's gracious initiative in providing escape from the morass of spiritual pollution.

Taylor's reading of man's nature, however, had rendered nugatory God's elaborate plan for human salvation. First, he had wandered off the point in claiming infants to be innocent and then had compounded misunderstanding by construing death as a "remedy" or palliative for wickedness. As a result, Christ's salvation of man from death becomes a farce. Or as Edwards scoffed, "It's ridiculous, to talk of persons needing a medicine, or a physician, to save 'em from an excellent medicine; or of a remedy from a happy remedy" (p. 355). Furthermore, Taylor insisted on talking about responsibilities and duties being proportional to the capacities which God had bestowed upon men. In reply to Watts, he had assured his readers of the com-

7. JE would not, however, agree that the word "death" meant annihilation. Notes for his arguments on this subject and death generally may be found in the "Book of Controversies":

> "Punishment cannot be without a subject, that which has no being can suffer no punishment. [sec. 23]
>
> The death threatened in the covenant of works and the punishment thereby due to infants not annihilation. [sec. 22]
>
> But it [is] very manifest that what is intimated in these places in Ezekiel is not that the sinner shall surely suffer temporal death for 'tis exceeding plain by the nature of the thing and by the context that it is some death that the righteous shall surely be delivered from (Ezek. 3:21 etc.). But this is not temporal death, it is not any kind of temporal death, it is not an untimely temporal death, nor is it a violent temporal death. All good men die a temporal death. (Yale Collection, Folder 28, p. 97).

See also secs. 12, 15, 19, 24, 31, 44, 59, and 79.

fortable doctrine that "If I have no power, or . . . sufficient power to do my duty, then it is evident . . . that I have no duty to do." [8] Since God gives men different powers and talents, it seemed quite reasonable to Taylor to conclude that "our duty must be measured by our powers," and "to a lower but just beginning degree of power, a lower or less degree of duty must be incumbent." [9] And what more clearly stood out in this manner of interpreting man's estate than that "we should make a due use of the powers we already have, before we receive and in order to our receiving, further help"? [1] Edwards believed that to follow this line of reasoning was nothing less than disastrous for the gospel scheme, for if men do have a duty to God which they can fulfill of themselves, Christianity is thrown back into that works righteousness from which Paul and the Reformers had rescued it (p. 356). Furthermore, Taylor's position hinged on the highly suspect axiom that God would require of man no more than man is capable of offering in return, by which device man would always be able to excuse himself from wrongdoing on the grounds that obligations had been met up to the limits of his powers. This in turn impugns God's right to demand more than man will fulfill, since divine purposes then must be scaled downward to meet the level of human purposes and achievements. These conclusions reduce to rubble the gospel plan of salvation in denying to God his sovereign authority over his creatures.

Taylor had laid himself open to attack from another angle when he admitted that men sometimes by their folly did entangle themselves in vile passions and evil appetites from which they were unable to release themselves. But if Taylor were to be taken at his own word, the release offered by Christ's redemptive work would bring no salvation. If men are in a bondage too strong to be overcome, this evil then must be counted as "necessary," and Taylor had already argued that "necessary evil can be no moral evil." So there is no evil from which to be saved! And if Taylor wanted to backtrack to the source of evils which lie in the moral capacities of man himself, Edwards reminded him that he had insisted formerly that man's abilities were sufficient to prevent this debacle and therefore from the be-

8. *Scripture-Doctrine,* p. 339. As for Kant, this line of reasoning was considered to be a clincher for the Arminian cause.

9. Ibid., p. 345.

1. Ibid., p. 256.

ginning of man's existence there had been no need of a savior. On Taylor's grounds, it follows then "that none of mankind, . . . ever did, or ever could stand in any need of a savior" (p. 358).

Of course, Taylor had never denied the fact of sin. He could even use the language of orthodox Calvinism in affirming "the degeneracy of mankind . . . as a point never deny'd or doubted by any that I know of." [2] Furthermore, sin, if not universal, at least was extraordinarily widespread in the world. Why then did Edwards not see eye to eye with him in identifying sin? The explanation lies in the difference which they found in the meaning of the term "sin." Edwards had long maintained a sharp distinction between a natural morality or righteousness and a true holiness or virtue.[3] Even in a graceless state, men do have a moral conscience by which they can devise a reasonably decent mode of life, but such virtues as attach to this natural morality never rise to the heights of a true virtue. Taylor, on the other hand, could make nothing of this distinction. For him there was nothing inferior about a morality that men strove earnestly to achieve by their own free and reasonable efforts; and when they failed, which many, if not all, did, their sin consisted in violations of the moral law, which they had transgressed by foolishness, ignorance, or habit. Sin was a blemish of character, but it was not an inexpungible event brought about by some inherent depravity of the soul.

In making his case for the universality of sin, Edwards was willing to count moral failures of the type that Taylor admitted as evidence, but he pushed his case further. Sin was not simply the grosser immoralities of mankind; it was the failure to be possessed of that "relish" and "taste" for divine things, that loving consent to Being as such, which comprised true virtue. What men fell short of was both the moral law and the constant enjoyment of the glory of God for his own sake. Immorality was sin, but so also was lack of holiness, and both counted against man. Yet, the reason the former was counted to

2. Ibid., p. 306.

3. This distinction runs through his *Distinguishing Marks of a Work of the Spirit of God,* the *Religious Affections,* and *The Nature of True Virtue* and appears in *Qualifications for Full Communion, Misrepresentations Corrected* and his observations *Concerning Faith* and *Concerning Efficacious Grace.* "When a man commits sin and is sensible of it, his soul has a natural sense of the propriety of punishment in such a case" (*Concerning Faith,* Worcester ed., *4,* 433).

be evil was that it indicated the latter, the loss of the supernatural principles in Adam, which otherwise would have insured man's faithful obedience and enjoyment of the transcendent beauty of deity. Thus, when Taylor offered examples of men doing deeds of charity and honesty to offset the grim picture of human existence the Calvinists offered, Edwards argued that such deeds did not belong to man's unregenerate or natural estate but were to be credited to the operations of divine grace. Taylor was, as it were, bent on plastering together the occasional remnants of natural virtues and offering this shoddy product as a full-scale image of a humanity that could, on the basis of a morally defensible status, stand before the great God. To Edwards, this was a subterfuge, which he completely disdained.

Of what use is it, he asked, to enumerate virtuous deeds and evil deeds and then try to balance the books in man's favor? After all, the root question is not over *quantity* but *quality*. A truly virtuous deed involves the heart of man, his inclination to savor the divine riches, but the heart can have no tendency to make itself better, till it begins to have a better tendency. And this is precisely the essential factor in true virtue, which is quite beyond the capacity of the self to achieve. Similarly with sin, it is the essential character of sin which outweighs the diverse acts of natural righteousness whereon Taylor had built his case. Sin, for Edwards, was not to be construed as a series of wicked acts strung out on the neutral strand of human personality, among which were interspersed an equal number of beneficent deeds. Such a superficial reading of human character bypassed the crucial truth that both true virtue and genuine sin resided in the very core of the self.

The time was near at hand, as Taylor's treatise clearly showed, when the distinctions between holiness and moral virtue and sin and ethical malfeasance would become meaningless. They were too subtle to have "cash value" in an age moving toward moralism, and people could no longer either undergo or imagine such distinctions. Therefore, Edwards accurately saw that he must deal a deathblow to all attempts that mangled his precious distinctions and generated unresolvable debates over how many good and bad deeds mankind piled up. He had carefully noted in his "Book of Controversies" the place where Francis Hutcheson gave voice to the current optimism of those who wanted to engage in moralistic arithmetic, and he found

Turnbull and Taylor echoing the same sentiments.[4] Taylor appealed to common sense by arguing that "we must not take the measure of our health and enjoyments from a lazar-house, nor of our understanding from Bedlam, nor of our morals from a gaol, nor of this [sexual] passion from harlots and debauches."[5] Turnbull's *Principles of Moral Philosophy* had carried the same refrain, reminding men not to forget "the prevailing innocency, good-nature, industry, felicity and chearfulness of the greater part of mankind at all times" (p. 3).

Taylor, however, had let fall an incautious remark, upon which Edwards seized with great satisfaction. He had said that the law of God gave sin "a deadly force, subjecting every transgression to the penalty of death."[6] Here Taylor had opened just the gate Edwards was looking for, and he could now move from evidences of the universality of sin to an examination of the character of sin itself. If it led to death, then sin must indeed be a far more horrendous affair than the bulk of Taylor's writing expressed, for the clear implication of his remark was that one infringement of the law ruined man as effectively and irretrievably as a dozen, and thereby he had admitted to a peculiar viciousness inherent in sin which, as Edwards put it, "outweighs all effects or consequences of any supposed good." To reason otherwise would be as absurd as to argue that "the state of that ship is good, to cross the Atlantick Ocean in, that is such as cannot hold together through the voyage, but will infallibly founder and sink by the way; under a notion that it may probably go great

4. In the "Book of Controversies" JE appears to have quoted from Hutcheson's *An Essay on the Nature and Conduct of the Passions and Affections, with Illustrations on the Moral Sense* (3rd ed. Dublin, 1728), p. 121, although on p. 109 of *Original Sin* (Yale ed.) he credits Turnbull with the same expressions. Hutcheson wrote, "It is of more consequence to consider what evidences there are that vice and misery in the world are smaller than we sometimes in our melancholy hours imagine. There are no doubt many furious starts of passion in which malice may seem to have place in our constitution; but how seldom and how short in comparison of years spent in fixed kind pursuits of the good of a family, a party, a country." In terms nearly identical with those attributed by JE to Turnbull and Taylor, Hutcheson continued by pointing out that judgments concerning mankind should not be made on the basis of what one sees in a court of justice, or estimates of the healthfulness of a climate by the examination of hospitals. See "Book of Controversies," p. 257, where the pagination of Hutcheson is given as p. 185.

5. *Scripture-Doctrine*, p. 353.

6. Ibid., p. 207.

part of the way before it sinks, or that it will proceed and sail above water more hours than it will be in sinking" (p. 129), or, in another striking figure, to count a wife faithful "because, although she committed adultery, and that with the slaves and scoundrels sometimes, yet she did not do this so often as she did the duties of a wife" (p. 133). What conceivable benefit is there in enumerating good deeds, as Taylor was fond of doing, when these actions exist on a totally different scale from that employed by God in judging sinfulness? [7]

To make clear in a more formal way the intrinsically detestable nature of sin, Edwards returned to an argument he had frequently used in his revival sermons and to which Anselm had centuries before given classic formulation.[8] The heinousness of sin arises from the fact that sin is in proportion to the infinite worthiness of regard man owes an infinite being. Man owes God this infinite regard; it is a debt owed in all justice "in the nature of things." Consequently, if man paid it, it would only be what he justly owed the deity; it would count nothing to his own credit. But man's failure to do so, and this is man's present condition, amounts to an infinite demerit. And if sin is an infinite demerit, it is rightly punished by an infinite punishment. The excellence of the nature of the object against which sin is committed determines both the enormity of the sin and its punishment. Man's good actions simply are disproportionate to the infinite demerit he has incurred by contemning the justice, love, and glory of God (p. 130). So humanity has nothing to cast onto the scales to balance the heinousness of its crime and is in a natural state of corruption, which quite properly, unless God intervenes, culminates in eternal misery and torment.

The delicate question of the manner in which a finite being could incur an infinite debt Edwards did not treat at this point, but in the "Miscellanies" (No. 44) he attempted a formulation which would relieve the apparent injustice implied by it. He phrased the question as follows: "Seeing that the malicious or evil principle, which is the essence of the sin, is not infinite, though the God against whom sin is

7. Ibid., pp. 333–8.

8. *St. Anselm,* trans. Sidney N. Deane (LaSalle, Ill., Open Court Publishing Co., 1951), Bk. I, ch. 21, pp. 228–30; F. H. Foster, *A Genetic History of the New England Theology* (Chicago, University of Chicago Press, 1907), p. 85; Friedrich Loofs, *Lietfaden der Dogmengeschichte* (Halle, 1893), pp. 271–5. JE develops the argument in "Miscellanies," No. 713.

committed be infinite, how can it be just to punish sin with an infinite punishment?" His answer ran, "the crime or injury done, in itself considered, is really infinite, yet is finite in the idea or mind committing [it], that is, is in itself infinite but is not committed infinitely; so it is with the punishment. It is really in itself . . . infinite but is never suffered infinitely." The intrinsic quality of sin is infinite because it is against an infinite being, but in the view which the human mind takes, it is finite in extent or duration. The human mind is finite and can entertain the idea of an infinite degree, but only in the mind of God is sin infinite both in inherent quality and in duration, as is also punishment. "Sin against God, in God's idea, is infinite . . . and the punishment is infinite no otherwise but in the idea of God; for all that is past and all that is to come, that is not comprehended in finite ideas is not anywhere else but in the divine idea." But if this is so, no man as a finite being experiences either infinite sin or infinite punishment, since it might be argued that both are infinite only from the standpoint of God, whereas Edwards' argument in the *Original Sin* supposes that he can demonstrate to other finite men the infinite enormity of sin. To place infinity or heinousness of sin and infinity or duration of punishment in the mind of God would be to place it quite beyond the reach of the understanding of those Edwards wished to confute. If he remembered this line of argument as developed in the "Miscellanies" when he wrote *Original Sin,* he was doubtless wise not to include it!

By his insistence upon the infinitely heinous character of all sin, he was running close to dangerous shoal waters, for he apparently admitted that there were no degrees of sinfulness. Once sin appeared, nothing that followed could add more weight to its infinitely detestable nature. "White lies" and murder would stand on the same footing, and ethical discriminations of even the most rudimentary kind would count for nothing.[9] Edwards did not see fit to explore this line of reasoning, but in *The Nature of True Virtue* and in a

9. This problem haunted the Reformers in their treatments of original sin. JE's line of thought on the issue seems to have paralleled theirs, although he makes no explicit reference to sources. Emil Brunner, interpreting the Reformers on the subject, claims, "Within Original Sin the distinction between 'good' and 'evil' has not been obliterated. . . . The Reformers, too, frankly admitted this fact—although they obstinately and passionately resisted the inferences which Catholic theology drew from it—and to this sphere (the realm of relative ethical judgments) they gave the name of the *justitia civilis*" (*Man in Revolt,* Philadelphia, Westminster Press, 1947, pp. 153–4).

few places in the *Original Sin* he offered indications of the direction he would take had he done so. Once the basic differences between sin and virtue, nature and grace, were established, he was prepared to admit that men grow in sin as they do in grace and that there are degrees of sin and virtue. He can therefore speak without obvious contradiction of "that increasing iniquity" derived from natural depravity and affirm that "dispositions to evil are commonly much stronger in adult persons, than in children" (p. 137). He finds that "every one who comes to act in the world as a moral agent, is, in a greater or lesser degree, guilty of sin" (p. 114) and that Noah's descendants "had been gradually growing more and more corrupt" (p. 165). In fact, his notion of the dynamic, productive character of both sin and grace would seem to lead directly to a concept of degrees of intensity in both areas.[1]

One of the principal advantages which Edwards believed he had won over his opponents by his demonstration of sin's heinousness was that he had shown the justice of God in punishing men for it. When he swept aside all moralistic arithmetic and insisted on studying man in his natural state apart from grace, he had opened the way to that vindication of God's moral attributes which the Arminians charged the Calvinists with defacing. "The controversy," as he put it bluntly, "is not, what grace will do, but what justice might do" (p. 111). Infinite sin calls for infinite punishment, and God's justice is exhibited in bringing this result to pass; that he saves only certain men from this fate is simply beside the point when the issue is one of man's natural posture. God would not be a god of righteousness, in Edwards' view, if he temporized with human vileness. The logic is clear. Just as justice in this world demands punishment, so divine justice demands infinite punishment, and therefore the slightest breath of criticism cannot be reasonably raised against this exhibition of divine righteousness.

THE CAUSE AND TRANSMISSION OF SIN

Having amassed the evidence for the universality of sin and argued its heinousness, Edwards went to the root of the matter by ex-

1. In the Corollary to "Miscellanies," No. 713, JE referred to the problem of all sins being equally heinous as "hardly worth mentioning," but went on to argue ingeniously that the infinite heinousness of sin "don't hinder but that some sins may be more aggravated & heinous than others in other respects as if we suppose a cylinder infinitely long it can't be greater in that respect . . .

plaining its cause. What lay behind all instances of overt sinfulness was nothing other than a constant and preponderating tendency in human nature. Reason demands for recurrent events a recurrent cause, and on this causal principle Edwards stubbornly insisted. "A steady effect argues a steady cause" (p. 121), and that steady cause was the vicious tendency which lay in the human heart. This inference was to be justified in turn by reasoning from the evidence which he had collected. "We obtain a notion of such a thing as tendency, no other way than by observation: and we can observe nothing but events: and 'tis the commonness or constancy of events, that gives us a notion of tendency in all cases" (p. 121; see also pp. 119–23, 190–92).

He was then prepared to deal with those attempts of Taylor and others to blame sin on the general order of things or other external circumstances which would keep depravity at arm's length. "In God's sight no man living can be justified," he explained, and "this is true of persons of all constitutions, capacities, conditions, manners, opinions and educations; in all countries, climates, nations and ages; and through all the mighty changes and revolutions, which have come to pass in the habitable world" (p. 124). If this sweeping evaluation were maintained, then the fault must lie in the nature of man as such and not in the furnishings of his world. Taylor had lamented that this ordering of the present world was not one calculated to encourage virtue, and he speculated that, given a different world, humanity, with its present nature, would have had a better opportunity to practice virtue than even Adam had.[2] But this kind of idealistic vaporing Edwards sees as circular, signifying only that if sin had already been conquered, then there would be no sin! And what point can there be in fleeing to such elysian dreams when the stark facts of this world, not of another, insistently call for an accounting? Above all, what sense is there in decrying present circumstances while insisting in the same breath that men are here and now capable of virtue?

Edwards met efforts to blame on the world's system what in fact belongs to human nature with further argument drawn from his Neoplatonic vision of reality. "If any creature be of such a nature that it proves evil in its proper place, or in the situation which God has assigned it in the universe, it is of an evil nature. That part of

---

yet it may be doubled & trebled yea & made a thousand fold more by the increase of other dimensions." So with sin, it may "be vastly more dreadful on other accounts."

2. *Scripture-Doctrine*, p. 236.

the system is not good, which is not good in its place in the system: and those inherent qualities of that part of the system, which are not good, but corrupt, in that place, are justly looked upon as evil inherent qualities" (p. 125). The whole system of existence is supposed to be an interlocking, harmonious structure, but if one element therein can throw the whole into disorder, it must be that there is a radical defect in that element, not in the system itself. And this is precisely how men judge the nature of anything—by observing what course it takes when seen in its proper context. Thus, the discovery of propensities depends on observing what the entity in question does or aims at accomplishing within the general structure of which it is a component. Or, as Edwards would have it, "Propensities are no propensities, any otherwise, than as taken with their objects" (p. 126). If men do evil in this world where God obviously intended them to dwell, they are evil.

In anticipation of an argument to be used later, Edwards went on to remind Taylor that those who blamed man's sin on purely external circumstances had not moved one step nearer to solving the question of the origin of sin, but had only postponed decision on that score. And if they would not accept the fact that man's inherently corrupt nature was compatible with the present divine constitution in human affairs, the embarrassing question remained as to who or what had established and ordered "external circumstances" so that men would fall into sin as surely in this way as in the manner upon which the Calvinists insisted (p. 126). The Arminian–Pelagian gambit succeeded only in splitting its advocates on the point of impugning God's moral excellencies, an option most abhorrent because God's more amiable moral attributes served as a court of last appeal to support their own outraged denials of human depravity.

If sin's occurrence could not be fobbed off on the punishment, it must find its origin in the human self. But Taylor had his alternative reply ready. Sin does arise in the individual, not because of any naturally depraved state, but by the free choice of the person. Men misuse their God-given natural propensities by choosing to follow base appetites and drives. Here, thought Taylor, was the explanation which commended itself by its patent intelligibility. Adam and Eve went astray by "prostituting reason to appetite," but, Taylor quickly pointed out, they involved themselves and no one else in their sin.[3] It is the same with all men; they corrupt their natures by their own

3. Ibid., pp. 8, 13, 19–20, 96, 168.

choices. Their moral delinquencies owe nothing to the baleful inheritance from Adam. You ought to blame or condemn yourself alone, warned Taylor, not Adam.[4] Those nobler powers of reason and choice that God has bestowed upon man lift man above the beasts, and sin appears only when "sensual appetites and passions" become excessive and irregular because of reason's abdication of authority over them.[5] If sin comes by necessary consequence, with no act of choice on the part of the individual, there would, properly speaking, be no sin, "for whatever is necessary, whatever cannot be helped, before it comes to pass, is no sin; because no body can be blamed for it." [6] Or to put the whole matter succinctly: "If we come into the world infected, and depraved with sinful dispositions, then sin must be natural to us; and if natural, then necessary, and if necessary, then no sin." [7] But, to go round the circle again, man's nature can be corrupted only by "the depraved choice of a moral agent" and for this reason, Taylor cried defiantly, "none can corrupt my nature or make me wicked, but I myself." [8] Of course, men will repeatedly fall away into iniquity, but this is to be expected since we do not come into the world perfect, Taylor observed in a dangerous concession. And since we are here in a "state of probation, where we are to be tried and purified in order to future and everlasting happiness," we are liable to be seduced "by bodily appetites and the things of sense and time and to disregard the laws of reason and truth" and thereby neglect "spiritual and eternal concernment." [9]

Edwards had been over this weary, well-trodden track before in *Freedom of the Will,* and he refers his readers to that work, where he had "fully and largely considered" the absurdities attendant upon the notion of the will's self-determining power (p. 228). Nevertheless, he plunged ahead into a shortened version of his principal contentions in that treatise. Buttressed by his argument from causality, he could inquire of Taylor "how it comes to pass that mankind so universally agree in this evil exercise of their free will?" If men are as free to choose good as evil, why haven't affairs worked out so that there is as much good as evil in the world? "If the cause is indifferent,

4. Ibid., pp. 257–8, 351.
5. Ibid., pp. 352–3.
6. Ibid., pp. 129, 98, 339.
7. Ibid., pp. 200, 125, 420.
8. Ibid., p. 188.
9. Ibid., pp. 299, 311.

why is not the effect in some measure indifferent?" If free will implies contingency in its most radical sense, then no previous inclination affects a particular choice, and certainly nothing could be "more unfixed than that." Yet there is a universal and unswerving obedience to sin in the world, which even Taylor admitted, and how else can it be explained except on the grounds that "a steady effect requires a steady cause"? (p. 194)

Taylor's cherished notion that virtue or vice presupposes the reflective choice of a moral agent was thoroughly dismantled. The general principle to which Edwards appealed for his demolition work was "not that principles derive their goodness from actions, but that actions derive their goodness from the principles whence they proceed." So, in the case of virtue, "the act of choosing that which is good, is no further virtuous than it proceeds from a good principle, or virtuous disposition of mind." The conclusion follows quickly: if a virtuous disposition antedates the act of choice, then virtue or vice cannot depend on choice itself (p. 225).[1] Taylor, furthermore, had made a damaging concession in asserting that all Christian virtue is resolvable into the single principle of love. Edwards pounced on the contradiction: therefore, "no act of volition or choice can have any moral rectitude, that takes place before this principle exists . . . yet the principle of benevolence itself, can't be virtuous, unless it proceeds from choice." Surely Taylor cannot have it both ways. "Virtuous love, as the principle of all virtue, must go before virtuous choice, and be the principle or spring of it; and yet virtuous choice must go before virtuous benevolence, and be the spring of that" (p. 226). How much further can incoherence go?

When Taylor argued that the cause of every effect is "chargeable" with the effect it produces, he had only dug his grave deeper, for Edwards was more than eager to show him that he had once more entangled himself by twisted logic. If nothing, for example, can be sin except what derives from choice, then how is it possible to argue that only the cause itself, i.e. choice, is "chargeable with all the blame"? (p. 377) Then, with his favorite device of the infinite regress to absurdity, Edwards took Taylor to task for having designated the choice itself as faulty. "If the choice itself be sin, and there be no sin but what proceeds from a sinful choice, then the sinful choice must proceed from another *antecedent* choice"; this choice must be ex-

1. In expanded form this argument is found in *Freedom of the Will,* Yale ed., *1,* 340–1.

plained by another previous choice, and so on back to a first choice. But the first choice of the chain, being by definition first, must be necessary, since we can retire no further to other choices (p. 378). It must be that choice arises from a necessarily evil nature, or else there is no explanation of either evil or good to be found.

A morally necessary action or principle does not deliver the agent from blame, because the agent's nature involves the will; it is part of his nature and he is therefore, properly speaking, "willing" the action or principle. And in the case of sin, as he confided to the "Miscellanies," "It don't at all excuse persons for not doing such duties as loving God, accepting of Christ, etc. that they can't do it of themselves, unless they would if they could i.e. unless they would do it from good principles; for that woulding is as good as no would at all that is in no wise from any good principle." [2]

Furthermore, as already proved, the very nature of the sin committed and intended is itself odious, and God has so judged it. It must be, then, that God in his wisdom counts a necessary evil nature subject to moral blame. The chimera of free choice cannot be used by sinful men to bargain with God for exemption from moral responsibility.

Taylor's efforts to explain human sin on the basis of free choice thus failed. His case had hinged on the proposition "if natural, then necessary; if necessary, then no sin," and with that principle demolished, all elaborations based on it fall to the ground. Returning once more to his favorite line, Edwards vigorously claimed that only a powerful, fixed, steady cause, constitutive of man's fundamental nature, explained universal wickedness (p. 193).

Edwards more briefly disposed of two other favorite sallies. Taylor had suggested that men sin because they are corrupted by bad examples. This superficial answer Edwards reduced to triviality by pointing out that " 'tis accounting for the thing by the thing itself," or accounting for the corruption of humanity by simple affirmation of it. It is to offer a description in place of an explanation of sin. And why are there so many bad examples which men follow so avidly, unless there is a native propensity to evil both in the examples and in those who imitate them? (pp. 196–99) An equally innocuous explanation of sin on the grounds that the senses and appetites got a head start on the rational faculty had been offered by Turnbull, who was enchanted with the idea that by training man developed from a state of

2. No. 631; see also No. 43, in Worcester ed., *5*, 454.

animalistic sensibilities to that of rational, moral self-control. But what purpose does such an explanation serve? All it comes to is that men are brought into existence in those precise circumstances in which they will inevitably sin. "That strength, which sensitive appetites and animal passions come to by their habitual exercise, before persons come to the exercise of their rational powers, amounts to a strong propensity to sin, when they first come to the exercise of those rational powers" (p. 202). And what was worse for the Arminian position was that it had succeeded in placing men in this state while they were in no position to oppose it. This, for Edwards, meant that men are necessarily in sin in their primitive condition and that God is responsible as the architect of their fate (pp. 202–04). But these conclusions, to the dismay of the liberal mind, were precisely the conclusions they most wished to avoid and had urged as objections against the orthodox scheme.

There was one line of Taylor's argument which particularly endangered Edwards' insistence upon man's corrupt nature. If Taylor could establish the point that the doctrine was an unnecessary hypothesis for accounting for Adam's sin, he could conclude that it was equally irrelevant in accounting for the sin of Adam's posterity. He set up a neat dilemma for the Calvinists when he reminded them of their insistence upon Adam's original righteousness and their equal insistence upon his fall. Certainly, Adam fell, and for this there must be an adequate cause. But if he fell from a righteous state, there is no need for a doctrine of original sin as an explanation, because original sin is ruled out by definition, Adam being righteous when created. It follows, then, that if the notion of a depraved nature is unnecessary as an explanation of Adam's sin, it is equally useless in explaining the sin of his posterity.[3] It is simply an otiose hypothesis.

To ward off this threat, Edwards had to show that the notion of original sin was irrelevant to Adam's sinning, but that it was absolutely essential for giving an account of man's sin. To accomplish this, he had to establish the fact that his argument for human depravity rested upon a ground different from that which explained the original fall itself. He therefore proceeded to refute Taylor by introducing some basic clarifications. It is conformable to reason to argue constancy of cause from constancy of effect, but, he asks, "is it the manner of men to conclude, that whatever they see others once do, they have a fixed abiding inclination to do?" (p. 192). As great

3. *Scripture-Doctrine,* pp. 127, 231–2.

and aggravated as was the sin of Adam and, for that matter, the angels, it was not a permanent or fixed affair. These "first acts, considered in themselves, were no permanent continued effects" (p. 192). True, a first act may lead to a "settled habit or propensity," but simply considered as a first act, such as Adam's was, nothing can be inferred as to an abidingly corrupt nature. The extensive harm of Adam's misstep cannot be employed as evidence of the permanence of a fixed inclination, for many can do wrong a first time, as did the angels, thereby multiplying instances of evil without revealing by these multiple, single, first acts the control of a steady propensity to evil. Unlike the circumstances from which Edwards had drawn his evidence for man's corrupt nature, those in which Adam and the angels stood offered no possibility of a "trial of a vast variety of circumstances attending a permanent effect, to shew the fixed cause to be internal" (pp. 192–93). Since man's nature has been put to the test in so many different contexts and still has poured forth in a torrent of wickedness, it is altogether proper to conclude that men are possessed of an inherent bent to evil. Therefore, Taylor, having overlooked the difference between the conditions in which Adam sinned and those in which his posterity sin, has missed the whole point of the controversy. The term "original sin" cannot properly be assigned to Adam; it must be applied to humanity at large. The doctrine of man's depraved nature must be retained, for it is by no means a futile hypothesis.

Taylor also wanted to push the argument further by insisting that just as there was no reason to suppose that the doctrine of original sin explained Adam's fall, neither were there grounds for affirming Adam's original righteousness. Adam, as we have seen, fell as all men fall, by the misuse of his freedom and reason. Not even God, Taylor argued, can create a virtuous man, because virtue implies rational choice, "for 'tis obvious to the common sense of all mankind, that whatever is wrought in my nature without my knowledge and consent, cannot possibly be either sin or righteousness in me. . . . It is mere instinct." And since the Scriptures offer no evidence of Adam's original righteousness, Taylor concluded "it appears to me, that the common scheme of original righteousness, as well as that of original sin, is without any foundation in Scripture, or the reason and nature of things." [4] But, answered Edwards, since Adam's sin was his first sin, and since God had at first smiled upon and favored him, it must follow that Adam was perfectly innocent by nature (pp. 228, 229). By

4. Ibid., pp. 437–43.

identifying righteousness with innocence rather than with a rectitude wrought out by the personal endeavors of Adam, Edwards set the issue of Adam's righteousness in a different light from that in which Taylor viewed it. Edwards argued that Adam was immediately capable of behaving as a moral agent under the rule and principle of right action. If Taylor wished to contend that Adam could not sin without an inclination thereto, Edwards was willing to claim, by parity of reasoning, that Adam could not have acted rightly prior to the fall without an inclination to right action. As Adam had acted righteously at first, he must have been created with an inclination to good, from which his virtuous behavior stemmed.

If he were righteous initially, the starting up of sin for the first time in Adam was correspondingly more difficult to account for. Hence, Edwards had to show just how it was possible for a perfectly virtuous being to slide off into rebellion against his Maker. He set about the task by pointing out that Taylor had labored under the misapprehension that Calvinists believed that human nature was despoiled by God's having implanted some positive evil within it. "There is not the least need of supposing any evil quality *infused, implanted,* or *wrought* into the nature of man, by any . . . cause, or influence whatsoever, either from God, or the creature" (p. 380). All it is necessary to recognize about original man, Edwards contended, is that he was created with certain natural principles, such as self-love, and natural appetites and passions, and added to these were superior or supernatural principles "wherein consisted the spiritual image of God, and man's righteousness and true holiness" (p. 381). Even though these supernatural principles were to be withdrawn, "human nature would be human nature still; man's nature as such, being entire without these divine principles" (p. 382).[5] However,

5. JE labored over this distinction in the footnote on this page to be sure that, in spite of his use of the terms "natural" and "supernatural" in an "uncommon sense," he was to be understood as distinguishing mere human nature (man as such) from man as truly virtuous, holy, and spiritual. Both sets of principles began in Adam and "are necessary to the perfection and well-being" of humanity, but supernatural principles are not essential to "the constitution of it, or necessary to its being." In his two sermons on Rom. 7:14, he said that supernatural principles were no proof of human nature (Yale Collection, MS. VI). Miller detected in this footnote JE's move toward a naturalistic outlook, since the "supernatural" for JE arises as a special kind of taste or perception, out of sensation (cf. *Jonathan Edwards,* pp. 275–6). A clear description of the distinction between the natural and the spiritual man is to be found in the *Religious Affections,* Yale ed., 2, 208 ff.

when Adam failed, these superior principles were withdrawn, and the release of the natural principles in an orgy of self-love and passion brought forth the horror, confusion, and evil which has wracked human history ever since. "The inferior principles of self-love and natural appetite, which were given only to serve, being alone, and left to themselves, of course became reigning principles; . . . they became absolute masters of the heart" (p. 382). Or, as recorded in the "Miscellanies," sin is "only the same self-love" that on the removal of the superior principles "will certainly, without anything else, produce or rather will become all those sinful inclinations which are in the corrupted nature of man." [6] Thus, the origin of sin is not due to any positive factor, but to the withdrawal of influences which God justly effects, since it would be derogatory to his nature to continue in company with a rebellious subject.[7] In a figure that did not find its way into the text of *Original Sin,* Edwards described the process of sin's origination on the mechanistic model of a scale: "If there be weight in opposite scales the balance may be kept even but if the weight of one scale be removed the other will have the entire government and will put the balance out of order without any addition." [8] The important phrase here, of course, is "without any addition," and if employed in the completed text it would have reemphasized the privative character of sin's origin.

6. No. 301.

7. JE, in this analysis of a privative cause of sin, follows closely a line of thought used by Aquinas, a similarity that Miller noted (*Jonathan Edwards,* pp. 276–7).

8. "Book of Controversies," p. 252. The figure was not original with JE. He cites in this place, probably from Lord Kames' *Essays on the Principles of Morality and Natural Religion* (Edinburgh, 1751), a description of man whose author JE identified at the bottom of the page as a "Scotch author of essays on the principles of morality": "Man is a complex machine composed of various principles which may be conceived as so many springs and weights counteracting and balancing one another. Those being accurately adjusted the movement of life is beautiful because regular and uniform. But if some springs or weights be withdrawn those which remain acting now without opposition from their antagonist [faults?] with disorder the balance and derange the whole machine." To this quotation JE added his own conclusion, "by the withdrawnment of one kind of principle that balanced, limited and regulated others those others properly increase strength without any positive cause or without putting any positive thing into 'em by strength be meant efficacy and governing power." The same figure of speech is in the *Religious Affections,* Yale ed., *2,* 179. On Kames, see Yale ed., *1,* 443–52.

The sequence of events in Adam's fall leaves Edwards mired in a difficulty from which he never successfully freed himself. Once having established Adam's original righteousness, how could he explain the take-over of the lower faculties? The withdrawal of the supernatural principles followed and did not precede or cause the fall itself. Whence then arose Adam's inclination to sin, since, by Edwards' own oft-repeated thesis, a cause must be found for every act? In a brief footnote he attempted to meet Taylor's charge that Adam could not have sinned without an antecedent sinful inclination. He haltingly conceded as much when he claimed that there was "no natural sinful inclination in Adam" and yet insisted that there was "an inclination to that sin of eating the forbidden fruit" which "was begotten in him by the delusion and error he was led into" (p. 229). This appears to be nothing more than circular reasoning. How could a delusion be "begotten in him" or how could he be "led into" delusion without presupposing a sinful propensity to which the temptation could appeal? God, who created him righteous, could not have led him astray without contradicting himself. Satan could not be expected to gain a purchase on a mind created in pristine innocence. Edwards, of course, could not argue for a spontaneous or free choice, since this would have played directly into the hands of the Arminians.[9] He could not consistently hold that there was no cause for the fall, though it happened only once and therefore was a unique event. He did allow that sin's coming into existence might be explained "from the imperfection which properly belongs to a creature as such," but this was a damaging concession, inasmuch as imperfections in the creature as created would redound only to the discredit of the Creator. He seems therefore to have given over this line of reasoning in the *Freedom of the Will* after employing it in an ad hoc manner to offset the charge that sin came into the world by God's express command.[1] He had tried another explanation in which he identified original righteousness with innocence. Adam and Eve before their fall had been acting in artless simplicity, and the tempter beguiled them by leading them to believe "that their disobedience should be followed with no destruction or calamity at all to themselves (and

9. "Nothing that the Arminians say, about the contingence, or self-determining power of man's will, can serve to explain with less difficulty, how the first sinful volition of mankind could take place, and man be justly charged with the blame of it" (Yale ed., *1*, 414).

1. Ibid., p. 413.

therefore not to their posterity) but on the contrary, with a great increase and advancement of dignity and happiness" (p. 193). Hence, their ignorance or innocence proved incapable of recognizing temptation when confronted by it, and they fell in with the suggestion of eating the apple. Therefore, the first sin might be traced to ignorance. But this way of reasoning seemed only to lead back to Taylor's contention that the original parents sinned in the same manner in which all men do, by errors of judgment made in ignorance of consequences and with free exercise of choice; or it leads to a contemning of God's creatorship, since he knew beforehand that ignorance would lead to this disastrous consequence. Moreover, Edwards had explicitly stated that Adam and Eve in their primordial condition practiced both internal and external duties to God; they loved him as they ought. This is nothing other than positive virtue; it does not bespeak an estate of ignorant simplicity (p. 230).

Edwards ended lamely. He could affirm only that sin had come about and that God had permitted it to do so. "The first arising or existing of that evil disposition in the heart of Adam, was by God's *permission;* who could have prevented it, if he had pleased, by giving such influences of his spirit, as would have been absolutely effectual to hinder it; . . . and whatever mystery may be supposed in the affair, yet no Christian will presume to say, it was not in perfect consistence with God's holiness and righteousness, notwithstanding Adam had been guilty of no offense before." (p. 394) If any Arminians wanted to argue with this resolution, they could do so, but Edwards had blunted in advance any further caviling on their part. In the *Freedom of the Will* he had resorted to two devices with which to confound them. First, he put the alternatives: events, including moral actions, are disposed either by "blind and undesigning causes" or by a being of infinite sagacity. Which would the Arminians take? "Is it not better, that the good and evil which happens in God's world, should be ordered, regulated, bounded and determined by the good pleasure of an infinitely wise Being, who perfectly comprehends . . . the universality of things . . . than to leave these things to fall out by chance, and to be determined by those causes which have no understanding or aim?" [2] If Arminians were convinced that they lived in a pointless, dumb world, working out their destinies, they could have it so, but clearly, they must accept all the implications of the choice. Edwards, for his part, would not sur-

2. Ibid., p. 405.

render his conviction of divine sovereignty; better to hold to both evil and purposeful realization under God's sway than to yield either. And certainly no Arminian worth his salt would be expected to settle for a "chance" universe! Why not then follow to its conclusion the other alternative, that of God's infinitely wise direction of all that does happen, even including sin's entry into the world? Edwards had defiantly flung the challenge to his opponents to find a better solution to sin's advent, knowing full well that whatever proposals they offered were all infected with irrationality. What could one expect of people who persisted in placing a first act of will before a first act of will in Adam to explain a second first act? He remarked dryly that it was "an odd way of solving difficulties to advance greater, in order to do it." And to prattle of accidents causing sins was only to compound nonsense, for that is to say no more than that there is no cause at all! Having rehearsed and shown the absurdities of Arminian thought processes in the *Freedom of the Will,* he roundly asserted that nothing they had to say on the subject of sin's origin could "explain with less difficulty, how the first sinful volition of mankind could take place" than his own theory.[3] He was willing to stand by this contention in the *Original Sin.*

Edwards may have made heavy weather of explaining the origin of sin, but even stormier weather lay ahead in making sense of the doctrine of imputation. Nothing in the whole controversy over original sin so outraged the Arminian mentality as the idea that Adam represented humanity in such a fashion that his guilt as well as his sin was passed on to a hapless humanity who had had neither hand nor choice in his fall. Each person is wholly responsible for himself, said Taylor, and no one can take his place. "A representative of moral action is what I can by no means digest," he complained when faced with the notion of Adam's standing for the whole human race.[4] And he proceeded to sum up the case against imputation in words that fairly shook with indignation:

> But that any man, without my knowledge or consent, should so represent me, that when he is guilty I am to be reputed guilty, and when he transgresses I shall be accountable and punishable for his transgression, and thereby subjected to the wrath and curse of God, nay further that his wickedness shall give me a sin-

3. Ibid., p. 414.
4. *Scripture-Doctrine,* p. 384.

> ful nature, and all this before I am born and consequently while I am in no capacity of knowing, helping, or hindering what he doth; surely anyone who dares use his understanding, must clearly see this is unreasonable, and altogether inconsistent with the truth and goodness of God.[5]

After correcting Taylor on the point that Scripture explicitly and implicitly includes Adam's posterity in God's judgment on Adam (pp. 252–57) and shows Adam to be "the public head and representative of his posterity" (pp. 247, 383), Edwards demonstrated how the constituted relation between Adam and the human race operates and what the moral justification of that arrangement is. The factual question must first be dealt with, and the hard fact is that God does deal with mankind as a unity. "It signifies nothing, to exclaim against plain fact" (p. 394). Since men come into the world in a state which universally manifests itself in sin, and since God treats them in this condition as one with Adam and not as innocent individuals, it makes little difference whether Taylor and his ilk liked the constitution of unity or not. "Fact obliges us to get over the difficulty, either by finding out some solution, or by shutting our mouths, and acknowledging the weakness and scantiness of our understandings" (p. 395). Humanity is organically one by virtue of "an established method and order of events, settled and limited by divine wisdom," and it existed in Adam as the branches and fruit of a tree are in the tree (cf. pp. 386, 389).

As Taylor understood the matter, imputation meant blaming sin and guilt on millions of discrete individuals far removed in times, places, and nature from Adam. To burden others with sin and guilt from Adam or any other person seemed to him the rankest miscarriage of justice and good sense. However, the trouble, as Edwards

5. Ibid., p. 385. In a remarkable passage from the controversy over the formation of the council that finally recommended his dismissal from the Northampton church, JE used an argument that agreed with the sentiment expressed in Taylor's statement. It seems to contradict flatly the theme used in *Original Sin*. "No persons professing Protestant principles will maintain, that Christians of the present generation are bound, in affairs of religion and the worship of God, by the determination of their forefathers, unless they have adopted the act of their forefathers and made it in some way or other their own, by their own act and consent, either express or implicit" (Dwight ed., *1*, 351, 381). Only by contending that the posterity of Adam was identical with Adam and that their sin was his, as his was theirs, could he dispel the contradictory impression which this passage leaves.

saw it, was that Taylor simply did not understand what imputation meant because he had not grasped the meaning of the concept of personal identity. To say that Adam and his posterity were identical and therefore were rightfully treated as one by God might sound odd, but once a clear understanding of identity was offered, the whole process of imputation would become intelligible. And this he proceeded to do in one of the most creative pieces of reasoning to be found in the treatise.

A mature person, Edwards pointed out, is in certain respects quite different from what he was as an infant. Many changes of "substances" have taken place between birth and maturity, yet in other respects the person is the same. It must be that there is a principle of unity in each person, established by God, and it is this same divinely ordained principle by which Adam and his posterity are counted as one (p. 398). But how is this principle of personal identity to be understood? John Locke had suggested that personal identity consisted in a sameness or continuity of consciousness in a person (pp. 398–99), and, earlier in the references to memory and personal identity in his "Notes on the Mind," Edwards had seemed inclined to accept that interpretation. "Well might Mr. Locke say, that identity . . . of person consisted in identity of consciousness." But on second thought he was troubled by the implications of Locke's doctrine: "Identity of person is what seems never yet to have been explained." Perhaps Locke's notion was a mistake "if by sameness of consciousness, be meant, having the same ideas hereafter, that I have now, with a notion or apprehension that I had them before." Edwards saw a problem in the possibility that God could create independent beings having the same ideas which he himself had, without his being aware of these new persons. In a sense, these beings were identical with him, if consciousness and memories were identical, but he did not see how it was possible that any of these persons should be "the same person" as himself "when I know nothing of his sufferings and am never the better for his joys." [6] Although ever ready to count Locke on his side, Edwards was not prepared to let the case for personal identity rest on the grounds of memory alone, lest an opponent argue that he had no memory of Adam's sin and therefore could reckon himself guiltless. Furthermore, he was quick to point out, sameness of conciousness or memory was not a self-operative process dependent only upon "a course of nature" which God,

6. Dwight ed., *1*, 680–1.

in a deistic fashion, once having created it, left to go on in its own fashion. Let it be remembered "who it is, gives the soul this nature," and, quoting Taylor against himself, that "the course of nature, separate from the agency of God, is no cause, or nothing." Turnbull's citation from Newton was also quarried to buttress Edwards' principal theses: "It is the will of the mind that is the first cause, that gives a subsistence and efficacy to all those laws, who is the efficient cause that produces the phenomena . . . according to these laws." And he nodded agreement to Turnbull's improvement of the passage, when Turnbull claimed that the same principle operated in moral philosophy. Thus, Edwards concluded that identity of consciousness depends on an "arbitrary divine constitution" and not on some independent function of the personality. God as efficient agent directly causes personal identity, and there is no possible recourse to some order in nature which operates by its own impetus (p. 399).

Edwards had yet to show more precisely in what way this immediate causal action of God laid the groundwork for the doctrine of imputation. He therefore set about elaborating the proposition "that God not only created all things, and gave them being at first, but continually preserves them, and upholds them in being" (p. 400). If this proposition, taken in its fullest extent, could be maintained successfully, he foresaw important implications following, by which to explain imputation itself. He began with the innocent truism that every created object in the world has dependent existence, thereby in a sense depositing the conclusion of the argument in the premise. Every object is, therefore, a caused thing. Its cause must lie either in an "antecedent existence" of that substance or in the power of the Creator. But it cannot owe its present existence to its own antecedent state because what existed a moment before is only a passive entity and not an active cause. Nor can any cause produce effects in a time or place where it is not existing. "In point of time, what is *past* entirely ceases, when *present* existence begins; otherwise it would not be *past*" (p. 400). The same principle holds in the case of space. In neither case does the cause exist with the effect, and so long as they do not coexist in the same fragment of time or space, no matter how close they are in respect to these dimensions, they are not in a cause-and-effect relation. Antecedent existence can no more cause a new existence than can the shopworn concept of the "course of nature" (cf. pp. 400–01). It must follow that "the existence of created substances, in each successive moment, must be the effect of the *immediate* agency, will, and power of God" (p. 401). And this conclusion does nothing more than maintain that God by his established laws is bringing into existence new things, moment by moment. Continuing creation out of nothing is identical with what men call preservation of created objects. Even to talk of preservation, however, is to reveal the dependent condition of all finite objects, for what point is there in speaking of preservation if there is no need to preserve them from falling out of existence? And the only difference between God's first creation and his continuing creation is purely circumstantial. In the first case, no previous creative act had taken place; in the second, his creative acts have been preceded by other creative acts (p. 402). But none of the effects of God's creative acts are thereby enabled to sustain themselves, for there is nothing in any given moment or segment of space which of itself insures that in the next moment or space a hitherto existing entity will continue to exist.[7]

Therefore, when God wills that in certain respects there be oneness or identity among successive acts, he communicates to them like "properties, relations, and circumstances," thereby leading men also to treat them as one. This arrangement Edwards boldly calls an "arbitrary constitution" because it depends on nothing but the divine will guided by divine wisdom. And this is precisely what nature in its broadest sense is, a system established and constantly renewed by the sovereign will of God. As all dependent beings are in "constant flux," they are renewed, or created anew, in every instant by that sovereign will, or else the whole would drop into nonexistence.

Taylor's objection, we recall, was that "no constitution can make those to be one, which are not one." Edwards, of course, was not arguing for a universal identity between Adam and posterity; what he

7. JE ingeniously fortified his line of argument by an extensive footnote (pp. 402 ff.), which drew upon the then current conceptions of constantly renewed images as the basis of perception of light, sound, physical solidity, and mirror reflections. The entire argument operates in an "occasionalistic" vein. It was roughed out in the "Book of Controversies" and ran in part as follows: "Perhaps in the beginning of that part that shall be covering imputed sin to have an introductory discourse wherein shew how that in all created identities divine sovereignty concerns that all depend on an arbitrary divine constitution. . . . Here shew and prove that every creature is every moment from God and every moment created by him as much as the first moment and that therefore the existence the 2nd moment is not individually the same with the existence [of] the first moment nor from it but immediately from G" (p. 92).

had established by his metaphysical excursion was the basic principle that in certain respects, degrees, and for various purposes, God made identical those things which in other respects were not one.[8] Taylor's fallacy lay in supposing that there could be a unity in created beings, acting as productive agents in the past, whereby "qualities and relations" are brought forth "distinct from, and prior to any oneness that can be supposed to be founded on divine constitution." However, the truth, as Edwards believed he had demonstrated fully, was "that a *divine constitution* is the thing which *makes truth,* in affairs of this nature" (p. 404). The bedrock structure of metaphysical truth determined what was true or false, and that bedrock was the will of God, the sheer arbitrary decisiveness of God, who makes things to be what they are. In this case, all personal identity, all awareness of past acts in an individual's life, and all continuation of qualities, properties, and relations of human and natural entities stand on the same footing, that of the divine constitution. The conclusion toward which Edwards had been heading all the time now became clear. Since no sober reason could be offered to contradict his line of reasoning to this point, he saw no reason to deny that God "may not establish a constitution whereby the natural posterity of Adam . . . should be treated as one with him . . . either of righteousness and communion in rewards, or of the loss of righteousness and consequent corruption and guilt" (p. 405). If God can and does unify one individual's life, there is no countervailing reason for his not unifying the life of the whole human race.

How then should the doctrine of imputation be understood? Having turned aside the charge of irrationality by demonstrating the grounds of the unity between Adam and his posterity, Edwards could then present the remainder of his case. Posterity was in Adam; it fell in him and with him, and in its present state is no more than the extension of that spiritual and moral pollution as it continues to recapitulate the first fall (p. 391). Sin and guilt belong to human nature

8. The direction of JE's argument is reminiscent of the distinction that both Anselm and Aquinas had made between "nature" and "person." Men as persons or individuals are not identical with Adam. What is passed on is a "nature" corrupted by Adam. The purely individualistic or idiosyncratic characteristics which make each person different from every other are not transmitted; they are given at birth. But that which makes each person a human being as such was transmitted as having inhered in the original parent, and this inheritance is a debility of the will. Cf. G. P. Fisher, "The Augustinian and Federal Theories of Original Sin Compared," *The New Englander,* 27 (1868), 480, 482–3.

as such, or as Edwards concisely put it, "The sin of the apostacy is not theirs, merely because God *imputes* it to them; but it is *truly* and *properly* theirs, and on that ground, God imputes it to them" (p. 408).[9]

All that was left for Edwards now was to reply to the charge that God's treatment of humanity as a unity was morally repellent to the conscience of mankind. In great part, if his case for identity were sustained, he had drawn the fangs of Taylor's charge that it was ethically inconceivable for God to attribute sin and guilt to a perfectly innocent person who did not even exist when Adam fell from his rightful obedience to divine authority. He had already shown that the notion of a "perfectly innocent" person was a myth, so that part of Taylor's objection fell to the ground. But Taylor had insisted upon the utter unfairness of any unitary arrangement by which Adam's descendants were penalized before they ever got started in the race of life.

Edwards calmly pointed out that there was nothing whatsoever unfair in God's appointing Adam as the "moral head" of humanity. Indeed, the greatest possible benefits could have been passed on to Adam's posterity had he not willfully disobeyed his Creator. Everything at the outset was in favor of a happy outcome. Adam, by his "capacity and natural talents," appeared to be headed for perfect obedience. Knowing that his descendants' eternal welfare depended on him, he had every reason to be careful in his behavior. He, unlike his posterity, came into the world already in the full state of mature manhood. His powers were at a height. The promise of an eternal happy life was set before him, another mark of God's graciousness, since he need not have promised a reward, but only demanded obedience under penalty of eternal death (pp. 396–97). Therefore, it was incomprehensible to Edwards that anyone could take the slightest exception to a scheme that from the beginning was fraught with enormous possibilities for human welfare and happiness. The outcome of Adam's abuse of opportunity, however, now worked through

9. In expounding on JE's improvements in theology, JE, Jr. explained that his father's followers had clarified the notion of imputation by showing that it does not signify a transfer of righteousness from Christ to the believer or of sin from Adam to his posterity, but rather a transfer of the beneficial or baneful consequences, as the case may be. The restatement of imputation, however, weakens JE's clear judgment that all mankind sins in Adam and does not simply inherit the consequences of Adam's fall (*The Works of Jonathan Edwards,* D.D., 2 vols., Andover, 1842, *1,* 486–7).

the very same structure which under other conditions would have poured untold richness of blessings upon mankind, and to affirm this is in no way to impugn the ethical respectability of God's design itself. God established the union of Adam and his posterity; God was just and even gracious in doing this; the arrangement itself was just and gracious; and therefore the whole scheme passed the test of ethical impeccability.

GOD THE AUTHOR OF SIN

According to Taylor, the Calvinist position demeaned not only the nature of man but also that of God. If one pursued to the bitter end the logic of orthodoxy, it led from man's depraved condition back to Adam and thence to the only conceivable proper cause, God himself. In short, Calvinism culminated in blasphemy by bypassing the plain deliverances of common and moral sense which show each man responsible for his own sins and virtues. God's hands are clean, therefore, since he had only created mankind with propensities, appetites, and reason, neutral as to sin or virtue, and left to human freedom the responsibility for the achievement of vice or righteousness.[1] The orthodox scheme binds both man and God into an intolerable union, to the discredit of both, and lands in a morass of unintelligible and impious attributions which no amount of tortured speculation could ever correct.

So warmly cherished was this Arminian criticism, and so acutely embarrassing was it to the whole structure of the case for original sin, that Edwards might be expected to mount a slashing attack upon it. Instead, in a relatively brief chapter (Pt. IV, Ch. 2), he patiently explained his theory of sin's origin as due to the privative action of God and wearily referred his readers to his discourse on *Freedom of the Will* for more information on the question. The only argument of substance advanced at this point was his contention that God permits sin to occur, but that he does not cause it (p. 384). Thus, if permissiveness on the part of deity were the issue involved in the problem of God's responsibility, he maintained that the Arminians were caught in the same embarrassment they had hoped to lodge against orthodoxy. They admitted that sin continues in this world, and it must be that it does so by divine permission. If they believed they could exonerate God from responsibility on the grounds that he permits sin to continue only after man once initiates it, the Calvinists

1. Cf. *Scripture-Doctrine,* pp. 420–1.

could do so on the same grounds. If it was unworthy to think that God caused sin to exist in the first place, it is equally unworthy for anyone to attribute to him the continuance of anything so hateful as sin (p. 387).

Edwards' answer to Taylor came close to being no more than a tu quoque argument and does much less than justice to the care with which he scouted this troublesome issue in the *Freedom of the Will* and elsewhere. To bring out his full defense of the position it is necessary, therefore, to look beyond the pages of the *Original Sin*. In the *Freedom of the Will* he had attempted to demonstrate that God's withdrawal of the superior, supernatural principles from Adam did not bring the deity under censure as the "author of sin." He clarified his usage of this phrase as follows: "If by 'the author of sin,' be meant the sinner, the agent, or actor of sin, or the *doer* of a wicked thing . . . I utterly deny God to be the author of sin. . . . But if by 'the author of sin,' is meant the permitter, or not a hinderer of sin; and at the same time, a disposer of the state of events . . . for wise, holy and most excellent ends and purposes . . . I don't deny that God is the author of sin (though I dislike and reject the phrase, as that which by use and custom is apt to carry another sense)." With a defiant flourish he added, "I don't deny, that God's being thus the author of sin, follows from what I have laid down; and I assert, that it equally follows from the doctrine which is maintained by most of the Arminian divines."[2] Anyone ought to be able to see that efficient causation and permissive causation belong to totally different categories and recognize that it is a misuse of language to employ the phrase "author of sin" in such a way as to imply a lack of holiness in God. "It would be strange arguing indeed," Edwards thought, "because men never commit sin, but only when God leaves 'em *to themselves,* and necessarily sin, when he does so, that therefore their sin is not *from themselves,* but from God; and so, that God must be a sinful being." This way of reasoning was just about as sensible as claiming that "because it is always dark when the sun is gone, and never dark when the sun is present, that therefore all darkness is from the sun, and that his disk and beams must needs be black."[3]

It was all very well for Edwards to pitch his argument on the principle of permissiveness by God, but he had still left unsettled the crucial issue of God's responsibility for sin. Some years later, James

2. Yale ed., *1,* 399.
3. Ibid., p. 404.

Dana was able to make a decisive attack on Edwards' distinction between permissiveness and efficient causation. He found Edwards insisting that God allows sin, yet also asserting God to be the determiner and orderer of the world in all parts. The latter must be positive rather than negative or privative action and must have relevance to sin's occurrence. If the efficient cause of sin be man himself, then, according to Dana, men do have the power of self-determination, a conclusion which would effectively undermine the entire argument of Edwards. On the other hand, if Edwards held consistently to his doctrine of divine sovereignty, he should also have admitted that God's "positive energy and action" introduced sin into the world, a verdict so offensive that "the moral perfections and government of God and revealed religion must be disbelieved." Somewhere in the process of sin's appearance there had to be efficient causation, if not in man's free choice then in God, who in the last analysis was the Creator of whatever capacities man possessed. Thus, in sympathy with Taylor, Dana decided, "The creature cannot be answerable for more than he hath received." With Edwards' distinction between permissive and efficient causation esteemed futile so far as it applied to God's action, if not to man's, Dana triumphantly concluded, "Whoever would defend his book must either shew, that the leading principles of it do not suppose the deity to be the efficient [cause] of moral evil; or else that such a supposition is no reproach to his character and government." [4]

What Edwards had written elsewhere certainly gave a basis for Dana's skillful attack, for in the *Observations on Divine Decrees* Edwards argued "that nothing can come to pass but what it is the will and pleasure of God should come to pass." The divine foreknowledge itself implies a decree, which is to say, whatever he permits, he decrees to permit. Hence, sin and its punishment have been permitted because he has so decided and decreed. Edwards was willing to go even further to state "God decrees all things, and even all sins." This extraordinarily strong language would seem to put Edwards in the position of making God the efficient cause of all evil and sin.

4. James Dana, *The "Examination of the Late Rev'd President Edwards' Enquiry on Freedom of Will" Continued* (New Haven, 1773), pp. 59–60, 63, 65, 141. A similar line of reasoning was offered by Charles Chauncy: "If they [men] must be corrupt creatures . . . it matters not whether, what is thus unavoidable, takes rise from positive or privative principles." And in any case, Scripture does not give "this absurd account of the matter" (*Five Dissertations on the Scripture Account of the Fall; and its Consequences,* London, 1785, p. 200).

What he seems to be saying, however, is that God decreed (efficient cause) to permit sin (negative or privative cause).[5]

In addition, Edwards had to wrestle with this problem by showing that God might decree sin in this sense and yet not be accounted a morally reprehensible being. Therefore, he resorted to a time-honored device of which Calvinists were fond, the distinction between God's will considered as revealed and as secret, as command or decree, or, as he put it in the *Freedom of the Will,* between God's preceptive and disposing wills.[6] This distinction enabled him to argue that, although in their content or nature certain attitudes and acts were inherently evil, nevertheless, by his disposing will, the deity could with full righteousness permit them to occur because, seen in the total context of his purposes, they may be brought to a good end in accordance with his sovereign will. This line of thought sounded suspiciously like the attribution of an inherent inconsistency within the Godhead, as though his wills were working in complete opposition to one another, but Edwards assured his readers that there was no inconsistency in God, because each of the wills has as its object a different entity. "To suppose God to have contrary wills towards the same object, is a contradiction; but it is not so, to suppose him to have contrary wills about different objects." Thus, sin in itself is evil; God stands unalterably opposed to it. The permission of sin, allowing it to happen, may be a good thing, and in this sense God decrees that it should come to pass. His object in the first instance is sin in itself; in the second instance, his object is the great good which will occur by his disposal of sin.[7] But this does not mean that God does evil in order that good will come from it, Edwards contended. Men commit evil for the sake of evil, simply considered, but God's permission of sin has as its object "the great good" which will follow from his employment of it in the divine economy. God does not do evil at all; he does only that which is in accordance with his supremely righteous will. "I do not argue that God may commit evil, that good may come of it; but that he may will that evil should come to pass, and permit that it may come to pass, that good may come of it." [8] On this slender thread hung much of Edwards' vindication of the divine righteousness.

5. Worcester ed., *5,* 361, 367, 387, 357, 378.
6. Cf. ibid., pp. 356, 362–3; Yale ed., *1,* 406–7.
7. Cf. Worcester ed., *5,* 411–12; Yale ed., *1,* 407–9.
8. Worcester ed., *5,* 410.

To understand more fully what God's righteousness is, Edwards claimed that it is necessary to recognize that God aims at one thing, the expression of his glory in the harmonious interplay of all elements within his world. "God inclines to excellency, which is harmony, but yet he may incline to suffer that which is unharmonious in itself, for the promotion of universal harmony, or for the promoting of the harmony. That then is in the universality, and making it shine the brighter." For the complete exposure of his glory, all of the divine attributes must reach their full exercise. Thus, sin and punishment must be decreed by God, or else the splendor of his "awful majesty, his authority and dreadful greatness, justice and holiness" would have had no play, nor would the "glory of his goodness, love and holiness" be properly exercised or appreciated.[9] Even the creatures' happiness is heightened by the full and balanced exercise of the divine attributes, for their lasting happiness consists in a full knowledge of God, of which they would be deprived if God did not communicate himself fully. And this means that there must be evil in the world, so that the fullest savor of the divine goodness may be tasted by contrast.[1]

Since evil does occur in this world, and since this is God's world, to what other conclusion can one come? The alternative would be that sin and virtue fall out by blind chance without the plan and design of an intelligent and wise being. And this conclusion would lead at best to the notion of a being seriously deficient in both wisdom and goodness or perhaps even to outright atheism.[2] In either case, God would be robbed of his glory, whereas by Edwards' interpretation, God receives his full due not only because any deprecation of the divine attributes is warded off, but because God's righteousness is shown forth in its most compelling and extensive form.

MISCELLANEOUS ARGUMENTS ANSWERED

Edwards, determined to carry through his announced aim of answering anything that had the appearance of a criticism, concluded his work by burying Taylor under an avalanche of criticisms. No less than twelve objections, some of which he had reduced to rubble in the body of the treatise, were thoroughly overhauled. Of particular

9. Cf. ibid., pp. 356–7. See also "Miscellanies," No. 553.
1. Cf. Worcester ed., *5*, 358.
2. Yale ed., *1*, 405, 410–11.

interest were those which Taylor offered as the results of accepting the doctrine of original sin. As he would have it, the acceptance of the doctrine encourages "all manner of iniquity," reduces men's efforts for reforming themselves and the world, discourages a proper humiliation and repentance, and produces a gloominess of mind and spirit which ill accords with cheerful obedience and love of God. In the end, the doctrine invites men to treat each other with contempt and hatred and robs men of dignity.[3] Talk like this Edwards scored as childish, sarcastically remarking that there are those who, being of a delicate taste, "can hear nothing but compliment and flattery." If, however, sin were indigenous to mankind, it would be a poor demonstration of one's solicitude for one's fellowmen to gloss over the extreme danger in which they stand and prevent them from recognizing the sovereign remedy God has provided for their disease (p. 424).[4] Indeed, attempts to stave off sin and guilt, instead of leading to benign feelings toward their fellows, directly embolden men to think better of themselves than they have a right to do, thereby leading them to pride, which in turn promotes that ill will and hatred of which the world already has a surfeit. The doctrine of original sin, on the other hand, when correctly understood, bends men to that humility which begets human compassion and peaceableness, for it "teaches us to think no worse of others, than of ourselves" (p. 424). Undoubtedly, men being sinners are fittingly brought low in melancholy and gloom when the truth strikes home, but Edwards sees nothing in the doctrine which obstructs comfort and joy when it is viewed in its proper context against the background of God's offer of grace and redemption. There is no denial of the dignity of men or contempt poured out upon them, for "no contempt is by this doctrine cast upon the noble faculties and capacities of man's nature, or the exalted business, and divine and immortal happiness he is made capable of" (p. 423). Rather, a compassionate understanding of the desperate plight wherein all stand, coupled with the comforting hope of

3. Cf. below p. 423 ff.

4. In the same vein he claimed that the palliative interpretations offered by the Arminians lead only to disillusionment by encouraging men in the days of their vigor with roseate views of their freedom and the possibility of their development of virtue by self-discipline. At life's close, when sickness and death approach and the normal vitalities, to which Arminianism appeals, ebb, then the optimistic views of JE's opponents will be shown up for the sham they are. Cf. *Notes on Efficacious Grace,* in Worcester ed., *5,* 418.

freedom and happiness offered by God, makes all men brothers and confers a dignity upon them unlike any possessed elsewhere in creation.

What the opponents of the doctrine could not be brought to see was the principle that human dignity or worth depended upon God's creative, judgmental, and saving action, instead of upon some autonomous virtue developed by men with their own free actions. For them, worth depended on virtue rather than on the deeper ground of God's concern for his creation as viewed in the complex drama of salvation provided for them.[5] Edwards' theocentrism could lead him in no other direction than one in which human worth derived from a divine action, which even human sinfulness could not nullify; his opponents could see no way of maintaining human depravity short of denying a doctrine which so demeaned man as to make him virtually worthless. Whereas they read the signs of man's efforts for goodness as indications of his innate capacity for high achievement and possible perfectibility, Edwards could see only that the worth of man must rest upon something more secure and abiding than the erratic, stumbling, and transient achievements of humankind. Man's worth had to be established upon that Being which provided the very energies out of which men lived, not upon the sinfulness or righteousness of men who made use of these same energies and structures given to them.

It was not sufficient for Edwards to answer the arguments of Taylor; he felt it necessary to warn readers against "some other things, besides arguments" which Taylor's book contained. The attitudinizing which Taylor affected with his references to his own sincerity, modesty, charity, lack of infallibility, openness to reasonable argument, as well as his "magisterial assurance" and open contempt for those who disagreed with him, profoundly irritated Edwards. Such protestations and assertions threatened to persuade readers, especially "juvenile and unwary readers," to misconstrue Scripture and fail to appreciate cogent argument when it was offered.[6] Edwards

5. Reinhold Niebuhr has commented on the same point: "The dignity of man is therefore no proof of his virtue; nor is the misery of man a proof of his bestiality" (*Faith and History,* New York, Charles Scribner's Sons, 1949, p. 124).

6. JE had originally listed the contradictory passages in Taylor, where that author had pleaded his modesty and charitableness of judgment on the one hand, and on the other, expressed himself dogmatically and contemptuously. He did not include these passages in the final draft. See Yale Collection, Folder 36, pp. 387 ff. See also below, Intro., Sec. 5.

did not openly charge Taylor and his stripe with conscious distortion in scriptural interpretation, but he noted, not without a trace of malice, that such tactics, approaching nearly artful design, would create an atmosphere in which the "peculiar sentiments" of his opponents would be advanced as successfully by indirection as by conscious intent. The novel, superficial interpretations proffered by Arminians wrenched awry the plain sense of Scripture, especially in the case of Paul, and thereby cast odium upon the divines and commentators of the past as well as on the biblical authors themselves. This presumptuous attitude of Taylor's group, who set themselves up as the heralds of a new enlightenment, Edwards ridiculed unmercifully. "It must be understood, that there is risen up, now at length in this happy age of light and liberty, a set of men, of a more free and generous turn of mind, a more inquisitive genius, and better discernment" (p. 435),[7] whose analyses of scriptural passages so subtilized them as to make them "evaporate into a thin cloud, that easily puts on any shape, and is moved in any direction, with a puff of wind, just as the manager pleases." Against this kind of art, Edwards owned, it was not in the nature and power of language to provide defense (p. 436). He offered the hope, however, that the inevitable "candid reader" would see through the subterfuges of his opponents and leave the outcome in the hands of God, who "is able to make his own truths prevail" (p. 437).

4. *Edwards' Sources*

The "Book of Controversies," "Miscellanies," and other preparatory writings indicate that Edwards had read widely over a considerable period of time before collecting his thoughts in the finished work.[8] However, remarkably few of the authors he had explored are cited in the first edition. Armed with his own studies of the Scriptures and redoubtable dialectical powers, Edwards seemed to have cut loose from these secondary sources and concentrated mainly upon Taylor and, to a lesser extent, Turnbull. Winder, although often referred to in the "Miscellanies," appears only briefly to sup-

7. JE was greatly irked by the high tone which the Arminians took toward orthodoxy. In a letter to the Reverend Thomas Gillespie, dated November 24, 1752, he observed "that these modern fashionable opinions, however called noble and liberal, are commonly attended, not only with a haughty contempt, but an inward malignant bitterness of heart, towards all the zealous professors and defenders of the contrary spiritual principles" (Dwight ed., *1*, 514).

8. See below, Intro., Sec. 2 for references to JE's sources.

port Edwards' contention that the world had fallen into spiritual and moral decline, and Locke is used principally in introducing Edwards' famous discussion of personal identity. Other writers whose citations plentifully decorated the "Miscellanies" were given attention in footnotes, with Buxtorf, Stapfer, and Poole most prominently in view, while Ainsworth, Gale, and Watts won only incidental mention.

JOHN TAYLOR (1694–1761)[9]

The most prominent place among the authors cited must go to Taylor. Born at Scotford in the parish of Lancaster, of a father who was a churchman and a mother of dissenting background, his formal education began in 1709 at Whitehaven, one of several nonconformist academies where Presbyterian and Congregational clergy were educated. Under the tutelage of Thomas Dixon, Taylor proved to be a gifted student, showing exceptional aptitude for Hebrew, even making for himself a Hebrew grammar. It is possible that he was exposed to the virus of Arminianism during this time, as it is known that the works of Philip von Limborch, a Dutch Arminian and friend and correspondent of John Locke, circulated at Whitehaven.[1] After leaving the academy, Taylor took tuition under Thomas Hill in classical studies, achieving a reputation "almost unrivaled," as Edward Harwood put it, although his skill in Latin seems to have been more mediocre than that in Hebrew. On completion of his studies with Hill, he took charge of a small chapel at Kirkstead, Lincolnshire, on April 7, 1716, and was ordained four days later. In 1733 he was called to Norwich as the junior colleague of Peter Finch, later succeeding him in the senior pastorate. In this period, Taylor appears to have been an orthodox Presbyterian, but the story runs that after having studied Samuel Clarke's *Scripture-Doctrine of the Trinity* with his congregation he gave over his Trinitarian belief. In 1737 he wrote in defense of a layman in another parish who had been excommunicated for his heterodox ideas on the Trinity; in 1740 he ex-

9. The information below is largely drawn from the *Dictionary of National Biography* (hereafter *DNB*), *55*, 439–40. See also Wright, *Beginnings of Unitarianism*, pp. 76–7; Smith, *Changing Conceptions of Original Sin*, pp. 13 ff.; Wilbur, *History of Unitarianism*, *2*, 267–8.

1. Jeremy Goring, "Calvinism in Decline," *Hibbert Journal*, *60* (1962), 206; J. Hay Colligan (*Eighteenth Century Nonconformity*, New York, Longmans, Green and Co., 1915) argues that the dissenting academies greatly assisted in spreading Arminianism among nonconformist groups.

plicitly identified himself with the rising Pelagian and Arminian tide by his attack upon the doctrine of original sin. He was attracted to Locke's views of Scripture interpretation and reworked Pauline theology and the church fathers in that direction, producing as companion pieces to his *Scripture-Doctrine of Original Sin, A Key to the Apostolic Writings and a Paraphrase with Notes on the Epistle to the Romans.* Nor had he neglected his interest in Hebraic studies in the late 1740s and early 1750s. He published in 1754 the first volume of a *Hebrew Concordance* based upon Buxtorf and Noldius, following it with other volumes until 1757. His diligent labors on this work caused it to be reckoned as the first scholarly study, at least in England, to fix the original meanings of Hebrew roots and to clarify the various uses of Hebrew terms. The first stone of the famous Octagon Chapel at Norwich was laid by Taylor on February 23, 1754, and it was opened two years later with a sermon by him in which he laid claim only to the name of Christian and disowned all party names and affiliations. In the same year, he was graced with an honorary doctorate of divinity from the University of Glasgow.

Near the close of 1757, the recently opened Warrington Academy called Taylor to the post of divinity tutor, a position which also called for instruction in moral philosophy. In this role he was not entirely happy or too well received. His haughty and magisterial style, which Edwards condemned in the closing pages of the *Original Sin,* seems to have borne some resemblance to his classroom performances. He was reputed to have been oracular in utterance, given to archaic studies, and oversensitive as to his reputation. His closing years were marked by failing health and petty disputes within the Academy. Rheumatism in the knees forced him to use crutches, but he continued his scholarly efforts and at his death left behind him unpublished *The Scripture-Account of Prayer, A Scheme of Scripture Divinity,* and a lengthy abridgment of Matthew Henry's *Exposition of the Old Testament.* He died peacefully in 1761 and was buried in the churchyard at Chowhent, Lancashire. In 1717 he had married, and his wife followed him to the grave within a few months of his passing, leaving behind three sons and a daughter.

Estimates of Taylor's writings and theological position tended to follow party lines. Job Orton in 1778 considered that "he had to the last a great deal of the puritan in him," in spite of his own earlier estimate that Taylor was a Socinian. John Wesley counted his views to be "old deism in new dress." He has been embraced by many as an early Unitarian, although his careful study of Scripture, his expression even concerning the prevalence of sin and the sovereignty of God, as well as his devotional nature, represented in the *Scripture-Account of Prayer,* showed him to be considerably removed from those forms of Unitarianism which flourished in post-Edwardean America. Unquestionably, his mode of thought, with its emphasis on the moral aspects of Christianity and distaste for the niceties of theological disputation, reflected, if it did not pioneer, a liberal Christianity well attuned to the commonsense rationalism and moralism of the Enlightenment. By his scrupulous attention to the biblical languages and his development of the paraphrase method of introducing and interpreting Scripture, he proved a doughty foe of the orthodox brethren and undoubtedly prompted Edwards to labor doggedly over alternative senses of key biblical terms, often sending him to Buxtorf for aid in ferreting out these alternative Hebrew meanings. Taylor published quite extensively, and his best work, from the standpoint of pure scholarship, probably lay in his linguistic studies, but his *Scripture-Doctrine of Original Sin* was destined to attract more attention from friends and foes. By the end of the century, his arguments in that work had become commonplace in many quarters and even had assumed a kind of orthodoxy of their own, which has lasted in liberal Christianity to the present.

GEORGE TURNBULL (1698–1748) [2]

Of Turnbull, Edwards' secondary target, less is known than of Taylor, although he published extensively. As McCosh remarked, he "has passed away from the public view so effectively that it is difficult now to procure materials for his biography, or even to get a sight of most of his works." [3]

He was born the son of the Reverend George Turnbull of the Church of Scotland in 1698 and was baptized on July 15 of that year. He graduated from the University of Edinburgh in April of 1721 and, in November of the same year, was appointed regent of Marischal College at Aberdeen, where, in a controversy between the masters and principal of that institution over the election of a rector, he

2. The information below is largely drawn from James McCosh, *The Scottish Philosophy* (New York, Robert Carter and Brothers, 1875), pp. 95–106. In the "Book of Controversies," JE often refers to Turnbull as Trumbull.

3. *Scottish Philosophy,* p. 95.

took sides with the masters. By April 14, 1726, he had led thirty-nine students to graduation through his course on philosophy, one of whom, Thomas Reid, was to be better known in Scottish philosophy than Turnbull himself. For their graduation, at which he presided, he prepared a thesis to be discussed by the candidates, entitled *De Pulcherrima Mundi Materialis tum Rationalis Constitutione.* In this essay he employed the new physics as the basis of arguments for the existence of God and took the view that natural science should be taught before moral philosophy. In the same vein he published while at Aberdeen a *Thesis on the Connection of Natural and Moral Philosophy.* In 1731 he came out with *A Philosophical Inquiry Concerning the Connection between the Doctrines and Miracles of Jesus Christ,* a work probably written in 1726, in which he made evident his break with orthodox Scottish theology by referring to the operation of the Spirit of God as merely assistance to the virtuous. The note of "common sense" to be developed further by the Scottish philosophers was clearly sounded in this work.

After resigning from Marischal College in the spring of 1727, he appears to have become a tutor to a family traveling to the Continent, where during a stay in Italy he undoubtedly gathered materials for his *Treatise on Ancient Painting* (1739). The University of Edinburgh conferred upon him the honorary degree of doctor of laws in 1732, the same year in which his *Christianity Neither False Nor Useless, Tho' Not As Old As Creation* appeared. His trail is next picked up in London, where he circulated in literary circles and won his way with persons of influence and prestige. The years in London seem to have been his most productive. In addition to the essay on ancient painting, he brought out a pamphlet in letter form entitled *An Impartial Enquiry into the Moral Character of Jesus Christ* (1740) and prepared his translation and illustrations for Heineccius' *A Methodical System of Universal Law,* which was not published until 1763. His most important works also came from this period. In February of 1740 *The Principles of Moral Philosophy* appeared, followed in the same year by his *Christian Philosophy.* Two years later he brought out *Observations upon Liberal Education,* in which he identifies himself as chaplain to the Prince of Wales and dedicates the book to Thomas, Lord Bishop of Derry. It therefore seems clear that he had left the Church of Scotland and taken orders in the Church of England. By the good offices of the

Bishop of Derry, he was appointed Rector of Drumachose, where he remained until ill health forced him to go abroad, where he died at The Hague on January 31, 1748.

Edwards was primarily concerned with Turnbull's *Principles of Moral Philosophy* and *Christian Philosophy,* but he also seems to have known of that author's *Liberal Education,* since he refers to it in his "Catalogue" of books as "a book newly come over." [4] He also notes in the "Catalogue" Turnbull's commendation of Butler's *Analogy,* a reference found in *Principles of Moral Philosophy.*[5] Three entries in the "Miscellanies," Nos. 1209, 1210, and 1211, are quotations from *Christian Philosophy,* and the "Book of Controversies" contains Edwards' reminder to himself to borrow Turnbull's *Moral Philosophy* when he sets out to write *Original Sin.*[6] This last item clearly suggests that he did not own the book, and this supposition is supported by the fact that he quoted a lengthy passage from that book which is identified by Turnbull as coming from Hutcheson's *On the Passions,* although Edwards in the first edition credits Turnbull and Taylor with the quotation. Edwards apparently identified the passage correctly in the "Book of Controversies" but, in carrying it over into the text, carelessly omitted reference to Hutcheson. Probably he did not have the book at hand and depended on the quotation he had copied out previously, remembering that he had found it in Turnbull.[7]

A study of *The Principles of Moral Philosophy* readily reveals why Edwards would find it an appropriate object of attack while at the same time agreeing with its method. In his fulsome dedication of the treatise to Philip, Earl of Stanhope, Turnbull stated his method as experimental, modeled on that of Newton. As he put it, the book contained "an enquiry into a real part of nature, which must be carried on in the same way with our researches into our own bodily contexture or into any other, whether vegetable or animal fabrick." He then continued in a vein which Edwards could also approve: " 'Tis only by an acurate [sic] inspection of this whole and its constituent parts, that we can come at the knowledge of the means and

4. P. 34, col. 2.

5. P. 32.

6. The "Book of Controversies" is littered with references to Turnbull, not only in connection with JE's notes for *Original Sin,* but for *True Virtue, Efficacious Grace,* and other works then in preparation.

7. See below, Intro., p. 109, n. 3.

causes, by which our inward constitution may be rendered or preserved sound and entire; or countrariwise, maimed, distorted, impaired and injured." [8]

Thus, starting with the same method as Edwards, Turnbull might be expected to reach conclusions parallel with those of Edwards, but such was not the case. Turnbull's investigation aimed "to vindicate human nature and the ways of God to man, by reducing the more remarkable appearances in the human system to excellent general laws; i.e. to powers and laws of powers, admirably adapted to produce a very noble species of being in the rising scale of life and perfection." [9] Where Edwards saw the debacle of sin enfolding human effort, Turnbull claimed to see gradual improvement possible by diligent cultivation of man's innate powers. Quoting Hutcheson, he strenuously objected to any idea of sheer evil in man: "there is no reason to think, there is any such thing as pure disinterested malice in the most vicious of mankind," since all vices are but corruptions of high and noble affections.[1] Nothing short of the most optimistic conclusions about mankind would please Turnbull as he summarized Part I of his treatise: "Man therefore is made (as all the better ancients ever believed and taught) for eternal progress in moral perfection and happiness, proportionally to his care and diligence to improve in it." [2]

Turnbull obligingly listed the authors upon whom he had drawn most heavily in this work: John Clark's *Sermons* at the Bayle Lectures, Bishop Berkeley, Butler's *Analogy,* Shaftesbury's *Characteristicks,* Pope's *Essay on Man,* and above all Hutcheson, especially his *Essay on the Nature and Conduct of the Passions and Affections.* Perhaps Edwards should not be blamed too severely for his incorrect identification of the passage from Hutcheson, since Turnbull admits that he has changed phrases, joined together passages some distance from each other, and intermixed "some things of my own with his reasonings." In fact, there is so much borrowing from other authors in the treatise that it is difficult to discover what originality Turnbull possessed. He bespeaks the same bland hopefulness which marked the cultured liberals of his day, and he pays his respects to

8. *The Principles of Moral Philosophy, An Enquiry into the Wise and Good Government of the Moral World* (London, 1740), p. i.

9. Ibid., p. iv.

1. Ibid., p. 298.

2. Ibid., p. 272.

the emergent "scientific use" of experimental models for philosophical discourse which identified him as a sophisticate of the period. His works apparently made no great stir in his own day, and he had the misfortune to advertise his *Moral Philosophy* at the same time that another Scot, David Hume, published his *Treatise of Human Nature*.

FRANCIS HUTCHESON (1694–1746)[3]

As in the case of Turnbull, Edwards found sentiments in Hutcheson with which he both agreed and disagreed. *The Nature of True Virtue* bears the impress of Hutcheson's influence and that of other "benevolence" moralists, although Hutcheson himself is mentioned only three times.[4] In that treatise Edwards found support from Hutcheson for the idea of a natural moral taste in mankind and that of virtue as consistency in a beauty of symmetry of the affections. However, he decisively parted company with Hutcheson when that philosopher was willing to settle for a natural happiness or utilitarian aim as the goal of man's moral effort, a level of achievement that Edwards relegated to a secondary status in respect to true virtue, which consisted in the cordial and aesthetically satisfying consent of individual beings to Being as such. In the "Book of Controversies," Edwards showed he had determined to deal with the "moral taste" notion, either in *Original Sin* or *True Virtue* "according as which is published first," but, contrary to his intention at this point, the *True Virtue,* which was published posthumously, rather than the *Original Sin,* which was completed before his death, carried on the analysis of man's moral taste. This idea was attributed to what he called "our modern philosopher," probably meaning Hutcheson. He found Hutcheson acceptable in identifying self-concern as "the common spring of vice and wickedness" and, this being the case, drew the conclusion that "all wickedness is an argument of the priority of self-love over benevolence." In a section entitled "Arg. against Original Sin," Hutcheson's *Nature and Conduct of the*

3. The information below is drawn from *DNB, 28,* 333 ff.; Thomas Fowler, *Shaftesbury and Hutcheson* (New York, G. P. Putnam's Sons, 1883), pp. 169 ff.; and McCosh, *Scottish Philosophy,* pp. 49 ff.

4. Worcester ed., *2,* 414, 451, 470; JE's "Catalogue" names Hutcheson's *Essay on the Passions* as cited in his *An Inquiry into the Original of Our Ideas of Beauty and Virtue* (p. 22). It also notes that Turnbull often cites Hutcheson on the passions "with great approbation" (p. 32). Major references to Hutcheson also occur in "Miscellanies," Nos. 1289, 1291, and 1356.

Passions is quoted, and this passage is incorporated into *Original Sin,* but credited to Turnbull.[5] Apart from this reference to Hutcheson, the *Original Sin* contains only two other quotations from that author. In the course of his argument against the idea of both Taylor and Turnbull that virtue must proceed only from choice, Edwards turned the tables by insisting that the act of choosing the good is no more virtuous than the principle or virtuous disposition of the mind from which it emanates. At this juncture he buttressed his argument by quoting Hutcheson, Turnbull's "admired author," who had stated that "Every action which we apprehend as either morally good or evil, is always supposed to flow from some affections toward sensitive natures. And whatever we call virtue or vice, is either some such affection, or some action *consequent upon it*" (p. 225). Hutcheson is again quoted on the next page to show that virtue may arise from an instinct or passion and not simply from an exercise of reason. Both citations are drawn from Hutcheson's *Inquiry Concerning Moral Good and Evil.* With the possible exception of the slightly slurring reference to Hutcheson's being Turnbull's "admired author," no criticism of Hutcheson is implied by Edwards. He was not willing to travel the whole road with Hutcheson, but it is clear, both here and in the *True Virtue,* that he had drawn upon him and coveted his support wherever appropriate to his own views.

Hutcheson's life was not spectacular. He was born of a Scottish Presbyterian family in North Ireland in 1694, and he lived much of his early life with a grandfather in Saintfield while acquiring a preparatory classical and philosophical training. In 1710 he entered the University of Glasgow, where he remained for six years, applying himself to the study of philosophy, classics, literature, and theology. After reading Samuel Clarke's *Being and Attributes of God,* he wrote to the author, questioning his use of a priori arguments for God's existence, but he received no reply.[6] Clarke, then a person of considerable eminence, apparently thought that it was beneath him to answer a mere student, but Hutcheson's inquiries suggest that he had already begun to follow that line of British empiricism and "commonsense realism" of the Scottish tradition, which was at odds

5. For references in the "Book of Controversies" see Yale Collection, Folder 28, pp. 180b, 160, and 256. Another brief reference to Hutcheson is found on p. 96.

6. Fowler, p. 170; McCosh claims that the reply was lost (p. 53).

with the excessively rationalistic trend in other quarters. More serious matters soon engaged the young Hutcheson. While at the university he had gradually been weaned away from the stricter elements of Calvinism, perhaps by the influence of John Simson, a professor who had gone so far astray from Calvinism as to favor free will, deny the justice of punishment for original sin only, and cast doubt upon the eternal necessity of Christ's coexistence with God. Hutcheson took his master's degree in 1712 and studied theology under Simson for about three years, leaving the university about 1716, by which time it is probable he had veered away from becoming a theologian because of the cantankerous theological squabbles in which Simson was being ensnared by the General Assembly.

He was licensed to preach by the Presbyterian Church in Ireland, but reports circulated that the doctrines he preached smacked too much of divine benevolence and too little of reprobation, original sin, and faith. He was easily prevailed upon to open an academy under nonconformist auspices in Dublin; after several doubts arose with the Irish bishop of the Established Church over his failure to subscribe to the canons of that church and to procure a license to teach, he was defended by Archbishop King of "De Origine Mali" fame and was able to carry on peaceably. In addition to his duties at the academy, he fell into the company of a group of friends who read papers to each other on philosophical themes, and it is likely that his first published work had its beginning in ideas stimulated by this club. *An Inquiry into the Original of Our Ideas of Beauty and Virtue* (1725) was published anonymously, and its favorable reception led to a second corrected and enlarged edition in 1726, which included the *Inquiry Concerning Moral Good and Evil.* His second major work, *An Essay on the Nature and Conduct of the Passions and Affections,* came out two years later. These works, along with his *Thoughts on Laughter* and critical observations on Mandeville's *Fable of the Bees,* had so placed him in the public eye that he was called to the University of Glasgow as professor of moral philosophy.

At the university he lectured on natural religion, ethics, jurisprudence, and government and read classical authors with his students. He was a popular lecturer and appears to have worked hard on preparing textbooks, such as his *Compend of Logic, Synopsis of Metaphysics,* and *Institutes of Philosophy.* He declined an offer to the same chair at the University of Edinburgh in 1745 and lived only one year more, dying August 8, 1746, in Dublin. He left behind *A System of Moral Philosophy,* which his son published in 1755. Reports of his presence and manner support the view which he had set forth in his works, that of a gentle, humane person of "benevolent feelings" and liberal theological tendencies, which he refrained from obtruding upon others. In his time he wielded a considerable influence over the new theology of the Church of Scotland through his students. Like Turnbull, he was to be overshadowed by his correspondent, David Hume, and by his former student, Adam Smith.

JOHN LOCKE (1632–1704)[7]

Edwards had read Locke's *Essay Concerning Human Understanding* when only fourteen, and it had made a great impression upon him. The *Essay* had been the result of nearly twenty years of reflection and had been completed only after many interruptions during the hectic days before and during the English Restoration. Locke was of Puritan parentage and had been educated at Westminster School and Christ Church, Oxford, where it is said he took "small satisfaction" in his studies. He remained at Oxford for fifteen years, taking his master's degree and achieving the status of senior scholar and tutor. His active and contentious mind bridled at the stodgy instruction he encountered at the university, but he found his way into medieval studies and conducted chemical experiments before leaving. Under the stimulus of the writings of Descartes, he turned increasingly away from any thought of ecclesiastical office and seems also to have waned appreciably in his sympathy for the Puritanical interests. His mind, enlivened by the reading of Descartes, turned to matters philosophical. In 1667 he met Lord Ashley, First Earl of Shaftesbury, who brought him to London as his secretary, where he lived for sixteen years, enjoying the cultured and influential company of such men as Boyle, Halifax, and Buckingham. There the *Essay* developed out of an informal meeting with friends, where an abstruse subject was being discussed to no purpose or conclusion. Finding themselves in confusion, the group prevailed upon Locke to put down some notes which would shed light on the issues involved, and these notes proved to be his first steps toward clarification of the

7. For additional biographical details, see H. C. Fraser, ed., *Essay Concerning Human Understanding* (2 vols. Oxford, 1894), *1,* xviii–liii. Ramsey discusses the relation of Locke to JE in respect to the *Freedom of the Will* in Yale ed. *1,* 47 ff.

way the mind works. They were to be expanded and refined until published as the *Essay* in 1690.

His work on the *Essay* went on intermittently because of the exigencies of Shaftesbury's political career and his own health. When Shaftesbury fell from influence in 1675, Locke went to France, where for four years, among other matters, he continued to formulate his ideas. On his return to England, in spite of his connections with Shaftesbury's wavering political fortunes, he labored on until suspicion lodged upon him as a politically dangerous personage, whereupon he exiled himself to Holland in 1683, with the *Essay* still incomplete. There he struck up a firm friendship with Philip von Limborch, the liberal Dutch theologian whose influence is traceable in the *Reasonableness of Christianity* and the *Letters on Toleration*. Locke returned to England in 1689, and the *Essay* appeared in the next year. Plagued by poor health and an asthmatic condition during much of his life, Locke passed his last years with the Masham family at Oates, where he died on October 28, 1704.

Edwards' high regard for Locke survived the years which passed since he had first read him as a youth. He had jotted down his evaluation of Locke's theory of personal identity in his *Notes on the Mind,* a source to which he may have turned in preparing Part IV, chapter 3, of the *Original Sin.*[8] He also counted Locke as a significant commentator upon the Scriptures, as his notations in the "Interleaved Bible" indicate, and his "Miscellanies" show his frequent reflections upon Lockean themes.[9] However, Locke does not figure prominently in the *Original Sin.* Citations from the *Essay* occur to support a natural knowledge of God's existence (p. 149) and to bring out more fully Edwards' conviction that men pay scant heed to their eternal welfare (p. 152). Edwards harked back briefly to the latter (p. 156) and again brings Locke into the picture in connection with the interpretation of the word "flesh" in the seventh and eighth chapters of Romans (p. 276). But the most significant reference to Locke occurs, almost in passing, in the development of Edwards' theory of personal identity as part of his argument for imputation (p. 398). In comparison with the *Freedom of the Will,* where Locke's

8. *Works,* Dwight ed. (1829), *1,* 680–1.

9. The "Interleaved Bible," Yale Collection, MS. VI, contains among other references a partial quotation or paraphrase of Locke on Rom. 6:19 (p. 803) and a reference to Locke's *Notes on Greatness* (p. 874). In "Miscellanies," No. 1060 and elsewhere, Locke is cited or mentioned.

views are obvious and important, the *Original Sin* uses Locke only incidentally as added confirmation of views that Edwards had advanced independently. Unless it is suggested that Edwards' thorough examination of human experience should be attributed to Locke's empirical bent—a superfluous supposition at best—there is little beyond the allusion to personal identity which calls for comment.

In defending and interpreting the doctrine of imputation, Edwards had advanced the idea that some things "simply considered" were distinct and separate entities, but when regarded more adequately, these objects were united into a sameness or unity by God's established law or constitution. Thus, trees and the bodies of men may change their constituent materials and forms several times over, yet at every point of their development God has communicated to each the appropriate unique properties by virtue of which each can properly be called "this tree" or "that man." In a man, the changes and differentiations of soul and body are similarly related by divine constitution, so that although the soul and the body are very different from each other, they nevertheless become parts of one man. Then Edwards went on to show wherein the personal identity consisted, in the course of which discussion he paid passing respects to Locke's theory of personal identity. He carefully stated both his agreement and disagreement with Locke in the problem of personal identity: "And if we come even to the *personal identity* of created intelligent beings, though this be not allowed to consist wholly in that which Mr. Locke places it in, i.e. *same consciousness;* yet I think it can't be denied, that this is one thing essential to it" (p. 398). Identity of consciousness or memory constitutes one major aspect of what makes a person the same person through temporal duration, but it was not the whole story for Edwards as it was for Locke. Here, Edwards undoubtedly refers to Book II, chapter 27, of the *Essay,* a chapter which did not appear in the first edition of that work but was added to the second edition at the suggestion of Molyneux in correspondence with Locke.[1]

Locke set out from the definition of a person as a thinking, intelligent being,

> that has reason and reflection, and can consider itself as itself, the same thinking thing, in different times and places; which it

1. JE used the eleventh edition of the *Essay*. In the *Freedom of the Will* he used the seventh edition (Yale ed., *1*, 53).

> does only by that consciousness which is inseparable from thinking, and, as it seems to me, essential to it. . . . For, since consciousness always accompanies thinking, and it is that which makes every one to be what he calls self, and thereby distinguishes himself from all thinking things, in this alone consists personal identity . . . and as far as this consciousness can be extended backwards to any past action or thought, so far reaches the identity of that person.[2]

If Locke is correct, the material substance which a person possesses does not constitute identity since it changes, nor can a kind of momentary flash of self-recognition provide the basis for a person's continuing selfhood, in spite of moments of forgetfulness. If the memory can bridge these momentary lapses into forgetfulness of past experience, the person from one moment to another is the same person. It is on the foundation of this retroactive operation of the mind that the whole apparatus of reward and punishment and moral responsibility rests. Substances are not subject to law or to penalties and benefactions, but persons are, and without consciousness there is no person. Then Locke added another dimension, of which Edwards presumably would have been suspicious. Since the personality extends itself to the past by consciousness, it thereby "becomes concerned and accountable; owns and imputes to itself past actions." This being the case, any actions it cannot "reconcile or appropriate to that present self by consciousness, it can be no more concerned in than if they had never been done." [3] If one has no awareness of a past deed, for example, the sin of Adam, it therefore does not belong to that person, or as Locke put it, "Supposing a *man* punished now for what he had done in another life, whereof he could be made to have no consciousness at all, what difference is there between that punishment and being *created* miserable?" [4] This unsavory conclusion was virtually the one to which the opponents of the doctrine of original sin had arrived, and it was also the conclusion which Edwards was attempting to fend off. If he were to follow Locke to the end, he would have to admit that if men had no memory of Adam's sin, it could not be theirs or imputed to them.

Charles Chauncy pounced upon Edwards just at this point. As Chauncy read the *Original Sin*, Edwards had gone all the way with

2. Fraser, ed., *Essay*, *1*, 448–9 ff.
3. Ibid., p. 467.
4. Ibid., p. 468.

Locke by affirming that "consciousness in intelligent beings is essential to personal identity," and then asking if it could be reasonably supposed that God "should make an identical complex one of Adam and his posterity . . . and at the same time, leave them, throughout all generations, without the least *consciousness* that they had thus sinned?"[5] But Edwards' reference to Locke had been more circumspect than Chauncy assumed. He explicitly stated that personal memory or consciousness was "one thing essential" to personal identity and then passed on to assert that consciousness itself was not self-sustained, but dependent upon the divine constitution, thus showing that Locke's formulation was acceptable only in part.

HENRY WINDER (1693–1752)[6]

Winder is remembered, if at all, for one cumbersome major work bearing the unwieldy title of *A Critical and Chronological History of the Rise, Progress, Declension and Revival of Knowledge, Chiefly Religious.* Edwards appears to have cherished this treatise, especially where it documented on a worldwide scale the sorry state to which religion fell among the pagans and made clear that, even among the most civilized and rational of peoples, idolatry and immorality flourished. Two references from Winder in the *Original Sin* (pp. 150–176) make these points to Edwards' acute satisfaction. There are other indications that Edwards respected Winder and studied him with care. His "Catalogue" (pp. 14–15, col. 2) contains a brief portion of a letter from Winder to a friend in Boston, dated May 15, 1746, and commendations by Winder of books which Edwards contemplated securing (p. 39). Among the "Miscellanies" there are extensive quotations from Winder, especially in numbers 1156 and 1350.

Winder, born at Hutton John, May 15, 1693, had been educated at Penruddock Grammar School and at Whitehaven Academy, where he was a fellow student of John Taylor. After two years of study in Dublin, 1712–14, he was licensed to preach and returned to England to take the pastorate of a dissenting congregation in Tunley, Lancashire. He received full ordination in 1716 and was called two years later to be minister of the Castle Hey congregation in Liverpool. His success as a pastor resulted in the construction of a new church which opened in July of 1727. His marriage to the

5. Chauncy, *Five Dissertations.*
6. See *DNB, 62,* 166–7.

widow Shawe brought to his household her son, William, whose education Winder supervised, taking him to the University of Glasgow in 1740, where he himself was honored with an honorary doctorate of divinity. In the course of educating young Shawe, he drew up a scheme of chronology of knowledge "on the Newtonian plan," and this grew into the major piece of his life. The final draft fell into two parts, the first covering the period from Adam to Moses, the second from Moses to Christ. These two volumes appeared in 1745 but did not receive much response. Nevertheless, the next year he brought out a second edition. A paralytic stroke that same year virtually ended his pastoral career, although he preached a few times from a reading desk after the seizure. He died August 9, 1752, and was buried in Liverpool. His large library was left to the congregation and was transferred to the Renshaw Street Chapel when the congregation moved again in 1811. His manuscripts and papers were scattered and, for the most part, lost in the nineteenth century.

OTHER AUTHORS

Edwards' footnotes mention or quote from several other authors. Johannes Buxtorf (1599–1664),[7] whose name frequently appears in the "Miscellanies" (No. 1008 and elsewhere), is referred to in only one footnote (p. 235), but it is reasonably clear that Edwards placed a great deal of confidence in this author's *Hebrew Concordance* when interpreting Hebrew words where Taylor's readings displeased him.[8] Buxtorf came of a scholarly family, largely engaged in linguistic studies. In 1662 he published *Lexicon Chaldaicum et Syriacum* as a companion piece to his father's *Rabbinical Bible.* He succeeded his father as professor of Hebrew at Basel in 1629 and became professor of Old Testament in 1654. He completed his father's *Lexicon Chaldaicum, Talmudicum, et Rabbinicum* and published his *Hebrew Concordance* during his tenure. Much of his career was taken up with disputes on the divine authority of the Scriptures, since he insisted that because the vowel points of the Hebrew texts were as old as the time of Ezra, they possessed divine authority. He also de-

7. See *Encyclopedia Britannica* (1960 ed.), *4*, 473, and J. C. B. Mohr, *Religion in Geschichte und Gegenwart* (Tubingen, 1957), *1*, 1558.

8. JE apparently possessed two books of Buxtorf; he records in the "Memo Book," p. 37, on October 27, 1747, that he loaned "my little Buxtorf." This was a small edition which it is believed his father gave him. He later purchased the large *Hebrew Concordance,* to which he refers in the *Original Sin.*

fended the integrity of the Massoretic text and the antiquity of the Hebrew characters. He provided for years a mine of information and interpretation for biblical scholars, and even Taylor based his *Concordance* upon Buxtorf's work. His conservative theological tendencies suited Calvinistic interests, but for the same reason he was eclipsed by more radical scholars with the passing of both time and Calvinism.[9]

The long footnote which appears near the close of the *Original Sin* contains a concatenation of quotations from Johann Friedrich Stapfer (1708–75).[1] Edwards drew heavily upon this author for the "Miscellanies,"[2] but he did not see fit to weave Stapfer's observations into the body of his own treatise. Stapfer was a favorite commentator for evangelical theologians, although he was of a more rationalistic bent than many who helped themselves from the pages of his major work, *Institutiones theologicae polemicae universae*. This study appeared in five volumes in the years 1743–47 and was followed shortly by a twelve-volume opus entitled *Grundlegung zur wahren Religion* (1746–53). The former work seems to have been more favorably received than the latter. Stapfer's *Institutiones* may have influenced Edwards' notions of imputation, and his frequent references to the *Institutiones* seem to indicate that this was the only treatise of Stapfer with which he was acquainted. Stapfer's principal use to Edwards was in the *Original Sin* to support the thesis that the Old Testament rabbis and other commentators cited by Stapfer believed in the sinfulness of man.

Stapfer studied at Bern and Marburg and was invited four times to accept a chair at the latter. After travel in Holland, a brief period as a military chaplain (1738–40), and ten years as a private tutor, he settled as pastor at Diessbach, where he remained in the midst of scholarly productivity until his death.

Another of Edwards' favorite biblical mentors was Matthew Poole (1624–79).[3] Like Stapfer and Buxtorf, this author found ready acceptance among Edwards' "Miscellanies" (No. 1309, 1349,

9. Fisher refers slightingly to him in "The Augustinian and Federal Theories of Original Sin Compared," p. 501.

1. See *The New Schaff-Herzog Religious Encyclopedia* (New York and London, Funk and Wagnalls, 1911), *14*, 64; Mohr, *6*, 335.

2. "Miscellanies," Nos. 1300–02, 1305, 1353, and 1358 contain substantial segments from the *Institutiones*.

3. See *DNB*, *46*, 99 ff.

1352, etc.) and in the "Interleaved Bible"[4] and is noted in the "Catalogue." However, in the present work, Edwards uses a battery of incidental quotations from Poole's *Synopsis* only to support his contention that man is sinful from birth (pp. 429ff.).

Poole (Pole or Pool) was born at York, studied at Emmanuel College, Cambridge, taking the B.A. in 1649 and the master's in 1652, and was made an M.A. at Oxford in 1657. He became concerned with the financial plight of young men preparing for the clergy and therefore launched a promising campaign in 1658 for a permanent fund to assist such candidates through the university. The plan won the support of Ralph Cudworth and Benjamin Whichcote but, after raising some nine hundred pounds, was brought to an end at the Restoration. Upon the passing of the Uniformity Act (1662), Poole resigned his position and wrote a tract on the religious conditions of the period, entitled *Vox Clamantis in Deserto,* which was published posthumously in 1698. Fortunately, he had come into a sum of money that enabled him to survive these turbulent ecclesiastical changes. William Lloyd, later to become Bishop of Worcester, suggested that Poole occupy himself with bringing together the critical labors of the known biblical commentators, and the result was the *Synopis Criticorum aliorumque Sacrae Scripturae Interpretum.* Poole began to write in 1666 and in the ensuing ten years brought out five volumes, the first of which appeared in 1669. The fifth volume appeared in 1676, and two years later a second edition was published in Frankfort, followed by three other editions, two from the same location, the third from Utrecht (1684–96).[5] Little material in the *Synopsis* was taken from Calvin and none from Luther, but Poole delved into Rabbinic and Roman Catholic sources as well as relatively obscure commentators. This treatise was placed on the *Index* by a decree of April 21, 1693, but clearly Poole had struck a vein of interest and usefulness, as the multiple editions testify. Late in life he published a tract on the *Nullity of the Romish Battle,* whereupon he became convinced that his life was in danger from Catholics and fled to Amsterdam, where he died on October 12, 1679.

Edwards rounded out his barrage of citations in the final footnote with brief quotations from Henry Ainsworth's (1571–1622) *Anno-*

4. Yale Collection, MS. VI, p. 9.

5. Poole's *Commentary on the Holy Bible* has survived to be published in the twientieth century in three volumes.

tations upon the First Book of Moses Called Genesis (1616) and Theophilus Gale's (1628–1678) *Court of the Gentiles* (1669). The latter was an extraordinary attempt to trace the origins of European languages and the theology, science, political theories, and literature of pagan antiquity to Hebrew traditions.[6] A final book quoted was Isaac Watts' *Ruin and Recovery of Mankind.*[7] Ainsworth [8] was an Elizabethan Puritan of Separatist tendencies, who lived much of his life in Amsterdam in extremely reduced circumstances. He does not appear to have been a university man but was largely self-taught in the areas of Old Testament and Rabbinical literature. Roger Williams referred to him as "that most despised (while living) and now much honoured Mr. Ainsworth" who "had scarce his peere amongst a thousand academicians, and yet he scarce set foot within a colledge walls." Ainsworth was accounted a learned authority along with Cotton, Doddridge, and Poole.

5. *Notes on the Manuscripts and Text*

In addition to the copious references to the doctrine of original sin found in the "Miscellanies," "Sermons," "Interleaved Bible," and "Memo Book," several substantial manuscript fragments have survived. The most important of these are the so-called "Book of Controversies" (Yale Collection, Folder 28); parts of a notebook marked with a large Roman numeral "V," written in the margins of Antoine Arnauld's *De la fréquente communion* (Folder 38); a manuscript in folio which may contain the next-to-the-last draft of the last third of the *Original Sin;* and another manuscript of superior quality which includes a major segment of Part I, Chapter 1, section 8. This piece may possibly be a portion of the "fair copy" which the printer used. These last two manuscripts are housed in Folder 36.

The "Book of Controversies" was written on sheets about 8″ x 12¼″, covered in heavy paper bearing the word "Sundries" at the top and, below, the title "Controversy, Book C." Edwards wrote in two columns with items boxed off on each side of a line drawn from the top to the bottom of the page. Some of these boxed items are lined through, suggesting that they had been used elsewhere. Twenty pages of the manuscript are divided into sections numbered

6. See Yale ed., *2,* 70–1.
7. See Yale ed., *1,* 89 ff.
8. See *DNB, 1,* 191.

from one to seventy-nine, at which point pagination begins with page 80, and titles referring to various contemplated works appear at the tops of the pages. Although several of the items prior to page 80 bear upon the subject of original sin, the first section clearly identified with a systematic working out of Edwards' ideas on the subject begins at page 80 and runs to page 104. The sequence of thought is broken at that point and resumes on page 250, where Edwards wrote, "This goes on from the end of p. 104." The passage continues through page 259 and is introduced by the words ORIGINAL SIN in large capitals. Edwards then returns to pages 158 through 163, where he wrote "** join this at p. 259c."

The contents of this piece show with what care Edwards had worked over Taylor's books and the manner in which he summoned to his aid some forty or more authors, few of whom won a citation in the completed manuscript. The manner in which his embryonic ideas, developed in the "Book of Controversies" may be traced to the first edition can be seen in connection with his argument on the problem of personal identity. He introduces this problem on page 92 of the manuscript.

> Method.
> Perhaps in the beginning of that Part that shall be concerning IMPUTED SIN to have an introductory discourse wherein shew how that in all created identities divine sovereignty concerns that all depend on an arbitrary divine constitution. Identity of bodies and spirits and personal identities. Here shew and prove that every creature is every moment from God and every moment created by Him as much as the first moment. and that therefore the existence the 2nd moment is not individually the same with the existence the first moment nor from it but immediately from G.

The development of this fragmentary notion appears in Part IV, chapter 3, in the course of which an extensive footnote is appended which discusses the natural phenomenon of visual sensations. "Thus it appears," he there concludes in respect to Adam and his posterity, "if we consider matters strictly, there is no such thing as any identity or oneness in created objects, existing at different times, but what depends on *God's sovereign constitution*" (p. 404).

The notebook in Folder 38 is a fragmentary affair written in the margins of Arnauld's booklet, which was sewn together and covered with a piece of the Boston *Gazette* dated Monday, April 26,

1756. The outside measurements of this piece are approximately 5½″ x 8¼″; it has margins of 1½″ on the sides and 1¾″ at the top and bottom. The numbered pages run from 65 to 100, the preceding pages having been cut out. Edwards turned the book upside down and began writing from the back page forward. Among his notes, two items are of passing interest. In a passage intended for the preface to his book he wrote, "I have heard an answer has been writ to Dr. T. by Dr. Jennings [illeg.] but this answer is very much unknown in these parts where Dr. Tr's [sic] Book is common" (see below, p. 102). A longer section bears upon Edwards' hopes concerning the reception of *Original Sin.*

> PROPOSALS.
> The Discourse on Original Sin will be more adapted to the understandings of the ~~unlearned &~~ [sic] of such as have not been conversant in the writings of the modern reasoners on the nature of virtue & Gods end in creating the ⊙ who have opposed the opinion of such as used to be esteemed studius [sic] divines on these heads, and may perhaps be more agreable [sic] to the taste of such as have no disposition or leisure to be at the trouble of acquainting themselves with those controversies.

The passage continues with a reference to the discourse, *The Nature of True Virtue,* wherein there may be found answers to those writers who have attempted to prove "that there is in the human nature as we bring it into the ⊙ a prevailing disposition to virtue etc."

The manuscript that contains a rough approximation of the last third of the *Original Sin* is a folio notebook measuring about 12¾″ x 8¼″, paginated from 157 to 224 and identified below as manuscript A. Inserts are found in it, usually written on letter coverings addressed to Edwards at Stockbridge and Northampton, several of them being pinned together (e.g. pp. 168–9). Page numbers found in the footnotes of the printed text are greatly expanded here. The large number of variations from the published work, including several major omissions and additions, establish the fact that this is not the copy which the printer had before him. It is possibly a corrected copy of an earlier draft, but probably another copy, a piece of which we may have in the other manuscript in Folder 36, went to the printer. In any case, this manuscript is so much at variance with the final production that it cannot be used as the text for the present edition. A comparison of a portion of this manuscript and the first edition serves to indicate the degree of variation to be found between the two pieces.

First edition, p. 253

Judge of all the earth. What grace therefore, worthy of being so celebrated, would there be in affording remedy and relief, after there had been brought on innocent mankind that which is (as Dr. T himself represents), the dreadful and universal destruction of their nature; being a striking demonstration how infinitely odious sin is to God! What grace in delivering, from such shocking ruin, them that did not deserve the least calamity! Our author says, "We could not *justly* lose communion with God by Adam's sin."

If so, then we could not justly lose our lives, and be annihilated, after a course of extreme pains and agonies of body and mind, without any restoration; which would be an eternal loss of communion with God, and all other good, besides the positive suffering. The Apostle, throughout this passage, represents the death, which is the consequence of Adam's transgression, as coming in a way of judgment and condemnation for sin; but deliverance and life through Christ, as by grace, and the free gift of God. Whereas, on the contrary, by Dr. Taylor's scheme, the death that comes by Adam, comes by grace, great grace; it being a great benefit, ordered in fatherly love and kindness, and on the foot of a Covenant of grace! But in the deliverance and restoration by Christ, there is no grace at all. . . .

I will first consider the sense he puts upon the two former, "judgment" and "condemnation." He often calls this condemnation a judicial act, and a sentence of condemnation. But, according to his scheme, 'tis a judicial

Manuscript A, folder 36, pp. 158, 159

judge of all the earth. What grace (worthy of being so celebrated) is there in affording remedy and relief, after G— has brought this on innocent mankind which was (as Dr. T himself calls it [p. 69]) a dreadful and universal destruction of our nature;

a striking demonstration how infinitely odious sin is to God. What grace in delivering from such shocking ruin them that did not deserve the least degree of calamity. Dr. T says (orig. p. 148d) "We could not justly lose communion with God by Adam's sin" (p. 148d).

If so, then we could not justly by his sin lose our lives, and be annihilated forever

without any restoration, which must have been an eternal loss of communion with God, and therefore these would have been no good in restoring to life and to communion. Thus Dr. Taylor's scheme is doubly contrary to the apostle's in this place. The apostle, throughout this passage, speaks of the consequences of Adam's sin as coming by sin and judgement and condemnation for sin, but the deliverance of the second Adam by grace and the free gift of G—. And it places contrarily from the death that comes by the first Adam, comes by grace great grace, it being a great benefit ordered in fatherly love and kindness.

But if this redemption then is the counterpart which we have by the second Adam, there is *no grace at all*. . . .

I will first consider the way of explaining the two former viz. judgement and condemnation. He often calls this condemnation a ~~sentence of~~ [sic] judicial

sentence of condemnation passed upon them.

act, and a sentence of condemnation. But according to his scheme, 'tis a judicial sentence of condemnation passed on them.

This manuscript reveals that Edwards had intended to show up what he regarded as Taylor's lack of candor by listing passages of contrasting sentiments. These passages were cited by page from Taylor's third edition, but were not included in Edwards' final draft. They appear in their original form in Manuscript A, pages 221–2. However, the relics of these citations remain as page numbers in the footnotes near the beginning of the Conclusion.

[Taylor's] Preface. I warrant nothing of my own in the following enquiry I undertake to make nothing good—I have honestly endeavoured to set things in a just light but under the weakness and improper feeling of a man. This I advertise thus of that in reading you may freely use your own judgment without any regard to more [illeg.]. I add a hardy wish that we may all seriously closely and impartially [illeg.]ly and in the spirit love study the scriptures that our knowledge of the principles of Christianity being just our faith may be strong, our comfort solid, and that the light of the glorious gospel of X who is the image of God shining into our minds may give us a conformity to the son of God in all virtue in meekness humility and brotherly kindness that soon entrance may be introduced unto us abundantly into his everlasting kingdom Amen.

p. 6. Pray don't forget that I am only helping you as well as I can. I impose nothing on your faith and conscience. I picture not to judge for you, you must judge freely for yourself, least of all do I pretend to be infallible, possibly I may be mistaken.

p. 237. Judge freely for yourself, for I am not infallible. But judge candidly for I have delivered my sentiments candidly and impartially.

p. 125. And therefore I should not scruple to say that this proposition in the assemblies constitution is false.

p. 110. When he addeth and more by nature children of wrath he cannot mean they were liable to divine wrath or punishment by that nature which they brought into the world at their birth. This is impossibly absurd. Men pretend self-abasement, but this is not to abase ourselves for our own evil deeds but to vilify the source of our being.

The sinful nature of infants is only imagined but with it [illeg.] on posterity be proved.

pp. 150, 151. How mankind who were perfectly innocent of Adam's sin could for that sin and upon no other account be justly brought under God's displeasure and curse we cannot understand. But on the contrary we do understand and by our fountain must necessarily judge according to all it is unjust and therefore unless our good understanding or perception of truth be false, that is unless we do not understand what we do understand or understand that to be true which other minds understand to be false, is most unjust [illeg.]. If my understanding discerneth that twice two is equal to four and another understanding discerneth that it is equal to fourteen,

p. 265. May the father of lights illuminate our understanding [illeg.] I am not in any doubt or uncertainty at present about anything I have delivered, but that is no proof that I am everywhere right. I make no pretension to infallibility. The word of God is infallible, and thus not anything I say or judge is the common rule of faith. And observe while we love the truth and honestly endeavour all our days to understand what G hath revealed, whether the knowledge we gain be more or less we discharge the duty of good Christians [illeg.] the word of God is the rule of faith and if I have pointed out the light shining therein it is well you ought to open your eyes to that light but as for me, I am a weak and imperfect man and may have said several weak and imperfect things.
p. 267. Readers—Hold the truth in love—regulate your passions and be constant in reading the scriptures, fervent in regard to God, kind and compassionate to all men—humble in all your deportment.
p. 451. The gospel teaches us to be humble patient and peaceable to pity and pray for the weak and misguided, to [illeg.] and in all methods of true wisdom to labour for the salvation of man counting daily for the coming of our lord and by faith and prayer daily speaking for direction and assistance to God the very fountain of life who giveth wisdom to the wise and knowledge to them that have understanding, who knoweth what is in the darkness and the light dwelleth with him.

then either his or my understanding is no understanding i.e. either he or I do understand what we do not understand—and pray consider what a God he must be who can be displeased with and curse his innocent creatures even before they have a being. Is that thy God a Christian [illeg.] I will be bold to say that neither from Eph. 2 to 3 nor from any other scripture can the proposition be possibly proved.
p. 159. (speaking of the assembly of divines) In vain hath JX brought the doctrine of life from heaven and lodged it in his word if man thro lovelessness or somewhat worse will thus wrest and pervert what he has taught. (and in the next p. speaking of the same) Lo men have solemnly perverted one [of] these texts, so prove that X will or may justly condemn us to all tortures of body and mind in hell fire without intermission to all eternity only for one sin committed thousands of years before we had a being without taking into account any of our own present iniquities, this is perfectly astonishing! Surely the heavenly rule of our faith shall not all wise be trampled on.
p. 161. Give me leave to commiserate the mistaken many with whom such points as these pose for articles of the Christian faith. Their eyes are covered with a thick cloud of errors in thought for astonished in the gloomy cave of superstition surrounded with a causeless fear terror and despair and resounding with the murmurs of blasphemy.
p. 183 (speaking of the assembly of divines, he ironically says) Here one cannot forbear observing what saving regards both be paid to the true sense of scripture. How careful the divines were to establish their doctrines upon a just and firm foundation in the word

of God and in the next p. the brightest revelation they wretchedly applied is worse than darkness of mere ignorance. It will not discern the truth but vindicate the greatest errors.
p. 188. But whence have these men this knowledge who sayeth not that here they talk of things beyond the reach of all human understanding.
p. 243. Now say that God while he beseeches persuading and by all the motions of love exerts us to the discharge of our duty at the same time knows we have not sufficiency of power to do it or that our perversions by no means proportionable to our duties, but vastly inferior to 'em is in effect to say he is a being that deserves no manner of regard.

Not content to let Taylor's words speak for themselves, Edwards continued his manuscript as follows:

> Dr. T's expositions here noted in the first column are fair colours. He indeed therein puts on the clothing of a lamb and I will not undertake to judge how it agrees with his heart. But anyone has a right to judge how it agrees with the language and style he uses and the manner in which he expresses himself in things in[clud]ed in the other column. On seeing only his positions and expressions on the left hand [one] would expect that nothing could come from such a man but what should breathe a spirit of [illeg.] humility and the meekness and gentleness of X. But the reader must judge whether the things on the right hand do truly savour of nothing but such a sp[irit.] And the impartial reader may be judge or consider it [sic] the arguments on both sides, whether there be so little appearance of spirit or reason for the doc[trine] of original sin. And such plain evidence of his falsehood, impiety and folly or evil will[,] we all afford. Sufficient warrant to a man in the midst of such manifest professions of humility and modesty in his enquiries and reasonings to treat this doc[trine] with such obedience, assurance, irony and contempt and then in effect to treat all these eminent divines that G[od] made the instruments of the Reformation and fathers of the established ch[urch]. For these maintain no other doctrines

> than have been maintained by the generality of divines and professing Xtians through the world, even from the first ages of Xtianity as he himself in effect owns from time to time which also was agreeable to the doctrine of the Jewish chh[children] before them and the doctrine of the wise heathens from age to age. [Marginal note: Goodness of the origin of Jews and heathens.]
>
> I who pretend such degree of modesty in writing as to profess to that I undertake to make nothing good (as Dr. T does) may clothe myself with some assurance in my turn, at least, so far as to be peremptory in it, that the evidences of original sin from the holy scripture and from plain fact among all nations and ages are too great to be confounded and refuted by a stern and magisterial countenance and by dogmatical and disdainful expositions.
>
> I shall not pretend to vie with Dr. T in professions of modesty and humbleness of mind. I know it would be quite insignificant in me, over and over to advertise my readers over [sic] that I have imperfections and am a poor imperfect man and am not infallible that it is not an impossible thing that in some things I may be mistaken. I know that no persons of common sense have any need that I should tell him that I am not infallible etc. or will believe so the more for my carefully advertising born of it, and that if I should advertise my readers of this no person of consideration will think that the true reason of my doing it is fear lest my readers should be mistaken and look upon me infallible and think me above the imperfections of a man.

In some ways, the most valuable manuscript is the one which parallels, with very few emendations, the present edition from page 170 to the top of page 183. Like the previously mentioned manuscript from Folder 36, it is written on foolscap folio, but it does not seem to be part of the same manuscript. The case for this manuscript's being the "fair copy" intended for the printer depends upon the following observations. There are few changes from the first edition, and these are trivial. For example, the total number of corrections is as follows, with the manuscript page given first and the page and reading of the present edition following: p. 45, "aught," p. 170, "ought"; p. 47, "However," p. 174, (omitted); "stretched out arm," p. 174, "outstretched arm"; p. 48, "Babilon" (twice), pp. 174, 175, "Babylon"; p. 49, "&," "instead," small compared," p. 176, "And," "instead" (first edition has "in Stead"), "small if compared"; p. 51, "his servant David," p. 179, "a great king, his servant David"; p. 52, "accounts given by the Evangelists represent," p. 181, "accounts given by the Evangelists"; p. 53, "or Sodom and Gomorrah," p. 181, "or even Sodom and Gomorrah"; p. 53, "antient," p. 182, "ancient." There are also several minor changes in punctuation.

Furthermore, compared with the previously mentioned manuscript, this piece has neater handwriting, clearer notes and cross-references, few eliminations of words and passages, and more carefully executed punctuation. Its biblical references are stylistically consistent. Chapter, part, and topic headings appear at the top of the pages; footnotes are marked with the same assortment of signs as in the first edition; and the first word of the next page to be turned is found at the foot of the preceding page. Most interesting of all is a marginal notation on page 46, which refers to "p. 81G." This notation correlates exactly with the pagination of the first edition, where the capital G, indicating the printer's gathering, appears at the bottom of page 81. The penmanship looks like that of Edwards, but it is possible that we have here a printer's mark. The several differences from the first edition, mentioned above, may simply be the printer's corrections. It seems justifiable, in any case, to proceed on the supposition that this fragment is the "fair copy."

Although the *Original Sin* did not prove to be as popular a work as the treatise on the freedom of the will, it passed through at least thirteen editions.[9] Six editions were published during the eighteenth century, beginning with the Boston issue of 1758, which had erroneous pagination beginning at page 144. This was followed by others in 1766, printed in Boston with a London reprint; 1768, printed in Glasgow with another printing in Dublin; 1771, printed in Wilmington; 1789, printed in Boston with a London reprint; 1790, printed in Amsterdam (a Dutch translation); and 1798, printed in Edinburgh. The nineteenth century saw six more editions, those of 1808, printed in Worcester with an advertisement for the forthcoming Worcester edition of Edwards' collected works; 1819, printed in Edinburgh and London; 1825, printed in Philadelphia in the form of "Extracts from a Work by the Learned and Celebrated President Edwards on Original Sin"; 1825, printed in New York as the third volume in *Views on Theology,* entitled *President Edwards' Doctrine of Original Sin. The Doctrine of Physical Depravity;* 1828, printed

9. Cf. Thomas H. Johnson, *The Printed Writings of Jonathan Edwards, 1703–1758,* a *Bibliography* (Princeton, Princeton University Press, 1940), pp. 72–76.

in New York; and 1838, printed in Edinburgh as a "New Edition." A Welsh translation appeared at Caernafon, without a date, at about this time.

The *Original Sin* was included in all the editions of the collected works, the earliest of which was the Leeds edition (1806–11), and the latest, a reprint of the Worcester edition (1881). Among the best known of these editions are the Worcester edition of eight volumes, called the "First American Edition" (1808–09), and the Converse edition of ten volumes, commonly known as the Dwight edition because it included the famous memoir of Edwards' life by Sereno Dwight (1829–30). Although the reprints of the Worcester edition, brought out in the years 1843, 1864, 1869, and 1881, purported to be identical with the original Worcester edition, it is clear that editorial liberties had been taken with the original Worcester. The editor of the Worcester often changed Edwards' sentences and modernized the eighteenth-century spelling, contractions, and punctuation, thereby losing something of the vigor of Edwards' style. He incorporated many of the footnotes of the first edition into the text, while omitting others. He also referred to the London edition of Taylor's major book instead of the Belfast edition, the third, which Edwards had used. In one case, he misread a footnote (Locke, p. 4, instead of B.4), and this error was faithfully reproduced in subsequent reprints of this edition. Dwight in the Converse edition also had no compunction about editing Edwards' sentences, so that the total effect is quite pallid compared with the original reading. He omitted whole paragraphs which he felt were unnecessary to the line of thought, notably in the introduction and the conclusion of the work.

The following comparison of manuscript A with the first and two other major editions is excerpted from the conclusion of the work.

(a) *Manuscript A, p. 224*

Thus the most unreasonable interpretations of Scripture are palliated and, if the simple reader don't clearly see with his own eyes, or has too much indolence, thoroughly to examine for himself (As few are willing to be at the pains of acquainting themselves so thoroughly with the Apostle's writings, and of comparing one part of them with another, so as to be fully able to judge of these men's pretences) as he is prepared by this fair pretext of

(b) *First edition (text pp. 566 ff.)*

By such insinuations, they seek advantage to their cause; and thus the most unreasonable and extravagant interpretations of Scripture are palliated and recommended: So that, if the simple reader is not very much on his guard, if he don't clearly see with his own eyes, or has too much indolence, or too little leisure, thoroughly to examine for himself (as few, alas, are willing to be at the pains of acquainting themselves so thoroughly with the

exalting the sagacity of the apostle, and by a parade of learning, criticism, and exact knowledge of the original, and discerning of wonderful connections, together with the airs they assume of magisterial positiveness, and contempt of old notions and expositions, I say, they are prepared to swallow their interpretations, as trusting to their supposed superior abilities.

Apostle's writings, and of comparing one part of them with another, so as to be fully able to judge of these gentlemen's glosses and pretences) in this case, he is in danger of being imposed on with delusive appearances; as he is prepared by this fair pretext of exalting the sagacity of the apostle, and by a parade of learning, criticism, exact version penetration into the true scope, and discerning of wonderful connections, together with the airs these writers assume of dictatorial peremptoriness, and contempt of old opinions and old expositions; I say, such an one is by these things prepared to swallow strange doctrine, as trusting to the superior abilities of these modern interpreters.

(c) *Dwight, p. 582*

By such insinuations, they seek advantage to their cause; and thus the most unreasonable and extravagant interpretations of scripture are palliated and recommended: So that if the simple reader is not very much on his guard, if he does not clearly see with his own eyes, or has too much indolence, or too little leisure, thoroughly to examine for himself, he is in danger of being imposed on with delusive appearances.

(d) *Worcester, p. 489*

By such insinuations, they seek advantage to their cause; and thus the most unreasonable and extravagant interpretations of scripture are palliated and recommended: So that, if the simple reader is not very much on his guard, if he does not clearly see with his own eyes, or has too much indolence, or too little leisure, thoroughly to examine for himself (as few, alas, are willing to be at the pains of acquainting themselves thoroughly with the apostle's writings, and of comparing one part of them with another, so as to be fully able to judge of these gentlemen's glosses and pretences) in this case, he is in danger of being imposed on with delusive appearances; as he is prepared by this fair pretext of exalting the sagacity of the apostle, and by a parade of learning, criticism, exact version, penetration into the new scope, and discerning of wonderful connexions, together with the airs these writers assume of dictatorial peremptoriness,

> and contempt of old opinions and old expositions; I say, such an one is by these things prepared to swallow strange doctrine, as trusting to the superior abilities of these modern interpreters.

The text reproduced in this book is that of the first edition of *Original Sin,* published in Boston by S. Kneeland "opposite to the Probate-Office in Queen Street" in 1758. It has been edited in accordance with the principles of the Yale Edition (See vol. 1, Ramsey: *Freedom of the Will,* pp. 118 ff.).

Minor changes have been made so as to make the reading more natural for the modern reader while yet preserving the vigorous style of Edwards. Most italics and capitals have been removed; nouns are capitalized only in accordance with twentieth century custom, and italics used only to indicate the first emphasis in a given paragraph, whereas Edwards capitalized all nouns and used frequent italics to indicate his emphasis throughout, habits which interrupt the modern reader's attention.

Spellings have been modernized when this does not change the pronunciation, e.g. "chuse" becomes "choose" and "threatning" is changed to "threatening." But spellings which indicate eighteenth century usage are retained, e.g. "ben't", "don't" after a singular subject, " 'em" for "them" and " 'tis" for "it is."

The printer's errata and other minor errors have been silently corrected. In a few cases, the punctuation has been changed slightly by omitting unnecessary commas or dashes, but the use of Edwards' rhetorical punctuation has been retained in order to preserve the rhythm of his sentences, since it produces an effect quite different from what would result from the use of modern syntactical punctuation.

When measured by the canons of contemporary scholarship, Edwards' use of quotations from his sources lacks precision. In garnering his references he often altered verb forms, omitted phrases and clauses that he deemed irrelevant to his argument, transformed articles and pronouns, and elided, without ellipsis marks, passages which in the primary source were separated from each other. Although in the case of Taylor, from whom he quoted extensively, he did not often translate that author's meaning into his own words, he did freely adapt Taylor's words and enclose them with his own minor emendations within quotation marks. Consequently, without substantively changing Taylor's meaning, scarcely any of the Taylor quotations are exact reproductions of the original. However, in accordance with the practice adopted in other volumes of this edition, these passages, as well as those from other sources, have been allowed to stand as they appear in the first edition. In several instances ellipsis marks have been introduced to indicate major elisions, and wherever Edwards made major changes in quoting Taylor the footnotes indicate the fact by the phrase, "JE's free paraphrase." All references to Taylor are from *The Scripture-Doctrine of Original Sin* (3d ed. Belfast, 1746) or *A Key to the Apostolic Writings and a Paraphrase with Notes on the Epistle to the Romans* (Dublin, 1746). All citations from these works, the Bible, and other sources have been located. Where Edwards wrongly identified or omitted specific references to his sources, corrections have been placed in the footnotes.

6. *Reception and Evaluations of the* Original Sin

The reception accorded the *Original Sin* has been a mixed one. In scholarly esteem, it has been largely overshadowed by its companion piece on the will, whose dialectical pyrotechnics made the *Original Sin* appear a jaded effort of Edwards' declining years. Its unimpressive literary style, heavily burdened by scriptural citations and commentary, made the reading of the work a formidable exercise in mental concentration. Moreover, its doctrine steadily lost ground with the passing of the years, until by the early twentieth century liberal theologians seemed to have permanently cast it out of the mainstream of speculation. To the more charitable it has appeared to be a period piece of only antiquarian interest; to the less charitable it has provided a dismal example of the frightful depths to which a warped imagination could sink when robbed of that benign light of human rationality which, inscrutably, had been withheld from the Massachusetts divine in the eighteenth century, but happily had been bestowed upon later generations.

Estimates of the work have generally followed party lines, but even opponents of the doctrine have paid occasional tributes to its vigor of argument and the ingenuity of Edwards' interpretation of imputation. Joseph Bellamy hailed the treatise as the final word on the doctrine, as did Peter Clark.[1] The *Memoirs* in the Worcester edition spoke approvingly of Edwards' judicious defense of various

1. Joseph Bellamy, "A Essay on the Nature and Glory of the Gospel of Jesus Christ" (1762) in *Works*, Dodge ed., *2*, 492; Peter Clark, "A Defense of

doctrines, especially as found in the *Freedom of the Will* and *Original Sin,* in the latter of which one could discover "the same penetrating turn, the same accuracy of discrimination, and the same closeness of reasoning" as was exhibited in the former.[2] Sereno Dwight had fallen in line with these opinions when he affirmed that the *Original Sin* was "not less conclusive in its reasonings" than the *Freedom of the Will,* a fact which "will not be doubted by any one who examines the controversy." The answer to Taylor, he thought, was so complete "that it admitted of no reply." Yet he was not completely convinced that Edwards had succeeded in clearing the matter of imputation. "With this exception," he continued, "the *Treatise on Original Sin* is regarded as the standard work on the subject of which it treats . . . and is doubtless the ablest defence of the doctrine of human depravity and of the doctrine that that depravity is the consequence of the sin of Adam, which has hitherto appeared.[3]

Other evaluations of the work in the eighteenth and early nineteenth centuries were far less complimentary. The anonymous reviewer of the *Monthly Review* (*36,* [1767], 18) called the treatise, in comparison with others before him, "by much the most important of them all," but he hastened to add that he had not analyzed the document because "where texts with texts a dreadful war maintain" it might appear tedious and trifling to readers. He admitted that Edwards had scored points on Taylor but concluded that "we are far from thinking, that in the main argument, he hath gained any real advantages over the Doctor." To be sure, Edwards, in his opinion, was an acute metaphysician who had undertaken to restore "the fallen fortunes of orthodoxy; with what success we shall leave others to determine. His scheme is however unlucky in this, that it will be unintelligible and useless to the bulk of people" (p. 20). The Mosaic history of the fall may be assumed to be true for "practical purposes—whenever we have occasion to speak upon a subject which seems to be without the reach of all our present powers of comprehension," he concluded in a sarcastic vein.

Few spoke more bitingly of the treatise than did Charles Chauncy, who scored the work from beginning to end. The section on imputation especially drew his scorn. After quoting Edwards at some length on the subject, he informed his readers that he had done so lest it be

the Doctrine of Original Sin, Further Vindicated," pp. 4, 128, n.d. (bound with pamphlets of Webster, Chauncy, and Bellamy, Yale University Library)

2. Worcester ed. *1,* 61, 96.

3. Dwight ed., *1,* 613, 557.

imagined that he had willfully misrepresented Edwards "so as to make him speak absurdly. . . . It is to me exceeding strange, that a gentleman of his understanding, should so impose on himself, as, in sober seriousness, to offer that for the truth of God which is not only a direct contradiction to the Scripture, but to that *moral discernment* mankind are naturally endowed with." [4] Edwards' talk of a divine constitution by which Adam and his posterity were made one he ridiculed as "not only an absurdity in speculation, but an impossibility in nature." The whole idea of all mankind eating the forbidden fruit with Adam "is as wild a conceit of a vain imagination as was ever published to the world. It cannot be paralleled with any thing unless the doctrine of transubstantiation." [5]

In a gentler vein, Jared Sparks in mid-nineteenth century observed that "the work has been considered by some as the greatest production of his pen. Though it is probable that such an estimate will hardly be sustained by the best judges, yet, in clearness, comprehensiveness, and force, it stands next to his work on the *Freedom of the Will.*" [6] G. P. Fisher's careful study of the doctrine led to the conclusion that Edwards had supported the formulations of Augustine and Aquinas. "His original speculations are to support this doctrine," he concluded, "but they do not materially modify it." [7] In a far less modulated tone, W. E. N. Lecky called the *Original Sin* "one of the most revolting books that have ever proceeded from the pen of man." [8] At the turn of the century, Henry Churchill King was echoing similar sentiments at the Edwards Bicentenary. He spoke of Edwards as one who totally lacked Christ's wonderful faith in men and who had painted the already dark hues of sin in even darker colors. "When one has made all possible qualifications," he continued, "then it is still a bitter, bitter heritage which comes down to us from Edwards' *Doctrine of Original Sin* and his imprecatory sermons." [9]

A slight amelioration in the evaluation of the treatise occurs with Williston Walker, who, although critical of the work, nevertheless

4. *Five Dissertations,* p. 264.

5. Ibid., pp. 270–1, 271–2.

6. "Jonathan Edwards," *American Biography* (New York, 1849), *8,* 140.

7. "The Augustinian and the Federal Theories of Original Sin Compared," p. 507.

8. *History of the Rise and Influence of the Spirit of Nationalism in Europe* (2 vols. New York, 1871), *1,* 368 n.

9. "Jonathan Edwards as Philosophical Theologian," *Edwards Bicentenary Celebration* (Hartford Seminary Press, 1903), p. 37.

said of it, "Of all his works none is more ingenious or intellectually acute, but none met so little acceptance. It may fairly be said to be a work that renders more difficult, if anything, one of the most mysterious problems of religion—the origin and universal pervasiveness of evil." [1] The beginnings of more affirmative responses to the work might be said to date from Frank H. Foster's *A Genetic History of the New England Theology* (1907). Compared to the denigrations or lukewarm approbation of the earlier post-Edwardean period, Foster's comments border upon the fulsome. "This treatise is no mere piece of reaction. He learns as he reads. He innovates as he writes. There is movement, change, life, in this work as in no preceding one. . . . Edwards now understands how to conserve the old, how to learn from even erroneous proposals, how to study the spirit of his age, how to change old forms as new light breaks upon him. He has arrived at last at the true position of a leader" (pp. 90–1). This encomium would not pass unchallenged in the years since Foster wrote, but at least he had read his source carefully and with understanding. Over a quarter of a century later, Clarence Faust found the book "a lucid and emphatic statement of conventional arguments for human depravity," marked by a bold reinterpretation of the doctrine of imputation and of God's responsibility for the human debacle. Nevertheless, he admitted, "in a century where deism was the gentleman's religion this treatise was out of the main stream." [2] In a similar vein, Ola E. Winslow paid tribute to the vigor of the treatise but saw its conclusions doomed "not because of John Taylor or any superiority in his argument, but because theology must reshape itself in accordance with a changing world" [3]—a judgment which raises again the specter of early criticisms that Edwards had failed to catch the spirit of his day. Yet E. M. Wilbur called it "one of his most powerful works," [4] and Conrad Wright placed it in importance above the *Freedom of the Will* in the Arminian controversy. "They [the Arminians] should have dismissed the *Freedom of the Will,* and concentrated on the *Treatise on Origi-*

1. *Ten New England Leaders,* pp. 257, 259. Walker's judgment was actually more adverse than the quotation above suggests. He went on to remark that Edwards' controversies were of "languid interest" to "our age," and Edwards' works on the will, original sin, and God's end in creation "we admire as feats of intellectual strength; but they do not move our hearts or altogether command the assent of our understandings" (p. 262).

2. Faust and Johnson, *Edwards Selections,* pp. lxix ff., 426.

3. *Jonathan Edwards, 1703–1758,* p. 307.

4. *History of Unitarianism, 2,* 384.

nal Sin, which complemented it. Moral necessity without total depravity loses all its sting." [5] H. Shelton Smith admitted that Edwards' theory of personal identity "fell flat," but felt that the book was "a potent force in keeping the controversy alive for many decades. . . . In point of dialectical skill *Original Sin* must be ranked with the *Freedom of Will.*" [6]

It remained for Perry Miller to see the wider implications of the treatise for Edwards' time and our own. "His *Original Sin* is a powerful indictment of utilitarian liberalism and of the profit-motive, but it is delivered in the name of what seems rather a glorified naturalism than an eternal transcendence. Thus I more than suspect the book leads us to the very secret of Jonathan Edwards." [7] Miller viewed approvingly the upshot of Edwards' argument on identity. "In the most profound moment of his philosophy" Edwards, Miller claimed, found the unity of the human race in the depths of sin, whereon he laid a basis "for a new definition of the brotherhood of man that merged all men into one conception, that discomfited the prosperous and the proud, the merchants and the river gods, by telling them that in the nature of things God treats them all as one, along with Negroes and Housatunnucks." "To Edwards," Miller continued, "retention of belief in the historic Christian doctrine, bulwarked by the testimony of history, was a profession that we must bear the shame for things not done, not only by ourselves, but by others with whom we are nearly concerned." [8] Probably Miller was overly impressed with the notion of a secret naturalism in Edwards, but his remarks attain a high water mark in recent evaluations of the treatise.

To be sure, the contemporary revival of interest in the problem of human sinfulness, found not only in major theologians, but also in the drama and literature of our day, owes little directly to Edwards' treatise, but so long as men debate in depth the source and meaning of that perversion of good intent which distressed even the rational Kant, Edwards' work will have a place in the ongoing dialogue between the sons of the Reformation and those of the Enlightenment.

C. A. Holbrook

Oberlin, Ohio
February 1968

5. *Beginnings of Unitarianism,* p. 104.
6. *Changing Conceptions,* p. 35.
7. *Jonathan Edwards,* p. 276.
8. Ibid., pp. 278–80, 282.

THE AUTHOR'S PREFACE

THE following discourse is intended, not merely as an answer to any particular book written against the doctrine of original sin, but as a *general defense* of that great important doctrine. Nevertheless, I have in this defense taken notice of the main things said against this doctrine, by such of the more noted opposers of it, as I have had opportunity to read; particularly those two late writers, Dr. Turnbull, and Dr. Taylor of Norwich; but especially the latter, in what he has published in those two books of his, the first entitled, *The Scripture-Doctrine of Original Sin Proposed to Free and Candid Examination;* the other, his *Key to the Apostolic Writings, with a Paraphrase and Notes on the Epistle to the Romans.* According to my observation, no one book has done so much towards rooting out of these western parts of New England, the principles and scheme of religion maintained by our pious and excellent forefathers, the divines and Christians who first settled this country, and alienating the minds of many from what I think are evidently some of the main doctrines of the gospel, as that which Dr. Taylor has published against the doctrine of original sin. The book has now for many years been spread abroad in the land, without any answer to it, as an antidote; and so has gone on to prevail with little control. I have indeed heard, that an answer to it has been published by Dr. Jennings of London: but never saw it, nor heard of its being in these American parts: so that, however sufficient it may be, it has been of no service to that purpose here. And inasmuch as about fifteen years (if I mistake not) have elapsed, since Dr. Taylor's piece has been in the hands of some, there is manifest need of some other antidote, for the sake of such as dwell in this part of the world. The providing one is what I have attempted in the following work; wherein I have closely attended to that piece, in all its parts, and have endeavored that no one thing there said, of any consequence in this controversy, should pass unnoticed, or that anything which has the appearance of an argument in opposition to this doctrine should be left unanswered. I look on the doctrine as of *great importance;* which everybody will doubtless own it is, if it be true. For, if the case be such indeed, that all mankind are by nature in a state of total ruin, both with respect to the moral evil they are subjects of, and the afflictive evil they are exposed to, the one as the consequence and punishment of the other, then doubtless the great salvation by Christ stands in direct relation to this ruin, as the remedy to the disease; and the whole gospel or doctrine of salvation, must suppose it; and all real belief, or true notion of that gospel, must be built upon it. Therefore, as I think the doctrine is most certainly both true and important, I hope, my attempting a *vindication* of it, will be candidly interpreted, and that what I have done towards its defense, will be impartially considered, by all that will give themselves the trouble to read the ensuing discourse.

N.B. I had finished my defense of the doctrine of original sin, and prepared the copy (as here you have it) for the press, and had wrote the preceding part of this preface, before I had received the least intimation of anything written or intended to be written, by the Rev. Mr. Niles, in answer to Dr. Taylor. But having heard, that his answer is chiefly confined to two parts of Dr. Taylor's *Scripture-Doctrine,* without so particularly replying to the third part of that book, or the large *Supplement;* and it being the design of the following discourse to examine everything material throughout the whole book, and many things in that other book of Dr. Taylor's, containing his *Key* and the *Exposition on Romans;* as also many things written in opposition to this doctrine by some *other* modern authors; and moreover, my discourse being not only intended for an answer to Dr. Taylor, and other opposers of the doctrine of original sin, but (as was observed above) for a general defense of that doctrine; producing the evidence of the truth of the doctrine, as well as answering objections made against it—considering these things, I say, I hope this attempt of mine will not be thought needless, nor be altogether useless. And possibly, even in those parts, where the same subjects and arguments are handled by us both, the two books may receive light from each other, and may confirm one another; and so the common design be the better subserved.

I would also hope, that the extensiveness of the plan of the following treatise will excuse the length of it. And that when it is considered, how much was absolutely requisite to the full executing of a design formed on such a plan; how much has been written against the doctrine of original sin, and with what plausibility; and how strong the prejudices of many are in favor of what is said in opposition to this doctrine; and that it can't be expected, [that] anything short of a full consideration of almost *every* argument advanced by the main opposers, especially by this late and specious writer, Dr. Taylor, will satisfy many readers; and also, how much must unavoidably be said in order to [have] a full handling of the arguments in defense of the doctrine; and how important the doctrine must be, if true; I say, when such circumstances as these are considered, I trust, the length of the following discourse will not be thought to exceed what the case really required. However, this must be left to the judgment of the intelligent and candid reader.

Stockbridge, May 26, 1757

THE GREAT CHRISTIAN DOCTRINE OF ORIGINAL SIN DEFENDED

PART ONE

Wherein Are Considered some Evidences of Original Sin from Facts and Events, as Found by Observation and Experience, together with Representations and Testimonies of Holy Scripture, and the Confession and Assertions of Opposers

CHAPTER I

THE EVIDENCE OF ORIGINAL SIN FROM WHAT APPEARS IN FACT OF THE SINFULNESS OF MANKIND

SECTION 1. ALL MANKIND DO CONSTANTLY IN ALL AGES, WITHOUT FAIL IN ANY ONE INSTANCE, RUN INTO THAT MORAL EVIL, WHICH IS IN EFFECT THEIR OWN UTTER AND ETERNAL PERDITION, IN A TOTAL PRIVATION OF GOD'S FAVOR AND SUFFERING OF HIS VENGEANCE AND WRATH

BY ORIGINAL sin, as the phrase has been most commonly used by divines, is meant the *innate sinful depravity of the heart.* But yet when the doctrine of original sin is spoken of, it is vulgarly understood in that latitude, as to include not only the depravity of nature, but the *imputation* of Adam's first sin; or in other words, the liableness or exposedness of Adam's posterity, in the divine judgment, to partake of the punishment of that sin. So far as I know, most of those who have held one of these, have maintained the other; and most of those who have opposed one, have opposed the other. Both are opposed by the author chiefly attended to in the following discourse, in his book against original sin. And it may perhaps appear in our future consideration of the subject, that they are closely connected, and that the arguments which prove the one establish the other, and that there are no more difficulties attending the allowing of one than the other.

I shall in the first place consider this doctrine more especially with regard to the corruption of nature; and as we treat of this, the other will naturally come into consideration in the prosecution of the discourse, as connected with it.

As all moral qualities, all principles, either of virtue or vice, lie in the disposition of the heart, I shall consider whether we have any evidence, that the heart of man is naturally of a corrupt and evil disposition. This is strenuously denied by many late writers, who are enemies to the doctrine of original sin, and particularly by Dr. Taylor.[1]

The way we come by the idea of any such thing as disposition or tendency, is by observing what is constant or general in event; especially under a great variety of circumstances; and above all, when the effect or event continues the same through great and various opposition, much and manifold force and means used to the contrary not prevailing to hinder the effect. I don't know that such a prevalence of effects is denied to be an evidence of prevailing tendency in causes and agents; or that it is expressly denied by the opposers of the doctrine of original sin, that if, in the course of events, it universally or generally proves that mankind are actually corrupt, this would be an evidence of a prior corrupt propensity in the world of mankind; whatever may be said by some, which, if taken with its plain consequences, may seem to imply a denial of this; which may be considered afterwards. But by many the fact is denied: that is, it is denied, that corruption and moral evil is commonly prevalent in the world. On the contrary, it is insisted on, that good preponderates, and that virtue has the ascendant.

To this purpose Dr. Turnbull says,[2]

> With regard to the prevalence of vice in the world, men are apt to let their imagination run out upon all the robberies, piracies, murders, perjuries, frauds, massacres, assassinations they have either heard of, or read in history; thence concluding all mankind to be very wicked. As if a court of justice were a proper place to make an estimate of the morals of mankind, or an hospital of the healthfulness of the climate. But ought they not to consider, that the number of honest citizens and farmers far surpasses that of all sorts of criminals in any state, and that the innocent and kind actions of even criminals themselves surpass their crimes in numbers; that it is the rarity of crimes, in comparison of innocent or good actions, which engages our attention to them, and makes them to be recorded in history, while honest, generous domestic actions are overlooked, only because they are so common? As one great danger, or one month's sickness shall become a frequently repeated story during a long life of health and safety. Let not the vices of mankind be multiplied or magnified. Let us make a fair

1. [See above, Intro., Sec. 4.]
2. [Ibid.]

> estimate of human life, and set over against the shocking, the astonishing instances of barbarity and wickedness that have been perpetrated in any age, not only the exceeding generous and brave actions with which history shines, but the prevailing innocency, good-nature, industry, felicity and cheerfulness of the greater part of mankind at all times; and we shall not find reason to cry out, as objectors against providence do on this occasion, that all men are vastly corrupt, and that there is hardly any such thing as virtue in the world. Upon a fair computation, the fact does indeed come out, that very great villainies have been very uncommon in all ages, and looked upon as monstrous; so general is the sense and esteem of virtue.[3]

It seems to be with a like view that Dr. Taylor says, "We must not take the measure of our health and enjoyments from a lazar-house, nor of our understanding from Bedlam, nor of our morals from a gaol." [4]

With respect to the propriety and pertinence of such a representation of things, and its force as to the consequence designed; I hope we shall be better able to judge, and in some measure to determine whether the natural disposition of the hearts of mankind be corrupt or not, when the things which follow have been considered.

But for the greater clearness, it may be proper here to premise one consideration, that is of great importance in this controversy, and is very much overlooked by the opposers of the doctrine of original sin in their disputing against it; which is this—

That is to be looked upon as the true tendency of the natural or innate disposition of man's heart, which appears to be its tendency when we consider things as they are in themselves, or in their own nature, without the *interposition of divine grace*. Thus, that state of man's nature, that disposition of the mind, is to be looked upon as evil and pernicious, which, as it is in itself, tends to extremely pernicious consequences, and would certainly end therein, were it not that the free mercy and kindness of God interposes to prevent that issue. It would be very strange, if any should argue that there is no evil tendency in the case, because the mere favor and compassion of the Most High may step in and oppose the tendency, and prevent

3. *Mor*[*al*] *Phil*[*osophy*], pp. 289–90.

4. [John Taylor, *The Scripture-Doctrine of Original Sin, Proposed to Free and Candid Examination* (3d ed., Belfast, 1746)], p. 353. [See above, Intro., Sec. 3, esp. p. 36.]

the sad effect tended to. Particularly, if there be anything in the nature of man, whereby he has an universal, unfailing tendency to that moral evil, which according to the real nature and true demerit of things, as they are in themselves, implies his utter ruin, that must be looked upon as an evil tendency or propensity; however divine grace may interpose, to save him from deserved ruin, and to overrule things to an issue contrary to that which they tend to of themselves. Grace is a sovereign thing, exercised according to the good pleasure of God, bringing good out of evil; the effect of it belongs not to the nature of things themselves, that otherwise have an ill tendency, any more than the remedy belongs to the disease; but is something altogether independent on it, introduced to oppose the natural tendency, and reverse the course of things. But the event that things tend to, according to their own demerit, and according to divine justice, that is the event which they tend to in their own nature; as Dr. Taylor's own words fully imply. "God alone," says he, "can declare whether he will pardon or punish the ungodliness and unrighteousness of mankind, which is in its own nature punishable." [5] Nothing is more precisely according to the truth of things, than divine justice; it weighs things in an even balance; it views and estimates things no otherwise than they are truly in their own nature. Therefore undoubtedly that which implies a tendency to ruin according to the estimate of divine justice, does indeed imply such a tendency in its own nature.

And then it must be remembered, that it is a *moral depravity* we are speaking of; and therefore when we are considering whether such depravity don't appear by a tendency to a bad effect or issue, 'tis a *moral tendency* to such an issue, that is what is to be taken into the account. A moral tendency or influence is by desert. Then it may be said, man's nature or state is attended with a pernicious or destructive tendency, in a moral sense, when it tends to that which deserves misery and destruction. And therefore it equally shews the moral depravity of the nature of mankind in their present state, whether that nature be universally attended with an effectual tendency to destructive vengeance actually executed, or to their deserving misery and ruin, or their just exposedness to destruction, how-

5. [John Taylor, *Key to the Apostolic Writings, with a Paraphrase and Notes on the Epistle to the Romans* (Dublin, 1746). JE refers to this work variously as the *Key, Notes on Romans,* and *Pref. to Par. on Rom.*], p. 187.

ever that fatal consequence may be prevented by grace, or whatever the actual event be.

One thing more is to be observed here, viz. that the topic mainly insisted on by the opposers of the doctrine of original sin, is the justice of God; both in their objections against the imputation of Adam's sin, and also against its being so ordered that men should come into the world with a corrupt and ruined nature, without having merited the displeasure of their Creator by any personal fault. But the latter is not repugnant to God's justice, if men can be, and actually are, born into the world with a tendency to sin, and to misery and ruin for their sin, which actually will be the consequence, unless *mere grace* steps in and prevents it. If this be allowed, the argument from *justice* is given up; for it is to suppose that their liableness to misery and ruin comes in a way of justice; otherwise there would be no need of the interposition of divine grace to save 'em. Justice alone would be sufficient security, if exercised, without grace. 'Tis all one in this dispute about what is just and righteous, whether men are born in a miserable state, by a tendency to ruin, which actually follows, and that justly; or whether they are born in such a state as tends to a desert of ruin, which might justly follow, and would actually follow, did not grace prevent. For the controversy is not, what grace will do, but what justice might do.

I have been the more particular on this head, because it enervates many of the reasonings and conclusions by which Dr. Taylor makes out his scheme; in which he argues from that state which mankind are in by divine grace, yea, which he himself supposes to be by divine grace; and yet not making any allowance for this, he from hence draws conclusions against what others suppose of the deplorable and ruined state, mankind are in by the fall.[6] Some of his argu-

6. [When JE refers to Taylor's writings simply by page, the reference is to the *Scripture-Doctrine of Original Sin.*]
He often speaks of death and affliction as coming on Adam's posterity in consequence of his sin; and in pp. 20–21 and many other places, he supposes that these things come in consequence of his sin, not as a punishment or a calamity, but as a benefit: but in p. 23 he supposes, these things would be a great calamity and misery, if it were not for the resurrection; which resurrection he there, and in the following pages, and many other places, speaks of as being by Christ; and often speaks of it as being by the grace of God in Christ.
pp. 63–64. Speaking of our being subjected to sorrow, labor and death, in consequence of Adam's sin; he represents these as evils that are reversed, and

ments and conclusions to this effect, in order to be made good, must depend on such a supposition as this; that God's dispensations of grace are rectifications or amendments of his foregoing constitutions and proceedings, which were merely legal; as though the dispensations of grace, which succeed those of mere law, implied an acknowledgement, that the preceding legal constitution would be unjust, if left as it was, or at least very hard dealing with mankind; and that the other were of the nature of a satisfaction to his creatures, for former injuries, or hard treatment: so that put together, the injury with the satisfaction, the legal and injurious dispensation taken with the following good dispensation, which our author calls grace, and the unfairness or improper severity of the former amended by the goodness of the latter, both together made up one righteous dispensation.

The reader is desired to bear this in mind, which I have said con-

---

turned into advantages, and that we are delivered from through grace in Christ. And in pp. 65–67, he speaks of God's thus turning death into an advantage through grace in Christ, as what vindicates the justice of God in bringing death by Adam.

pp. 152, 156. 'Tis one thing which he alleges against this proposition of the Assembly of Divines [Westminster Assembly, 1645–46] that we are by nature bond-slaves to Satan; that God hath been providing, from the beginning of the world to this day, various means and dispensations, to preserve and rescue mankind from the devil.

pp. 168, 169, 170. One thing alleged, in answer to that objection against his doctrine, that we are in worse circumstances than Adam, is the happy circumstances we are under by the provision and means furnished, through free grace in Christ.

p. 228. Among other things which he says, in answering that argument against his doctrine, and brought to shew men have corruption by nature, viz, that there is a law in our members . . . bringing us into captivity to the law of sin and death, spoken of in Rom. 7. He allows that the case of those who are under a law threatening death for every sin (which law he elsewhere says, shews us the natural and proper demerit of sin, and is perfectly consonant to everlasting truth and righteousness) must be quite deplorable, if they have no relief from the mercy of the lawgiver.

pp. 367–370. In opposition to what is supposed of thc miserable state mankind are brought into by Adam's sin, one thing he alleges, is the noble designs of love manifested by advancing a new and happy dispensation, founded on the obedience and righteousness of the son of God; and that although by Adam we are subjected to death, yet in this dispensation a resurrection is provided; and that in Adam's posterity are under a mild dispensation of grace, etc. pp. 388, 389. He vindicates God's dealings with Adam, in placing him at first under the rigor of law, transgress and die (which, as he expresses it, was

cerning the interposition of divine grace, its not altering the nature of things, as they are in themselves; and accordingly, when I speak of such and such an evil tendency of things, belonging to the present nature and state of mankind, understand me to mean their tendency *as they are in themselves,* abstracted from any consideration of that remedy the sovereign and infinite grace of God has provided.

Having premised these things, I now proceed to say, that mankind are all naturally in such a state, as is attended, without fail, with this consequence or issue; that they universally run themselves into that which is, in effect, their own utter eternal perdition, as being finally accursed of God, and the subjects of his remedy-less wrath, through sin.

From which I infer, that the natural state of the mind of man is attended with a propensity of nature, which is prevalent and effectual, to such an issue; and that therefore their nature is corrupt and depraved with a moral depravity, that amounts to and implies their utter undoing.

Here I would first consider the truth of the proposition; and then would shew the certainty of the consequences which I infer from it. If both can be clearly and certainly proved, then I trust, none will deny but that the doctrine of original depravity is evident, and so the falseness of Dr. Taylor's scheme demonstrated; the greatest part

---

putting his happiness on a foot extremely dangerous) by saying, that as God had before determined in his own breast, so he immediately established his covenant upon a quite different bottom, namely upon grace.

pp. 398, 399. Against what R. R. [Isaac Watts, *The Ruin and Recovery of Mankind* in *Collected Works* by David Jennings and Philip Doddridge, 1753] says, that God forsook man when he fell, and that mankind after Adam's sin were born without the divine favor, etc. He alleges among other things, Christ's coming to be the propitiation of the sins of the whole world . . . and the riches of God's mercy in giving the promise of a Redeemer to destroy the works of the devil, that he caught his sinning falling creature in the arms of his grace. In his *Note on Rom.* 5:20, p. 379 [Taylor, *Key*] he says as follows: "The law, I conceive, is not a dispensation suitable to the infirmity of the human nature in our present state; or it doth not seem congruous to the goodness of God, to afford us no other way of salvation but by law, which if we once transgress we are ruined forever. For who then from the beginning of the world could be saved? And therefore it seems to me, that the law was not absolutely intended to be a rule for obtaining life, even to Adam in paradise: grace was the dispensation God intended mankind should be under: and therefore Christ was foreordained before the foundation of the world." There are various other passages in this author's writings of the like kind.

of whose book, that he calls *The Scripture-Doctrine of Original Sin* etc. is against the doctrine of innate depravity. In p. 383 he speaks of the conveyance of a corrupt and sinful nature to Adam's posterity as the grand point to be proved by the maintenance of the doctrine of original sin.

In order to demonstrate what is asserted in the proposition laid down, there is need only that these two things should be made manifest: one is this fact, that all mankind come into the world in such a state, as without fail comes to this issue, namely, the universal commission of sin; or that every one who comes to act in the world as a moral agent, is, in a greater or lesser degree, guilty of sin. The other is, that all sin deserves and exposes to utter and eternal destruction, under God's wrath and curse; and would end in it, were it not for the interposition of divine grace to prevent the effect. Both which can be abundantly demonstrated to be agreeable to the word of God, and to Dr. Taylor's own doctrine.

That every one of mankind, at least of them that are capable of acting as moral agents, are guilty of sin (not now taking it for granted that they come guilty into the world) is a thing most clearly and abundantly evident from the holy Scriptures. (I Kgs. 8:46), "If any man sin against thee, for there is no man that sinneth not." (Eccles. 7:20), "There is not a just man upon earth that doth good, and sinneth not." (Job 9:2–3), "I know it is so of a truth" (i.e. as Bildad had just before said, that God would not cast away a perfect man, etc.), "but how should man be just with God? If he will contend with him, he cannot anwer him one of a thousand." To the like purpose (Ps. 143:2), "Enter not into judgment with thy servant; for in thy sight shall no man living be justified." So the words of the Apostle (in which he has apparent reference to those words of the Psalmist, Rom. 3:19–20), "That every mouth may be stopped, and all the world become guilty before God. Therefore by the deeds of the law there shall no flesh be justified in his sight: for by the law is the knowledge of sin." So Gal. 2:16, I John 1:7–10: "If we walk in the light, the blood of Christ cleanseth us from all sin. If we say that we have no sin, we deceive ourselves, and the truth is not in us. If we confess our sins, he is faithful and just to forgive us our sins, and to cleanse us from all unrighteousness. If we say that we have not sinned, we make him a liar, and his word is not in us." As in this place, so in innumerable other places, confession and repentance of sin are spoken of as duties proper for all; as also prayer to

God for pardon of sin; and forgiveness of those that injure us, from that motive, that we hope to be forgiven of God. Universal guilt of sin might also be demonstrated from the appointment, and the declared use and end, of the ancient sacrifices; and also from the ransom, which everyone that was numbered in Israel, was directed to pay, to make atonement for his soul (Ex. 30:11–16). All are represented, not only as being sinful, but as having great and manifold iniquity (Job 9:2,3; Jas. 3:1,2).

There are many scriptures which both declare the universal sinfulness of mankind, and also that all sin deserves and justly exposes to everlasting destruction, under the wrath and curse of God; and so demonstrate both parts of the proposition I have laid down. To which purpose, that in Gal. 3:10 is exceeding full. "For as many as are of the works of the law are under the curse; for it is written, cursed is every one that continueth not in all things which are written in the book of the law, to do them." How manifestly is it implied in the Apostle's meaning here, that there is no man but what fails in some instances of doing all things that are written in the book of the law, and therefore as many as have their dependence on their fulfilling the law, are under that curse which is pronounced on them that do fail of it. And hence the Apostle infers in the next verse, "that no man is justified by the law in the sight of God"; as he had said before in the preceding chapter, vv. 16, 17. "By the works of the law shall no flesh be justified" and that all that "seek to be justified by the works of the law, are found sinners." The Apostle shews us that he understands, that by this place which he cites from Deuteronomy, the Scripture hath concluded, or shut up, all under sin; as in ch. 3:22. So that here we are plainly taught, both that every one of mankind is a sinner, and that every sinner is under the curse of God.

To the like purpose is that, Rom. 4:14, and also II Cor. 3:6,7,9, where the law is called "the letter that kills, the ministration of death, and the ministration of condemnation." The wrath, condemnation and death which is threatened in the law to all its transgressors, is final perdition, the second death, eternal ruin; as is very plain, and is confessed. And this punishment which the law threatens for every sin, is a just punishment; being what every sin truly deserves; God's law being a righteous law, and the sentence of it a righteous sentence.

All these things are what Dr. Taylor himself confesses and asserts.

He says, that the law of God requires perfect obedience. (*Note on Rom.* 7:6, pp. 391, 392), "God can never require imperfect obedience, or by his holy law allow us to be guilty of any one sin, how small soever. And if the law as a rule of duty were in any respect abolished, then we might in some respects transgress the law, and yet not be guilty of sin. The moral law, or law of nature, is the truth, everlasting, unchangeable; and therefore, as such, can never be abrogated. On the contrary, our Lord Jesus Christ has promulgated it anew under the gospel, fuller and clearer than it was in the Mosaical constitution, or anywhere else; [. . .] having added to its precepts the sanction of his own divine authority." And many things which he says imply that all mankind do in some degree transgress the law. In p. 228, speaking of what may be gathered from Rom. 7 and 8, he says, "We are very apt, in a world full of temptation, to be deceived, and drawn into sin by bodily appetites, etc. And the case of those who are under a law threatening death to every sin, must be quite deplorable, if they have no relief from the mercy of the lawgiver." But this is very fully declared in what he says in his *Note on Romans* 5:20, pp. 378, 379. His words are as follows: "Indeed, as a rule of action prescribing our duty, it (the law) always was, and always must be a rule ordained for obtaining life; but not as a rule of justification, not as it subjects to death for every transgression. For if it could in its utmost rigour have given us life, then, as the Apostle argues, it would have been against the promise of God. For if there had been a law, in the strict and rigorous sense of law, *which could have made us live,* verily justification should have been by the law. But he supposes, no such law was ever given: and therefore there is need and room enough for the promises of grace; or as he argues (Gal. 2:21), it would have frustrated, or rendered useless the grace of God. For if justification came by the law, then truly Christ is dead in vain, then he died to accomplish what was, or *might have been effected* by law it self, without his death. Certainly the law was not brought in among the Jews to be a rule of justification, or to recover 'em out of a state of death, and to procure life by their sinless obedience to it: for in this, as well as in another respect, it was *weak;* not in itself, but through the *weakness* of our flesh. (Rom. 8:3). The law, I conceive, is not a dispensation suitable to the infirmity of the human nature in our present state; or it doth not seem congruous to the goodness of God to afford us no other way of salvation, but by *law: which if we once transgress, we are ruin'd forever.*

For who then from the beginning of the world could be saved? How clear and express are these things, that no one of mankind from the beginning of the world can ever be justified by law, because every one transgresses it? [7]

And here we also see, Dr. Taylor declares, that by the law men are sentenced to everlasting ruin for one transgression. To the like purpose he often expresses himself. So, p. 207: "The law requireth the most extensive obedience, discovering sin in all its branches. It gives sin a deadly force, subjecting every transgression to the penalty of death; and yet supplieth neither help nor hope to the sinner; but leaveth him under the power of sin, and sentence of death." In p. 213 he speaks of the law as extending to lust and irregular desires, and to every branch and principle of sin; and even to its latent principles, and minutest branches. Again (*Note on Rom.* 7:6, p. 391), to every sin, how small soever. And when he speaks of the law subjecting every transgression to the penalty of death, he means eternal death, as he from time to time explains the matter. In p. 212 he speaks of the law in the condemning power of it, as binding us in everlasting chains. In p. 396 he says that death which is the wages of sin, is the second death: and this (p. 78) he explains of [as] final perdition. In his *Key,* p. 155, no. 264 he says, "The curse of the law subjected men for every transgression to eternal death." So in *Note on Rom.* 5:20, p. 371, "The law of Moses subjected those who were under it to death, meaning by death eternal death." These are his words.

He also supposes, that this sentence of the law, thus subjecting men for every, even the *least sin,* and every minutest branch, and *latent principle of sin,* to so dreadful a punishment, is just and righteous, *agreeable to truth and the nature of things,* or to the natural and *proper demerits of sin.* This he is very full in. Thus in p. 21 "It was sin," says he, "which subjected to death by the law, justly threatening sin with death. Which law was given us, that sin might appear; might be set forth in its proper colours; when we saw it subjected us to death by a law perfectly holy, just, and good; that sin by the commandment, by the law, might be represented what it really

7. I am sensible, these things are quite inconsistent with what he says elsewhere, of sufficient power in all mankind constantly to do the whole duty which God requires of 'em, without a necessity of breaking God's law in any degree (pp. 339, 340, 344, 348). But I hope the reader will not think me accountable for his inconsistencies.

is, an exceeding great and deadly evil." So in *Note on Rom.* 5:20, p. 380. "The law or ministration of death, as it subjects to death for every transgression, is still of use to shew the natural and proper demerit of sin." (Ibid., p. 371, 372), "The language of the law, dying thou shalt die, is to be understood of the demerit of the transgression, that which it deserves." (Ibid., p. 379), The law was added, saith Mr. Locke on the place, because the Israelites, the posterity of Abraham, were transgressors as well as other men, to shew them their sins, and the punishment and death, which in strict justice they incurred by them. And this appears to be a true comment on Rom. 7:13—Sin, by virtue of the law, subjected you to death for this end, that sin, working death in us by that which is holy, just & good, perfectly consonant to everlasting truth and righteousness. . . . Consequently every sin is in strict justice deserving of wrath and punishment; and the law in its rigour was given to the Jews, to set home this awful truth upon their consciences, to shew them the evil and pernicious nature of sin; and that being conscious they had broke the law of God, this might convince them of the great need they had of the favour of the lawgiver, and oblige them, by faith in his goodness, to fly to his mercy for pardon and salvation.

If the law be holy, just and good, a constitution perfectly agreeable to God's holiness, justice and goodness; then he might have put it exactly in execution, agreeably to all these his perfections. Our author himself says (p. 409), "How that constitution, which establishes a law, the making of which is inconsistent with the justice and goodness of God, and the executing of it inconsistent with his holiness, can be a righteous constitution, I confess, is quite beyond my comprehension."

Now the reader is left to judge whether it ben't most plainly and fully agreeable to Dr. Taylor's own doctrine, that there never was any one person from the beginning of the world, who came to act in the world as a moral agent, and that it is not to be hoped there ever will be any, but what is a sinner or transgressor of the law of God; and that therefore this proves to be the issue and event of things, with respect to all mankind in all ages, that, by the natural and proper demerit of their own sinfulness, and in the judgment of the law of God, which is perfectly consonant to truth, and exhibits things in their true colors, they are the proper subjects of the curse of God, eternal death, and everlasting ruin; which must be the actual consequence, unless the grace or favor of the lawgiver interpose, and mercy prevail for their pardon and salvation. The reader has seen also how agreeable this is to the doctrine of the Holy Scripture.

And if so, and what has been observed concerning the interposition of divine grace be remembered, namely, that this alters not the nature of things as they are in themselves, and that it don't in the least affect the state of the controversy we are upon, concerning the true nature and tendency of the state that mankind come into the world in, whether grace prevents the fatal effect or no; I say, if these things are considered, I trust, none will deny, that the proposition that was laid down, is fully proved, as agreeable to the word of God, and Dr. Taylor's own words; viz. that mankind are all naturally in such a state, as is attended, without fail, with this consequence or issue, that they universally are the subjects of that guilt and sinfulness, which is, in effect, their utter and eternal ruin, being cast wholly out of the favor of God, and subjected to his everlasting wrath and curse.

SECTION 2. IT FOLLOWS FROM THE PROPOSITION PROVED IN THE FOREGOING SECTION, THAT ALL MANKIND ARE UNDER THE INFLUENCE OF A PREVAILING EFFECTUAL TENDENCY IN THEIR NATURE, TO THAT SIN AND WICKEDNESS, WHICH IMPLIES THEIR UTTER AND ETERNAL RUIN

THE proposition laid down being proved, the consequence of it remains to be made out, viz. that the mind of man has a *natural tendency* or propensity to that event, which has been shewn universally and infallibly to take place (if this ben't sufficiently evident of itself, without proof), and that this is a *corrupt* or *depraved* propensity.

I shall here consider the former part of this consequence, namely, whether such an universal, constant, infallible event is truly a proof of the being of any tendency or propensity to that event; leaving the evil and corrupt nature of such a propensity to be considered afterwards.

If any shall say, they don't think that its being a thing universal and infallible in event, that mankind commit some sin, is a proof of a prevailing tendency to sin; because they don't only sin, but also do good, and perhaps more good than evil: let them remember, that the question at present is not, how much sin there is a tendency to; but whether there be a prevailing propensity to that issue, which it is allowed all men do actually come to, that all fail of keeping the law perfectly, whether there ben't a tendency to such imperfection of obedience, as always without fail comes to pass; to that degree of sinfulness, at least, which all fall into; and so to that utter ruin, which that sinfulness implies and infers. Whether an effectual propensity to this be worth the name of depravity, because of the good that may be supposed to balance it, shall be considered by and by. If it were so, that all mankind, in all nations and ages, were at least one day in their lives deprived of the use of their reason, and run raving mad; or that all, even every individual person, once cut their own throats, or put out their own eyes; it might be an evidence of some tendency in the nature or natural state of mankind to such an event; though they might exercise reason many more days than they were distracted, and were kind to and tender of themselves oftener than they mortally and cruelly wounded themselves.[1]

To determine whether the unfailing constancy of the above-named event be an evidence of tendency, let it be considered, what can be meant by tendency, but a prevailing liableness or exposedness to such or such an event? Wherein consists the notion of any such thing, but some stated prevalence or preponderation in the nature or state of causes or occasions, that is followed by, and so proved to be effectual to, a stated prevalence or commonness of any particular kind of effect? Or, something in the permanent state of things, concerned in bringing a certain sort of event to pass, which is a foundation for the constancy, or strongly prevailing probability, of such an event? If we mean this by tendency (as I know not what else can be meant by it, but this, or something like this) then it is manifest, that where we see a stated prevalence of any kind of effect or event, there is a tendency to that effect in the nature and state of its causes. A common and steady effect shews, that there is somewhere a preponderation, a prevailing exposedness or liableness in the state of things, to what comes so steadily to pass. The natural dictate of reason shews, that where there is an effect, there is a cause, and a cause sufficient for the effect; because, if it were not sufficient, it would not be effectual: and that therefore, where there is a stated prevalence of the effect, there is a stated prevalence in the cause: a steady effect argues a steady cause.[2] We obtain a notion of such a thing as tendency, no other way than by observation: and we can observe nothing but events: and 'tis the commonness or constancy of events, that gives us a notion of tendency in all cases. Thus we judge of tendencies in the natural world. Thus we judge of the tendencies or propensities of nature in minerals, vegetables, animals, rational and irrational creatures. A notion of a stated tendency or fixed propensity is not obtained by observing only a single event. A stated preponderation in the cause or occasion, is argued only by a stated prevalence of the effect. If a die be once thrown, and it falls on a particular side, we don't argue from hence, that that side is the heaviest; but if

1. [Here JE appears to argue that a single event, occasion, or act provides evidence of a tendency. But this is inconsistent with the principal thrust of the argument which elsewhere (p. 108 and Pt. I, Ch. 1, sec. 9) insists on the need for continued observation for the establishment of a "fixed propensity."]

2. [On JE's controversial use of the term "cause" see Yale ed., *1*, 34–5, 118.]

it be thrown without skill or care, many thousands or millions of times going, and constantly falls on the same side, we have not the least doubt in our minds, but that there is something of propensity in the case, by superior weight of that side, or in some other respect. How ridiculous would he make himself, who should earnestly dispute against any tendency in the state of things to cold in winter, or heat in the summer; or should stand to it, that although it often happened that water quenched fire, yet there was no tendency in it to such an effect?

In the case we are upon, the human nature, as existing in such an immense diversity of persons and circumstances, and never failing in any one instance, of coming to that issue, viz. that sinfulness which implies extreme misery and eternal ruin, is as the die often cast. For it alters not the case in the least, as to the evidence of tendency, whether the subject of the constant event be an individual, or a nature and kind. Thus, if there be a succession of trees of the same sort, proceeding one from another, from the beginning of the world, growing in all countries, soils and climates, and otherwise in (as it were) an infinite variety of circumstances, all bearing ill fruit; it as much proves the nature and tendency of the kind, as if it were only one individual tree that had remained from the beginning of the world, had often been transplanted into different soils etc. and had continued to bear only bad fruit. So, if there were a particular family, which, from generation to generation, and through every remove to innumerable different countries and places of abode, all died of a consumption, or all run distracted, or all murdered themselves, it would be as much an evidence of the tendency of something in the nature or constitution of that race, as it would be of the tendency of something in the nature or state of an individual, if some one person had lived all that time, and some remarkable event had often appeared in him, which he had been the agent or subject of, from year to year and from age to age, continually and without fail.[3]

3. Here may be observed the weakness of that objection, made against the validity of the argument for a fixed propensity to sin, from the constancy and universality of the event, that Adam sinned in one instance, without a fixed propensity. Without doubt a single event is an evidence, that there was some cause or occasion of that event: but the thing, we are speaking of, is a fixed cause: propensity is a stated continued thing. We justly argue, that a stated effect must have a stated cause; and truly observe, that we obtain the notion of tendency, or stated preponderation in causes, no other way than by observing a stated prevalence of a particular kind of effect. But who ever argues a fixed

Thus a propensity attending the present nature or natural state of mankind, eternally to ruin themselves by sin, may certainly be inferred from apparent and acknowledged fact. And I would now observe further, that not only does this follow from facts that are acknowledged by Dr. Taylor, but the things he asserts, the expressions and words which he uses, do plainly imply that all mankind have such a propensity; yea, one of the highest kind, a propensity that is *invincible,* or a tendency which really amounts to a fixed constant unfailing *necessity.* There is a plain confession of a propensity or proneness to sin (p. 143). "Man, who drinketh in iniquity like water; who is attended with so many sensual appetites, and so apt to indulge them." And again (p. 228), "We are very apt, in a world full of temptation, to be deceiv'd, & drawn into sin by bodily appetites." If we are very apt or prone to be drawn into sin by bodily appetites, and sinfully to indulge them, and very apt or prone to yield to temptation to sin, then we are *prone to sin:* for to yield to temptation to sin, is sinful. In the same page he represents, that on this account, and on account of the consequences of this, the case of those who are under a law threatening death for every sin, must be quite deplorable, if they have no relief from the mercy of the lawgiver. Which implies, that their case is hopeless, as to an escape from death, the punishment of sin, by any other means than God's mercy. And that implies, that there is such an aptness to yield to temptation to sin, that 'tis hopeless that any of mankind should wholly avoid it. But he speaks of it elsewhere, over and over, as truly impossible, or what can't be; as in the words which were cited in the last section, from his *Note on Romans* 5:20, where he repeatedly speaks of the law, which subjects us to death for every transgression, as what cannot give life; and represents that if God offered us no other way of salvation, no man from the beginning of the world could be saved. In the same place he with approbation cites Mr. Locke's words, in which, speaking of the Israelites, he says, "All endeavours after righteousness was lost labour, since any one slip forfeited life, & it

---

propensity from a single effect? And is it not strange arguing, that because an event which once comes to pass, don't prove any stated tendency, therefore the unfailing constancy of an event is an evidence of no such thing?—But because Dr. Taylor makes so much of this objection, from Adam's sinning without a propensity, I shall hereafter consider it more particularly, in the beginning of the 9th section of this chapter; where will also be considered what is objected from the fall of the angels.

was impossible for them to expect aught but death."[4] Our author speaks of it as impossible for the law requiring sinless obedience, to give life, not that the law was weak in itself, but through the weakness of our flesh. Therefore, he says, he conceives the law not to be a dispensation suitable to the infirmity of the human nature in its present state. These things amount to a full confession, that the proneness in men to sin, and to a demerit of and just exposedness to eternal ruin by sin, is universally invincible, or, which is the same thing, amounts to absolute invincible necessity; which surely is the highest kind of tendency, or propensity: and that not the less for his laying this propensity to our infirmity or weakness, which may seem to intimate some defect, rather than anything positive: and 'tis agreeable to the sentiments of the best divines, that all sin originally comes from a defective or privative cause. But sin don't cease to be sin, or a thing not justly exposing to eternal ruin (as is implied in Dr. Taylor's own words) for arising from infirmity or defect; nor does an invincible propensity to sin cease to be a propensity to such demerit of eternal ruin, because the proneness arises from such a cause.

It is manifest, that this tendency which has been proved, don't consist in any particular external circumstances, that some or many are in, peculiarly tempting and influencing their minds; but is *inherent,* and is seated in that *nature* which is common to all mankind, which they carry with them wherever they go, and still remains the same, however circumstances may differ. For it is implied in what has been proved, and shewn to be confessed, that the same event comes to pass in all circumstances, that any of mankind ever are or can be under in the world. In God's sight no man living can be justified; but all are sinners, and exposed to condemnation. This is true of persons of all constitutions, capacities, conditions, manners, opinions and educations; in all countries, climates, nations and ages; and through all the mighty changes and revolutions, which have come to pass in the habitable world.

We have the same evidence, that the propensity in this case lies in the nature of the subject, and don't arise from any particular circumstances, as we have in any case whatsoever; which is only by the effects appearing to be the same in all changes of time and place, and under all varieties of circumstances. It is in this way only we judge, that any propensities, which we observe in mankind, are such as are seated in their nature, in all other cases. 'Tis thus we judge of

4. [Originally "ought."]

the mutual propensity betwixt the sexes, or of the dispositions which are exercised in any of the natural passions or appetites, that they truly belong to the nature of man; because they are observed in mankind in general, through all countries, nations and ages, and in all conditions.

If any should say, though it be evident that there is a tendency in the state of things to this general event, that all mankind should fail of perfect obedience, and should sin, and incur a demerit of eternal ruin; and also that this tendency don't lie in any distinguishing circumstances of any particular people, person or age—yet it may not lie in man's nature, but in the general constitution and frame of this world, into which men are born—though the nature of man may be good, without any evil propensity inherent in it; yet the nature and universal state of this earthly world may be such as to be full of so many and strong temptations everywhere, and of such a powerful influence on such a creature as man, dwelling in so infirm a body etc. that the result of the whole may be, a strong and infallible tendency in such a state of things, to the sin and eternal ruin of every one of mankind.

To this I would reply, that such an evasion will not at all avail to the purpose of those whom I oppose in this controversy. It alters not the case as to this question, whether man is not a creature that in his present state is depraved and ruined by propensities to sin. If any creature be of such a nature that it proves evil in its proper place, or in the situation which God has assigned it in the universe, it is of an evil nature. That part of the system is not good, which is not good in its place in the system: and those inherent qualities of that part of the system, which are not good, but corrupt, in that place, are justly looked upon as evil inherent qualities. That propensity is truly esteemed to belong to the *nature* of any being, or to be inherent in it, that is the necessary consequence of its nature, considered together with its proper situation in the universal system of existence, whether that propensity be good or bad. 'Tis the nature of a stone to be heavy; but yet, if it were placed, as it might be, at a distance from this world, it would have no such quality. But seeing a stone is of such a nature, that it will have this quality or tendency, in its proper place, here in this world, where God has made it, 'tis properly looked upon as a propensity belonging to its nature: and if it be a good propensity here in its proper place, then it is a good quality of its nature; but if it be contrariwise, it is an evil natural quality. So, if mankind are of such a nature, that they have an universal effectual tendency to sin and ruin in this world, where God has made and placed them, this is to be looked upon as a pernicious tendency belonging to their nature. There is, perhaps, scarce any such thing in beings not independent and self-existent, as any power or tendency, but what has some dependence on other beings, which they stand in some connection with, in the universal system of existence: propensities are no propensities, any otherwise, than as taken with their objects. Thus it is with the tendencies observed in natural bodies, such as gravity, magnetism, electricity etc. And thus it is with the propensities observed in the various kinds of animals; and thus it is with most of the propensities in created spirits.

It may further be observed, that it is exactly the same thing, as to the controversy concerning an agreeableness with God's moral perfections of such a disposal of things, that man should come into the world in a depraved ruined state, by a propensity to sin and ruin; whether God has so ordered it, that this propensity should lie in his nature considered alone, or with relation to its situation in the universe, and its connection with other parts of the system to which the Creator has united it; which is as much of God's ordering, as man's nature itself, most simply considered.

Dr. Taylor (pp. 188, 189), speaking of the attempt of some to solve the difficulty of God's being the author of our nature, and yet that our nature is polluted, by supposing that God makes the soul pure, but unites it to a polluted body (or a body so made, as tends to pollute the soul); he cries out of it as weak and insufficient, and too gross to be admitted: For, says he, who infused the soul into the body? And if it is polluted by being infused into the body, who is the author and cause of its pollution? And who created the body etc? But is not the case just the same, as to those who suppose that God made the soul pure, and places it in a polluted world, or a world tending by its natural state in which it is made, to pollute the soul, or to have such an influence upon it, that it shall without fail be polluted with sin, and eternally ruined? Here, mayn't I also cry out, on as good grounds as Dr. Taylor, Who placed the soul here in this world? And if the world be polluted, or so constituted as naturally and infallibly to pollute the soul with sin, who is the cause of this pollution? And, who created the world—?

Though in the place now cited, Dr. Taylor so insists upon it, that God must be answerable for the pollution of the soul, if he has infused or put the soul into a body that tends to pollute it; yet this is the very thing which he himself supposes to be fact, with respect to the soul's being created by God, in such a body as it is, and in such a world as it is; in a place which I have already had occasion to observe, where he says, "We are *apt,* in a world full of temptation, to be drawn into sin by bodily appetites." And if so, according to his way of reasoning, God must be the author and cause of this aptness to be drawn into sin. Again (p. 143), we have these words, "Who drinketh in iniquity like water; who is attended with so many sensual appetites, and so apt to indulge them." In these words our author in effect says that the individual thing that he cries out of as so gross, viz. the tendency of the body, as God has made it, to pollute the soul, which he has infused into it. These sensual appetites, which incline the soul, or make it apt to a sinful indulgence, are either from the body which God hath made, or otherwise a proneness to sinful indulgence is immediately and originally seated in the soul itself, which will not mend the matter, for Dr. Taylor.

I would lastly observe, that our author insists upon it (pp. 317, 318). That this lower world where we dwell, in its present state, "Is as it was, when, upon a review, God pronounced it, and all its furniture, very good. [. . .] And that the present form and furniture of the earth is full of God's riches, mercy & goodness, and of the most evident tokens of his love & bounty to the inhabitants." If so, there can be no room for such an evasion of the evidences from fact, of the universal infallible tendency of man's nature to sin and eternal perdition, as, that the tendency there is to this issue, don't lie in man's nature, but in the general constitution and frame of this earthly world, which God hath made to be the habitation of mankind.

Section 3. That propensity which has been proved to be in the nature of all mankind, must be a very evil, depraved and pernicious propensity; making it manifest that the soul of man, as it is by nature, is in a corrupt, fallen and ruined state: which is the other part of the consequence, drawn from the proposition laid down in the first section

THE question to be considered, in order to determine whether man's nature is not depraved and ruined, is not whether he is not inclined to perform as many *good deeds* as *bad ones,* but, which of these two he preponderates to, in the frame of his heart, and state of his nature, a state of innocence and righteousness, and favor with God; or a state of sin, guiltiness and abhorrence in the sight of God. Persevering sinless righteousness, or else the guilt of sin, is the alternative, on the decision of which depends (as is confessed) according to the nature and truth of things, as they are in themselves, and according to the rule of right and perfect justice, man's being approved and accepted of his Maker, and eternally blessed as good; or his being rejected, thrown away and cursed as bad. And therefore the determination of the tendency of man's heart and nature with respect to these terms, is that which is to be looked at, in order to determine whether his nature is good or evil, pure or corrupt, sound or ruined. If such be man's nature, and state of his heart, that he has an infallibly effectual propensity to the latter of those terms; then it is wholly impertinent, to talk of the innocent and kind actions, even of criminals themselves, surpassing their crimes in numbers; and of the prevailing innocence, good nature, industry, felicity and cheerfulness of the greater part of mankind. Let never so many thousands, or millions of acts of honesty, good nature, etc. be supposed; yet, by the supposition, there is an unfailing propensity to such moral evil, as in its dreadful consequences infinitely outweighs all effects or consequences of any supposed good. Surely that tendency, which, in effect, is an infallible tendency to eternal destruction, is an infinitely dreadful and pernicious tendency: and that nature and frame of mind, which implies such a tendency, must be an infinitely dreadful and pernicious frame of mind. It would be much more absurd, to suppose that such a state of nature is good, or not bad, under a notion of men's doing more honest and kind things, than evil ones; than to say, the state of that ship is good, to cross the Atlantick Ocean in, that is such as cannot hold together through the voyage, but will infallibly founder and sink by the way; under a notion that it may probably go great part of the way before it sinks, or that it will proceed and sail above water more hours than it will be sinking: or to pronounce that road a good road to go to such a place, the greater part of which is plain and safe, though some parts of it are dangerous, and certainly fatal to them that travel in it; or to call that a good propensity, which is an inflexible inclination to travel in such a way.

A propensity to that sin which brings God's eternal wrath and curse (which has been proved to belong to the nature of man) is not evil, only as it is calamitous and sorrowful, ending in great *natural evil;* but it is *odious* too, and *detestable;* as, by the supposition, it tends to that *moral evil,* by which the subject becomes odious in the sight of God, and liable, as such, to be condemned, and utterly rejected and cursed by him. This also makes it evident, that the state which it has been proved mankind are in, is a corrupt state in a moral sense, that it is inconsistent with the fulfillment of the law of God, which is the rule of moral rectitude and goodness. That tendency, which is opposite to that which the moral law requires and insists upon, and prone to that which the moral law utterly forbids, and eternally condemns the subject for, is doubtless a corrupt tendency, in a moral sense.

So that this depravity is both odious, and also pernicious, fatal and destructive, in the highest sense, as inevitably tending to that which implies man's eternal ruin; it shews, that man, as he is by nature, is in a deplorable and undone state, in the highest sense. And this proves that men don't come into the world perfectly innocent in the sight of God, and without any just exposedness to his displeasure. For the being by nature in a lost and ruined state, in the highest sense, is not consistent with being by nature in a state of favor with God.

But if any should still insist on a notion of men's good deeds exceeding their bad ones, and that seeing the good that is in men more than countervails the evil, they can't be properly denominated evil; all persons and things being most properly denominated from that which prevails, and has the ascendent in them: I would say further, that

I presume it will be allowed, that if there is in man's nature a tendency to guilt and ill-desert, in a vast over-balance to virtue and merit; or a propensity to that sin, the evil and demerit of which is so great, that the value and merit that is in him, or in all the virtuous acts that ever he performs, are as nothing to it; then truly the nature of man may be said to be corrupt and evil.

That this is the true case, may be demonstrated by what is evident of the infinite heinousness of sin against God, from the nature of things.[1] The heinousness of this must rise in some proportion to the obligation we are under to regard the Divine Being; and that must be in some proportion to his worthiness of regard; which doubtless is infinitely beyond the worthiness of any of our fellow creatures. But the merit of our respect or obedience to God is not infinite. The merit of respect to any being don't increase, but is rather diminished in proportion to the obligations we are under in strict justice to pay him that respect. There is no great merit in paying a debt we owe, and by the highest possible obligations in strict justice are obliged to pay; but there is great demerit in refusing to pay it. That on such accounts as these there is an infinite demerit in all sin against God, which must therefore immensely outweigh all the merit which can be supposed to be in our virtue, I think, is capable of full demonstration; and that the futility of the objections, which some have made against the argument, might most plainly be demonstrated. But I shall omit a particular consideration of the evidence of this matter from the nature of things, as I study brevity, and lest any should cry out, "Metaphysicks!" as the manner of some is, when any argument is handled, against any tenet they are fond of, with a close and exact consideration of the nature of things. And this is not so necessary in the present case, inasmuch as the point asserted, namely, that he who commits any one sin, has guilt and ill-desert which is so great, that the value and merit of all the good which it is possible he should do in his whole life, is as nothing to it; I say, this point is not only evident by metaphysics, but is plainly demonstrated by what has been shewn to be *fact,* with respect to God's own constitutions and dispensations towards mankind: as particularly by this, that whatever acts of virtue and obedience a man

1. [See above, Intro., Sec. 3, "The Fact and Nature of Sin."]

performs, yet if he trespasses in one point, is guilty of any the least sin, he, according to the law of God, and so according to the exact truth of things and the proper demerit of sin, is exposed to be wholly cast out of favor with God, and subjected to his curse, to be utterly and eternally destroyed. This has been proved; and shewn to be the doctrine which Dr. Taylor abundantly teaches. But how can it be agreeable to the nature of things, and exactly consonant to everlasting truth and righteousness, thus to deal with a creature for the least sinful act, though he should perform ever so many thousands of honest and virtuous acts, to countervail the evil of that sin? Or how can it be agreeable to the exact truth and real demerit of things, thus wholly to cast off the deficient creature, without any regard to the merit of all his good deeds, unless that be in truth the case, that the value and merit of all those good actions bear no proportion to the heinousness of the least sin? If it were not so, one would think, that however the offending person might have some proper punishment, yet seeing there is so much virtue to lay in the balance against the guilt, it would be agreeable to the nature of things, that he should find some favor, and not be altogether rejected, and made the subject of perfect and eternal destruction; and thus no account at all be made of all his virtue, so much as to procure him the least relief or hope. How can such a constitution represent sin in its proper colors and according to its true nature and desert (as Dr. Taylor says it does) unless this be its true nature, that it is so bad, that even in the least instance it perfectly swallows up all the value of the sinner's supposed good deeds, let 'em be ever so many? So that this matter is not left to our metaphysics or philosophy; the great Lawgiver and infallible Judge of the universe has clearly decided it, in the revelation he has made of what is agreeable to exact truth, justice and the nature of things, in his revealed law or rule of righteousness.

He that in any respect or degree is a transgressor of God's law, is a wicked man, yea, wholly wicked in the eye of the law; all his goodness being esteemed nothing, having no account made of it, when taken together with his wickedness. And therefore, without any regard to his righteousness, he is, by the sentence of the law, and so by the voice of truth and justice to be treated as worthy to be rejected, abhorred and cursed forever; and must be so, unless grace interposes, to cover his transgression. But men are really, in themselves, what they are in the eye of the law, and by the voice of strict equity and justice; however they may be looked upon, and treated by infinite and unmerited mercy.

So that, on the whole, it appears, all mankind have an infallibly effectual propensity to that moral evil, which infinitely outweighs the value of all the good that can be in them; and have such a disposition of heart, that the certain consequence of it is, their being, in the eye of perfect truth and righteousness, wicked men. And I leave all to judge, whether such a disposition be not in the eye of truth a depraved disposition.

Agreeable to these things, the Scripture represents all mankind, not only as having guilt, but immense guilt, which they can have no merit or worthiness to countervail. Such is the representation we have in Matt. 18:21, to the end. There, on Peter's inquiring how often his brother should trespass against him and he forgive him, whether until seven times? Christ replies, "I say not unto thee, until seven times, but until seventy times seven"; apparently meaning, that he should esteem no number of offenses too many, and no degree of injury it is possible our neighbor should be guilty of towards us, too great to be forgiven. For which this reason is given in the parable there following, that if ever we obtain forgiveness and favor with God, he must pardon that guilt and injury towards his majesty, which is immensely greater than the greatest injuries that ever men are guilty of, one towards another, yea, than the sum of all their injuries put together; let 'em be ever so many, and ever so great: so that the latter would be put as an hundred pence to ten thousand talents: which immense debt we owe to God, and have nothing to pay; which implies that we have no merit, to countervail any part of our guilt. And this must be because, if all that may be called virtue in us, be compared with our ill-desert, it is in the sight of God as nothing to it. The parable is not to represent *Peter*'s case in particular, but that of all who then were, or ever should be Christ's disciples. It appears by the conclusion of the discourse; "*So likewise shall my heavenly Father do* . . . if ye, from your hearts, forgive not every one his brother their trespasses."

Therefore how absurd must it be for Christians to object, against the depravity of man's nature, a greater number of innocent and kind actions, than of crimes; and to talk of a prevailing innocency, good nature, industry, and cheerfulness of the greater part of mankind? Infinitely more absurd, than it would be to insist, that the domestic of a prince was not a bad servant, because though sometimes he contemned and affronted his master to a great degree, yet he did not spit in his master's face so often as he performed acts of service; or, than it would be to affirm, that his spouse was a good wife to him, because, although she committed adultery, and that with the slaves and scoundrels sometimes, yet she did not do this so often as she did the duties of a wife. These notions would be absurd, because the crimes are too heinous to be atoned for, by many honest actions of the servant or spouse of the prince; there being a vast disproportion between the merit of the one, and the ill-desert of the other: but in no measure so great, nay infinitely less than that between the demerit of our offenses against God and the value of our acts of obedience.

Thus I have gone through with my first argument; having shewn the evidence of the truth of the proposition I laid down at first, and proved its consequence. But there are many other things, that manifest a very corrupt tendency or disposition in man's nature in his present state, which I shall take notice of in the following sections.

Section 4. The Depravity of Nature Appears by a Propensity in All to Sin Immediately, as Soon as They Are Capable of It, and to Sin Continually and Progressively; and Also by the Remains of Sin in the Best of Men

THE great depravity of man's nature appears, not only in that they universally commit sin, who spend any long time in the world, but in that men are naturally so prone to sin, that none ever fail of *immediately* transgressing God's law, and so of bringing infinite guilt on themselves, and exposing themselves to eternal perdition, as soon as they are capable of it.[1]

The Scriptures are so very express in it, that all mankind, *all flesh, all the world,* every man living, are guilty of sin; that it must at least be understood, everyone that is come to be capable of being active, in duty to God, or sin against him, is guilty of sin. There are multitudes in the world, who have but very lately begun to exert their faculties as moral agents; and so are but just entered on their state of trial, as acting for themselves. There are many thousands constantly in the world, who have not lived one month, or week, or day, since they have arrived to any period that can be assigned from their birth to twenty years of age. And if there be not a strong propensity in man's nature to sin, that should as it were hurry them on to speedy transgression, and they have no guilt previous to their personal sinning, what should hinder but that there might always be a great number of such as act for themselves on the stage of the world, and are answerable for themselves to God, who have hitherto kept themselves free from sin, and have perfectly obeyed God's law, and so are righteous in God's sight with the righteousness of the law; and if they should be called out of the world without any longer trial (as innumerable die at all periods of life) would be justified by the deeds of the law? And how then can it be true, that in God's sight no man living can be justified, that no man can be just with God, and that *by the deeds of the law no flesh can be justified,* because *by the law is the knowledge of sin?* And what should hinder but that

1. [See above, Intro., Sec. 3, "The Fact and Nature of Sin."]

there may always be many in the world, who are capable subjects of instruction and counsel, and of prayer to God, for whom the calls of God's word to repentance and to seek pardon through the blood of Christ, and to forgive others their injuries, because they need that God should forgive them, would not be proper; and for whom the Lord's prayer is not suitable, wherein Christ directs all his followers to pray, that God would forgive their sins, as they forgive those that trespass against them?

If there are any in the world, though but lately become capable of acting for themselves, as subjects of the law of God, who are perfectly free from sin, such are most likely to be found among the children of Christian parents, who give 'em the most pious education, and set them the best examples: and therefore such would never be so likely to be found in any part or age of the world, as in the primitive Christian church, in the first age of Christianity (the age of the church's greatest purity) so long after Christianity had been established, that there had been time for great numbers of children to be born, and educated by those primitive Christians. It was in that age, and in such a part of that age, that the apostle John wrote his first epistle to the Christians that then were. But if there was then a number of them, come to understanding, who were perfectly free from sin, why does he write as he does? (I John 1:8,9, 10), "If we say that we have no sin, we deceive ourselves, and the truth is not in us. If we confess our sins, he is faithful and just to forgive us our sins, and to cleanse us from all unrighteousness. If we say that we have not sinned, we make him a liar, and the truth is not in us." [2]

2. If any should object, that this is an overstraining of things; and that it supposes a greater niceness and exactness, than is observed in scripture representations and expressions, to infer from these expressions, that all men sin immediately, as soon as ever they are capable of it: to this I would say, that I think the arguments used are truly solid, and do really and justly conclude, either that men are born guilty, and so are chargeable with sin before they come to act for themselves, or else commit sin immediately, without the least time intervening after they are capable of understanding their obligations to God, and reflecting on themselves; and that the Scripture clearly determines, there is not one such person in the world, free from sin. But whether this be a straining things up to too great an exactness, or not; yet I suppose, none that don't entirely set aside the sense of such scriptures as have been mentioned, and deny those propositions which Dr. Taylor himself allows to be contained in some of 'em, will deny they prove, that no considerable time passes after men are capable of acting for themselves, as the subjects of God's law, before they

Again, the reality and greatness of the depravity of man's nature appears in this, that he has a prevailing propensity to be *continually* sinning against God. What has been observed above, will clearly prove this. That same disposition of nature, which is an effectual propensity to immediate sin, amounts to a propensity to continual sin. For a being prone to continual sinning is nothing but a proneness to immediate sin continued. Such appears to be the tendency of nature to sin, that as soon as ever man is capable, it causes him immediately to sin, without suffering any considerable time to pass without sin. And therefore, if the same propensity be continued undiminished, there will be an equal tendency to immediate sinning again, without any considerable time passing. And so the same will always be a disposition still immediately to sin, with as little time passing without sin afterwards, as at first. The only reason that can be given why sinning must be immediate at first, is that the disposition is so great, that it will not suffer any considerable time to pass without sin: and therefore, the same disposition being continued in equal degree, without some new restraint, or contrary tendency, it will still equally tend to the same effect. And though it is true, the propensity may be diminished, or have restraints laid upon it, by gracious disposals of providence, or merciful influences of God's spirit; yet this is not owing to nature. That strong propensity of nature, by which men are so prone to immediate sinning at first, has no tendency in itself to a diminution; but rather to an increase; as the continued exercise of an evil disposition, in repeated actual sins, tends to strengthen it more and more: agreeable to that observation of Dr. Taylor's (p. 228). "We are apt to be drawn into sin by bodily appetites, and when once we are under the government of these appetites, it is at least exceeding difficult, if not impracticable, to recover ourselves, by the mere force of reason." The increase of strength of disposition in such a case, is as in a falling body, the strength of its

are guilty of sin; because if the time were considerable, it would be great enough to deserve to be taken notice of, as an exception to such universal propositions, as, "In thy sight shall no man living be justified," etc. And if this be allowed, that men are so prone to sin, that in fact all mankind do sin, as it were, immediately, after they come to be capable of it, or fail not to sin so soon, that no considerable time passes before they run into transgression against God; it don't much alter the case, as to the present argument. If the time of freedom from sin be so small, as not to be worthy of notice in the forementioned universal propositions of Scripture, it is also so small, as not to be worthy of notice in the present argument.

tendency to descend is continually increased, so long as its motion is continued. Not only a constant commission of sin, but a constant increase in the habits and practice of wickedness, is the true tendency of man's depraved nature, if unrestrained by divine grace; as the true tendency of the nature of an heavy body, if obstacles are removed, is not only to fall with a continual motion, but with a constantly increasing motion. And we see, that increasing iniquity is actually the consequence of natural depravity, in most men, notwithstanding all the restraints they have. Dispositions to evil are commonly much stronger in adult persons, than in children, when they first begin to act in the world as rational creatures.

If sin be such a thing as Dr. Taylor himself represents it (p. 69), "A thing of an odious and destructive nature, the corruption and ruin of our nature, and infinitely hateful to God"; then such a propensity to continual and increasing sin, must be a very evil disposition. And if we may judge of the perniciousness of an inclination of nature, by the evil of the effect it naturally tends to, the propensity of man's nature must be evil indeed: for the soul being immortal, as Dr. Taylor acknowledges (p. 370), it will follow from what has been observed above, that man has a natural disposition to one of these two things; either to an increase of wickedness without end, or till wickedness comes to be so great, that the capacity of his nature will not allow it to be greater. This being what his wickedness will come to by its natural tendency, if divine grace don't prevent, it may as truly be said to be the effect which man's natural corruption tends to, as that an acorn in a proper soil truly tends by its nature to become a great tree.

Again, that sin which is remaining in the hearts of the best men on earth, makes it evident, that man's nature is corrupt, as he comes into the world. A remaining depravity of heart in the greatest saints, may be argued from the sins of most of those who are set forth in Scripture as the most eminent instances and examples of virtue and piety: and is also manifest from this, that the Scripture represents all God's children as standing in need of chastisement. (Heb. 12:6,7, 8), "For whom the Lord loveth, he chasteneth; and scourgeth every son whom he receiveth. . . . What son is he, whom the father chasteneth not? If ye are without chastisement . . . then are ye bastards, and not sons." But this is directly and fully asserted in some places; as in that forementioned Eccles. 7:20: "There is not a just man upon earth, that doeth good and sinneth not." Which is as much as to say, there is no man on earth, that is so just, as to have attained to such a degree of righteousness, as not to commit any sin. Yea, the Apostle speaks of all Christians as often sinning, or committing many sins; even in that primitive age of the Christian church, an age distinguished from all others by eminent attainments in holiness; (Jas. 3:2) "In many things we all offend." And that there is pollution in the hearts of all, as the remainder of moral filth that was there antecedent to all attempts of means for purification, is very plainly declared in Prov. 20:9: "Who can say, I have made my heart clean, I am pure from my sin?"

According to Dr. Taylor, men come into the world wholly free from sinful propensities. And if so, it appears from what has been already said, there would be nothing to hinder, but that many, without being better than they are by nature, might perfectly avoid the commission of sin. But much more might this be the case with men after they had, by care, diligence and good practice, attained those positive habits of virtue, whereby they are at a much greater distance from sin, than they were naturally: which this writer supposes to be the case with many good men. But since the Scripture teaches us, that the best men in the world do often commit sin, and have remaining pollution of heart, this makes it abundantly evident, that men, when they are no otherwise than they were by nature, without any of those virtuous attainments, have a sinful depravity; yea, must have great corruption of nature.

Section 5. The Depravity of Nature Appears, in That the General Consequence of the State and Tendency of Man's Nature Is a Much Greater Degree of Sin, Than Righteousness; Not Only with Respect to Value and Demerit, but Matter and Quantity

I HAVE before shewn, that there is a propensity in man's nature to that sin, which in heinousness and ill-desert immensely outweighs all the value and merit of any supposed good, that may be in him, or that he can do. I now proceed to say further, that such is man's nature, in his present state, that it tends to this lamentable effect, that there should at all times, through the course of his life, be at least, much more sin than righteousness; not only as to weight and value, but as to *matter* and *measure;* more disagreement of heart and practice from the law of God, and from the law of nature and reason, than agreement and conformity.

The law of God is the rule of right, as Dr. Taylor often calls it: it is the measure of virtue and sin: so much agreement as there is with this rule, so much is there of rectitude, righteousness, or true virtue, and no more; and so much disagreement as there is with this rule, so much sin is there.

Having premised this, the following things may be here observed.

I. The degree of disagreement from this rule of right is to be determined, not only by the degree of distance from it in *excess,* but also in *defect;* or in other words, not only in positive transgression, or doing what is forbidden, but also in withholding what is required. The divine lawgiver does as much prohibit the one as the other, and does as much charge the latter as a sinful breach of his law, exposing to the eternal wrath and curse, as the former. Thus at the day of judgment, as described [in] Matt. 25. The wicked are condemned, as cursed, to everlasting fire, for their sin in defect and omission: "I was anhungered, and ye gave me no meat," etc. and the case is thus, not only when the defect is in word or behavior, but in the inward temper and exercise of the mind. (I Cor. 16:22), "If any man love not the Lord Jesus Christ, let him be anathema maranatha." Dr. Taylor, speaking of the sentence and punishment of the wicked (Matt. 25:41,46) says, "It was manifestly for want of benevolence, love and compassion to their fellow creatures, that they were condemned" (pp. 158–9). And elsewhere, as was observed before, he says, that the law of God extends to the latent principles of sin, to forbid them, and to condemn to eternal destruction for them. And if so, it doubtless also extends to the inward principles of holiness, to require them, and in like manner to condemn for the want of them.

II. The sum of our duty to God, required in his law, is *love to God;* taking love in a large sense, for the true regard of our hearts to God, implying esteem, honor, benevolence, gratitude, complacency, etc. This is not only very plain by the Scripture, but it is evident in itself. The sum of what the law of God requires, is doubtless obedience to that law: no law can require more than that it be obeyed. But 'tis manifest, that obedience to God is nothing, any otherwise than as a testimony of the respect of our hearts to God: without the heart, man's external acts are no more than the motions of the limbs of a wooden image: have no more of the nature of either sin or righteousness.[1] It must therefore needs be so, that love to God, or the respect of the heart, must be the sum of the duty required towards God in his law.

III. It therefore appears from the premises, that whosoever withholds more of that love or respect of heart from God which his law requires, than he affords, has more sin than righteousness. Not only he that has less divine love, than passions and affections which are opposite; but also he that don't love God half so much as he ought, or has reason to do, has justly more wrong than right, imputed to him, according to the law of God, and the law of reason; he has more irregularity than rectitude, with regard to the law of love. The sinful disrespect or unrespectfulness of his heart to God, is greater than his respect to him.

But what considerate person is there, even among the more virtuous part of mankind, but what would be ashamed to say, and profess before God or men, that he loves God half so much as he ought to do; or that he exercises one half of that esteem, honor and gratitude towards God, which would be altogether becoming him; considering what God is, and what great manifestations he has made of his transcendent excellency and goodness, and what benefits he re-

1. ["True religion, in great part, consists in holy affections" (*Religious Affections,* Yale ed. 2, 95).]

ceives from him? And if few or none of the best of men can with reason and truth make even such a profession, how far from it must the generality of mankind be?

The chief and most fundamental of all the commands of the moral law, requires us "to love the Lord our God with all our hearts, and with all our souls, with all our strength, and all our minds": that is plainly, with all that is within us, or to the utmost capacity of our nature: all that belongs to, or is comprehended within the utmost extent or capacity of our heart and soul, and mind and strength, is required. God is in himself worthy of infinitely greater love, than any creature can exercise towards him: he is worthy of love equal to his perfections, which are infinite: God loves himself with no greater love than he is worthy of, when he loves himself infinitely: but we can give God no more than we have. Therefore, if we give him so much, if we love him to the utmost extent of the faculties of our nature, we are excused: but when what is proposed, is only that we should love him as much as our capacity will allow, this excuse of want of capacity ceases, and obligation takes hold of us; and we are doubtless obliged to love God to the utmost of what is possible for us, with such faculties, and such opportunities and advantages to know God, as we have. And 'tis evidently implied in this great commandment of the law, that our love to God should be so great, as to have the most absolute possession of all the soul, and the perfect government of all the principles and springs of action that are in our nature.

Though it is not easy, precisely to fix the limits of man's capacity, as to love to God; yet in general we may determine, that his capacity of love is coextended with his capacity of knowledge: the exercise of the understanding opens the way for the exercise of the other faculty.[2] Now, though we can't have any proper positive understanding of God's infinite excellency; yet the capacity of the human understanding is very great, and may be extended far. 'Tis needless to dispute, how far man's knowledge may be said to be strictly comprehensive of the things that are very great, as of the extent of the expanse of the heavens, or of the dimensions of the globe of the earth; and of such a great number, as of the many millions of its inhabitants. The word "comprehensive" seems to be ambiguous. But

2. ["Holy affections are not heat without light; but evermore arise from some information of the understanding, some spiritual instruction that the mind receives, some light or actual knowledge" (ibid., p. 266).]

doubtless we are capable of some proper positive understanding of the greatness of these things, in comparison of other things that we know, as unspeakably exceeding them. We are capable of some clear understanding of the greatness or considerableness of a whole nation, or of the whole world of mankind, as vastly exceeding that of a particular person or family. We can positively understand, that the whole globe of the earth is vastly greater, than a particular hill or mountain. And [we] can have some good positive apprehension of the starry heavens, as so greatly exceeding the globe of the earth, that the latter is as it were nothing to it. So the human faculties are capable of a real and clear understanding of the greatness, glory and goodness of God, and of our dependence upon him, from the manifestations which God has made of himself to mankind, as being beyond all expression above that of the most excellent human friend or earthly object. And so we are capable of an esteem and love to God, which shall be proportionable, and as much exceeding that which we have to any creature.

These things may help us to form some judgment, how vastly the generality of mankind fall below their duty, with respect to love to God; yea, how far they are from coming half-way to that height of love, which is agreeable to the rule of right. Surely if our esteem of God, desires after him, and delight in him were such as become us, considering the things forementioned, they would exceed our regard to other things, as the heavens are high above the earth, and would swallow up all other affections, like a deluge. But how far, how exceeding far, are the generality of the world from any appearance of being influenced and governed by such a degree of divine love as this!

If we consider the love of God with respect to that one kind of exercise of it, namely, gratitude, how far indeed do the generality of mankind come short of the rule of right and reason in this! If we consider how various, innumerable and vast the benefits are we receive from God, and how infinitely great and wonderful that grace of his is, which is revealed and offered to them that live under the Gospel, in that eternal salvation which is procured by God's giving his only begotten Son to die for sinners; and also how unworthy we are all, deserving (as Dr. Taylor confesses) eternal perdition under God's wrath and curse: how great is the gratitude, that would become us, who are the subjects of so many and great benefits, and have such grace towards poor sinful lost mankind set before us in so affecting a manner, as in the extreme sufferings of the Son of God, being carried through those pains by a love stronger than death, a love that conquered those mighty agonies, a love whose length and breadth and depth and height passes knowledge? But oh, what poor returns! How little the gratitude! How low, how cold and inconstant the affection in the best, compared with the obligation! And what then shall be said of the gratitude of the generality? Or rather, who can express the ingratitude?

If it were so, that the greater part of them that are called Christians, were no enemies to Christ in heart and practice, were not governed by principles opposite to him and his gospel, but had some real love and gratitude; yet if their love falls vastly short of the obligation or occasion given, they are guilty of shameful and odious ingratitude. As when a man has been the subject of some instance of transcendent generosity, whereby he has been relieved from the most extreme calamity, and brought into very opulent, honorable and happy circumstances, by a benefactor of excellent character; and yet expresses no more gratitude on such an occasion, than would be requisite for some kindness comparatively infinitely small, he may justly fall under the imputation of vile unthankfulness, and of much more ingratitude, than gratitude; though he may have no ill will to his benefactor, or no positive affection of mind contrary to thankfulness and benevolence: what is odious in him is his defect, whereby he falls so vastly below his duty.

Dr. Turnbull abundantly insists that the forces of the affections naturally in man are well proportioned; and often puts a question to this purpose—how man's nature could have been better constituted in this respect? How the affections of his heart could have been better proportioned? I will now mention one instance, out of many that might be mentioned. Man, if his heart were not depraved, might have had a disposition to gratitude to God for his goodness, in proportion to his disposition to anger towards men for their injuries. When I say, "in proportion," I mean considering the greatness and number of favors and injuries, and the degree in which the one and the other are unmerited, and the benefit received by the former, and the damage sustained by the latter. Is there not an apparent and vast difference and inequality in the dispositions to these two kinds of affection, in the generality of both old and young, adult persons and little children? How ready is resentment for injuries received from men? And how easily is it raised in most, at least, to an equal-ity with the desert? And is it so with respect to gratitude for benefits received from God, in any degree of comparison? Dr. Turnbull pleads for the natural disposition to anger for injuries as being good and useful: but surely gratitude to God, if we were inclined to it, would be at least as good and useful as the other.

How far the generality of mankind are from their duty with respect to love to God, will further appear, if we consider, that we are obliged not only to love him with a love of gratitude for benefits received; but true love to God primarily consists in a supreme regard to him for what he is in himself. The tendency of true virtue is to treat everything as it is, and according to its nature. And if we regard the Most High according to the infinite dignity and glory of his nature, we shall esteem and love him with all our heart and soul, and to the utmost of the capacity of our nature, on this account; and not primarily because he has promoted our interest. If God be infinitely excellent in himself, then he is infinitely lovely on that account; or in other words, infinitely worthy to be loved. And doubtless, if he be worthy to be loved for this, then he ought to be loved for this. And 'tis manifest, there can be no true love to him, if he be not loved for what he is in himself. For if we love him not for his own sake, but for something else, then our love is not terminated on him, but on something else, as its ultimate object. That is no true value for infinite worth, which implies no value for that worthiness in itself considered, but only on the account of something foreign. Our esteem of God is fundamentally defective, if it be not primarily for the excellency of his nature, which is the foundation of all that is valuable in him in any respect. If we love not God because he is what he is, but only because he is profitable to us, in truth we love him not at all.[3] If we seem to love him, our love is not to him, but to something else.

And now I must leave it to everyone to judge for himself, from his own opportunities of observation and information concerning mankind, how little there is of this disinterested love to God, this pure divine affection, in the world. How very little indeed in comparison of other affections altogether diverse, which perpetually urge, actuate and govern mankind, and keep the world, through all nations

3. ["But my meaning is, that no affections towards particular persons, or Beings, are of the nature of true virtue, but such as arise from a generally benevolent temper, or from that habit or frame of mind, wherein consists a disposition to love Being in general" (*The Nature of True Virtue,* Worcester ed., 2, 398).]

and ages, in a continual agitation and commotion! This is an evidence of an horrid contempt of God, reigning in the world of mankind. It would be justly esteemed a great instance of disrespect and contempt of a prince, if one of his subjects, when he came in to his house, should set him below his meanest slave. But in setting the infinite Jehovah below earthly objects and enjoyments, men degrade him below those things, between which and him there is an infinitely greater distance, than between the highest earthly potentate and the most abject of mortals. Such a conduct as the generality of men are guilty of towards God, continually and through all ages, in innumerable respects, would be accounted the most vile contemptuous treatment of a fellow creature, of distinguished dignity. Particularly men's treatment of the offers God makes of himself to them as their friend, their father, their God and everlasting portion; their treatment of the exhibitions he has made of his unmeasurable love, and the boundless riches of his grace in Christ, attended with earnest repeated calls, counsels, expostulations, and entreaties; as also of the most dreadful threatenings of his eternal displeasure and vengeance.

Before I finish this section, it may be proper to say something in reply to an objection, some may be ready to make against the force of that argument, which has been used to prove, that men in general have more sin than righteousness, namely, that they don't come half way to that degree of love to God, which becomes them, and is their duty.

The *objection* is this: that the argument seems to prove too much, in that it will prove, that even good men themselves have more sin than holiness; which also has been supposed. But if this were true, it would follow, that sin is the prevalent principle even in good men, and that it is the principle which has the predominancy in the heart and practice of the truly pious; which is plainly contrary to the Word of God.

I answer, if it be indeed so, that there is more sin, consisting in defect of required holiness, than there is of holiness in good men in this world; yet it will not follow, that sin has the chief government of their heart and practice, for two reasons.

1. They may love God more than other things, and yet there may not be so much love, as there is want of due love; or in other words, they may love God more than the world, and therefore the love of God may be predominant, and yet may not love God near half so much as they ought to do. This need not be esteemed a paradox: a

person may love a father, or some great friend and benefactor, of a very excellent character, more than some other object, a thousand times less worthy of his esteem and affection, and yet love him ten times less than he ought; and so be chargeable, all things considered, with a deficiency in respect and gratitude, that is very unbecoming and hateful. If love to God prevails above the love of other things, then virtue will prevail above evil affections, or positive principles of sin; by which principles it is, that sin has a positive power and influence. For evil affections radically consist in inordinate love to other things besides God. And therefore, virtue prevailing beyond these, will have the governing influence. The predominancy of the love of God in the hearts of good men is more from the nature of the object loved, and the nature of the principle of true love, than the degree of the principle. The object is one of supreme loveliness; immensely above all other objects in worthiness of regard; and 'tis by such a transcendent excellency, that he is God, and worthy to be regarded and adored as God, and he that truly loves God, loves him as God. True love acknowledges him to be God, or to be divinely and supremely excellent, and must arise from some knowledge, sense and conviction of his worthiness of supreme respect. And though the sense and view of it may be very imperfect, and the love that arises from it in like manner imperfect; yet if there be any realizing view of such divine excellency, it must cause the heart to respect God above all.

2. Another reason, why a principle of holiness maintains the dominion in the hearts of good men, is the nature of the Covenant of Grace, and the promises of that covenant, on which true Christian virtue relies, and which engage God's strength and assistance to be on its side, and to help it against its enemy, that it may not be overcome. The just live by faith. Holiness in the Christian, or his spiritual life, is maintained, as it has respect by faith to its Author and Finisher, and derives strength and efficacy from the divine Fountain, and by this means overcomes. For, as the Apostle says, "This is the victory that overcomes the world, even our faith" (I John 5:4). 'Tis our faith in him who has promised, never to leave nor forsake his people, and not to forsake the work of his own hands, nor suffer his people to be tempted above their ability, and that his grace shall be sufficient for them, and that his strength shall be made perfect in weakness, and that where he has begun a good work he will carry it on to the day of Christ.

Section 6. The Corruption of Man's Nature Appears by Its Tendency, in Its Present State, to an Extreme Degree of Folly and Stupidity in Matters of Religion

It appears, that man's nature is greatly depraved, by an apparent proneness to an exceeding stupidity and sottishness in those things wherein his duty and main interest are chiefly concerned.

I shall instance in two things; viz. men's proneness to *idolatry* and so general and great a *disregard of eternal things,* as appears in them that live under the light of the gospel.

'Tis manifest, that man's nature in its present state is attended with a great propensity to forsake the acknowledgment and worship of the true God, and to fall into the most stupid idolatry. This has been sufficiently proved by known fact, on abundant trial: inasmuch as the world of mankind in general (excepting one small people, miraculously delivered and preserved) through all nations, in all parts of the world, ages after ages, continued without the knowledge and worship of the true God, and overwhelmed in gross idolatry, without the least appearance or prospect of its recovering itself from so great blindness, or returning from its brutish principles and customs, till delivered by divine grace.

In order to the most just arguing from fact, concerning the tendency of man's nature, as that is in itself, it should be inquired what the event has been, where nature has been left to itself, to operate according to its own tendency, with least opposition made to it by anything supernatural; rather than in exempt places, where the infinite power and grace of God have interposed, and extraordinary means have been used to stem the current, and bring men to true religion and virtue. As to the means by which God's people of old, in the line of Abraham, were delivered and preserved from idolatry, they were miraculous, and of mere grace: notwithstanding which, they were often relapsing into the notions and ways of the heathen: and when they had backslidden, never were recovered, but by divine gracious interposition. And as to the means by which many Gentile nations have been delivered, since the days of the gospel, they are such as have been wholly owing to most wonderful, miraculous and infinite grace. God was under no obligation to bestow on the heathen world greater advantages than they had in the ages of their gross darkness; as appears by the fact, that God actually did not, for so long a time, bestow greater advantages.

Dr. Taylor himself observes (*Key,* p. 1), "That in about 400 years after the flood, the generality of mankind were fallen into idolatry." And thus it was everywhere through the world, excepting among that people that was saved, and preserved by a constant series of miracles, through a variety of countries, nations and climates, great enough, and through successive changes, revolutions and ages, numerous enough, to be a sufficient trial of what mankind are prone to; if there be any such thing as a sufficient trial.

That men should forsake the true God for idols, is an evidence of the most astonishing folly and stupidity, by God's own testimony. (Jer. 2:12–13), "Be astonished, O ye heavens, at this, and be ye horribly afraid, be ye very desolate, saith the Lord: for my people have committed two evils; they have forsaken me the fountain of living waters, and have hewed out to themselves cisterns, broken cisterns, that can hold no water." And that mankind in general did thus, so soon after the flood, was from the evil propensity of their hearts, and because they did not like to retain God in their knowledge; as is evident by Rom. 1:28. And the universality of the effect shews that the cause was universal, and not anything belonging to the particular circumstances of one, or only some nations or ages, but something belonging to that nature that is common to all nations, and that remains the same through all ages. And what other cause could this great effect possibly arise from, but a depraved disposition, natural to all mankind? It could not arise from want of a sufficient capacity or means of knowledge. This is in effect confessed on all hands. Dr. Turnbull (*Christian Philosophy,* p. 21) says as follows: "The existence of one infinitely powerful, wise and good mind, the author, creator, upholder and governour of all things, is a truth that lies plain and obvious to all that will but think." And (Ibid., p. 245), "Moral knowledge, which is the most important of all knowledge, may easily be acquired by all men." And again (Ibid., p. 292), "Every man by himself, if he would duly employ his mind, in the contemplation of the works of God about him, or in the examination of his own frame, . . . might make very great progress in the knowledge of the wisdom and goodness of God. This all men, generally speaking, might do, with very little assistance; for they have all sufficient abilities for thus employing their minds, and have all sufficient time for it." Mr. Locke says (*Hum. Und.* Bk. IV, ch. 4, p. 242, ed. 11),[1] "Our own existence, and the sensible parts of the universe, offer the proofs of a deity so clearly and cogently to our thoughts, that I deem it impossible for a considerate man to withstand them. For I judge it as certain and clear a truth, as can anywhere be delivered, that the invisible things of God are clearly seen from the creation of the world, being understood by the things that are made, even his eternal power and godhead." And Dr. Taylor himself (in p. 78) says, "The light given to all ages and nations of the world, is sufficient for the knowledge and practice of their duty." And in pp. 111, 112, [after] citing those words of the Apostle (Rom. 2:14,15), says, "This clearly supposes that the Gentiles, who were then in the world, might have done the things contained in the law by nature, or their natural power." And in one of the next sentences, he says, "The Apostle in Rom. 1:19,20,21, affirms that the Gentiles had light sufficient to have seen God's eternal power and godhead, in the works of creation; and that the reason why they did not glorify him as God, was because they became vain in their imaginations, and had darkened their foolish heart; so that they were without excuse." And in his paraphrase on those verses in the first of Romans he speaks of the "very heathens, that were without a written revelation, as having that clear and evident discovery of God's being and perfections, that they are inexcusable in not glorifying him, suitably to his excellent nature, and as the author of their being and enjoyments." And in p. 422, he says, "God affords every man sufficient light to know his duty." If all ages and nations of the world have sufficient light for the knowledge of God, and their duty to him, then even such nations and ages, in which the most brutish ignorance and barbarity prevailed, had sufficient light, if they had had but a disposition to improve it; and then much more those of the heathen, which were more knowing and polished, and in ages wherein arts and learning had made greatest advances. But even in such nations and ages, there was no advance made towards true reli-

1. [John Locke, *Essay Concerning Human Understanding,* 1st ed. 1690. See above Intro., Sec. 4.]

gion; as Dr. Winder observes (*His. of Knowl.* vol. 2, p. 336) [2] in the following words:

"The pagan religion degenerated into greater absurdity, the further it proceeded, and it prevailed in all its height of absurdity when the pagan nations were polished to the height. Though they set out with the talents of reason, and had solid foundations of information to build upon, it in fact proved, that with all their strengthened faculties, and growing powers of reason, the edifice of religion rose in the most absurd deformities and disproportions, and gradually went on in the most irrational disproportioned, incongruous systems, of which the most easy dictates of reason would have demonstrated the absurdity. They were contrary to all just calculations in moral mathematicks." He observes, "That their grossest abominations first began in Egypt, where was an ostentation of the greatest progress in learning and science: and they never renounced clearly any of their abominations, or openly returned to the worship of the one true God, the Creator of all things, and to the original, genuine sentiments of the highest, and most venerable antiquity. The pagan religion continued in this deep state of corruption to the last. The pagan philosophers, and inquisitive men, made great improvements in many sciences, and even in morality itself; yet the inveterate absurdities of pagan idolatry remained without remedy. Every temple smoked with incense to the sun and moon, & other inanimate, material luminaries, and earthly elements, to Jupiter, Juno, Mars and Venus, &c., the patrons and examples of almost every vice. Hecatombs bled on the altars of a thousand gods, as mad superstition inspired. And this was not the disgrace of our ignorant, untaught northern countries only; but even at Athens itself, the infamy reigned, and circulated through all Greece: and finally prevailed, amidst all their learning and politeness, under the Ptolemys in Egypt, and the Caesars in Rome. Now if the knowledge of the pagan world, in religion, proceeded no further than this; if they retained all their deities, even the most absurd of them all, their deified beasts, and deified men, even to the last breath of pagan power; we may justly ascribe the great

2. [Henry Winder, *A Critical and Chronological History of the Rise, Progress, Declension, and Revival of Knowledge, Chiefly Religious,* 1745. See above, Intro., Sec. 4.]

improvements in the world on the subject of religion, to divine revelation; either vouchsafed in the beginning, when this knowledge was competently clear and copious; or at the death of paganism, when this light shone forth in its consummate lustre, at the coming of Christ."

Dr. Taylor often speaks of the idolatry of the heathen world, as great wickedness, in which they were wholly inexcusable: and yet often speaks of their case as remedy-less, as being dead in sin, and unable to recover themselves. And if so, and yet, according to his own doctrine, every age, and every nation, and every man, had sufficient light afforded, to know God, and to know and do their whole duty to him; then their inability to deliver themselves must be a moral inability, consisting in a desperate depravity, and most evil disposition of heart.

And if there had not been sufficient trial of the propensity of the hearts of mankind, through all those ages that passed from Abraham to Christ, the trial has been continued down to this day, in all those vast regions of the face of the earth, that have remained without any effects of the light of the gospel; and the dismal effect continues everywhere unvaried. How was it with that multitude of nations inhabiting South and North America? What appearance was there, when the Europeans first came hither, of their being recovered, or recovering, in any degree from the grossest ignorance, delusions, and most stupid paganism? And how is it at this day, in those parts of Africa and Asia, into which the light of the gospel has not penetrated?

This strong and universally prevalent disposition of mankind to idolatry, of which there has been such great trial, and so notorious and vast proof, in fact, is a most glaring evidence of the exceeding depravity of the human nature; as 'tis a propensity, in the utmost degree, contrary to the highest end, the main business and chief happiness of mankind, consisting in the knowledge, service and enjoyment of the living God, the Creator and Governor of the world; in the highest degree contrary to that for which mainly God gave mankind more understanding than the beasts of the earth, and made them wiser than the fowls of heaven: which was, that they might be capable of the knowledge of God; and in the highest degree contrary to the first and greatest commandment of the moral law, that we should have no other gods before Jehovah, and that we should love and adore him with all our heart, soul, mind and strength. The Scriptures are abundant in representing the idolatry of the heathen world as their exceeding wickedness, and their most brutish stupidity. They that worship and trust in idols, are said themselves to be like the lifeless statues they worship, like mere senseless stocks and stones (Ps. 115:4–8, and 135:15–18).

A second instance of the natural stupidity of the minds of mankind, that I shall observe, is that great disregard of their own eternal interest; which appears so remarkably, so generally, among them that live under the gospel.

> As Mr. Locke observes (*Hum. Und.* vol. 1 [Bk. 2], p. 207), "Were the will determined by the views of good, as it appears in contemplation, greater or less to the understanding, it could never get loose from the infinite eternal joys of heaven, once proposed, and considered as possible: the eternal condition of a future state infinitely outweighing the expectation of riches or honor, or any other worldly pleasure, which we can propose to ourselves; though we should grant these the more probable to be obtained." Again (pp. 228, 229), "He that will not be so far a rational creature, as to reflect seriously upon infinite happiness and misery, must needs condemn himself, as not making that use of his understanding he should. The rewards and punishments of another life, which the Almighty has established, as the enforcements of his laws, are of weight enough to determine the choice, against whatsoever pleasure or pain this life can show. When the eternal state is considered but in its bare possibility, which nobody can make any doubt of, he that will allow exquisite and endless happiness to be but the possible consequences of a good life here, and the contrary state the possible reward of a bad one, must own himself to judge very much amiss, if he does not conclude that a virtuous life, with the certain expectation of everlasting bliss, which may come, is to be preferred to a vicious one, with the fear of that dreadful state of misery, which 'tis very possible may overtake the guilty, or at least the terrible uncertain hope of annihilation. This is so evidently so; though the virtuous life here had nothing but pain, and the vicious continual pleasure; which yet is for the most part quite otherwise, and wicked men have not much the odds to brag of, even in their present possession; nay, all things rightly considered, have I think even

the worst part here. But when infinite happiness is put in one scale, against infinite misery in the other; if the worst that comes to the pious man, if he mistakes, be the best that the wicked man can attain to, if he be in the right; who can, without madness, run the venture: Who in his wits would choose to come within a possibility of infinite misery? Which if he miss, there is yet nothing to be got by that hazard: whereas, on the other side, the sober man ventures nothing, against infinite happiness to be got, if his expectations come to pass."

That disposition of mind which is a propensity to act contrary to reason, is a depraved disposition. 'Tis not because the faculty of reason, which God has given to mankind, is not sufficient fully to discover to 'em that forty, sixty, or an hundred years, is as nothing in comparison of eternity, infinitely less than a second of time to an hundred years, that the greatest wordly prosperity and pleasure is not treated with most perfect disregard, in all cases where there is any degree of competition of earthly things, with salvation from exquisite eternal misery, and the enjoyment of everlasting glory and felicity; as certainly it would be, if men acted according to reason. But is it a matter of doubt or controversy, whether men in general don't shew a strong disposition to act far otherwise, from their infancy, till death is in a sensible approach? In things that concern men's temporal interest, they easily discern the difference between things of a long and short continuance. 'Tis no hard matter to convince men of the difference between a being admitted to the accommodations, and entertainments of a convenient, beautiful, well-furnished habitation, and to partake of the provisions and produce of a plentiful estate, for a day or a night; and having all given to them and settled upon them as their own, to possess as long as they live, and to be theirs, and their heirs' forever: there would be no need of men's preaching sermons, and spending their strength and life to convince men of the difference. Men know how to adjust things in their dealings and contracts one with another, according to the length of time in which anything agreed for is to be used or enjoyed. In temporal affairs, men are sensible that it concerns 'em to provide for future time, as well as for the present. Thus common prudence teaches 'em to take care in summer to lay up for winter; yea, to provide a fund, and get a solid estate, whence they may be supplied for a long time to come. And not only so, but they are willing and forward to spend and be spent, to provide that which will stand their children in stead, after they are dead; though it be quite uncertain, who shall use and enjoy what they lay up, after they have left the world; and if their children should have the comfort of it, as they desire, they will not partake with them in that comfort, or have any more a portion in anything under the sun. In things which relate to men's temporal interest, they seem very sensible of the uncertainty of life, especially of the lives of others; and to make answerable provision for the security of their worldly interest, that no considerable part of it may rest only on so uncertain a foundation, as the life of a neighbor or friend. Common discretion leads men to take good care, that their outward possessions be well secured, by a good and firm title. In worldly concerns, men are discerning of their opportunities, and careful to improve 'em before they are passed. The husbandman is careful to plow his ground, and sow his seed, in the proper season; otherwise he knows he can't expect a crop: and when the harvest is come, he will not sleep away the time; for he knows, if he does so, the crop will soon be lost. How careful and eagle-eyed is the merchant to observe and improve his opportunities and advantages, to enrich himself? How apt are men to be alarmed at the appearance of danger to their worldly estate, or anything that remarkably threatens great loss or damage to their outward interest? And how will they bestir themselves in such a case, if possible to avoid the threatened calamity? In things purely secular, and not of a moral or spiritual nature, men easily receive conviction by past experience, when anything, on repeated trial, proves unprofitable or prejudicial; and are ready to take warning by what they have found themselves, and also by the experience of their neighbors and forefathers.

But if we consider how men generally conduct themselves in things on which their well-being does infinitely more depend, how vast is the diversity? In these things, how cold, lifeless and dilatory? With what difficulty are a few of multitudes excited to any tolerable degree of care and diligence, by the innumerable means used with men to make 'em wise for themselves? And when some vigilance and activity is excited, how apt is it to die away, like a mere force against a natural tendency? What need of a constant repetition of admonitions and counsels, to keep the heart from falling asleep? How many objections are made? And how are difficulties magnified? And how soon is the mind discouraged? How many arguments, and often renewed, and variously and elaborately enforced, do men stand in need of, to convince 'em of things that are self-evident? As that things which are eternal, are infinitely more important than things temporal, and the like. And after all, how very few convinced effectually, or in such a manner as to induce to a practical preference of eternal things? How senseless are men of the necessity of improving their time to provide for futurity, as to their spiritual interest, and their welfare in another world? Though it be an endless futurity, and though it be their own personal, infinitely important good, after they are dead, that is to be cared for, and not the good of their children, which they shall have no share in. Though men are so sensible of the uncertainty of their neighbors' lives, when any considerable part of their estates depends on the continuance of them; how stupidly senseless do they seem to be of the uncertainty of their own lives, when their preservation from immensely great, remedyless and endless misery, is risked by a present delay, through a dependence on future opportunity? What a dreadful venture will men carelessly and boldly run, and repeat and multiply, with regard to their eternal salvation, who are very careful to have everything in a deed or bond firm, and without a flaw? How negligent are they of their special advantages and opportunities for their soul's good? How hardly awakened by the most evident and imminent dangers, threatening eternal destruction, yea, though put in mind of 'em, and much pains taken to point them forth, shew them plainly, and fully to represent them, if possible to engage their attention to 'em? How are they like the horse, that boldly rushes into the battle? How hardly are men convinced by their own frequent and abundant experience, of the unsatisfactory nature of earthly things, and the instability of their own hearts in their good frames and intentions? And how hardly convinced by their own observation, and the experience of all past generations, of the uncertainty of life and its enjoyments? (Ps. 49:11, etc.), "Their inward thought is, that their houses shall continue forever. . . . Nevertheless, man being in honor, abideth not; he is like the beasts that perish. This their way is their folly: yet their posterity approve their sayings. Like sheep are they laid in the grave."

In these things, men that are prudent for their temporal interest, act as if they were bereft of reason: "They have eyes, and see not; ears, and hear not; neither do they understand: They are like the horse and mule, that have no understanding" (Mark 8:18, Ps. 32:9).

(Jer. 8:7), "The stork in the heaven knoweth her appointed times; and the turtle, and the crane, and the swallow, observe the time of their coming: but my people know not the judgment of the Lord."

These things are often mentioned in Scripture, as evidences of extreme folly and stupidity, wherein men act as great enemies to themselves, as though they loved their own ruin (Prov. 8:36), laying wait for their own blood (Prov. 1:18). And how can these things be accounted for, but by supposing a most wretched depravity of nature? Why otherwise should not men be as wise for themselves in spiritual and eternal things, as in temporal? All Christians will confess, that man's faculty of reason was given him chiefly to enable him to understand the former, wherein his main interest, and true happiness consists. This faculty would therefore undoubtedly be every way as fit for the understanding of them, as the latter, if not depraved. The reason why these are understood and not the other, is not that such things as have been mentioned, belonging to men's spiritual and eternal interest, are more obscure and abstruse in their own nature. For instance, the difference between long and short, the need of providing for futurity, the importance of improving proper opportunities, and of having good security, and a sure foundation, in affairs wherein our interest is greatly concerned, etc., these things are as plain in themselves in religious matters, as in other matters. And we have far greater means to assist us to be wise for ourselves in eternal, than in temporal things. We have the abundant instruction of perfect and infinite wisdom itself, to lead and conduct us in the paths of righteousness, so that we may not err. And the reasons of things are most clearly, variously and abundantly set before us in the word of God; which is adapted to the faculties of mankind, tending greatly to enlighten and convince the mind: whereas, we have no such excellent and perfect rules to instruct and direct us in things pertaining to our temporal interest, nor anything to be compared to it.

If any should say, 'tis true, if men gave full credit to what they are told concerning eternal things, and these appeared to 'em as real and certain things, it would be an evidence of a sort of madness in them, that they shew no greater regard to 'em in practice: but there is reason to think, this is not the case; the things of another world, being unseen things, appear to men as things of a very doubtful nature, and attended with great uncertainty. In answer, I would observe, agreeable to what has been cited from Mr. Locke, though eternal things were considered in their bare possibility, if men acted rationally, they would infinitely outweigh all temporal things in their influence on their hearts. And I would also observe, that the supposing eternal things not to be fully believed, at least by them who enjoy the light of the gospel, does not weaken, but rather strengthen the argument for the depravity of nature. For the eternal world being what God had chiefly in view in the creation of men, and the things of this world being made to be wholly subordinate to other, man's state here being only a state of probation, preparation and progression, with respect to the future state, and so eternal things being in effect men's all, their whole concern: to understand and know which it chiefly was, that they had understanding given 'em; and it concerning them infinitely more to know the truth of eternal things than any other, as all that are not infidels will own; therefore, we may undoubtedly conclude, that if men have not respect to 'em as real and certain things, it cannot be for want of sufficient evidence of their truth, to induce 'em so to regard them; especially as to them that live under that light, which God has appointed as the most proper exhibition of the nature and evidence of these things: but it must be from a dreadful stupidity of mind, occasioning a sottish insensibility of their truth and importance, when manifested by the clearest evidence.

Section 7. That man's nature is corrupt, appears, in that vastly the greater part of mankind, in all ages, have been wicked men

The depravity of man's nature appears, not only in its propensity to sin in some degree, which renders a man an evil or wicked man in the eye of the law, and strict justice, as was before shewn; but it is so corrupt, that its depravity, either shews that men *are,* or tends to make them *to be,* of such an evil character, as shall denominate them wicked men, according to the tenor of the Covenant of Grace.

This may be argued from several things which have been already observed: as from a tendency to continual sin; a tendency to much greater degree of sin than righteousness, and from the general extreme stupidity of mankind. But yet the present state of man's nature, as implying, or tending to a *wicked character,* may be worthy to be more particularly considered, and directly proved. And in general, this appears, in that there have been so very few in the world, from age to age, ever since the world has stood, that have been of any other character.

'Tis abundantly evident in Scripture, and is what I suppose none that call themselves Christians will deny, that the whole world is divided into good and bad, and that all mankind at the day of judgment will either be approved as righteous, or condemned as wicked; either glorified, as children of the kingdom, or cast into a furnace of fire, as children of the wicked one.

I need not stand to shew what things belong to the character of such as shall hereafter be accepted as righteous, according to the word of God. It may be sufficient for my present purpose, to observe what Dr. Taylor himself speaks of as belonging essentially to the character of such. In p. 203 he says, "This is infallibly the character of true Christians, and what is essential to such, that they have really mortified the flesh, with its lusts; They are dead to sin, and live no longer therein; the old man is crucified, and the body of sin destroyed: they yield themselves to God, as those that are alive from the dead, and their members as instruments of righteousness to God, and as servants of righteousness to holiness." [1] There is more to the like purpose in the two next pages. In p. 228 he says, "Whatsoever is evil and corrupt in us, we ought to condemn; not so, as it shall still remain in us, that we may always be condemning it, but that we may speedily reform, and be effectually delivered from it; otherwise certainly we do not come up to the character of the true disciples of Christ."

In p. 248 he says, "Unless God's favor be preferred before all other enjoyments whatsoever, unless there be a delight in the worship of God, and in converse with him, unless every appetite be brought into subjection to reason and truth, and unless there be a kind and benevolent disposition towards our fellow-creatures, how can the mind be fit to dwell with God, in his house and family, to do him service in his kingdom, and to promote the happiness of any part of his creation?" And in his *Key* no. 255, p. 145, etc. shewing there, *what it is to be a true Christian,* he says, among other things, "That he is one who has such a sense and persuasion of the love of God in Christ, that he devotes his life to the honor and service of God, in hope of eternal glory. And that to the character of a true Christian, it is absolutely necessary, that he diligently study the things that are freely given him of God, viz. his election, regeneration, &c. that he may gain a just knowledge of those inestimable privileges, may taste that the Lord is gracious, and rejoice in the gospel-salvation, as his greatest happiness and glory. . . . 'Tis necessary, that he work these blessings on his heart, till they become a vital principle, producing in him the love of God, engaging him to all cheerful obedience to his will, giving him a proper dignity and elevation of soul, raising him above the best and worst of this world, carrying his heart into heaven, and fixing his affections and regards upon his everlasting inheritance, and the crown of glory laid up for him there. . . . Thus he is armed against all the temptations and trials, resulting from any pleasure or pain, hopes or fears, gain or loss, in the present world. None of these things move him, from a faithful discharge of any part of his duty, or from a firm attachment to truth and righteousness: neither counts he his very life dear to him, that he may do the will of God, and finish his course with joy, in a sense of the love of God and Christ. He maintains daily communion with God, by reading and meditating on his Word. In a

1. [JE's free paraphrase.]

sense of his own infirmity, and the readiness of the divine favor to succour him, he daily addresses the throne of grace, for the renewal of spiritual strength; and in assurance of obtaining it, through one mediator Christ Jesus, enlightened and directed by the heavenly doctrine of the gospel, &c." [2]

Now I leave it to be judged by everyone that has any degree of impartiality, whether there be not sufficient grounds to think, from what appears everywhere, that it is but a very small part indeed, of the many myriads and millions which overspread this globe, who are of a character that in any wise answers these descriptions. However, Dr. Taylor insists, that all nations, and every man on the face of the earth, have light and means sufficient to do the whole will of God, even they that live in the grossest darkness of paganism.

Dr. Taylor in answer to arguments of this kind, very impertinently from time to time objects [3] that we are no judges of the viciousness of men's character, nor are able to decide in what degree they are virtuous or vicious. As though we could have no good grounds to judge, that anything, appertaining to the qualities or properties of the mind, which is invisible, is general or prevailing among a multitude or collective body, unless we can determine how it is with each individual. I think, I have sufficient reason, from what I know and have heard of the American Indians, to judge, that there are not many good philosophers among them; though the thoughts of their hearts, and the ideas and knowledge they have in their minds, are things invisible; and though I have never seen so much as the thousandth part of the Indians; and with respect to most of them, should not be able to pronounce peremptorily, concerning any one, that he was not very knowing in the nature of things, if all should singly pass before me. And Dr. Taylor himself seems to be sensible of the falseness of his own conclusions, that he so often urges against others; if we may judge by his practice, and the liberties he takes, in judging of a multitude himself. He, it seems, is sensible that a man may have good grounds to judge, that wickedness of character is general in a collective body; because he openly does it himself (*Key*, p. 147). After declaring the things which belong to the character of a true Christian, he judges of the generality of Christians, that they have cast off these things, that they are a people

2. What Dr. Turnbull says of the character of a good man, is also worthy to be observed, *Chris*[*tian*] *Phil*[*osophy*], pp. 86, 258, 288, 375, 409, 410.

3. Pp. 327, 339, 340, 343, 344, 348.

that do err in their hearts, and have not known God's ways. [On] p. 259, he judges, that the generality of Christians are the most wicked of all mankind—when he thinks it will throw some disgrace on the opinion of such as he opposes. The like we have from time to time in other places, as p. 168, p. 258, *Key* p. 182.

But if men are not sufficient judges, whether there are few of the world of mankind but what are wicked, yet doubtless God is sufficient, and his judgment, often declared in his Word, determines the matter. (Matt. 7:13,14), "Enter ye in at the strait gate: for wide is the gate, and broad is the way, that leadeth to destruction, and many there be that go in thereat; because strait is the gate, and narrow is the way that leadeth to life, and few there be that find it." 'Tis manifest, that here Christ is not only describing the state of things, as it was at that day, and don't mention the comparative smallness of the number of them that are saved, as a consequence of the peculiar perverseness of that people, and of that generation; but as a consequence of the general circumstances of the way to life, and the way to destruction, the broadness of the one, and narrowness of the other. In the straitness of the gate, etc. I suppose none will deny, that Christ has respect to the strictness of those rules, which he had insisted on in the preceding sermon, and which render the way to life very difficult to mankind. But certainly these amiable rules would not be difficult, were they not contrary to the natural inclinations of men's hearts; and they would not be contrary to those inclinations, were these not depraved. Consequently the wideness of the gate, and broadness of the way that leads to destruction, in consequence of which many go in thereat, must imply the agreeableness of this way to men's natural inclinations. The like reason is given by Christ, why few are saved. (Luke 13:23,24), "Then said one unto him, Lord, are there few [that be] saved? And he said unto them, Strive to enter in at the strait gate: for many, I say unto you, will seek to enter in, and shall not be able." That there are generally but few good men in the world, even among them that have those most distinguishing and glorious advantages for it, which they are favored with that live under the gospel, is evident by that saying of our Lord, from time to time in his mouth, "Many are called, but few are chosen" (Matt. 22:14). And if there are but few among these, how few, how very few indeed, must persons of this character be, compared with the whole world of mankind? The exceeding smallness of the number of true saints, compared with the whole world, appears by the representations often made of them as distinguished from the world; in which they are spoken of as called and chosen out of the world; redeemed from the earth, redeemed from among men; as being those that are of God, while the whole world lieth in wickedness, and the like. And if we look into the Old Testament, we shall find the same testimony given. (Prov. 20:6), "Most men will proclaim every man his own goodness: but a faithful man who can find?" By a faithful man, as the phrase is used in Scripture, is intended much the same as a sincere, upright or truly good man; as in Ps. 12:1 and 31:23 and 101:6 and other places. Again (Eccles. 7:25–29), "I applied mine heart to know and to search, and to find out wisdom, and the reason of things, and to know the wickedness of folly, even of foolishness and madness: and I find more bitter than death the woman whose heart is snares, etc. . . . Behold, this have I found, saith the preacher, counting one by one, to find out the account, which yet my soul seeketh, but I find not: one man among a thousand have I found; but a woman among all these have I not found. Lo, this only have I found, that God [hath] made man upright; but they have sought out many inventions." Solomon here signifies, that when he set himself diligently to find out the account or proportion of true wisdom or thorough uprightness among men, the result was, that he found it to be but as one to a thousand, etc. Dr. Taylor on this place (p. 184), says, "The wise man in the context is inquiring into the corruption and depravity of mankind, of the men and women that lived in his time." As though what he said represented nothing of the state of things in the world in general, but *only in his time.* But does Dr. Taylor or anybody else suppose this only to be the design of that book, to represent the vanity and evil of the world in that time, and to shew that all was vanity and vexation of spirit in Solomon's day? (Which day truly we have reason to think, was a day of the greatest smiles of heaven on that nation, that ever had been on any nation from the foundation of the world.) Not only does the subject and argument of the whole book shew it to be otherwise; but also the declared design of the book in the first chapter; where the world is represented as very much the same, as to the vanity and evil it is full of, from age to age, making little or no progress, after all its revolutions and restless motions, labors and pursuits, like the sea, that has all the rivers constantly emptying themselves into it, from age to age, and yet is never the fuller. As to that place (Prov. 20:6), "A faithful man who can find?" there is no more reason to suppose, that the wise man has respect only to *his* time, in these words, than in those immediately preceding, "Counsel in the heart of a man is like deep waters; but a man of understanding will draw it out." Or in the words next following, "The just man walketh in his integrity: his children are blessed after him." Or in any other proverb in the whole book. And if it were so, that Solomon in these things meant only to describe his own times, it would not at all weaken the argument. For if we observe the history of the Old Testament, there is reason to think there never was any time from Joshua to the captivity, wherein wickedness was more restrained, and virtue and religion more encouraged and promoted, than in David's and Solomon's times. And if there was so little true piety in that nation that was the only people of God under heaven, even in their very best times, what may we suppose concerning the world in general, take one time with another?

Notwithstanding what some authors advance concerning the prevalence of virtue, honesty, good neighborhood, cheerfulness, etc. in the world, Solomon, whom we may justly esteem as wise and just an observer of human nature, and the state of the world of mankind, as most in these days (besides, Christians ought to remember that he wrote by divine inspiration) judged the world to be so full of wickedness, that it was better never to be born, than to be born to live only in such a world. (Eccles. 4 at the beginning), "So I returned and considered all the oppressions that are done under the sun; and behold, the tears of such as were oppressed, and they had no comforter: and on the side of their oppressors there was power; but they had no comforter. Wherefore, I praised the dead, which were already dead more than the living which are yet alive. Yea, better is he than both they, which hath not yet been; who hath not seen the evil work that is done under the sun." Surely it will not be said, that Solomon has only respect to *his* times here too, when he speaks of the oppressions of them that were in power; since he himself, and others appointed by him, and wholly under his control, were the men that were in power, in that land, and in almost all neighboring countries.

The same inspired writer says (Eccles. 9:3), "The heart of the sons of men is full of evil; and madness is in their heart while they live; and after that they go to the dead." If these general expressions are to be understood only of some, and those the lesser part, when in general, truth, honesty, good-nature, etc. govern the world, why are such general expressions from time to time used? Why don't this wise and noble, and great-souled prince express himself in a more generous and benevolent strain as well as more agreeable to truth, and say, "Wisdom is in the hearts of the sons of men while they live, etc."—instead of leaving in his writings so many sly, ill-natured suggestions, which pour such contempt on the human nature, and tend so much to excite mutual jealousy and malevolence, to taint the minds of mankind through all generations after him?

If we consider the various successive parts and periods of the duration of the world, it will, if possible, be yet more evident, that vastly the greater part of mankind have in all ages been of a wicked character. The short accounts we have of Adam and his family are such as lead us to suppose, that far the greater part of his posterity, in his lifetime, yea, in the former part of his life, were wicked. It appears, that his eldest son, Cain, was a very wicked man, who slew his righteous brother Abel. And Adam lived an hundred and thirty years before Seth was born: and by that time, we may suppose, his posterity began to be considerably numerous: when he was born his mother "called his name Seth: for God, said she, hath appointed me another seed, instead of Abel." Which naturally suggests this to our thoughts; that of all her seed now existing, none were of any such note for religion and virtue, as that their parents could have any great comfort in them, or expectation from 'em on that account. And by the brief history we have, it looks as if (however there might be some intervals of a revival of religion, yet) in the general, mankind grew more and more corrupt till the flood. 'Tis signified, that when men began to multiply on the face of the earth, wickedness prevailed exceedingly (Gen. 6, at the beginning). And that before God appeared to Noah, to command him to build the ark, 120 years before the flood, the world had long continued obstinate in great and general wickedness, and the disease was become inveterate. The expression we have in the 3[d], 5th, and 6th verses of that chapter suggest as much: "And the Lord said, My spirit shall not *always* strive with man. . . . And God saw, that the wickedness of man was great on the earth, and that every imagination of the thoughts of his heart was evil, only evil *continually;* and it repented the Lord, that he had made man on the earth, and it grieved him at his heart." And by that time "all flesh had corrupted his way upon the earth" (v. 12). And as Dr. Taylor himself observes (p. 122), "Mankind were universally debauched into lust, sensuality, rapine and injustice."

And with respect to the period after the flood, to the calling of Abraham; Dr. Taylor says, as has been already observed, that in about 400 years after the flood, the generality of mankind were fallen into idolatry. Which was before the passing away of one generation; or before all they were dead, that came out of the ark. And it can't be thought, the world jumped into that so general and extreme degree of corruption, all at once; but that they had been gradually growing more and more corrupt; though it is true, it must be by very swift degrees (however soon we may suppose they began)—to get to that pass in one age.

And as to the period from the calling of Abraham to the coming of Christ, Dr. Taylor justly observes as follows (*Key* p. 190), "If we reckon from the call of Abraham to the coming of Christ, the Jewish dispensation continued one thousand nine hundred and twenty-one years: during which period, the other families and nations of the earth, not only lay out of God's peculiar kingdom, but also lived in idolatry, great ignorance, and wickedness." And with regard to that one only exempt family or nation of the Israelites, 'tis evident that wickedness was the generally prevailing character among them, from age to age. If we consider how it was with Jacob's family, the behavior of Reuben with his father's concubine, the behavior of Judah with Tamar, the conduct of Jacob's sons in general (though Simeon and Levi were leading) towards the Shechemites, the behavior of Joseph's ten brethren in their cruel treatment of him; we can't think, that the character of true piety belonged to many of them, according to Dr. Taylor's own notion of such a character; though it be true, they might afterwards repent. And with respect to the time the children of Israel were in Egypt; the Scripture, speaking of them in general, or as a collective body, often represents them as complying with the abominable idolatries of the country.[4] And as to that generation which went out of Egypt, and wandered in the wilderness; they are abundantly represented as extremely and almost universally wicked, perverse, and children of divine wrath. And after Joshua's death, the Scripture is very express, that wickedness was the prevailing character in the nation, from age to age. So it was till Samuel's time. (I Sam. 8:7,8), "They have rejected me, that I should not

4. Lev. 17:7, Josh. 5:9, 24:14, Ezek. 20:7,8, and 23:3.

reign over them; according to all their works which they have done, since the day that I brought them out of Egypt, unto this day." Yea, so it was till Jeremiah's and Ezekiel's time. (Jer. 32:30,31), "For the children of Israel, and the children of Judah, have only done evil before me from their youth: for the children of Israel have only provoked me to anger with the work of their hands, saith the Lord: for this city hath been to me [as] a provocation of mine anger, and of my fury, from the day they built it, even unto this day" (cf. ch. 5:21 and 23, and ch. 7:25,26,27). So Ezek. 2:3,4. "I sent thee to the children of Israel, to a rebellious nation, that hath rebelled against me, they and their fathers have transgressed against me even unto this very day: for they are impudent children, and stiff-hearted." And it appears by the discourse of Stephen (Acts 7) that this was generally the case with that nation, from their first rise, even to the days of the apostles. After his summary rehearsal of the instances of their perverseness from the very time of their selling Joseph into Egypt, he concludes (vv. 51,52,53), "Ye stiff-necked and uncircumcised in heart and ears, ye do always resist the Holy Ghost. As your fathers did, so do ye. Which of the prophets have not your fathers persecuted? And they have slain them which shewed before of the coming of that just one; of whom ye have been now the betrayers and murderers: who have received the law by the disposition of angels, and have not kept it."

Thus it appears, that wickedness was the generally prevailing character in all the nations of mankind, till Christ came. And so also it appears to have been since his coming, to this day. So in the age of the apostles: though then, among those that were converted to Christianity, were great numbers of persons eminent for piety; yet this was not the case with the greater part of the world, or the greater part of any one nation in it. There was a great number of persons of a truly pious character in the latter part of the apostolic age, when multitudes of converts had been made, and Christianity was as yet in its primitive purity. But what says the apostle John of the church of God at that time, as compared with the rest of the world? (I John 5:19), "We know that we are of God, and the whole world lieth in wickedness." And after Christianity came to prevail, to that degree that Christians had the upper hand in nations and civil communities, still the greater part of mankind remained in their old heathen state; which Dr. Taylor speaks of as a state of great ignorance and wickedness. And besides, this is noted in all ecclesiastical history, that as the Christians gained in power and secular advantages, true piety declined, and corruption and wickedness prevailed among them. And as to the state of the Christian world, since Christianity began to be established by human laws, wickedness for the most part has greatly prevailed; as is very notorious, and is implied in what Dr. Taylor himself says: he, in giving an account how the doctrine of original sin came to prevail among Christians, says (p. 443) "That the Christian religion was very early and grievously corrupted, by dreaming, ignorant, superstitious monks." In p. 259 he says, "The generality of Christians have embraced this persuasion concerning original sin; and the consequence has been, that the generality of Christians have been the most wicked, lewd, bloody and treacherous of all mankind."

Thus, a view of the several successive periods of the past duration of the world, from the beginning to this day, shews, that wickedness has ever been exceeding prevalent, and has had vastly the superiority in the world. And Dr. Taylor himself in effect owns, that it has been so ever since Adam first turned into the way of transgression. (p. 168), "It is certain," says he, "the moral circumstances of mankind, since the time Adam first turned into the way of transgression, have been very different from a state of innocence. So far as we can judge from history, or what we know at present, the greatest part of mankind, have been, and still are very corrupt; though not equally so in every age and place." And lower in the same page, he speaks of "Adam's posterity, as having sunk themselves into the most lamentable degrees of ignorance, superstition, idolatry, injustice, debauchery, etc."

These things clearly determine the point, concerning the tendency of man's nature to wickedness; if we may be allowed to proceed according to such rules and methods of reasoning, as are universally made use of, and never denied, or doubted to be good and sure, in experimental philosophy; [5] or may reason from experience and facts, in that manner which common sense leads all mankind to in other cases. If experience and trial will evince anything at all concerning the natural disposition of the hearts of mankind, one would

5. Dr. Turnbull, though so great an enemy to the doctrine of the depravity of nature, yet greatly insists upon it, that the experimental method of reasoning ought to be gone into in moral matters, and things pertaining to the human nature; and should chiefly be relied upon, in moral, as well as natural philosophy. See *Introduction to Moral Philosophy* [see above, Intro., Sec. 5].

think the experience of so many ages as have elapsed since the beginning of the world, and the trial as it were made by hundreds of different nations together, for so long a time, should be sufficient to convince all, that wickedness is agreeable to the nature of mankind in its present state.

Here, to strengthen the argument, if there were any need of it, I might observe some further evidences than those which have been already mentioned, not only of the extent and generality of the prevalence of wickedness in the world, but of the *height* to which it has risen, and the *degree* in which it has reigned. Among innumerable things which shew this, I shall now only observe this, viz. the degree in which mankind have from age to age been hurtful one to another. Many kinds of brute animals are esteemed very noxious and destructive, many of 'em very fierce, voracious, and many very poisonous, and the destroying of 'em has always been looked upon as a public benefit: but have not mankind been a thousand times as hurtful and destructive as any one of them, yea, as all the noyous beasts, birds, fishes and reptiles in the earth, air and water, put together, at least, of all kinds of animals that are visible? And no creature can be found anywhere so destructive of its own kind, as mankind are. All others for the most part are harmless and peaceable, with regard to their own species. Where one wolf is destroyed by another wolf, one viper by another, probably a thousand of mankind are destroyed by those of their own species. Well therefore might our blessed Lord say, when sending forth his disciples into the world (Matt. 10:16,17), "Behold, I send you forth as sheep in the midst of wolves . . . but beware of men." As much to say, I send you forth as sheep among wolves, but why do I say, wolves? I send you forth into the wide world of men, that are far more hurtful and pernicious, and that you had much more need to beware of than wolves.

It would be strange indeed, that this should be the state of the world of mankind, the chief of the lower creation, distinguished above all by reason, to that end that they might be capable of religion, which summarily consists in love, if men, as they come into the world, are in their nature innocent and harmless, undepraved and perfectly free from all evil propensities.

SECTION 8. THE NATIVE DEPRAVITY OF MANKIND APPEARS, IN THAT THERE HAS BEEN SO LITTLE GOOD EFFECT OF SO MANIFOLD AND GREAT MEANS, USED TO PROMOTE VIRTUE IN THE WORLD

THE evidence of the native corruption of mankind appears much more glaring, when it is considered that the world has been so generally, so constantly, and so exceedingly corrupt, notwithstanding the *various, great* and *continual means,* that have been used to restrain men from sin, and promote virtue and true religion among them.

Dr. Taylor supposes, all that sorrow and death, which came on mankind, in consequence of Adam's sin, was brought on them by God, in great favor to them; as a benevolent father exercising an wholesome discipline towards his children; to restrain 'em from sin, by increasing the vanity of all earthly things, to abate their force to tempt and delude; to induce 'em to be moderate in gratifying the appetites of the body; to mortify pride and ambition; and that men might always have before their eyes a striking demonstration, that sin is infinitely hateful to God, by a sight of that, than which nothing is more proper to give them the utmost abhorrence of iniquity, and to fix in their minds a sense of the dreadful consequences of sin, etc. etc. And in general, that they don't come as punishments, but purely as means to keep men from vice, and to make them better. If it be so, surely they are great means indeed. Here is a mighty alteration: mankind, once so easy and happy, healthful, vigorous and beautiful, rich in all the pleasant and abundant blessings of paradise, now turned out destitute, weak and decaying, into a wide barren world, yielding briars and thorns, instead of the delightful growth and sweet fruit in the garden of Eden, to wear out life in sorrow and toil, on the ground cursed for his sake; and at last, either through long languishing and lingering decay, or severe pain and acute disease, to expire and turn to putrefaction and dust. If these are only used as medicines, to prevent and to cure the diseases of the mind, they are sharp medicines indeed; especially death; which, to use Hezekiah's representation, is as it were breaking all his bones:

and one would think, should be very effectual, if the subject had no depravity, no evil and contrary bias, to resist and hinder a proper effect; especially in the old world, when the thing which was the first occasion of this terrible alteration, this severity of means, was fresh in memory; Adam continuing alive near two thirds of the time that passed before the flood; so that a very great part of those that were alive till the flood, might have opportunity of seeing and conversing with him, and hearing from his mouth, not only an account of his fall, and the introduction of the awful consequences of it, but also of his first finding himself in existence in the new-created world, and of the creation of Eve, and the things [1] which passed between him and his Creator in paradise.[2]

But what was the success of these great means, to restrain men from sin, and to induce them to virtue? Did they prove sufficient? Instead of this, the world soon grew exceeding corrupt; till it came to that, to use our author's own words, "That mankind were universally debauched into lust, sensuality, rapine and injustice" (p. 122).

Then God used further means: he sent Noah, a preacher of righteousness, to warn the world of the universal destruction which would come upon them by a flood of waters, if they went on in sin. Which warning he delivered with these circumstances, tending to strike their minds, and command their attention; that he immediately went about building that vast structure of the ark; in which he must employ a great number of hands, and probably spent all he had in the world to save himself and his family. And under these uncommon means, God waited upon them 120 years. But all to no effect. The whole world, for aught appears, continued obstinate, and absolutely incorrigible: so that nothing remained to be done with them, but utterly to destroy the inhabitants of the earth; and to begin a new world, from that single family who had distinguished themselves by their virtue; that from them might be propagated a new and purer race. Accordingly this was done: and the inhabitants of the new world, of Noah's posterity, had these new and extraordi-

1. [The "fair copy" MS begins here. See above, Intro., Sec. 5.]

2. [Here JE begins to use the Bible as a source book of universal history to buttress his theology. "To object against a book's being divine, merely because it is historical, is a poor objection; just as if that could not be the word of God which gives an account of what is past" (*A History of the Work of Redemption,* Worcester ed., 2, 171). He used the King James version. Passages have been checked. He may also have depended on Winder's *Critical and Chronological History*. See also above, Intro., Sec. 3, n. 1.]

nary means to restrain sin and excite [to] [3] virtue, in addition to the toil, sorrow, and common mortality, which the world had been subjected to before in consequence of Adam's sin; viz. that God had newly testified his dreadful displeasure for sin, in destroying the many millions of mankind, all at one blow, old and young, men, women and children, without pity on any for all the dismal shrieks and cries which the world was filled with; when they themselves, the remaining family, were so wonderfully distinguished by God's preserving goodness, that they might be a holy seed, being delivered from the corrupting examples of the old world; and being all the offspring of a living parent, whose pious instructions and counsels they had, to enforce these things upon them, to prevent sin, and engage them to their duty. And these inhabitants of the new earth must, for a long time, have before their eyes many evident, and as it were fresh and striking effects and signs of that universal destruction, to be a continual affecting admonition to 'em. And besides all this, God now shortened the life of man, to about one half of what it used to be. The shortening of man's life, Dr. Taylor says (p. 68), "was, that the wild range of ambition and lust might be brought into narrower bounds, and have less opportunity of doing mischief; and that death, being still nearer to our view, might be a more powerful motive to regard less the things of a transitory world, and to attend to the rules of truth and wisdom."

And now let us observe the consequence. These new and extraordinary means, in addition to the former, were so far from proving sufficient, that the new world degenerated, and became corrupt, by such swift degrees, that, as Dr. Taylor observes, mankind in general were sunk into idolatry, in about 400 years after the flood, and so in about 50 years after Noah's death: they became so wicked and brutish, as to forsake the true God, and turn to the worship of inanimate creatures.

When things were come to this dreadful pass, God was pleased, for a remedy, to introduce a new and wonderful dispensation; separating a particular family and people, from all the rest of the world, by a series of most astonishing miracles, done in the open view of the world; and fixing their dwelling, as it were in the midst of the earth, between Asia, Europe and Africa, and in the midst of those nations which were most considerable and famous for power, knowledge and arts; that God might, in an extraordinary manner, dwell

3. [Supplied from MS.]

amongst that people, in visible tokens of his presence, manifesting himself there, and from thence to the world, by a course of great and miraculous operations and effects, for many ages: that people might be holy to God, and as a kingdom of priests, and might stand as a city on an hill, to be a light to the world: withal gradually shortening man's life, till it was brought to be but about one twelfth part of what it used to be before the flood; and so, according to Dr. Taylor, vastly cutting off and diminishing his temptations to sin, and increasing his excitements to holiness. And now let us consider what the success of these means was, both as to the Gentile world, and the nation of Israel.

Dr. Taylor justly observes (*Key*, no. 50),[4] "The Jewish dispensation had respect to the nations of the world, to spread the knowledge and obedience of God in the earth; and was established for the benefit of all mankind." But how unsuccessful were these means, and all other means used with the heathen nations, so long as this dispensation lasted? Abraham was a person noted in all the principal nations that were then in the world; as in Egypt, and the eastern monarchies: God made his name famous by his wonderful distinguishing dispensations towards him, particularly by so miraculously subduing before him, and his trained servants, those armies of the four eastern kings. This great work of the most high God, Possessor of Heaven and Earth, was greatly taken notice of by Melchizedek; and one would think, should have been sufficient to have awakened the attention and consideration of all the nations in that part of the world, and to have led them to the knowledge and worship of the only true God; especially if considered in conjunction with that miraculous and most terrible destruction of Sodom, and all the cities of the plain, for their wickedness, with Lot's miraculous deliverance; which doubtless were facts, that in their day were much famed abroad in the world. But there is not the least appearance, in any accounts we have, of any considerable good effect. On the contrary, those nations which were most in the way of observing and being affected with these things, even the nations of Canaan, grew worse and worse, till their iniquity came to the full, in Joshua's time. And the posterity of Lot, the saint so wonderfully distinguished, soon became some of the most gross idolaters; as they appear to have been in Moses' time. (See Num. 25) Yea, and the far greater part even of Abraham's posterity, the children of Ishmael, Zimran, Johshan,

4. [*Key* no. 60.]

Medan, Midian, Ishbak, and Shuah, and Esau, soon forget the true God, and fell off to heathenism.

Great things were done in the sight of the nations of the world, tending to awaken them, and lead them to the knowledge and obedience of the true God, in Jacob's and Joseph's time; in that God did miraculously, by the hand of Joseph, preserve from perishing by famine, as it were the whole world; as appears by Gen. 41:56,57. Agreeably to which, the name that Pharaoh gave to Joseph, Zaphnath-Paaneah, as is said, in the Egyptian language, signifies "savior of the world." But there does not appear to have been any good abiding effect of this; no, not so much as in the nation of the Egyptians (which seems to have been the chief of all the heathen nations at that day) who had these great works of Jehovah in their most immediate view: on the contrary, they grew worse and worse, and seem to be far more gross in their idolatries, and ignorance of the true God, and every way more wicked, and ripe for ruin, when Moses was sent to Pharaoh, than they were in Joseph's time.

After this, in Moses and Joshua's time, the great God was pleased to manifest himself in a series of the most astonishing miracles, for about fifty years together, wrought in the most public manner, in Egypt, in the wilderness, and in Canaan, in the view as it were of the whole world; miracles by which the world was shaken, the whole frame of the visible creation, earth, seas and rivers, the atmosphere, the clouds, sun, moon and stars, were affected; miracles greatly tending to convince the nations of the world of the vanity of their false gods, shewing Jehovah to be infinitely above them, in the thing wherein they dealt most proudly, and exhibiting God's awful displeasure at the wickedness of the heathen world. And these things are expressly spoken of as one end of these great miracles, in Ex. 9:15, Num. 14:21, Josh. 14:23,24, and other places. However, no reformation followed these things; but by the Scripture account, the nations which had them most in view, were dreadfully hardened, stupidly refusing all conviction and reformation, and obstinately went on in an opposition to the living God, to their own destruction.

After this, God did from time to time, very publicly manifest himself to the nations of the world, by wonderful works wrought in the time of the Judges, of a like tendency with those already mentioned. Particularly in so miraculously destroying by the hand of Gideón, almost the whole of that vast army of the Midianites, Amalekites, and all the children of the East, consisting of about 135,000 men (Judg. 7:12, and 8:12). But no reformation followed this or the other great works of God, wrought in the times of Deborah and Barak, Jephthah and Samson.

After these things, God used new, and in some respects much greater means with the heathen world, to bring them to the knowledge and service of the true God, in the days of David and Solomon. He raised up David, a man after his own heart, a most fervent worshipper of the true God, and zealous hater of idols, and subdued before him almost all the nations between Egypt and Euphrates; often miraculously assisting him in his battles with his enemies: and he confirmed Solomon his son in the full and quiet possession of that great empire, for about forty years; and made him the wisest, richest, most magnificent, and every way the greatest monarch that ever had been in the world; and by far the most famous, and of greatest name among the nations; especially for his wisdom, and things concerning the name of his God; particularly the temple he built, which was "exceeding mangificent, that it might be of fame and glory throughout all lands (I Chron. 22:5)." And we are told, that there came of all people to hear the wisdom of Solomon, from all kings of the earth (I Kgs. 4:34 and 10:24). And the Scripture informs us, that these great things were done, that the nations in far countries might hear of God's great name, and of his outstretched arm; that all the people of the earth might fear him, as well as his people Israel, and that all the people of the earth might know, that the Lord was God, and that there was none else (I Kgs. 8:41, 42,43,60). But still there is no appearance of any considerable abiding effect, with regard to any one heathen nation.

After this, before the captivity into Babylon, many great things were done in the sight of the Gentile nations, very much tending to enlighten, affect and persuade them. As God's destroying the army of the Ethiopians, of a thousand thousand, before Asa; Elijah's and Elisha's miracles; especially Elijah's miraculously confounding Baal's prophets and worshippers; Elisha's healing Naaman, the King of Syria's prime minister, and the miraculous victories obtained through Elisha's prayers, over the Syrians, Moabites and Edomites; the miraculous destruction of the vast united army of the children of Moab, Ammon, and Edom, at Jehoshaphat's prayer (II Chron. 20), Jonah's preaching at Nineveh, together with the miracle of his deliverance from the whale's belly; which was published, and well attested, as a sign to confirm his preaching: but more especially that great work of God, in destroying Sennacherib's army by an angel, for his contempt of the God of Israel, as if he had been no more than the gods of the heathen.

When all these things proved ineffectual, God took a new method with the heathen world, and used, in some respects, much greater means to convince and reclaim them, than ever before. In the first place, his people, the Jews, were removed to Babylon, the head and heart of the heathen world (Chaldea having been very much the fountain of idolatry) to carry thither the revelations which God had made of himself, contained in the sacred writings; and there to bear their testimony against idolatry; as some of them, particularly Daniel, Shadrach, Meshach and Abednego, did, in a very open manner, before the king, and the greatest men of the empire, with such circumstances as made their testimony very famous in the world; God confirming it with great miracles; which were published through the empire, by order of its monarch, as the mighty works of the God of Israel, shewing him to be above all gods: Daniel, that great prophet, at the same time being exalted to be governor of all the wise men of Babylon, and one of the chief officers of Nebuchadnezzar's court.

After this, God raised up Cyrus, to destroy Babylon, for its obstinate contempt of the true God, and injuriousness towards his people; according to the prophecies of Isaiah, speaking of him by name, instructing him concerning the nature and dominion of the true God (Is. 45). Which prophecies were probably shewn to him, whereby he was induced to publish his testimony concerning the god of Israel, as *the God* (Ezra 1:2,3). Daniel, about the same time, being advanced to be prime minister of state in the new empire, erected under Darius, and in that place appeared openly as a worshipper of the God of Israel, and him alone; God confirming his testimony for him, before the king, and all the grandees of his kingdom, by preserving him in the den of lions; whereby Darius was induced to publish to all people, nations and languages, that dwelt in all the earth, his testimony, that the God of Israel was the living God and steadfast forever, etc.

When after the destruction of Babylon, some of the Jews returned to their own land, multitudes never returned, but were dispersed abroad, through many parts of the vast Persian empire; as appears by the book of Esther. And many of 'em afterwards, as good histories inform, were removed into the more western parts of the world; and so were dispersed as it were all over the heathen world, having the holy Scriptures with them, and synagogues everywhere, for the worship of the true God. And so it continued to be, to the days of Christ and his apostles; as appears by the Acts of the Apostles. Thus that light, which God had given them, was in the providence of God, carried abroad into all parts of the world; so that now they had far greater advantages, to come to the knowledge of the truth, in matters of religion, if they had been disposed to improve their advantages.

And besides all these things, from about Cyrus' time, learning and philosophy increased, and was carried to a great height. God raised up a number of men of prodigious genius, to instruct others, and improve their reason and understanding, in the nature of things: and philosophic knowledge having gone on to increase for several ages, seemed to be got to its height before Christ came, or about that time.

And now let it be considered what was the effect of all these things. Instead of a reformation, or any appearance or prospect of it, the heathen world in general rather grew worse. As Dr. Winder observes,[5] "The inveterate absurdities of pagan idolatry continued without remedy, and increased as arts and learning increased; and paganism prevailed in all its height of absurdity, when pagan nations were polished to the height, and in the most polite cities and countries; and thus continued to the last breath of pagan power." And so it was with respect to wickedness in general, as well as idolatry; as appear by what the apostle Paul observes in Rom. 1—Dr. Taylor, speaking of the time when the gospel-scheme was introduced (*Key* no. 257) says, "The moral and religious state of the heathen was very deplorable, being generally sunk into great ignorance, gross idolatry, & abominable vice." Abominable vices prevailed, not only among the common people, but even among their philosophers themselves, yea, some of the chief of them, and of greatest genius; so Dr. Taylor himself observes, as to that detestable vice of sodomy, which they commonly and openly allowed and practised without shame. (See Dr. Taylor's *Note on Rom.* 1:27)

Having thus considered the state of the heathen world, with regard to the effect of means used for its reformation, during the Jewish dispensation, from the first foundation of it in Abraham's time; let us now consider how it was with that people themselves, that

5. [JE's free paraphrase; Winder, pp. 335, 336, 337.]

were distinguished with the peculiar privileges of that dispensation. The means used with the heathen nations, were great; but they were small, if compared with those used with the Israelites. The advantages by which that people were distinguished, are represented in Scripture as vastly above all parallel, in passages which Dr. Taylor takes notice of (*Key* no. 39). And he reckons these privileges among those which he calls antecedent blessings, consisting in motives to virtue and obedience; and says (*Key* no. 51), "That this was the very end and design of the dispensation of God's extraordinary favors to the Jews, viz. to engage them to duty and obedience, or that it was a scheme for promoting virtue, is clear beyond dispute, from every part of the Old Testament." Nevertheless, as has been already shewn, the generality of that people, through all the successive periods of that dispensation, were men of a wicked character. But it will be more abundantly manifest, how strong the natural bias to iniquity appeared to be among that people, by considering more particularly how things were with them from time to time.

Notwithstanding the great things God had done in the times of Abraham, Isaac and Jacob, to separate them and their posterity from the idolatrous world, that they might be a holy people to himself; yet in about 200 years after Jacob's death, and in less than 150 years after the death of Joseph, and while some were alive that had seen Joseph, the people had in a great measure lost the true religion, and were apace conforming to the heathen world: when, for a remedy, and the more effectually to alienate them from idols, and engage them to the God of their fathers, God appeared to bring 'em out from among the Egyptians, and separate them from the heathen world, and to reveal himself in his glory and majesty, in so affecting and astonishing a manner, as tended most deeply and durably to impress their minds; that they might never forsake him more. But so perverse were they, that they murmured even in the midst of the miracles that God wrought for 'em in Egypt, and murmured at the Red Sea, in a few days after God had brought them out with such a mighty hand. When he had led them through the sea, they sang his praise, but soon forgat his works. Before they got to Mount Sinai, they openly manifested their perverseness from time to time; so that God says of 'em (Ex. 16:28), "How long refuse ye to keep my commandments, and my laws?" Afterwards they murmured again at Rephedim.

In about two months after they came out of Egypt, they came to

Mount Sinai; where God entered into a most solemn covenant with the people, that they should be an holy people unto him, with such astonishing manifestations of his power, majesty and holiness, as were altogether unparalleled: as God puts the people in mind (Deut. 4:32–34), "For ask now of the days that are past, which were before thee, since the day that God created man upon the earth; and ask from one side of heaven unto the other; whether there has been any such thing as this great thing is, or hath been heard like it. Did ever people hear the voice of God speaking out of the midst of the fire, as thou hast heard, and live? Or hath God assayed to go and take him a nation from the midst of another nation" etc. And these great things were to that end, to impress their minds with such a conviction and sense of divine truth, and their obligations to their duty, that they might never forget them: as God says (Ex. 19:9), "Lo, I come unto thee in a thick cloud, that the people may hear when I speak with thee, and believe thee forever." But what was the effect of all? Why, it was not more than two or three months, before that people, there, under that very mountain, returned to their old Egyptian idolatry, and were singing and dancing before a golden calf, which they had set up to worship. And after such awful manifestations as there were of God's displeasure for that sin, and so much done to bring 'em to repentance, and confirm 'em in obedience, it was but a few months before they came to that violence of spirit, in open rebellion against God, that with the utmost vehemence they declared their resolution to follow God no longer, but to make them a captain to return into Egypt. And thus they went on in ways of perverse opposition to the Most High, from time to time, repeating their open acts of rebellion, in the midst of continued astonishing miracles, till that generation was destroyed. And though the following generation seems to have been the best that ever was in Israel; yet notwithstanding their good example, and notwithstanding all the wonders of God's power and love to that people, in Joshua's time, how soon did that people degenerate, and begin to forsake God, and join with the heathen in their idolatries, till God by severe means, and by sending prophets and judges, extraordinarily influenced from above, reclaimed them? But when they were brought to some reformation by such means, they soon fell away again into the practice of idolatry; and so from time to time, from one age to another; and nothing proved effectual for any abiding reformation.

After things had gone on thus for several hundred years, God used new methods with his people, in two respects; first, he raised up a great prophet, under whom a number of young men were trained up in schools, that from among them there might be a constant succession of great prophets in Israel, of such as God should choose; which seems to have been continued for more than 500 years. Secondly, God raised up a great king, David, one eminent for wisdom, piety and fortitude, to subdue all their heathen neighbors, who used to be such a snare to 'em; and to confirm, adorn and perfect the institutions of his public worship; and by him to make a more full revelation of the great salvation, and future glorious kingdom of the Messiah. And after him, raised up his son Solomon, the wisest and greatest prince that ever was on earth, more fully to settle and establish those things which his father David had begun, concerning the public worship of God in Israel, and to build a glorious temple for the honor of Jehovah, and the institutions of his worship, and to instruct the neighbor nations in true wisdom and religion. But as to the success of these new and extraordinary means, if we take Dr. Taylor for our expositor of Scripture, the nation must be extremely corrupt in David's time: for he supposes, he has respect to his own times, in those words (Ps. 14:2,3), "The Lord looked down from heaven . . . to see if there were any that did understand, and seek God: they are all gone aside; they are together become filthy; there is none that doth good; no, not one." But whether Dr. Taylor be in the right in this, or not, yet if we consider what appeared in Israel, in Absolom's and Sheba's rebellion, we shall not see cause to think that the greater part of the nation at that day were men of true wisdom and piety. As to Solomon's time, Dr. Taylor supposes, as has been already observed, that Solomon speaks of his own times, when he says he had found but one in a thousand that was a thoroughly upright man. However, it appears that all those great means used to promote and establish virtue and true religion, in Samuel's, David's and Solomon's times, were so far from having any general abiding good effect in Israel, that Solomon himself, with all his wisdom, and notwithstanding the unparalleled favors of God to him, had his mind corrupted, so as openly to tolerate idolatry in the land, and greatly to provoke God against him. And as soon as he was dead, ten tribes of the twelve forsook the true worship of God, and instead of it, openly established the like idolatry, that the people fell into at Mount Sinai, when they made the golden calf; and continued finally obstinate in this apostacy, notwithstanding all means that could be used with them by the prophets, which God sent, one after another, to reprove, counsel and warn them, for about 250 years; especially those two great prophets, Elijah and Elisha. Of all the kings that reigned over them there was not so much as one but what was of a wicked character. And at last it came to that, that their case seemed utterly desperate; so that nothing remained to be done with them, but to remove 'em out of God's sight. Thus the Scripture represents the matter (II Kgs. 17).

And as to the other two tribes; though their kings were always of the family of David, and they were favored in many respects, far beyond their brethren, yet they were generally exceeding corrupt: their kings were most of 'em wicked men, and their other magistrates, and priests and people, were generally agreed in the corruption. Thus the matter is represented in the Scripture-history, and the books of the prophets. And when they had seen how God had cast off the ten tribes, instead of taking warning, they made themselves vastly more vile than ever the other had done; as appears by II Kgs. 17:18,19; Ezek. 16:46,47,51. God indeed waited longer upon them, for his servant David's sake, and for Jerusalem's sake, that he had chosen; and used more extraordinary means with them; especially by those great prophets, Isaiah and Jeremiah; but to no effect. So that at last it came to this, as the prophets represent the matter, that they were like a body universally and desperately diseased and corrupted, that would admit of no cure, the whole head sick, and the whole heart faint, etc. Things being come to that pass, God took this method with them: he utterly destroyed their city and land, and the temple which he had among them, made thorough work in purging the land of 'em; as when a man empties a dish, wipes it, and turns it upside down; or when a vessel is cast into a fierce fire, till its filthiness is thoroughly burnt out (II Kgs. 21:13. Ezek. 24). They were carried into captivity, and there left till that wicked generation was dead, and those old rebels were purged out; that afterwards the land might be resettled with a more pure generation.

After the return from the captivity, and God had built the Jewish church again in their own land, by a series of wonderful providences; yet they corrupted themselves again, to so great a degree, that the transgressors were come to the full again in the days of Antiochus Epiphanes; as the matter is represented in the prophecy of Daniel (Dan. 8:28). And then God made them the subjects of a dispensation, little, if anything, less terrible than that which had been in Nebuchadnezzar's days. And after God had again delivered 'em, and restored the state of religion among them, by the instrumentality of the Maccabees, they degenerated again: so that when Christ came, they were arrived to that extreme degree of corruption, which is represented in the accounts given by the evangelists.

It may be observed here in general, that the Jews, though so vastly distinguished with advantages, means and motives to holiness, yet are represented as coming, from time to time, to that degree of corruption and guilt, that they were more wicked, in the sight of God, than the very worst of the heathen. As of old, God sware by his life, that the wickedness of Sodom was small, compared with that of the Jews (Ezek. 16:47,48 etc., also ch. 5:5–10). So, Christ speaking of the Jews, in his time, represents 'em as having much greater guilt than the inhabitants of Tyre and Sidon, or even Sodom and Gomorrah.

But we are now come to the time when the grandest scene was displayed, that ever was opened on earth. After all other schemes had been so long and so thoroughly tried, and had so greatly failed of success, both among Jews and Gentiles; that wonderful dispensation was at length introduced, which was the greatest scheme for the suppressing and restraining iniquity among mankind, that ever infinite wisdom and mercy contrived; even the glorious gospel of Jesus Christ. "A new dispensation of grace was erected," to use Dr. Taylor's own words (pp. 239, 240), "for the more certain, and effectual sanctification of mankind, into the image of God; the delivering them from sin and wickedness, into which they might fall, or were already fallen; to redeem 'em from all iniquity, and bring 'em to the knowledge and obedience of God." In whatever high and exalted terms the Scripture speaks of the means and motives which the Jews enjoyed of old; yet their privileges are represented as having no glory, in comparison of the advantages of the gospel. Dr. Taylor's words in p. 233 are worthy to be here repeated.

> "Even the heathen," says he, "knew God, and might have glorified him as God, but under the glorious light of the gospel, we have very clear ideas of the divine perfections, and particularly of the love of God as our father, and as the God and father of our Lord and Savior Jesus Christ. We see our duty in the utmost extent, and the most cogent reasons to perform it: we have etern-

ity opened to us, even an endless state of honor and felicity, the reward of virtuous actions; and the spirit of God promised for our direction and assistance. And all this may and ought to be applied to the purifying our minds, and the perfecting of holiness. And to these happy advantages, we are born: for which we are bound for ever to praise and magnify the rich grace of God in the Redeemer." And he elsewhere says, "The gospel-constitution is a scheme the most perfect and effectual for restoring true religion, and promoting virtue and happiness, that ever the world has yet seen." [6] And "admirably adapted to enlighten our minds and sanctify our hearts"; [7] and "never were motives so divine and powerful proposed, to induce us to the practice of all virtue and goodness." [8]

And yet even these means have been ineffectual upon the far greater part of them with whom they have been used; of the many that have been called, few have been chosen.

As to the Jews, God's ancient people, with whom they were used in the first place, and used long by Christ and his apostles, the generality of them rejected Christ and his gospel, with extreme pertinaciousness of spirit. They not only went on still in that career of corruption, which had been increasing from the time of the Maccabees; but Christ's coming, and his doctrine and miracles, and the preaching of his followers, and the glorious things that attended the same, were the occasion, through their perverse improvement, of an infinite increase of their wickedness. They crucified the Lord of Glory, with the utmost malice and cruelty, and persecuted his followers; they pleased not God, and were contrary to all men; and went on to grow worse and worse, till they filled up the measure of their sin, and wrath came upon them to the uttermost; and they were destroyed, and cast out of God's sight, with unspeakably greater tokens of the divine abhorrence and indignation, than in the days of Nebuchadnezzar. The bigger part of the whole nation were slain, and the rest were scattered abroad through the earth, in the most abject and forlorn circumstances. And in the same spirit of unbelief and malice against Christ and the gospel, and in their miserable dispersed circumstances, do they remain to this day.

6. *Key* no. 139.
7. *Note on Rom.* 1:16.
8. *Pref. to Par. on Rom.*, p. 203.

And as to the Gentile nations, though there was a glorious success of the gospel amongst them, in the apostles' days; yet probably not one in ten of those that had the gospel preached to 'em, embraced it. The powers of the world were set against it, and persecuted it with insatiable malignity. And among the professors of Christianity, there presently appeared in many a disposition to corruption, and to abuse the gospel unto the service of pride and licentiousness. And the apostles in their days foretold a grand apostacy of the Christian world, which should continue many ages; and observed, that there appeared a disposition to such an apostacy, among the professing Christians, even in that day (II Thess. 2:7). And the greater part of the ages which have now elapsed, have been spent in the duration of that grand and general apostacy, under which the Christian world, as it is called, has been transformed into that which has been vastly more deformed, more dishonorable and hateful to God, and repugnant to true virtue, than the state of the heathen world before: which is agreeable to the prophetical descriptions given of it by the Holy Spirit.

In these latter ages of the Christian church, God has raised up a number of great and good men, to bear testimony against the corruptions of the Church of Rome, and by their means introduced that light into the world, by which, in a short time, at least one third part of Europe were delivered from the more gross enormities of Antichrist: which was attended at first with a great reformation, as to vital and practical religion. But how is the gold soon become dim! To what a pass are things come in Protestant countries at this day, and in our nation in particular! To what a prodigious height has a deluge of infidelity, profaneness, luxury, debauchery and wickedness of every kind, arisen! The poor savage Americans are mere babes and fools (if I may so speak) as to proficiency in wickedness, in comparison of multitudes that the Christian world throngs with. Dr. Taylor himself, as was before observed, represents, that the "generality of Christians have been the most wicked, lewd, bloody and treacherous, of all mankind"; and says (*Key* no. 356), "The wickedness of the Christian world renders it so much like the heathen, that the good effects of our change to Christianity are but little seen."

And with respect to the dreadful corruption of the present day, it is to be considered, besides the advantages already mentioned, that great advances in learning and philosophic knowledge have been made in the present and past century, giving great advantage for a proper and enlarged exercise of our rational powers, and for our seeing the bright manifestation of God's perfections in his works. And it is to be observed, that the means and inducements to virtue, which this age enjoys, are in addition to most of those which were mentioned before, as given of old; and among other things, in addition to the shortening of man's life, to 70 or 80 years, from near a thousand. And with regard to this, I would observe that as the case now is in Christendom, take one with another of them that ever come to years [of] discretion, their life is not [9] more than forty or forty-five years; which is but about the twentieth part of what it once was: and not so much in great cities, places where profaneness, sensuality and debauchery, commonly prevail to the greatest degree.

Dr. Taylor (*Key* no. 1) truly observes, that God has from the beginning exercised wonderful and infinite wisdom, in the methods he has, from age to age, made use of to oppose vice, cure corruption, and promote virtue in the world; and introduced several schemes to that end. 'Tis indeed remarkable, how many schemes and methods were tried of old, both before and after the flood; how many were used in the times of the Old Testament, both with Jews and heathens; and ineffectual all these ancient methods proved, for 4000 years together, till God introduced that grand dispensation, for the redeeming [of] men from all iniquity, and purifying them to himself, a people zealous of good works; which the Scripture represents as the subject of the admiration of angels. But even this has, now so long, proved so ineffectual, with respect to the generality, that Dr. Taylor thinks "there is need of a new dispensation, Christians being now," as he says, "in a manner reduced to a state of religion, as low as that of heathenism, & may be ranked among the dead; the present light of the gospel proving insufficient for the full reformation of the Christian world" (*Note on Rom.* 1:27). And yet all these things, according to him, without any natural bias to the contrary; no stream of natural inclination or propensity at all, to oppose inducements to goodness; no native opposition of heart, to withstand those gracious means, which God has ever used with mankind, from the beginning of the world to this day; any more than there was in the heart of Adam, the moment God created him in perfect innocence.

Surely Dr. Taylor's scheme is attended with strange paradoxes. And that his mysterious tenets may appear in a true light, it must be

9. [The "fair copy" MS breaks off here.]

observed, at the same time while he supposes these means, even the very greatest and best of 'em, to have proved so ineffectual, that help from them, as to any general reformation, is to be despaired of; yet he maintains, that all mankind, even the heathen in all parts of the world, yea, every single person in it (which must include every Indian in America, before the Europeans came hither; and every inhabitant of the unknown parts of Africa, and Terra Australis) has ability, light, and means sufficient, to do their whole duty; yea (as many passages in his writings plainly suppose) to perform perfect obedience to God's law, without the least degree of vice or iniquity.[1]

But I must not omit to observe, Dr. Taylor supposes that the reason why the gospel-dispensation has been so ineffectual, is that it has been greatly misunderstood and perverted. In [*Key*] p. 183 he says, "Wrong representations of the scheme of the gospel have greatly obscured the glory of divine grace, and contributed much to the corruption of its professors. Such doctrines have been almost universally taught and received, as quite subvert it. Mistaken notions about nature, grace, election and reprobation, justification, regeneration, redemption, calling, adoption, etc. have quite taken away the very ground of the Christian life."

But how came the gospel to be so universally and exceedingly misunderstood? Is it because it is in itself so very dark and unintelligible, and not adapted to the apprehension of the human faculties? If so, how is the possession of such an obscure and unintelligible thing, so unspeakable and glorious an advantage? Or is it because of the native blindness, corruption and superstition of mankind? But this is giving up the thing in question, and allowing a great depravity of nature. And Dr. Taylor speaks of the gospel as far otherwise than dark and unintelligible; he represents it as exhibiting the clearest and most glorious light, to deliver the world from darkness, and bring 'em into marvellous light. He speaks of the light which the Jews had, under the Mosaic dispensation, as vastly exceeding the light of nature, which the heathen enjoyed: and yet he supposes, that even the latter was so clear, as to be sufficient to lead men to the knowledge of God, and their whole duty to him. And he speaks of the light of the gospel as vastly exceeding the light of the Old Testament. He says of the apostle Paul in particular, "That he wrote with great perspicuity; that he takes great care to explain every part of his subject; that he has left no part of it unexplained

1. See pp. 259, 339, 340, 348.

and unguarded; and that never was an author more exact and cautious in this." [2] Is it not strange therefore, that the Christian world, without any native depravity to prejudice and darken their minds, should be so blind in the midst of such glaring light, as to be all, or the generality, agreed, from age to age, so essentially to misunderstand that which is made so very plain?

Dr. Taylor says (p. 443), " 'Tis my opinion, that the Christian religion was very early and grievously corrupted, by dreaming, ignorant, superstitious monks, too conceited to be satisfied with plain gospel; and has long remained in that deplorable state." But how came the whole Christian world, without any blinding depravity, to hearken to these ignorant foolish men, rather than unto wiser and better teachers? Especially, when the latter had *plain gospel* on their side, and the doctrines of the other were (as our author supposes) so very contrary not only to the plain gospel, but to men's reason and common sense! Or were all the teachers of the Christian church nothing but a parcel of *ignorant dreamers?* If so, this is very strange indeed, unless mankind naturally love darkness, rather than light; seeing in all parts of the Christian world, there was so great a multitude of those in the work of the ministry, who had the gospel in their hands, and whose whole business it was to study and teach it; and therefore had infinitely greater advantages to become truly wise, than the heathen philosophers. But if it did happen so, by some strange and inconceivable means, that notwithstanding all these glorious advantages, all the teachers of the Christian church through the world, without any native evil propensity, very early became silly dreamers, and also in their dreaming, generally stumbled on the same individual monstrous opinions, and so the world might be blinded for a while; yet why did not they hearken to that wise and great man, Pelagius, and others like him, when he plainly held forth the truth to the Christian world? Especially seeing his instructions were so agreeable to the plain doctrines, and the bright and clear light of the gospel of Christ, and also so agreeable to the plainest dictates of the common sense and understanding of all mankind; but the other so repugnant to it, that (according to our author) if they were true, it would prove *understanding to be no understanding,* and *the word of God to be no rule of truth,* nor at all to be relied upon, and *God to be a being worthy of no regard!*

And besides, if the ineffectualness of the gospel to restrain sin and

2. *Pref. to Par. on Rom.* [Sec. IV, p. cxlvi.]

promote virtue, be owing to the general prevalence of these doctrines, which are supposed to be so absurd and contrary to the gospel, here is this further to be accounted for; namely, why, since there has been so great an increase of light in religious matters (as must be supposed on Dr. Taylor's scheme) in this and the last age, and these monstrous doctrines of original sin, election, reprobation, justification, regeneration, etc. have been so much exploded, especially in our nation, there has been no reformation attending this great advancement of light and truth: but on the contrary, vice and everything that is opposite to practical Christianity, has gone on to increase, with such a prodigious celerity, as to become like an overflowing deluge, threatening, unless God mercifully interposes, speedily to swallow up all that is left of what is virtuous and praiseworthy.

Many other things might have been mentioned under this head, of the means which mankind have had to restrain vice, and promote virtue; such as—wickedness being many ways contrary to men's temporal interest and comfort in this world, and their having continually before their eyes so many instances of persons made miserable by their vices; the restraints of human laws, without which men cannot live in society; the judgments of God brought on men for their wickedness, with which history abounds, and the providential rewards of virtue; and innumerable particular means, that God has used from age to age, to curb the wickedness of mankind, which I have omitted. But there would be no end of a particular enumeration of such things. Enough has been said. They that will not be convinced by the instances which have been mentioned, probably would not be convinced, if the world had stood a thousand times so long, and we had the most authentic and certain accounts of means having been used from the beginning, in a thousand times greater variety; and new dispensations had been introduced, after others had been tried in vain, ever so often, and still to little effect. He that won't be convinced by a thousand good witnesses, 'tis not likely that he would be convinced by a thousand thousand. The proofs that have been extant in the world, from trial and fact, of the depravity of men's nature, are inexpressible, and as it were infinite, beyond the representation of all comparison and similitude. If there were a piece of ground, which abounded with briars and thorns, or some poisonous plant, and all mankind had used their endeavors, for a thousand years together, to suppress that evil growth, and to bring that ground by manure and cultivation, planting and sowing, to produce better fruit, but all in vain, it would still be overrun with the same noxious growth; it would not be a proof, that such a produce was agreeable to the nature of that soil, in any wise to be compared to that which is given in divine providence, that wickedness is a produce agreeable to the nature of the field of the world of mankind; which has had means used with it, that have been so various, great and wonderful, contrived by the unsearchable and boundless wisdom of God; medicines procured with infinite expense, exhibited with so vast an apparatus; so marvelous a succession of dispensations, introduced one after another, displaying an incomprehensible length and breadth, depth and height, of divine wisdom, love and power, and every perfection of the Godhead, to the eternal admiration of the principalities and powers in heavenly places.

SECTION 9. SEVERAL EVASIONS OF THE ARGUMENTS FOR THE DEPRAVITY OF NATURE, FROM TRIAL AND EVENTS, CONSIDERED

EVASION I. Dr. Taylor says (pp. 231, 232),

"Adam's nature, it is allowed, was very far from being sinful; yet he sinned. And therefore, the common doctrine of original sin, is no more necessary to account for the sin that hath been in the world, than it is to account for Adam's sin."

Again (p. 328, etc.), "If we allow mankind to be as wicked as R.R.[1] represented them to be; and suppose that there is not one upon earth that is truly righteous, and without sin, and that some are very enormous sinners, yet it will not thence follow, that they are naturally corrupt. . . . For, if sinful action infers [implies] a nature originally corrupt, then, whereas *Adam* (according to them that hold the doctrine of original sin) committed the most heinous and aggravated sin, that ever was committed in the world; for, according to them, he had greater light than any other man in the world, to know his duty, and greater power than any other man to fulfill it, and was under greater obligations than any other men to obedience; he sinned when he knew he was the representative of millions, and that the happy or miserable state of all mankind depended on his conduct; which never was, nor can be, the case of any other man in the world:—then, I say, it will follow, that *his* nature was originally *corrupt,* etc. . . . Thus, their argument from the wickedness of mankind, to prove a sinful and corrupt nature, must inevitably and irrecoverably fall to the ground—which will appear more abundantly, if we take in the case of the angels; who in numbers sinned and kept not their first estate, though created with a nature superior to Adam's." Again (p. 421) "When it is enquired, how it comes to pass that our appetites and passions are not so irregular and strong, as that not one person has resisted them, so as to keep himself pure and innocent? If this be the case, if such

1. [Watts, *Ruin and Recovery of Mankind,* 1740.]

as make the enquiry will tell the world, how it came to pass that Adam's appetites and passions were so irregular and strong, that he did not resist them, so as to keep himself pure and innocent, when upon their principles he was far more able to have resisted them; I also will tell them how it comes to pass, that his posterity don't resist them. Sin doth not alter its nature, by its being general; and therefore, how far soever it spreads, it must come upon all just as it came upon Adam."

These things are delivered with much assurance. But is there any reason in such a way of talking? One thing implied in it, and the main thing, if anything at all to the purpose, is, that because an effect's being general don't alter the nature of the effect, therefore nothing more can be argued concerning the cause, from its happening constantly, and in the most steady manner, than from its happening but once. But how contrary is this to reason? If such a case should happen, that a person, through the deceitful persuasions of a pretended friend, once takes an unwholesome and poisonous draught, of a liquor which he had no inclination to before; but after he has once taken of it, he be observed to act as one that has an insatiable, incurable thirst after more of the same in his constant practice, and acts often repeated, and obstinately continued in as long as he lives, against all possible arguments and endeavors used to dissuade him from it; and we should from hence argue a fixed inclination, and begin to suspect that this is the nature and operation of the poison, to produce such an inclination, or that this strong propensity is some way the consequence of the first draught; in such a case, could it be said with good reason, that a fixed propensity can no more be argued from his consequent constant practice, than from his first draught? Or, if we suppose a young man, no otherwise than soberly inclined, and enticed by wicked companions, should drink to excess, until he had got a habit of excessive drinking and should come under the power of a greedy appetite after strong drink, so that drunkenness should become a common and constant practice with him; and some observer, arguing from this his general practice, should say, "It must needs be, that this young man has a fixed inclination to that sin; otherwise, how should it come to pass that he should make such a trade of it?" And another, ridiculing the weakness of his arguing, should reply, "Do you tell me how it came to pass, that he was guilty of that sin the first time without a fixed inclination, and I'll tell you how he is guilty of it so generally without a fixed inclination. Sin don't alter its nature by being general: and therefore, how common soever it becomes, it must come at all times by the same means that it came at first." I leave it to everyone to judge, who would be chargeable with weak arguing in such a case.

'Tis true, as was observed before, there is no effect without some cause, occasion, ground or reason of that effect, and some cause answerable to the effect. But certainly it will not follow from thence, that a *transient* effect requires a *permanent* cause, or a fixed influence and propensity. An effect's happening once, though the effect may be great, yea, though it may come to pass on the same occasion in many subjects at the same time, will not prove any fixed propensity, or permanent influence. 'Tis true, it proves an influence great and extensive, answerable to the effect, once exerted, or once effectual; but it proves nothing in the cause fixed or constant. If a particular tree, or a great number of trees standing together, have blasted fruit on their branches at a particular season, yea, if the fruit be very much blasted, and entirely spoiled, it is evident that something was the occasion of such an effect at that time; but this alone don't prove the nature of the tree to be bad. But if it be observed, that those trees, and all other trees of the kind, wherever planted, and in all soils, countries, climates and seasons, and however cultivated and managed, still bear ill fruit, from year to year, and in all ages, it is a good evidence of the evil nature of the tree: and if the fruit, at all these times, and in all these cases, be very bad, it proves the nature of the tree to be very bad. And if we argue in like manner from what appears among men, 'tis easy to determine, whether the universal sinfulness of mankind, and their all sinning immediately, as soon as capable of it, and all sinning continually, and generally being of a wicked character, at all times, in all ages, and all places, and under all possible circumstances, against means and motives inexpressibly manifold and great, and in the utmost conceivable variety, be from a permanent internal great cause.

If the voice of common sense were attended to, and heard, there would be no occasion for labor in multiplying arguments, and instances, to shew, that one act don't prove a fixed inclination; but that constant practice and pursuit does. We see that it is in fact agreeable to the reason of all mankind, to argue fixed principles, tempers and prevailing inclinations, from repeated and continued actions, though the actions are voluntary, and performed of choice; and thus to judge of the tempers and inclinations of persons, ages, sexes, tribes and nations. But is it the manner of men to conclude, that whatever they see others once do, they have a fixed abiding inclination to do? Yea, there may be several acts seen, and yet they not be taken as good evidence of an established propensity; nay, though attended with that circumstance, that one act, or those several acts are followed with such constant practice, as afterwards evidences fixed disposition. As for example; there may be several instances of a man's drinking some spiritous liquor, and they be no sign of a fixed inclination to that liquor: but these acts may be introductory to a settled habit or propensity, which may be made very manifest afterwards by constant practice.

From these things it is plain, that what is alleged concerning the first sin of Adam, and of the angels, without a previous fixed disposition to sin, can't in the least injure or weaken the arguments which have been brought to prove a fixed propensity to sin in mankind in their present state. The thing which the permanence of the cause has been argued from, is the permanence of the effect. And that the permanent cause consists in an internal fixed propensity, and not any particular external circumstances, has been argued from the effect's being the same, through a vast variety and change of circumstances. Which things don't take place with respect to the first act of sin that Adam or the angels were guilty of; which first acts, considered in themselves, were no permanent continued effects. And though a great number of the angels sinned, and the effect on that account was the greater, and more extensive; yet this *extent* of the effect is a very different thing from that *permanence,* or settled continuance of the effect, which is supposed to shew a permanent cause, or fixed influence or propensity.[2] Neither was there any trial of a

2. [JE wrestled at length with the problem of the angels' fall, as several "Miscellanies" numbers indicate. In No. 664b, he suggested that the angels' rebellion was due to jealousy because man's destiny was to be more glorious than their own. In No. 320, "It seems to me probable that the temptation of the angels that occasioned their rebellion, was that . . . God declared . . . that one of that human nature should be his son." In No. 939, he found the reason for the fall of angels to be their violation of the purpose of their creation, which was that of being "ministering spirits to Christ in the great work of his exalting & glorifying beloved mankind. Hence we may infer that the occasion of their fall was God's revealing this their end & special service to them & their not complying with it that must be the occasion of their fall." See also Nos. 710 and 823.]

vast variety of circumstances attending a permanent effect, to shew the fixed cause to be internal, consisting in a settled disposition of nature, in the instances objected. And however great the sin of Adam, or of the angels, was, and however great means, motives and obligations they sinned against; whatever may be thence argued concerning the transient cause, occasion or temptation, as being very subtile, remarkably tending to deceive and seduce, or otherwise great; yet it argues nothing of any *settled* disposition, or *fixed* cause at all, either great or small; the effect both in the angels and our first parents, being in itself transient, and for aught appears, happening in each of them, under one system or coincidence of influential circumstances.

The general continued wickedness of mankind, against such means and motives, proves each of these things, viz. that the cause is fixed, and that the fixed cause is *internal,* in man's nature, and also that it is very *powerful.* It proves the first, namely, that the cause is fixed, because the effect is so abiding, through so many changes. It proves the second, that is, that the fixed cause is internal, because the circumstances are so various: the variety of means and motives is one thing that is to be referred to the head of variety of circumstances: and they are that kind of circumstances, which above all others proves this; for they are such circumstances as can't possibly cause the effect, being most opposite to the effect in their tendency. And it proves the third, viz. the greatness of the internal cause, or the powerfulness of the propensity; because the means which have opposed its influence, have been so great, and yet have been statedly overcome.

But here I may observe by the way, that with regard to the motives and obligations which our first father sinned against, it is not reasonably alleged, that he sinned when he knew his sin would have destructive consequences to all his posterity, and might, in process of time, pave the whole globe with skulls, etc. Seeing 'tis so evident, by the plain account the Scripture gives us of the temptation which prevailed with our first parents to commit that sin, that it was so contrived by the subtlety of the tempter, as first to blind and deceive 'em as to that matter, and to make them believe that their disobedience should be followed with no destruction or calamity at all to themselves (and therefore not to their posterity) but on the contrary, with a great increase and advancement of dignity and happiness.

Evasion II. Let the wickedness of the world be ever so general and great, there is no necessity of supposing any depravity of nature to be the cause: man's own *free will* is cause sufficient. Let mankind be more or less corrupt, they make themselves corrupt, by their own free choice. This Dr. Taylor abundantly insists upon, in many parts of his book.[3]

But I would ask, how it comes to pass that mankind so universally agree in this evil exercise of their free will? If their wills are in the first place as free to good as evil, what is it to be ascribed to, that the world of mankind consisting of so many millions in so many successive generations, without consultation, all agree to exercise their freedom in favor of evil? If there be no natural tendency of preponderation in the case, then there is as good a chance for the will's being determined to good as evil. If the cause is indifferent, why is not the effect in some measure indifferent? If the balance be no heavier at one end than the other, why does it perpetually and as it were infinitely preponderate one way? [4] How comes it to pass, that the free will of mankind has been determined to evil, in like manner before the flood, and after the flood; under the law, and under the gospel; among both Jews and Gentiles, under the Old Testament; and since that, among Christians, Jews, Mohametans; among Papists and Protestants; in those nations where civility, politeness, arts and learning most prevail, and among the Negroes and Hottentots in Africa, the Tartars in Asia, and Indians in America, towards both the poles, and on every side of the globe; in greatest cities, and obscurest villages; in palaces, and in huts, wigwams and cells under ground? Is it enough, to reply, it happens so, that men everywhere, and at all times choose thus to determine their own wills, and so to make themselves sinful, as soon as ever they are capable of it, and to sin constantly as long as they live, and universally to choose never to come up half way to their duty?

As has been often observed, a steady effect requires a steady cause; but free will, without any previous propensity, to influence its determinations, is no permanent cause; nothing can be conceived of, further from it: for the very notion of freedom of will consisting in self-determining power, implies contingence: and if the will is free in that sense, that it is perfectly free from any government of previous inclination, its freedom must imply the most *absolute* and *perfect*

3. Pp. 257, 258, 328, 329, 344, 421, 422, and many other places.

4. [See above, Intro., Sec. 3, The Cause and Transmission of Sin.]

contingence: and surely nothing can be conceived of, more unfixed than that. The notion of liberty of will, in this sense, implies perfect freedom from everything that should previously fix, bind or determine it; that it may be left to be fixed and determined wholly by itself: therefore, its determinations must be previously altogether unfixed. And can that which is so unfixed, so contingent, be a cause sufficient to account for an effect, in such a manner and to such a degree, permanent, fixed and constant?

When men see only one particular person going on in a certain course with great constancy, against all manner of means to dissuade him, do they judge this to be no argument of any fixed disposition of mind, because he being free may determine to do so, if he will, without any such disposition? Or if they see a nation or people that differ greatly from other nations, in such and such instances of their constant conduct, as though their tempers and inclinations were very diverse, and any should deny it to be from any such cause, and should say, we can't judge at all of the temper or disposition of any nation or people by anything observable in their constant practice or behavior, because they have all free will, and therefore may all choose to act so, if they please, without anything in their temper or inclination to bias 'em; would such an account of such effects be satisfying to the reason of mankind? But infinitely further would it be from satisfying a considerate mind, to account for the constant and universal sinfulness of mankind, by saying, that the will of all mankind is free, and therefore all mankind may, if they please, make themselves wicked: they are free when they first begin to act as moral agents, and therefore all may, if they please, begin to sin as soon as they begin to act: they are free as long as they continue to act in the world; and therefore they may all commit sin continually, if they will: men of all nations are free, and therefore all nations may act alike in these respects, if they please (though some don't know how other nations do act)—men of high and low condition, learned and ignorant, are free; and therefore they may agree in acting wickedly, if they please (though they don't consult together)—men in all ages are free, and therefore men in one age may all agree with men in every other age in wickedness, if they please (though they don't know how men in other ages have acted) etc. etc. Let everyone judge whether such an account of things can satisfy reason.

Evasion III. 'Tis said by many of the opposers of the doctrine of original sin, that the corruption of the world of mankind may be owing, not to a depraved nature, but to bad example. And I think we must understand Dr. Taylor as having respect to the powerful influence of bad instruction and example, when he says (p. 118), "The Gentiles in their heathen state, when incorporated into the body of the Gentile world, were without strength, unable to help or recover themselves." And in several other places to the like purpose. If there was no depravity of nature, what else could there be but bad instruction and example, to hinder the heathen world, as a collective body (for as such Dr. Taylor speaks of 'em, as may be seen pp. 117, 118), from emerging out of their corruption, on the rise of each new generation? As to their bad instruction, our author insists upon it, that the heathen, notwithstanding all their disadvantages, had sufficient light to know God, and do their whole duty to him, as we have observed from time to time. Therefore it must be chiefly bad example, that we must suppose, according to him, rendered their case helpless.

Now concerning this way of accounting for the corruption of the world, by the influence of bad example, I would observe the following things:

1. 'Tis accounting for the thing by the thing itself. It is accounting for the corruption of the world by the corruption of the world. For, that bad examples are general all over the world to be followed by others, and have been so from the beginning, is only an instance, or rather a description of that corruption of the world which is to be accounted for. If mankind are naturally no more inclined to evil than good, then how comes there to be so many more bad examples, than good ones, in all ages? And if there are not, how come the bad examples that are set, to be so much more followed, than the good? If the propensity of man's nature be not to evil, how comes the current of general example, everywhere, and at all times, to be so much to evil? And when opposition has been made by good examples, how comes it to pass that it has had so little effect to stem the stream of general wicked practice?

I think, from the brief account the Scripture gives us of the behavior of the first parents of mankind, the expressions of their faith and hope in God's mercy revealed to them, we have reason to suppose, that before ever they had any children, they repented, and were pardoned, and became truly pious. So that God planted the world at first with a noble vine; and at the beginning of the generations of mankind, he set the stream of example the right way. And we see, that children are more apt to follow the example of their parents, than of any others; especially in early youth, their forming time, when those habits are generally contracted, which abide by them all their days. And besides, Adam's children had no other examples to follow, but those of their parents. How therefore came the stream so soon to turn, and to proceed the contrary way, with so violent a current? Then, when mankind became so universally and desperately corrupt, as not to be fit to live on earth any longer, and the world was everywhere full of bad examples, God destroyed 'em all at once, but only righteous Noah, and his family, to remove those bad examples, and that the world of mankind might be planted again with good example, and the stream again turned the right way: how therefore came it to pass, that Noah's posterity did not follow his good example, especially when they had such extraordinary things to enforce his example, but so generally, even in his lifetime, became so exceeding corrupt? One would think, the first generations at least, while all lived together as one family, under Noah, their venerable father, might have followed his good example: and if they had done so, then, when the earth came to be divided in Peleg's time, the heads of the several families would have set out their particular colonies with good examples, and the stream would have been turned the right way in all the various divisions, colonies and nations of the world. But we see verily the fact was, that in about fifty years after Noah's death the world in general was overrun with dreadful corruption; so that all virtue and goodness was like soon to perish from among mankind, unless something extraordinary should be done to prevent it.

Then, for a remedy, God separated Abraham and his family from all the rest of the world, that they might be delivered from the influence of bad example, that in his posterity he might have a holy seed. Thus God again planted a noble vine; Abraham, Isaac, and Jacob being eminently pious. But how soon did their posterity degenerate, till true religion was like to be swallowed up? We see how desperately, and almost universally corrupt they were, when God brought 'em out of Egypt, and led them in the wilderness.

Then God was pleased, before he planted his people [in] Canaan, to destroy that perverse generation in the wilderness, that he might plant 'em there a *noble vine, wholly a right seed,* and set 'em out with good example, in the land where they were to have their settled abode (Jer. 2:21). It is evident, that the generation which came with Joshua into Canaan, was an excellent generation, by innumerable things said of 'em.[5] But how soon did that people, nevertheless, become the degenerate plant of a strange vine?

And when the nation had a long time proved themselves desperately and incurably corrupt, God destroyed them, and sent 'em into captivity, till the old rebels were dead and purged out, to deliver their children from their evil example: and when the following generation were purified as in a furnace, God planted 'em again, in the land of Israel, a *noble vine,* and set 'em out with good example; which yet was not followed by their posterity.

When again the corruption was become inveterate and desperate, the Christian church was planted by a glorious outpouring of the spirit of God, causing true virtue and piety to be exemplified in the first age of the church of Christ, far beyond whatever had been on earth before; and the Christian church was planted a *noble vine.* But that primitive good example has not prevailed, to cause virtue to be generally and steadfastly maintained in the Christian world: to how great a degree it has been otherwise, has already been observed.

After many ages of general and dreadful apostacy, God was pleased to erect the Protestant church, as separated from the more corrupt part of Christendom; and true piety flourished very much in it at first; God planted it a noble vine. But notwithstanding the good examples of the first reformers, what a melancholy pass is the Protestant world come to at this day?

When England grew very corrupt, God brought over a number of pious persons, and planted 'em in New England, and this land was planted with a noble vine. But how is the gold become dim! How greatly have we forsaken the pious examples of our fathers!

So prone have mankind always proved themselves to degeneracy, and bent to backsliding, which shews plainly their natural propensity; and that when good had revived, and been promoted among men, it has been by some divine interposition, to oppose the natural current; the fruit of some extraordinary means, the efficacy of which has soon been overcome by constant natural bias, and the effect of good example presently lost, and evil has regained and maintained the dominion: like an heavy body, which may by some great power be caused to ascend, against its nature, a little while, but soon goes

5. See Jer. 2:23; Ps. 68:14; Josh. 22:2 and 23:8; Deut. 4:3–4; Hos. 11:1 and 9:10; Judg. 2:7,17,22 and many other places.

back again towards the center, to which it naturally and constantly tends.

So that evil example will in no wise account for the corruption of mankind, without supposing a natural proneness to sin. The tendency of example alone will not account for general wicked practice, as consequent on good example. And if the influence of bad example is a reason of some of the wickedness that is in the world, that alone will not account for men's becoming worse than the example set, and degenerating more and more, and growing worse and worse, which is the manner of mankind.

2. There has been given to the world an example of virtue, which, were it not for a dreadful depravity of nature, would have influence on them that live under the gospel, far beyond all other examples; and that is the example of Jesus Christ.

God, who knew the human nature, and how apt men are to be influenced by example, has made answerable provision. His infinite wisdom has contrived that we should have set before us the most amiable and perfect example, in such circumstances as should have the greatest tendency to influence all the principles of man's nature, but his corruption. Men are apt to be moved by the example of others like themselves, or in their own nature: therefore this example was given in our nature. Men are ready to follow the examples of the great and honorable: and this example, though it was of one in our nature, yet it was one of infinitely higher and more honorable than kings or angels. A people are apt to follow the example of their prince: this is the example of that glorious person, who stands in a peculiar relation to Christians, as their Lord and King, the Supreme Head of the church; and not only so, but the King of Kings, Supreme Head of the universe, and Head over all things to the church. Children are apt to follow the example of their parents: this is the example of the Author of our being, and one who is in a peculiar and extraordinary manner our Father, as he is the Author of our holy and happy being; besides his being the Creator of the world, and everlasting Father of the universe. Men are very apt to follow the example of their friends: the example of Christ is of one that is infinitely our greatest Friend, standing in the most endearing relations of our Brother, Redeemer, Spiritual Head and Husband: whose grace and love expressed to us, transcends all other love and friendship, as much as heaven is higher than the earth. And the virtues and acts of his example were exhibited to us in the most endearing and engaging circumstances that can possibly be conceived of: his obedience and submission to God, his humility, meekness, patience, charity, self-denial, etc. being exercised and expressed in a work of infinite grace, love, condescension and beneficence to us; and had all their highest expression in his laying down his life for us, and meekly, patiently and cheerfully undergoing such extreme and unutterable suffering, for our eternal salvation. Men are peculiarly apt to follow the example of such as they have great benefits from: but it is utterly impossible to conceive of greater benefits, that we could have by the virtues of any person, than we have by the virtuous acts of Christ; who depend upon being thereby saved from eternal destruction, and brought to inconceivable immortal glory at God's right hand. Surely if it were not for an extreme corruption of the heart of men, such an example would have that strong influence on the heart, that would as it were swallow up the power of all the evil and hateful examples of a generation of vipers.

3. The influence of bad example, without corruption of nature, will not account for children's universally committing sin as soon as capable of it; which, I think, is a fact that has been made evident by the Scripture. It will not account for this, in the children of eminently pious parents; the first examples, that are set in their view, being very good; which, as has been observed, was especially the case of many children in Christian families in the apostles' days, when the apostle John supposes that every individual person had sin to repent of, and confess to God.

4. What Dr. Taylor supposes to have been fact with respect to a great part of mankind, cannot consistently be accounted for from the influence of bad example, viz. the state of the heathen world, which he supposes, considered as a collective body, was helpless, dead in sin, and unable to recover itself. Not evil example alone, no nor as united with evil instruction, can be supposed a sufficient reason why every new generation that arose among them, should not be able to emerge from the idolatry and wickedness of their ancestors, in any consistency with his scheme. The ill example of ancestors could have no power to oblige them to sin, any other way than as a strong temptation. But Dr. Taylor himself says (p. 348), "To suppose men's temptations to be superior to their powers, will impeach the goodness and justice of God, who appoints every man's trial." And as to bad instructions, as was observed before, he supposes that

they all, yea every individual person, had light sufficient to know God, and do their whole duty. And if each one could do this for himself, then surely they might all be agreed in it through the power of free will, as well as the whole world be agreed in corruption by the same power.

Evasion IV. Some modern opposers of the doctrine of original sin do thus account for the general prevalence of wickedness, viz., that in a course of nature our senses grow up first, and the animal passions get the start of reason. So Dr. Turnbull says,[6] "Sensitive objects first affect us, and inasmuch as reason is a principle, which, in the nature of things, must be advanced to strength and vigor, by gradual cultivation, and these objects are continually assailing and soliciting us; so that, unless a very happy education prevents, our sensitive appetites must have become very strong, before reason can have force enough to call them to an account, and assume authority over them." From hence Dr. Turnbull supposes it comes to pass,[7] "That though some few may, through the influence of virtuous example, be said to be sanctified from the womb, so liberal, so generous, so virtuous, so truly noble is their cast of mind; yet, generally speaking, the whole world lieth in such wickedness, that, with respect to the far greater part of mankind, the study of virtue is beginning to reform, and is a severe struggle against bad habits, early contracted, and deeply rooted; it is therefore putting off an old inveterate corrupt nature, and putting on a new form and temper; it is moulding ourselves anew; it is a being born again, and becoming as children. . . . And how few are there in the world, who escape its pollutions, so as not to be early in that class, or to be among the righteous that need no repentance?"

Dr. Taylor, though he is not so explicit, seems to hint at the same thing (p. 192), " 'Tis by slow degrees," says he, "that children come to the use of understanding; the animal passions being for some years the governing part of their constitution. And therefore, though they may be froward and apt to displease us, yet how far this is sin in them, we are not capable of judging. But it may suffice to say, that 'tis the will of God that children should have appetites and passions to regulate and restrain, that he hath given parents instructions and commands to discipline and inform their minds, that if parents first learned true wisdom for themselves, and then endea-

6. See *Mor[al] Phil[osophy]* p. 279 and *Chris[tian] Phil[osophy]* p. 274.

7. *Chris[tian] Phil[osophy]* pp. 282, 283.

vored to bring up their children in the way of virtue, there would be less wickedness in the world."

Concerning these things I would observe, that such a scheme is attended with the very same difficulties, which they that advance it would avoid by it; liable to the same objections, which they make against God's ordering it so that men should be brought into being with a prevailing propensity to sin. For this scheme supposes, the Author of nature has so ordered things, that men should come into being as moral agents, that is, should first have existence in a state and capacity of moral agency, under a prevailing propensity to sin. For that strength, which sensitive appetites and animal passions come to by their habitual exercise, before persons come to the exercise of their rational powers, amounts to a strong propensity to sin, when they first come to the exercise of those rational powers, by the supposition: because this is given as a reason why the scale is turned for sin among mankind, and why *"generally speaking, the whole world lies in wickedness, and . . . the study of virtue . . . is a severe struggle against bad habits, early contracted, and deeply rooted."* These deeply rooted habits must imply a tendency to sin; otherwise they could not account for that which they are brought to account for, namely, prevailing wickedness in the world: for that cause can't account for an effect, which is supposed to have no tendency to that effect. And this tendency which is supposed, is altogether equivalent to a *natural tendency:* 'tis as necessary to the subject. For it is supposed to be brought on the person who is the subject of it, when he has no power to withstand or oppose it: the habit, as Dr. Turnbull says, becoming very strong, before reason can have force enough to call the passions to account, or assume authority over them. And 'tis supposed, that this necessity, by which men become subject to this propensity to sin, is from the ordering and disposal of the Author of nature; and therefore must be as much from his hand, and as much without the hand of the person himself, as if he were first brought into being with such a propensity. Moreover, it is supposed that the effect, which the tendency is to, is truly wickedness. For 'tis alleged as a cause or reason why the whole world lies in wickedness, and why all but a very few are first in the class of the wicked, and not among the righteous that need no repentance. If they need repentance, what they are guilty of is truly and properly wickedness, or moral evil; for certainly men need no repentance for that which is no sin, or blameable evil. If it be so, that as a consequence of this propensity, the world lies in wickedness, and the far greater part are of a wicked character, without doubt, the far greater part go to eternal perdition: for death don't pick and choose, only for men of a righteous character. And certainly that is an evil corrupt state of things, which naturally tends to, and issues in that consequence, that as it were the whole world lies and lives in wickedness, and dies in wickedness, and perishes eternally. And this by the supposition is a state of things wholly of the ordering of the Author of nature, before mankind are capable of having any hand in the affair. And is this any relief to the difficulties, which these writers object against the doctrine of natural depravity?

And I might here also observe, that this way of accounting for the wickedness of the world, amounts to just the same thing with that solution of man's depravity, which was mentioned before, that Dr. Taylor cries out of as too gross to be admitted (pp. 188, 189), viz. God's creating the soul pure, and putting it into such a body, as naturally tends to pollute it. For this scheme supposes, that God creates the soul pure, and puts it into a body, and into such a state in that body, that the natural consequence is a strong propensity to sin, as soon as the soul is capable of sinning.

Dr. Turnbull seems to suppose, that the matter could not have been ordered otherwise, consistent with the nature of things, than that animal passions should be so aforehand with reason, as that the consequence should be that which has been mentioned; because reason is a faculty of such a nature, that it can have strength and vigor no otherwise than by exercise and culture.[8] But can there be any force in this? Is there anything in nature, to make it impossible, but that the superior principles of man's nature should be so proportioned to the inferior, as to prevent such a dreadful consequence, as the moral and natural ruin, and eternal perdition of the far greater part of mankind? Could not those superior principles be in vastly greater strength at first, and yet be capable of endless improvement? And what should hinder its being so ordered by the Creator, that they should improve by vastly swifter degrees than they do? If we are Christians, we must be forced to allow it to be possible in the nature of things, that the principles of human nature should be so balanced, that the consequence should be no propensity to sin, in the first beginning of a capacity of moral agency; because we must own, that it was so in fact in Adam, when first created, and also in the

8. *Mor*[*al*] *Phil*[*osophy*] p. 311.

man Christ Jesus; though the faculties of the latter were such as grew by culture and improvement, so that he increased in wisdom, as he grew in stature.

Evasion V. Seeing men in this world are in a state of trial, it is fit that their virtue should meet with trials, and consequently that it should have opposition and temptation to overcome; not only from without, but from within, in the animal passions and appetites we have to struggle with; that by the conflict and victory our virtue may be refined and established. Agreeable to this Dr. Taylor (p. 253) says, "Without a right use and application of our powers, were they naturally ever so perfect, we could not be judged fit to enter into the kingdom of God. . . . This gives a good reason why we are now in a state of trial and temptation, viz. to prove and discipline our minds, to season our virtue, and to fit us for the kingdom of God; for which, in the judgment of infinite wisdom, we cannot be qualified, but by overcoming our present temptations." And in p. 354 he says, "We are upon trial, and it is the will of our father that our constitution should be attended with various passions and appetites, as well as our outward condition with various temptations." He says the like in several other places. To the same purpose very often Dr. Turnbull: (particularly, *Chris. Phil.* p. 310), "What merit," says he, "except from combat? What virtue without the encounter of such enemies, such temptations as arise both from within, and from abroad? To be virtuous, is to prefer the pleasures of virtue, to those which come into competition with it, and vice holds forth to tempt us; and to dare to adhere to truth and goodness, whatever pains and hardships it may cost. There must therefore, in order to the formation and trial, in order to the very being of virtue, be pleasures of a certain kind to make temptations to vice."

In reply to these things I would say, either the state of temptation which is supposed to be ordered for men's trials, amounts on the whole to a prevailing tendency to that state of general wickedness and ruin, which has been proved to take place, or it does not. If it does not amount to a tendency to such an effect, then how does it account for it? When it is inquired, by what cause such an effect should come to pass, is it not absurd to allege a cause, which is owned at the same time to have no tendency to such an effect? Which is as much as to confess, that it will not account for it. I think it has been demonstrated that this effect must be owing to some prevailing tendency. If the other part of the dilemma be taken, and it be said, that this state of things does imply a prevailing tendency to that effect which has been proved, viz. that all mankind, without the exception of so much as one, sin against God, to their own deserved and just eternal ruin; and not only so, but sin thus immediately, as soon as capable of it, and sin continually, and have more sin than virtue, and have guilt that infinitely outweighs the value of all the goodness any ever have, and that the generality of the world in all ages are extremely stupid and foolish, and of a wicked character, and actually perish forever; I say, if the state of temptation implies a natural tendency to such an effect as this, it is a very evil, corrupt and dreadful state of things, as has been already largely shewn.

Besides, such a state has a tendency to defeat its own supposed end, which is to refine, ripen and perfect virtue in mankind, and so to fit men for the greater eternal happiness and glory: whereas, the effect it tends to, is the reverse of this, viz. general, eternal infamy and ruin, in all generations. 'Tis supposed, that men's virtue must have passions and appetites to struggle with, in order to have the glory and reward of victory: but the consequence is, a prevailing, continual, and generally effectual tendency, not to men's victory over evil appetites and passions, and the glorious reward of that victory, but to the victory of evil appetites and lusts over men, and utterly and eternally destroying them. If a trial of virtue be requisite, yet the question is, whence comes so general a failing in the trial, if there be no depravity of nature? If conflict and war be necessary, yet surely there is no necessity that there should be more cowards than good soldiers; unless it be necessary that men should be overcome and destroyed: especially is it not necessary that the whole world as it were should lie in wickedness, and so lie and die in cowardice.

I might also here observe, that Dr. Turnbull is not very consistent, in supposing that combat with temptation is requisite to the very being of virtue. For I think it clearly follows from his own notion of virtue, that virtue must have a being prior to any virtuous or praiseworthy combat with temptation. For by his principles, all virtue lies in good affection, and no actions can be virtuous, but what proceed from good affection.[9] Therefore, surely the combat itself can have no virtue in it, unless it proceeds from virtuous affection: and therefore virtue must have an existence before the combat, and be the cause of it.

9. *Chris*[*tian*] *Phil*[*osophy*] pp. 113, 114, 115.

CHAPTER II

UNIVERSAL MORTALITY PROVES ORIGINAL SIN; PARTICULARLY THE DEATH OF INFANTS, WITH ITS VARIOUS CIRCUMSTANCES

THE universal reign of *death,* over persons of all ages indiscriminately, with the awful circumstances and attendants of death, proves that men come sinful into the world.[1]

It is needless here particularly to inquire, whether God has not a sovereign right to set bounds to the lives of his own creatures, be they sinful or not; and as he gives life, so to take it away when he pleases. Or how far God has a right to bring extreme suffering and calamity on an innocent moral agent. For death, with the pains and agonies with which it is usually brought on, is not merely a limiting of existence, but is a most terrible calamity; and to such a creature as man, capable of conceiving of immortality, and made with so earnest a desire after it, and capable of foresight and of reflection on approaching death, and that has such an extreme dread of it, is a calamity above all others terrible, to such as are able to reflect upon it. I say, 'tis needless, elaborately to consider, whether God may not, consistent with his perfections, by absolute sovereignty, bring so great a calamity on mankind when perfectly innocent. It is sufficient, if we have good evidence from Scripture, that 'tis not agreeable to God's manner of dealing with mankind, so to do.

'Tis manifest, that mankind were not originally subjected to this calamity: God brought it on them afterwards, on occasion of man's sin, at a time of the manifestation of God's great displeasure for sin, and by a denunciation and sentence pronounced by him, as acting the part of a Judge; as Dr. Taylor often confesses. Sin entered into the world, and death by sin, as the Apostle says. Which certainly leads us to suppose, that this affair was ordered of God, not merely by the sovereignty of a Creator, but by the righteousness of a Judge.

1. [See above, Intro., Sec. 3, The Fact and Nature of Sin.]

And the Scripture everywhere speaks of all great afflictions and calamities, which God in his providence brings on mankind, as testimonies of his displeasure for sin, in the subject of those calamities; excepting those sufferings which are to atone for the sins of others. He ever taught his people to look on such calamities as his rod, the rod of his anger, his frowns, the hidings of his face in displeasure. Hence such calamities are in Scripture so often called by the name of judgments, being what God brings on men as a Judge, executing a righteous sentence for transgression: yea, they are often called by the name of wrath, especially calamities consisting or issuing in death.[2] And hence also is that which Dr. Taylor would have us take so much notice of, that sometimes in the Scripture, calamity and suffering is called by such names as sin, iniquity, being guilty, etc., which is evidently by a metonymy of the cause for the effect. 'Tis not likely, that in the language in use of old among God's people, calamity or suffering would have been called even by the names of sin and guilt, if it had been so far from having any connection with sin, that even death itself, which is always spoken of as the most terrible of calamities, is not so much as any sign of the sinfulness of the subject, or any testimony of God's displeasure for any guilt of his, as Dr. Taylor supposes.

Death is spoken of in Scripture as the chief of calamities, the most extreme and terrible of all those natural evils, which come on mankind in this world. Deadly destruction is spoken of as "the most terrible destruction" (I Sam. 5:11). Deadly sorrow, as "the most extreme sorrow" (Is. 17:11; Matt. 26:38), and deadly enemies, as "the most bitter and terrible enemies" (Ps. 17:9). The extremity of Christ's sufferings is represented by his suffering unto death (Phil. 2:8 and other places). Hence the greatest testimonies of God's anger for the sins of men in this world, have been by inflicting death: as on the sinners of the old world, on the inhabitants of Sodom and Gomorrah, on Onan, Pharaoh and the Egyptians, Nadab and Abihu, Korah and his company, and the rest of the rebels in the wilderness, on the wicked inhabitants of Canaan, on Hophni and Phineas, Ananias and Sapphira, the unbelieving Jews, upon whom wrath came to the uttermost in the time of the last destruction of Jerusalem. This calamity is often spoken of as in a peculiar manner the fruit of the guilt of sin. (Ex. 28:43), "That they bear not iniq-

2. See Lev. 10:6; Num. 1:53 and 18:5; Josh. 9:20; II Chron. 24:18 and 19:2,10 and 28:13 and 32:25; Ezra 7:23; Neh. 13:18; Zech. 7:12, and many other places.

uity and die." (Lev. 22:9), "Lest they bear sin for it and die." So Num. 18:22 compared with Lev. 10:1–22, the very light of nature, or tradition from ancient revelation, led the heathen to conceive of death as in a peculiar manner an evidence of divine vengeance. Thus we have an account (Acts 28:4) that when the barbarians saw the venomous beast hang on Paul's hand, they said among themselves, "No doubt this man is a murderer, whom though he hath escaped the seas, yet vengeance suffereth not to live."

Calamities that are very small in comparison of the universal temporal destruction of the whole world of mankind by death, are spoken of as manifest indications of God's great displeasure for the sinfulness of the subject; such as the destruction of particular cities, countries or numbers of men, by war or pestilence. (Deut. 29:24), "All nations shall say, wherefore hath the Lord done thus unto this land? what meaneth the heat of this great anger?" Here compare Deut. 32:30, I Kings 9:8, and Jer. 22:8–9. These calamities, thus spoken of as plain testimonies of God's great anger, consisted only in hastening on that death, which otherwise, by God's disposal, would most certainly come in a short time. Now the taking off of 30 or 40 years from 70 or 80 (if we should suppose it to be so much, one with another, in the time of these extraordinary judgments) is but a small matter, in comparison of God's first making man mortal, cutting off his hoped for immortality, subjecting him to inevitable death, which his nature so exceedingly dreads; and afterwards shortening his life further, by cutting off more than 800 years of it: so bringing it to be less than a twelfth part of what it was in the first ages of the world. Besides that, innumerable multitudes in the common course of things, without any extraordinary judgment, die in youth, in childhood and infancy. Therefore how inconsiderable a thing is the additional or hastened destruction, that is sometimes brought on a particular city or country by war, compared with that universal havoc which death makes of the whole race of mankind, from generation to generation, without distinction of sex, age, quality or condition, with all the infinitely various dismal circumstances, torments and agonies which attend the death of old and young, adult persons and little infants? If those particular and comparatively trivial calamities, extending perhaps not to more than a thousandth part of the men of one generation, are clear evidences of God's great anger; certainly this universal vast destruction, by which the whole world in all generations is swallowed up, as by a flood, that nothing can resist, must be a most glaring manifestation of God's anger for the sinfulness of mankind. Yea, the Scripture is express in it, that it is so. (Ps. 90:3, etc.), "Thou turnest man to destruction, and sayest 'Return, ye children of men.' . . . Thou carriest them away as with a flood; they are as asleep; in the morning they are like grass, which groweth up; in the morning it flourisheth and groweth up; in the evening it is cut down, and withereth. For we are consumed by thine anger, and by thy wrath are we troubled. Thou hast set our iniquities before thee, our secret sins in the light of thy countenance. For all our days are passed away in thy wrath: we spend our years as a tale that is told. The days of our years are three-score years and ten: and if by reason of strength they be four-score years, yet is their strength labour and sorrow; for it is soon cut off, and we fly away. Who knoweth the power of thine anger? Even according to thy fear, so is thy wrath. So teach us to number our days, that we may apply our hearts unto wisdom." How plain and full is this testimony, that the general mortality of mankind is an evidence of God's anger for the sin of those who are the subjects of such a dispensation?

Abimelech speaks of it as a thing which he had reason to conclude from God's nature and perfection, that he would not slay a righteous nation (Gen. 20:4). By righteous, evidently meaning innocent. And if so, much less will God slay a righteous world (consisting of so many nations—repeating the great slaughter in every generation) or subject the whole world of mankind to death, when they are considered as innocent, as Dr. Taylor supposes. We have from time to time in Scripture such phrases as "worthy of death" and "guilty of death": but certainly the righteous Judge of all the earth won't bring death on thousands of millions, not only that are not worthy of death, but are worthy of no punishment at all.

Dr. Taylor from time to time speaks of affliction and death as a great benefit, as they increase the vanity of all earthly things, and tend to excite sober reflections, and to induce us to be moderate in gratifying the appetites of the body, and to mortify pride and ambition, etc.[3] To this I would say,

1. 'Tis not denied but God may see it needful for mankind in their present state, that they should be mortal, and subject to outward afflictions, to restrain their lusts, and mortify their pride and ambition, etc. But then is it not an evidence of man's depravity, that it is so? Is it not an evidence of distemper of mind, yea, strong dis-

3. Pp. 21, 67 and other places.

ease, when man stands in need of such sharp medicines, such severe and terrible means to restrain his lusts, keep down his pride, and make him willing to be obedient to God? It must be because of a corrupt and ungrateful heart, if the riches of God's bounty, in bestowing life and prosperity, and things comfortable and pleasant, won't engage the heart to God, and to virtue and child-like love and obedience, but that he must always have the rod held over him, and be often chastised, and held under the apprehensions of death, to keep him from running wild, in pride, contempt and rebellion, ungratefully using the blessings dealt forth from his hand, in sinning against him, and serving his enemies. If man has no natural disingenuity of heart, it must be a mysterious thing indeed, that the sweet blessings of God's bounty have not as powerful an influence to restrain him from sinning against God, as terrible afflictions. If anything can be proof of a perverse and vile disposition, this must be a proof of it, that men should be most apt to forget and despise God, when his providence is most kind; and that they should need to have God chastise them with great severity, and even to kill them, to keep them in order. If we were as much disposed to gratitude to God for his benefits, as we are to anger at our fellow creatures for injuries, as we must be (so far as I can see) if we are not of a depraved heart, the sweetness of the divine bounty, if continued in life, and the height of every enjoyment that is pleasant to innocent human nature, would be as powerful incentives to a proper regard to God, tending as much to promote religion and virtue, as to have the world filled with calamity, and to have God (to use the language of Hezekiah (Is. 38:13), describing death and its agonies) "as a lion, breaking all our bones, and from day even to night, making an end of us."

Dr. Taylor himself (p. 252) says, "That our first parents before the fall were placed in a condition proper to engage their gratitude, love and obedience." Which is as much as to say, proper to engage them to the exercise and practice of all religion. And if the paradisiacal state was proper to engage to all religion and duty, and men still come into the world with hearts as good as the two first of the species, why is it not proper to engage 'em to it still? What need of so vastly changing man's state, depriving him of all those blessings, and instead of them allotting to him a world full of briars and thorns, affliction, calamity and death, to engage him to it? The taking away of life, and all those pleasant enjoyments man had at first, by a permanent constitution, would be no stated benefit to mankind, unless there were a stated disposition in them to abuse such blessings. The taking them away is supposed to be a benefit under the notion of their being things that tend to lead men to sin: but they would have no such tendency, at least in a stated manner, unless there were in men a fixed tendency to make that unreasonable improvement of 'em. Such a temper of mind as amounts to a disposition to make such an improvement of blessings of that kind, is often spoken of in Scripture, as most astonishingly vile and perverse. So concerning Israel's abusing the blessings of Canaan, that land flowing with milk and honey; their ingratitude in it is spoken of by the prophets, as enough to astonish all heaven and earth, and as more than brutish stupidity and vileness. (Jer. 2:7), "I brought you into a plentiful country, to eat the fruit thereof, and the goodness thereof. But when ye entered, ye defiled my land, etc." See the following verses, especially v. 12, "Be astonished, O ye heavens, at this." So Is. 1:1–4: "Hear, O heavens, and give ear, O earth; I have nourished and brought up children, and they have rebelled against me. The ox knows his owner and the ass his master's crib; but my people doth not know, Israel doth not consider. Ah, sinful nation! a people laden with iniquity, a seed of evil-doers, children that are corrupters."

Compare Deut. 32:6–19. If it showed so great depravity, to be disposed thus to abuse the blessings of so fruitful and pleasant a land as Canaan, surely it would be an evidence of a no less astonishing corruption, to be inclined to abuse the blessings of Eden, and the garden of God there.

2. If death be brought on mankind only as a benefit, and in that manner which Dr. Taylor mentions, viz. to mortify, or moderate their carnal appetites and affections, wean 'em from the world, excite 'em to sober reflections, and lead 'em to the fear and obedience of God, etc.—is it not strange, that it should fall so heavy on infants, who are not capable of making any such improvement of it; so that many more of mankind suffer death in infancy, than in any other equal part of the age of man? Our author sometimes hints, that the death of infants may be for the good of parents, and those that are adult, and may be for the correction and punishment of the sins of parents: but hath God any need of such methods to add to parents' afflictions? Are there not ways enough that he might increase their trouble, without destroying the lives of such multitudes of those that are perfectly innocent, and have in no respect any sin belonging to

'em: on whom death comes, at an age, when not only the subjects are not capable of any reflection, or making any improvement of it, either in the suffering, or expectation of it; but also at an age, when parents and friends, who alone can make a good improvement and whom Dr. Taylor supposes alone to be punished by it, suffer least by being bereaved of them; though the infants themselves sometimes suffer to great extremity?

3. To suppose, as Dr. Taylor does, that death is brought on mankind in consequence of Adam's sin, not at all as a calamity, but only as a favor and benefit, is contrary to the doctrine of the gospel; which teaches, that when Christ, as the second Adam, comes to remove and destroy that death, which came by the first Adam, he finds it not as a friend, but an enemy. (I Cor. 15:22), "For as in Adam all die, so in Christ shall all be made alive," with vv. 25 and 26, "For he must reign, till he hath put all enemies under his feet. The last enemy that shall be destroyed, is death."

Dr. Taylor urges, that the afflictions which mankind are subjected to, and particularly their common mortality, are represented in Scripture as the chastisements of our heavenly Father; and therefore are designed for our spiritual good: and consequently are not of the nature of punishments. So in pp. 68, 69, 314, 315.

Though I think the thing asserted far from being true, viz. that the Scripture represents the afflictions of mankind in general, and particularly their common mortality, as the chastisements of an heavenly Father; yet 'tis needless to stand to dispute that matter: for if it be so, it will be no argument that the afflictions and death of mankind are not evidences of their sinfulness. Those would be strange chastisements from the hand of a wise and good Father, which are wholly for nothing; especially such severe chastisements, as to break the child's bones; when at the same time the Father don't suppose any guilt, fault or offense, in any respect, belonging to the child; but it is chastised in this terrible manner, only for fear that it will be faulty hereafter. I say, these would be a strange sort of chastisements; yea, though he should be able to make it up to the child afterwards. Dr. Taylor tells of representations made by the whole current of Scripture: I am certain, it is not agreeable to the current of Scripture, to represent divine fatherly chastisements after this manner. 'Tis true, that the Scripture supposes such chastenings to be the fruit of God's goodness; yet at the same time it evermore represents them as being for the sin of the subject, and as evidence of the divine displeasure for its sinfulness. Thus the Apostle in I Cor. 11:31, 32, speaks of God's chastening his people by mortal sickness, for their good, "that they might not be condemned with the world," and yet signifies that it was "for their sin; for this cause many are weak and sickly among you, and many sleep"; that is, for the profaneness and sinful disorder before-mentioned. So Elihu (Job 33:16ff.) speaks of the same chastening by sickness, as for men's good; "to withdraw man from his [sinful] [4] purpose, and to hide pride from man, and keep back his soul from the pit; . . . that therefore God chastens man with pain on his bed, and the multitude of his bones with strong pain." But these chastenings are for his sins, as appears by what follows (v. 28), where 'tis observed, that when God by this means has brought men to repent, and humbly confess their sins, he delivers them. Again, the same Elihu, speaking of the unfailing love of God to the righteous, even when he "chastens them, and they are bound in fetters, and holden in cords of affliction" (ch. 36:8 etc.), yet speaks of these chastenings as being for their sins (v. 9), "Then he sheweth them their work, and their transgressions, that they have exceeded." So David (Ps. 30), speaks of God's chastening by sore afflictions, as being for his good, and issuing joyfully; and yet being the fruit of God's anger for his sin (v. 5). "God's anger endureth but for a moment." Compare Ps. 119:67,71, 75. God's fatherly chastisements are spoken of as being for sin (II Sam. 7:14,15), "I will be his father, and he shall be my son. If he commit iniquity, I will chasten him with the rod of men, and with the stripes of the children of men; but my mercy shall not depart away from him." So the prophet Jeremiah speaks of the great affliction that God's people of the young generation suffered in the time of the captivity, as being for their good (Lam. 3:25, etc.). But yet these chastisements are spoken of as being for their sin (see especially vv. 39, 40). So Christ says (Rev. 2:19), "As many as I love, I rebuke and chasten." But the words following shew, that these chastenings from love are for sin that should be repented of: "Be zealous therefore, and repent." And though Christ tells us, they are blessed that are persecuted for righteousness' sake, and have reason to rejoice and be exceeding glad; yet even the persecutions of God's people, as ordered in divine providence, are spoken of as divine chastenings for sin, like the just corrections of a father, when the children deserve them (Heb. 12). The Apostle there speaking to the Chris-

4. [JE adds this word.]

tians, concerning the persecutions which they suffered, called their sufferings by the name of divine rebukes; which implies testifying against a fault: and that they mayn't be discouraged, puts them in mind, that "whom the Lord loveth, he chasteneth, and scourgeth every son that he receiveth." 'Tis also very plain, that the persecutions of God's people, as they are from the disposing hand of God, are chastisements for sin (from I Pet. 4:17,18 compared with Prov. 11:31. See also Ps. 69:4–9).

If divine chastisements in general are certain evidences that the subjects are not wholly without sin, some way belonging to them then in a peculiar manner is death so; for these reasons:

(1) Because slaying, or delivering to death, is often spoken of as in general a more awful thing than the chastisements that are endured in this life. (So, Ps. 118:17,18), "I shall not die, but live, and declare the works of the Lord. The Lord hath chastened me sore; but he hath not given me over unto death." So the psalmist in Ps. 88:15, setting forth the extremity of his affliction, represents it by this, that it was next to death. "I am afflicted, and ready to die, while I suffer thy terrors, I am distracted." (So David, I Sam. 20:3). So God's tenderness towards persons under chastisement, is from time to time set forth by that, that he did not proceed so far as to make an end of 'em by death (as in Ps. 78:38,39, and Ps. 103:9 with vv. 14,15; Ps. 30:2,3,9; Job 33:22,23,24). So we have God's people often praying when under great affliction, that God would not proceed to this, as being the greatest extremity. (Ps. 13:3), "Consider, and hear me, O Lord my God; lighten mine eyes lest I sleep the sleep of death." (So Job 10:9; Ps. 6:1–5 and 88:9,10,11; 143:7).

Especially may death be looked upon as the most extreme of all temporal sufferings, when attended with such dreadful circumstances, and extreme pains, as those with which providence sometimes brings it on infants; as on the children that were offered up to Moloch, and some other idols, who were tormented to death in burning brass. Dr. Taylor says (pp. 359 and 404), "The Lord of all being can never want time and place and power to compensate abundantly any sufferings infants now undergo in subserviency to his good providence." But there are no bounds to such a license, in evading evidences from fact. It might as well be said, that there is not and cannot be any such thing as evidence, from events, of God's displeasure; which is most contrary to the whole current of Scripture, as may appear in part from things which have been observed.

This gentleman might as well go further still, and say, that God may cast guiltless persons into hell-fire, to remain there in the most unutterable torments for ages of ages (which bear no greater proportion to eternity than a quarter of an hour), and if he does so, it is no evidence of God's displeasure; because he can never want time, place and power, abundantly to compensate their sufferings afterwards. If it be so, it is not to the purpose, as long as the Scripture does so abundantly teach us to look on great calamities and sufferings which God brings on men, especially death, as marks of his displeasure for sin, and for sin belonging to them that suffer.

(2) Another thing, which may well lead us to suppose death, in a peculiar manner, above other temporal sufferings, intended as a testimony of God's displeasure for sin, is that death is a thing attended with that awful appearance, that gloomy and terrible aspect, that naturally suggests to our minds God's awful displeasure. Which is a thing that Dr. Taylor himself takes particular notice of (p. 69). Speaking of death, "Herein," says he, "have we before our eyes a striking demonstration, that sin is infinitely hateful to God, and the corruption and ruin of our nature. . . . Nothing is more proper than such a sight to give us the utmost abhorrence of all iniquity etc." Now if death be no testimony of God's displeasure for sin, no evidence that the subject is looked upon, by him who inflicts it, as any other than perfectly innocent, free from all manner of imputation of guilt, and treated only as an object of favor, is it not strange, that God should annex to it such affecting appearances of his hatred and anger for sin, more than to other chastisements, which yet the Scripture teaches us are always for sin? These gloomy and striking manifestations of God's hatred of sin attending death, are equivalent to awful frowns of God attending the stroke of his hand. If we should see a wise and just father chastising his child, mixing terrible frowns with severe strokes, we should justly argue, that the father considered his child as having something in him displeasing to him, and that he did not thus treat his child only under a notion of mortifying him, and preventing his being faulty hereafter, and making it up to him afterwards, when he had been perfectly innocent, and without fault, either of action or disposition hitherto.

We may well argue from these things, that infants are not looked upon by God as sinless, but that they are by nature children of wrath, seeing this terrible evil comes so heavily on mankind in infancy. But besides these things, which are observable concerning the mortality of infants in general, there are some particular cases of the death of infants, which the Scripture sets before us, that are attended with circumstances, in a peculiar manner, giving evidences of the sinfulness of such, and their just exposedness to divine wrath. As particularly,

The destroying the infants in Sodom, and the neighboring cities: which cities, destroyed in so extraordinary miraculous and awful a manner, are set forth as a signal example of God's dreadful vengeance for sin to the world in all generations; agreeable to that of the Apostle (Jude 7). God did not reprove, but manifestly countenanced Abraham, when he said, with respect to the destruction of Sodom (Gen. 18:23,25), "Wilt thou . . . destroy the righteous with the wicked? . . . That be far from thee, to do after this manner, to slay the righteous with the wicked: and the righteous should be as the wicked, that be far from thee. Shall not the judge of all the earth do right?" Abraham's words imply that God would not destroy the innocent with the guilty. We may well understand "innocent" as included in the word "righteous," according to the language usual in Scripture, in speaking of such cases of judgment and punishment; as is plain in Gen. 20:4; Ex. 23:7; Deut. 25:1; II Sam. 4:11; II Chron. 6:23; and Prov. 18:5. Eliphaz says (Job 4:7), "Who ever perished, being innocent? or where were the righteous cut off?" We see what great care God took that Lot should not be involved in that destruction. He was miraculously rescued by angels, sent on purpose; who laid hold on him, and brought him, and set him without the gates of the city; and told him that they could do nothing till he was out of the way (Gen. 19:22). And not only was he thus miraculously delivered, but his two wicked daughters for his sake. The whole affair, both the destruction, and the rescue of them that escaped, was miraculous: and God could as easily have delivered the infants which were in those cities. And if they had been without sin, their perfect innocency, one should think, would have pleaded much more strongly for them, than those lewd women's relation to Lot pleaded for them. When in such a case, we must suppose these infants much further from deserving to be involved in that destruction, than even Lot himself. To say here, that God could make it up to those infants in another world, must be an insufficient reply. For so he could as easily have made it up to Lot, or to ten or fifty righteous, if they had been destroyed in the same fire; nevertheless it is plainly signified, that this would not have been agreeable to the wise and holy proceedings of the Judge of all the earth.

Since God declared, that if there had been found but ten righteous in Sodom, he would have spared the whole city for their sake, may we not well suppose, if infants are perfectly innocent, that he would have spared the old world, in which there were, without doubt, many hundred thousand infants, and in general, one in every family, whose perfect innocence pleaded for its preservation? Especially when such vast care was taken to save Noah and his family (some of whom, one at least, seem to have been none of the best), that they might not be involved in that destruction. If the perfect sinlessness of infants had been a notion entertained among the people of God of old, in the ages next following the flood, handed down from Noah and his children, who well knew that vast multitudes of infants perished in the flood, is it likely that Eliphaz, who lived within a few generations of Shem and Noah, would have said to Job, as he does in that forementioned Job 4:7, "Who ever perish, being innocent? and where were the righteous cut off?" Especially since in the same discourse (ch. 5:1) he appeals to the tradition of the ancients for a confirmation of this very point; as he also does in ch. 15:7–10, and 22:15,16. In which last place, he mentions that very thing, the destruction of the wicked by the flood, as an instance of that perishing of the wicked, which he supposes to be peculiar to them, for Job's conviction; in which "the wicked were cut down out of time, whose foundation being overflown with a flood." Where 'tis also observable, that he speaks of such an untimeliness of death as they suffered by the flood, as one evidence of guilt; as he also does (ch. 15:32,33), "It shall be accomplished before his time; and his branch shall not be green." But those that were destroyed by the flood in infancy, above all the rest were cut down out of time; when instead of living above 900 years, according to the common period of man's life, many were cut down before they were one year old.

And when God executed vengeance on the ancient inhabitants of Canaan, not only did he not spare their cities and families for the sake of the infants that were therein, nor take any care that they should not be involved in the destruction; but often with particular care repeated his express commands, that their infants should not be spared, but should be utterly destroyed, without any pity; while Rahab the harlot (who had been far from innocence, though she expressed her faith in entertaining, and safely dismissing the spies) was preserved, and all her friends for her sake. And when God executed his wrath on the Egyptians by slaying their first born, though the children of Israel, who were most of 'em wicked men, as was before shewn, were wonderfully spared by the destroying angel, yet such first born of the Egyptians as were infants, were not spared. They not only were not rescued by the angel, and no miracle wrought to save 'em (as was observed in the case of the infants of Sodom), but the angel destroyed 'em by his own immediate hand, and a miracle was wrought to kill them.

Here not to stay to be particular concerning the command by Moses, concerning the destruction of the infants of the Midianites (Num. 31:17). And that given to Saul to destroy all the infants of the Amalekites (I Sam. 15:3), and what is said concerning Edom (Ps. 137:4), "Happy shall he be that shall take thy little ones, and dash them against the stones." I proceed to take notice of something remarkable concerning the destruction of Jerusalem, represented in Ezek. 9, when command was given to them that had charge over the city, to destroy the inhabitants (vv. 1–8). And this reason is given for it, that their iniquity required it, and it was a just recompense of their sin (vv. 9, 10). And God at the same time was most particular and exact in his care that such should by no means be involved in the slaughter, as had proved by their behavior, that they were not partakers in the abominations of the city. Command was given to the angel, to go through the city, and set a mark upon their foreheads, and the destroying angel had a strict charge not to come near any man on whom was the mark; yet the infants were not marked, nor a word said of sparing them: on the contrary, infants were expressly mentioned as those that should be utterly destroyed, without pity. (vv. 5, 6), "Go through the city, and smite: let not your eye spare, neither have ye pity. Slay utterly old and young, both maids and little children: but come not near any man upon whom is the mark."

And if any should suspect that such instances as these were peculiar to a more severe dispensation, under the Old Testament, let us consider a remarkable instance in the days of the glorious gospel of the grace of God; even the last destruction of Jerusalem; which was far more terrible, and with greater testimonies of God's wrath and indignation, than the destruction of Sodom, or of Jerusalem in Nebuchadnezzar's time, or anything that ever had happened to any city or people, from the beginning of the world to that time: agreeable to Matt. 24:21 and Luke 21:22,23. But at that time particular care was taken to distinguish and deliver God's people, as was foretold (Dan. 12:1). And we have in the New Testament a particular account of the care Christ took for the preservation of his followers: he gave them a sign, by which they might know when the desolation of the city was nigh, that they that were in Jerusalem might flee to the mountains, and escape. And as history gives account, the Christians followed the directions given, and escaped to a place in the mountains called Pella, and were preserved. Yet no care was taken to preserve the infants of the city, in general; but according to the predictions of that event, they were involved with others in that great destruction: so heavily did the calamity fall upon them, that those words were verified. (Luke 23:29), "Behold the days are coming, in which they shall say, 'Blessed are the barren, and the wombs that never bare, and the paps which never gave suck.' " And that prophecy in Deut. 32:21–25, which has undoubtedly special respect to this very time, and is so applied by the best commentators. "I will move them to jealousy, with those that are not a people: . . . for a fire is kindled in mine anger, and it shall burn to the lowest hell . . . I will heap mischiefs upon them; and I will spend mine arrows upon them. They shall be burnt with hunger, and devoured with burning heat, and bitter destruction. . . . The sword without, and terror within, shall destroy both the young man and the virgin, the suckling also, with the man of gray hairs." And it appears by the history of that destruction, that at that time was a remarkable fulfilment of that in Deut. 28:53–57, concerning "parents eating their children in the siege . . . and the tender and delicate woman eating her new-born child." And here it must be remembered, that these very destructions of that city and land are spoken of in those places fore-mentioned, as clear evidences of God's wrath to all nations, which shall behold them. And if so, they were evidences of God's wrath towards infants; who, equally with the rest, were the subjects of destruction. If a particular kind or rank of persons, which made a very considerable part of the inhabitants, were from time to time partakers of the overthrow, without any distinction made in divine providence, and yet this was no evidence at all of God's displeasure with any of 'em; then a being the subjects of such a calamity could not be an evidence of God's wrath against any of the inhabitants, to the reason of all nations, or any nation, or so much as one person.

PART TWO.

Containing Observations on Particular Parts of the Holy Scripture, Which Prove the Doctrine of Original Sin

CHAPTER I

OBSERVATIONS RELATING TO THINGS CONTAINED IN THE THREE FIRST CHAPTERS OF GENESIS, WITH REFERENCE TO THE DOCTRINE OF ORIGINAL SIN

SECTION 1. CONCERNING ORIGINAL RIGHTEOUSNESS: AND WHETHER OUR FIRST PARENTS WERE CREATED WITH RIGHTEOUSNESS OR MORAL RECTITUDE OF HEART?

THE doctrine of *original righteousness,* or the creation of our first parents with holy principles and dispositions, has a close connection, in several respects, with the doctrine of original sin. Dr. Taylor was sensible of this; and accordingly he strenuously opposes this doctrine, in his book against original sin. And therefore in handling the subject, I would in the first place remove this author's main objection against this doctrine; and then shew how the doctrine may be inferred from the account which Moses gives us, in the three first chapters of Genesis.

Dr. Taylor's grand objection against this doctrine, which he abundantly insists on, is this: that it is utterly inconsistent with the nature of virtue, that it should be concreated with any person; because, if so, it must be by an act of God's absolute power, without our knowledge or concurrence; and that moral virtue, in its very nature, implieth the choice and consent of the moral agent, without which it cannot be virtue and holiness: that a necessary holiness, is no holiness. So pp. 179, 180, where he observes, "That Adam must exist, he must be created, yea he must exercise thought and reflection, before he was righteous." (See also pp. 250, 251.) In p. 437 he says, "To say, that God not only endowed Adam with a capacity of being righteous, but moreover that righteousness and true holiness were created with him, or wrought into his nature, at the same time he was made, is to affirm a contradiction, or what is inconsistent with the very nature of righteousness." And in like manner Dr.

Turnbull in many places insists upon it, that it is necessary to the very being of virtue, that it be owing to our own choice, and diligent culture.

With respect to this, I would observe, that it consists in a notion of virtue quite inconsistent with the nature of things, and the common notions of mankind; and also inconsistent with Dr. Taylor's own notions of virtue. Therefore, if it be truly so, that to affirm that to be virtue or holiness which is not the fruit of preceding thought, reflection and choice, is to affirm a contradiction, I shall shew plainly, that for him to affirm otherwise, is a contradiction to himself.

In the first place, I think it a contradiction to the nature of things, as judged of by the common sense of mankind. It is agreeable to the sense of the minds of men in all nations and ages, not only that the fruit or effect of a good choice is virtuous, but the good choice itself, from whence that effect proceeds; yea, and not only so, but also the antecedent good disposition, temper or affection of mind, from whence proceeds that good choice, is virtuous. This is the general notion, not that principles derive their goodness from actions, but that actions derive their goodness from the principles whence they proceed; and so that the act of choosing that which is good, is no further virtuous than it proceeds from a good principle, or virtuous disposition of mind. Which supposes, that a virtuous disposition of mind may be before a virtuous act of choice; and that therefore it is not necessary that there should first be thought, reflection and choice, before there can be any virtuous disposition. If the choice be first, before the existence of a good disposition of heart, what signifies that choice? There can, according to our natural notions, be no virtue in a choice which proceeds from no virtuous principle, but from mere self-love, ambition, or some animal appetite. And therefore a virtuous temper of mind may be before a good act of choice, as a tree may be before the fruit, and the fountain before the stream which proceeds from it.

The following things in Mr. Hutcheson's *Inquiry* concerning moral good and evil, are evidently agreeable to the nature of things, and the voice of human sense and reason.[1] (Sec. II, pp. 132, 133),

1. [Francis Hutcheson, *An Inquiry into the Original of Our Ideas of Beauty and Virtue in Two Treatises: 1. Concerning Beauty, Order, Harmony, Design. 2. Concerning Moral Good and Evil* (London, 1738). See also above, Intro., Sec. 4.]

"Every action which we apprehend as either morally good or evil, is always supposed to flow from some affections towards sensitive natures. And whatever we call virtue or vice, is either some such affection, or some action *consequent upon it*. . . . All the actions counted religious in any country, are supposed by those who count them so, to flow from some affections towards the Deity: and whatever we call social virtue, we still suppose to *flow from* affections towards our fellow-creatures. . . . Prudence, if it is only employed in promoting private interest, is never imagined to be a virtue." In these things Dr. Turnbull expressly agrees with Mr. Hutcheson, who is his admired author.[2]

If a virtuous disposition or affection is before acts that proceed from it, then they are before those virtuous acts of choice which proceed from it. And therefore there is no necessity that all virtuous dispositions or affections should be the effect of choice: and so no such supposed necessity can be a good objection against such a disposition's being natural, or from a kind of instinct, implanted in the mind in its creation. Agreeable to what Mr. Hutcheson says (ibid. Sec. III, pp. 196, 197), "I know not," says he, "for what reason some will not allow that to be virtue, which flows from instinct of passions. But how do they help themselves? They say, virtue arises from reason. What is reason, but the sagacity we have in prosecuting any end? The ultimate end proposed by common moralists, is the happiness of the agent himself. And this certainly he is determined to pursue from instinct. Now may not another instinct towards the public, or the good of others, be as proper a principle of virtue, as the instinct towards private happiness? . . . If it be said, that actions from instinct are not the effect of prudence and choice, this objection will hold full as strongly against the actions which flow from self-love."

And if we consider what Dr. Taylor declares as his own notion of the essence of virtue, we shall find, what he so confidently and often affirms, of its being essential to all virtue that it should follow choice and proceed from it, is no less repugnant to that, than it is to the nature of things, and the general notions of mankind. For 'tis his notion, as well as Mr. Hutcheson's, that the essence of virtue lies in good affections, and particularly in benevolence or love: as he very fully declares in these words in his *Key:*[3] "That the word that signifies goodness and mercy, should also signify moral rectitude in

2. *Mor*[*al*] *Phil*[*osophy*] pp. 112–115, p. 142 et alibi passim.

3. Marginal note annexed to no. 326.

general, will not seem strange, if we consider that love is the fulfilling of the law. Goodness according to the sense of Scripture, and the nature of things, includes all moral rectitude; which, I reckon, may every part of it, where it is true and genuine, be resolved into this single principle." If it be so indeed, then certainly no act whatsoever can have moral rectitude, but what proceeds from this principle. And consequently no act of volition or choice can have any moral rectitude, that takes place before this principle exists. And yet he most confidently affirms, that thought, reflection and choice must go before virtue, and that all virtue or righteousness must be the fruit of preceding choice. This brings his scheme to an evident contradiction. For no act of choice can be virtuous but what proceeds from a principle of benevolence or love; for he insists that all genuine moral rectitude, in every part of it, is resolved into this single principle: and yet the principle of benevolence itself, can't be virtuous, unless it proceeds from choice; for he affirms that nothing can have the nature of virtue but what comes from choice. So that virtuous love, as the principle of all virtue, must go before virtuous choice, and be the principle or spring of it; and yet virtuous choice must go before virtuous benevolence, and be the spring of that. If a virtuous act of choice goes before a principle of benevolence, and produces it, then this virtuous act is something distinct from that principle which follows it, and is its effect. So that here is at least one part of virtue, yea, the spring and source of all virtue, viz. a virtuous choice, that cannot be resolved into that single principle of love.

Here also it is worthy to be observed, that Dr. Taylor (p. 128) says, "The cause of every effect, alone, is chargeable with the effect it produceth, or which proceedeth from it"; and so he argues, that if the effect be bad, the cause alone is sinful. According to which reasoning, when the effect is good, the cause alone is righteous or virtuous; to the cause is to be ascribed all the praise of the good effect it produceth. And by the same reasoning it will follow, that if, as Dr. Taylor says, Adam must choose to be righteous, before he was righteous, and if it be essential to the nature of righteousness or moral rectitude, that it be the effect of choice, and hence a principle of benevolence can't have moral rectitude, unless it proceeds from choice; then not to the principle of benevolence, which is the effect, but to the foregoing choice alone, is to be ascribed all the virtue or righteousness that is in the case. And so, instead of all moral rectitude, in every part of it, being resolved into that single principle of benevolence, no moral rectitude, in any part of it, is to be resolved into that principle; but all is to be resolved into the foregoing choice, which is the cause.

But yet it follows from these inconsistent principles, there is no moral rectitude or virtue in the first act of choice, that is the cause of all consequent virtue. This follows two ways: 1. Because every part of virtue lies in the benevolent principle, which is the effect; and therefore no part of it can lie in the cause. 2. The choice of virtue, as to the first act at least, can have no virtue or righteousness at all, because it don't proceed from any foregoing choice. For Dr. Taylor insists, that a man must first have reflection and choice, before he can have righteousness; and that it is essential to holiness, that it proceed from choice. So that the first choice of holiness, which holiness proceeds from, can have no virtue at all, because by the supposition it don't proceed from choice, being the first choice. Hence if it be essential to holiness, that it proceeds from choice, it must proceed from an unholy choice; unless the first holy choice can be before itself, or there be a virtuous act of choice before that which is first of all.

And with respect to Adam, let us consider how upon Dr. Taylor's principles, it was possible he ever should have any such thing as righteousness, by any means at all. In the state wherein God created him, he could have no such thing as love to God, or any love or benevolence in his heart. For if so, there would have been original righteousness; there would have been genuine moral recitude; nothing would be wanting: for our author says, "True genuine moral rectitude, in every part of it, is to be resolved into this single principle." But if he were wholly without any such thing as love to God, or any virtuous love, how should he come by virtue? The answer doubtless will be, by act of choice: he must first choose to be virtuous. But what if he did choose to be virtuous? It could not be from love to God, or any virtuous principle, that he chose it; for by the supposition, he has no such principle in his heart: and if he chooses it without such a principle, still, according to this author, there is no virtue in his choice; for all virtue, he says, is to be resolved into that single principle of love. Or will he say, there may be produced in the heart a virtuous benevolence by an act or acts of choice, that are not virtuous? But this don't consist with what he implicitly asserts, that to the cause alone is to be ascribed what is in the effect. So that there is no way can possibly be devised, in consistence with Dr. Taylor's scheme, in which Adam ever could have any righteousness, or could ever either obtain any principle of virtue, or perform any one virtuous act.

These confused inconsistent assertions, concerning virtue and moral rectitude, arise from the absurd notions in vogue, concerning freedom of will, as if it consisted in the will's *self-determining power,* supposed to be necessary to moral agency, virtue and vice. The absurdities of which, with the grounds of these errors, and what the truth is respecting these matters, with the evidences of it, I have, according to my ability, fully and largely considered, in my *Enquiry* on that subject; [4] to which I must refer the reader, that desires further satisfaction, and is willing to give himself the trouble of reading that discourse.

Having considered this great argument, and pretended demonstration of Dr. Taylor's against original righteousness; I proceed to the proofs of the doctrine. And in the first place, I would consider, whether there be not evidence of it in the three first chapters of Genesis: or whether the history there delivered, don't lead us to suppose, that our first parents were created in a state of moral rectitude and holiness.

I. This history leads us to suppose, Adam's sin, with relation to the forbidden fruit, was the *first* sin he committed. Which could not have been, had he not always, till then, been perfectly righteous, righteous from the first [5] moment of his existence; and consequently, created or brought into existence righteous. In a moral agent, subject to moral obligations, it is the same thing, to be perfectly *innocent,* as to be perfectly *righteous.* It must be the same, because there can no more be any *medium* between sin and righteousness, or between being right and being wrong, in a moral sense, than there can be a medium between straight and crooked, in a natural sense. Adam was brought into existence capable of acting immediately, as a moral agent; and therefore he was immediately under a rule of right action: he was obliged as soon as he existed, to act right. And if he was obliged to act right as soon as he existed, he was obliged even then to be *inclined* to act right. Dr. Taylor says (p. 442), "Adam could not sin without a sinful inclination"; [6] and just for

4. [*A Careful and Strict Enquiry into . . . Freedom of the Will,* 1754.]

5. [Erroneous pagination in the first ed. occurs here and continues for seven pages. With page 153 correct pagination returns.]

6. This is doubtless true: for although there was no natural sinful inclina-

the same reason, he could not do right, without an inclination to right action. And as he was obliged to act right from the first moment of his existence, and did do so, till he sinned in the affair of the forbidden fruit, he must have an inclination or disposition of heart to do right the first moment of his existence; and that is the same as to be created, or brought into existence, with an inclination to right action, or, which is the same thing, a virtuous and holy disposition of heart.[7]

Here it will be in vain to say, 'tis true, that it was Adam's duty to have a good disposition or inclination as soon as it was possible to be obtained, in the nature of things: but as it could not be without time to establish such an habit, which requires antecedent thought, reflection, and repeated right action; therefore all that Adam could be obliged to in the first place, was to reflect and consider things in a right manner, and apply himself to right action, in order to obtain a right disposition. For this supposes, that even this reflection and consideration, which he was obliged to, was *right action:* Surely he was obliged to it no otherwise than as a thing that was right: and therefore he must have an *inclination* to this right action immediately, before he could perform those first right actions. And as the inclination to them should be right, the principle or disposition from which he performed even these actions must be good. Otherwise, the actions would not be right in the sight of him who looks at the heart; nor would they answer the man's obligations, or be a doing his duty, if he had done them for some sinister end, and not from a regard to God and his duty. Therefore there must be a regard to God and his duty implanted in him at his first existence. Otherwise, 'tis certain, he would have done nothing from a regard to God and his duty; no, not so much as to reflect and consider, and try to obtain such a disposition. The very supposition of a *disposition* to right *action* being first obtained by repeated right action, is grossly inconsistent with itself: for it supposes a course of right action, *before* there is a disposition to perform any right action.

These are no invented quibbles, or sophisms. If God expected of Adam any obedience or duty to him at all, when he first made him, whether it was in reflecting, considering, or any way exerting the

---

tion in Adam, yet an inclination to that sin of eating the forbidden fruit, was begotten in him by the delusion and error he was led into; and this inclination to eat the forbidden fruit, must precede his actual eating.

7. [See above, Intro., Sec. 3, God the Author of Sin.]

faculties he had given him, then God expected he should immediately exercise love and regard to him. For how could it be expected, that Adam should have a strict and perfect regard to God's commands and authority, and his duty to him, when he had no love nor regard to him in his heart, nor could it be expected he should have any? If Adam from the beginning did his duty to God, and had more respect to the will of his Creator, than to other things, and as much respect to him as he ought to have; then from the beginning he had a supreme and perfect respect and love to God: and if so, he was created with such a principle. There is no avoiding the consequence. Not only external duties, but internal duties, such as summarily consist in love, must be immediately required of Adam, as soon as he existed, if any duty at all was required. For 'tis most apparently absurd, to talk of a spiritual being, with the faculties of understanding and will, being required to per[form] [8] external duties, without internal. Dr. Taylor himself observes, that love is the fulfilling of the law, and that "all moral rectitude, even every part of it, must be resolved into that single principle." Therefore, if any morally right act at all, reflection, consideration, or anything else, was required of Adam immediately, on his first existence, and was performed as required; then he must, the first moment of his existence, have his heart possessed of that principle of divine love; which implies the whole of moral rectitude in every part of it, according to our author's own doctrine; and so the whole of moral rectitude or righteousness must begin with his existence: which is the thing taught in the doctrine of original righteousness.

And let us consider how it could be otherwise, than that Adam was always, in every moment of his existence, obliged to exercise such regard or respect of heart towards every object or thing, as was agreeable to the apparent merit of that object. For instance, would it not at any time have been a becoming thing in Adam, on the exhibition to his mind of God's infinite goodness to him, for him to have exercised answerable gratitude; and the contrary have been unbecoming and odious? And if something had been presented to Adam's view, transcendently amiable in itself, as for instance, the glorious perfection of the divine nature, would it not have become him to love, relish and delight in it? Would not such an object have merited this? And if the view of an object so amiable in itself did not affect his mind with complacence, would it not, according to the

8. [Missing in first edition.]

plain dictates of our understanding, have shown an unbecoming temper of mind? To say, that he had not had time, by culture, to form and establish a good disposition or relish, is not what would have taken off the disagreeableness and odiousness of the temper. And if there had been ever [9] so much time, I don't see, how it could be expected he should improve it aright, in order to obtain a good disposition, if he had not already some good disposition to engage him to it.

That belonging to the will and disposition of the heart, which is in itself either odious or amiable, unbecoming or decent, always would have been Adam's virtue or sin, at any moment of his existence; if there be any such thing as virtue or vice; by which nothing can be meant, but that in our moral disposition and behavior, which is becoming or unbecoming, amiable or odious.

Human nature must be created with some dispositions; a disposition to relish some things as good and amiable, and to be averse to other things as odious and disagreeable. Otherwise, it must be without any such thing as inclination or will. It must be perfectly indifferent, without preference, without choice or aversion towards anything, as agreeable or disagreeable. But if it had any concreated dispositions at all, they must be either right or wrong, either agreeable or disagreeable to the nature of things. If man had at first the highest relish of those things that were most excellent and beautiful, a disposition to have the quickest and highest delight in those things that were most worthy of it, then his dispositions were morally right and amiable, and never can be decent and excellent in a higher sense. But if he had a disposition to love most those things that were inferior and less worthy, then his dispositions were vicious. And 'tis evident there can be no medium between these.

II. This notion of Adam's being created without a principle of holiness in his heart, taken with the rest of Dr. Taylor's scheme, is inconsistent with what the history in the beginning of Genesis leads us to suppose of the great favors and smiles of heaven, which Adam enjoyed, while he remained in innocency. The Mosaic account suggests to us, that till Adam sinned, he was in happy circumstances, surrounded with testimonies and fruits of God's favor. This is implicitly owned by Dr. Taylor when he says (p. 252), "That in the dispensation our first parents were under, before the fall, they were placed in a condition proper to engage their gratitude, love and obe-

9. [In first edition, "never."]

dience." But it will follow on our author's principles, that Adam while in innocency, was placed in far worse circumstances, than he was in after his disobedience, and infinitely worse than his posterity are in; under unspeakably greater disadvantages for the avoiding [of] sin, and the performance of duty. For by his doctrine Adam's posterity come into the world with their hearts as free from any propensity to sin as he, and he was made as destitute of any propensity to righteousness as they: and yet God, in favor to them, does great things to restrain them from sin, and excite them to virtue, which he never did for Adam in innocency, but laid him, in the highest degree, under contrary disadvantages. God, as an instance of his great favor and fatherly love to man, since the fall, has denied him the ease and pleasures of paradise, which gratified and allured his senses and bodily appetites; that he might diminish his temptations to sin: and as a still greater means to restrain from sin, and promote virtue, has subjected him to labor, toil, and sorrow in the world: and not only so, but as a means to promote his spiritual and eternal good far beyond this, has doomed him to death: and when all this was found insufficient, he, in further prosecution of the designs of his love, shortened men's lives exceedingly, made them twelve or thirteen times shorter than in the first ages. And yet this, with all the innumerable calamities, which God in great favor to mankind has brought on the world, whereby their temptations are so vastly cut short, and the means and inducements to virtue heaped one upon another, to so great a degree, all have proved insufficient, now for so many thousand years together, to restrain from wickedness in any considerable degree; innocent human nature, all along, coming into the world with the same purity and harmless dispositions that our first parents had in paradise. What vast disadvantages indeed then must Adam and Eve be in, that had no more in their nature to keep them from sin, or incline 'em to virtue, than their posterity, and yet were without all these additional and extraordinary means! Not only without such exceeding great means as we now have, when our lives are made so very short, but having vastly less advantages than their antediluvian posterity, who to prevent their being wicked and to make 'em good, had so much labor and toil, sweat and sorrow, briars and thorns, with a body gradually decaying and returning to the dust; when our first parents had the extreme disadvantage of being placed in the midst of so many and exceeding great temptations; not only without toil or sorrow, pain or disease, to humble and mortify 'em, and a sentence of death to wean 'em from the world, but in the midst of the most exquisite and alluring sensitive delights, the reverse in every respect, and to the highest degree of that most gracious state of requisite means, and great advantages, which mankind now enjoy! If mankind now under these vast restraints, and great advantages, are not restrained from general, and as it were universal wickedness, how could it be expected that Adam and Eve, created with no better hearts than men bring into the world now, and destitute of all these advantages, and in the midst of all contrary disadvantages, should escape it?

These things are not agreeable to Moses' account; which represents an happy state of peculiar favors and blessings before the fall, and the curse coming afterwards: but according to this scheme, the curse was before the fall, and the great favors and testimonies of love followed the apostacy. And the curse before the fall must be a curse with a witness, being to so high a degree the reverse of such means, means so necessary for such a creature as innocent man, and in all their multitude and fullness proving too little. Paradise therefore must be a mere delusion! There was indeed a great shew of favor, in placing man in the midst of such delights. But this delightful garden, it seems, with all its beauty and sweetness, was in its real tendency worse than the apples of Sodom. It was but a mere bait (God forbid the blasphemy) the more effectually enticing by its beauty and deliciousness, to Adam's eternal ruin: which might be the more expected to be fatal to him, seeing that he was the first man that ever existed, having no superiority of capacity to his posterity, and wholly without the advantage of the observations, experiences and improvements of preceding generations; which his posterity have.

I proceed now to take notice of an additional proof of the doctrine we are upon, from another part of the holy Scripture. A very clear text for original righteousness is that in Eccles. 7:29. "Lo, this only have I found, that God made man upright; but they have sought out many inventions."

It is an observation of no weight, which Dr. Taylor makes on this text, that the word "man" is commonly used to signify mankind in general, or mankind collectively taken. It is true, it often signifies the species of mankind: but then it is used to signify the species with regard to its duration and succession from its beginning, as well as with regard to its extent. The English word "mankind" is used to signify the species: but what if it be so? Would it be an improper or unintelligible way of speaking, to say, that when God first made mankind, he placed them in a pleasant paradise (meaning their first parents) but now they live in the midst of briars and thorns? And 'tis certain, that to speak of God's making mankind in such a meaning, viz. his giving the species an existence in their first parents, at the creation of the world, is agreeable to the Scripture use of such an expression. As in Deut. 4:32: "Since the day that God created man upon the earth." (Job 20:4), "Knowest thou not this of old, since man was placed upon the earth." (Is. 45:12), "I have made the earth, and created man upon it: I, even my hands, have stretched out the heavens." (Jer. 27:5), "I have made the earth, the man and the beast that are upon the ground, by my great power." All these texts speak of God's making man, by the word "man" signifying the species of mankind; and yet they all plainly have respect to God's making man at first, when God made the earth, and stretched out the heavens, and created the first parents of mankind. In all these places the same word "Adam" is used, as here in Ecclesiastes; and in the last of them, used with "he" *emphaticum,* as it is here; though Dr. Taylor omits it, when he tells us, he gives us a catalogue of all the places in Scripture, where the word is used. And it argues nothing to the doctor's purpose, that the pronoun "they" is used. "*They* have sought out many inventions." Which is properly applied to the species, which God made at first upright: God having begun the species with more than one, and it being continued in a multitude. As Christ speaks of the two sexes, in the relation of man and wife, as continued in successive generations. (Matt. 19:4), "He that made them at the beginning, made them male and female"; having reference to Adam and Eve.

No less impertinent, and also very unfair is his criticism on the word "jashar," translated "upright." Because the word sometimes signifies "right," he would from thence infer, that it don't properly signify a moral rectitude, even when used to express the character of moral agents. He might as well insist, that the English word "upright," sometimes, and in its most original meaning, signifying "right up," or in an erect posture, therefore it don't properly signify any moral character, when applied to moral agents: and indeed less unreasonably; for 'tis known, that in the Hebrew language, in a peculiar manner, most words used to signify moral and spiritual things, are taken from things external and natural. The word "jashar" is used, as applied to moral agents, or to the words and actions of such (if I have not mis-reckoned) [1] about 110 times in Scripture; and about an 100 of them, without all dispute, to signify virtue, or moral rectitude (though Dr. Taylor is pleased to say, the word don't generally signify a moral character); and for the most part it signifies *true virtue,* or virtue in such a sense, as distinguishes it from all false appearances of virtue, or what is only virtue in some respects, but not truly so in the sight of God. It is used at least 80 times in this sense. And scarce any word can be found in the Hebrew language more significant of this. It is thus used constantly in Solomon's writings (where 'tis often found) when used to express a character or property of moral agents. And it is beyond all controversy, that he uses it in this place in the 7th of Eccles. to signify a moral rectitude, or character of real virtue and integrity. For the wise man, in this context, is speaking of men with respect to their moral character, inquiring into the corruption and depravity of mankind (as is confessed, p. 184) and he here declares, he had not found more than one among a thousand, of the right stamp, truly and thoroughly virtuous and upright: which appeared a strange thing! But in this text he clears God, and lays the blame to man. Man was not made thus at first. He was made of the right stamp, altogether good in his kind (as all other things were), truly and thoroughly virtuous, as he ought to be; but "they have sought out many inventions." Which last expression signifies things sinful, or morally evil; as is confessed (p. 185). And this expression, used to signify those moral evils he found in man, which he sets in opposition to the uprightness man was made in, shews, that by "uprightness" he means the most true and sincere goodness. The word rendered "inventions" most naturally and aptly signifies the subtil devices, and crooked and deceitful ways of hypocrites, wherein they are of a character contrary to men of simplicity and godly sincerity; who, though wise in that which is good, are simple concerning evil. Thus the same wise man in Prov. 12:2 sets a truly good man in opposition to a man of wicked devices, whom God will condemn. Solomon had occasion to observe many who put on an artful disguise and fair shew of goodness; but on searching thoroughly, he found very few truly upright. As he says (Prov. 20:6), "Most men will proclaim every one his own goodness, but a faithful man who can find?" So that it is exceeding plain, that

1. Making use of Buxtorf's *Concordance,* which according to the author's professed design, directs to all the places where the word is used.

by "uprightness," in this place in Ecclesiastes, Solomon means true moral goodness.

What our author urges concerning many inventions being spoken of, whereas Adam's eating the forbidden fruit was but one invention, is of as little weight as the rest of what he says on this text. For the many lusts and corruptions of mankind, appearing in innumerable ways of sinning, are all the consequences of that sin. The great corruption men are fallen into by the original apostacy, appears in the multitude of wicked ways they are inclined to. And therefore these are properly mentioned as the fruits and evidences of the greatness of that apostacy and corruption.

SECTION 2. CONCERNING THE KIND OF DEATH, THREATENED TO OUR FIRST PARENTS, IF THEY SHOULD EAT OF THE FORBIDDEN FRUIT

DR. TAYLOR in his observations on the three first chapters of Genesis, says (p. 7), "The threatening to man in case of transgression was, that he should surely die. . . . Death is the losing of life. Death is opposed to life, and must be understood according to the nature of that life, to which it is opposed. Now the death here threatened can, with any certainty, be opposed only to the life God gave Adam, when he created him (v. 7). Anything besides this must be pure conjecture, without solid foundation."

To this I would say, 'tis true, "death is opposed to life, and must be understood according to the nature of that life, to which it is opposed"; but does it therefore follow, that nothing can be meant by it but the *loss* of life? Misery is opposed to happiness, and sorrow is in Scripture often opposed to joy: but can we conclude from thence, that nothing is meant in Scripture by sorrow, but the loss of joy? Or that there is no more in misery, than the loss or absence of happiness? And if it be so, that the death threatened to Adam can, with certainty, be opposed only to the life given to Adam, when God created him; I think, a state of perfect, perpetual and hopeless misery is properly opposed to that state Adam was in, when God created him. For I suppose, it won't be denied, that the life Adam had, was truly a happy life; happy in perfect innocency, in the favor of his Maker, surrounded with the happy fruits and testimonies of his love: and I think it has been proved, that he also was happy in a state of perfect righteousness. And nothing is more manifest, than that it is agreeable to a very common acceptation of the word "life" in Scripture, that it be understood as signifying a state of excellent and happy existence. Now that which is most opposite to that life and state Adam was created in, is a state of total confirmed wickedness, and perfect hopeless misery, under the divine displeasure and curse; not excluding temporal death or the destruction of the body, as an introduction to it.

And besides, that which is much more evident, than anything Dr.

Taylor says on this head, is this, viz. that the death, which was to come on Adam as the *punishment of his disobedience,* was opposed to that life which he would have had as the reward of his *obedience,* in case he had not sinned. *Obedience* and *disobedience* are contraries; and the threatenings and promises, that are sanctions of a law, are set in direct opposition: and the promised rewards, and threatened punishments, are what are most properly taken as each other's opposites. But none will deny, that the life which would have been Adam's reward, if he had persisted in obedience, was eternal life. And therefore we argue justly, that the death which "stands opposed to that life" (Dr. Taylor himself being judge, p. 396) "is manifestly eternal death, a death widely different from the death we now die," to use his own words. If Adam, for his persevering obedience, was to have had everlasting life and happiness, in perfect holiness, union with his Maker, and enjoyment of his favor, and this was the life which was to be confirmed by the tree of life; then doubtless the death threatened in case of disobedience, which stands in direct opposition to this, was a being given over to everlasting wickedness and misery, in separation from God and in enduring his wrath.

And it may with the greatest reason be supposed, that when God first made mankind, and made known to them the methods of his moral government towards them, in the revelation he made of himself to the natural head of the whole species; and let him know, that obedience to him was expected as his duty, and enforced this duty with the sanction of a threatened punishment, called by the name of *death;* I say, we may with the greatest reason suppose in such a case, that by death was meant that same death which God esteemed to be the most proper punishment of the sin of mankind, and which he speaks of under that name, throughout the Scripture, as the proper wages of the sin of man, and was always from the beginning understood to be so in the church of God. It would be strange indeed, if it should be otherwise. It would have been strange, if when the law of God was first given, and enforced by the threatening of a punishment, nothing at all had been mentioned of that great punishment, ever spoken of under the name of death (in the revelations which he has given to mankind from age to age) as the proper punishment of the sin of mankind. And it would be no less strange, if when the punishment which was mentioned and threatened on that occasion was called by the same name, even death, yet we must not understand it to mean the same thing, but something infinitely diverse, and infinitely more inconsiderable.

But now, let us consider what that death is, which the Scripture ever speaks of as the proper wages of the sin of mankind, and is spoken of as such by God's saints in all ages of the church, from the first beginning of a written revelation, to the conclusion of it. I'll begin with the New Testament. When the apostle Paul says (Rom. 6:23), "The wages of sin is death," Dr. Taylor tells us (p. 396) that "this means eternal death, the second death, a death widely different from the death we now die." The same Apostle speaks of death as the proper punishment due for sin (in Rom. 7:5 and 8:13; II Cor. 3:7; I Cor. 15:56). In all which places, Dr. Taylor himself supposes the Apostle to intend eternal death.[1] And when the apostle James speaks of death, as the proper reward, fruit and end of sin (Jas. 1:15), "Sin, when it is finished, bringeth forth death," 'tis manifest, that our author supposes eternal destruction to be meant.[2] And the apostle John, agreeable to Dr. Taylor's sense, speaks of the second death, as that which sin unrepented of will bring all men to at last (Rev. 20:6,14 and 21:8 and 2:11). In the same sense the apostle John uses the word in his first epistle (ch. 3:14), "We know, that we have passed from death to life, because we love the brethren: he that hateth his brother, abideth in death." In the same manner Christ used the word from time to time, when he was on earth, and spake concerning the punishment and issue of sin. (John 5:24), "He that heareth my word, and believeth . . . hath everlasting life; and shall not come into condemnation: but is passed from death unto life." Where, according to Dr. Taylor's own way of arguing, it can't be the death which we now die, that Christ speaks of, but eternal death, because it is set in opposition to everlasting life. (John 6:50), "This is the bread which cometh down from heaven, that a man may eat thereof, and not die." (ch. 8:51), "Verily, verily, I say unto you, if a man keep my saying, he shall never see death." (ch. 11:26), "And whosoever liveth and believeth in me, shall never die." In which places 'tis plain, Christ don't mean that believers shall never see temporal death. (See also Matt. 10:29 and Luke 10:28). In like

1. See p. 78 *Note on Rom.* 7:5 and note on v. 6. *Note on Rom.* 5:20, 7:8.

2. By comparing what he says (p. 126) with what he often says of that death and destruction which is the demerit and end of personal sin, which he says is the *second death,* or *eternal destruction.*

manner, the word was commonly used by the prophets of old, when they spake of death as the proper end and recompense of sin. So, abundantly by the prophet Ezekiel (Ezek. 3:18), "When I say unto the wicked man, thou shalt surely die." In the original, "dying thou shalt die."—The same form of expression, which God used in the threatening to Adam. We have the same words again (ch. 33:18). In ch. 18:4 it is said, "The soul that sinneth, it shall die." To the like purpose are ch. 3:19,20 and 18:4,5,10,14,17,18,19,20,21,24,26,28; ch. 33:8,9,12,13,14,19,20. And that temporal death is not meant in these places, is plain, because it is promised most absolutely that the righteous shall not die the death spoken of (ch. 17:21), "He shall surely live, he shall not die." (So, vv. 9, 17, 19 and 22 and ch. 3:21.) And 'tis evident, the prophet Jeremiah uses the word in the same sense. (Jer. 31:30), "Every one shall die for his own iniquity." And the same death is spoken of by the prophet Isaiah. (Is. 11:4), "With the breath of his lips shall he slay the wicked." (See also ch. 61:16 with v. 24). Solomon, who we must suppose was thoroughly acquainted with the sense in which the word was used by the wise, and by the ancients, continually speaks of death as the proper fruit, issue and recompense of sin, using the word only in this sense. (ch. 11:19), "As righteousness tendeth to life, so he that pursueth evil, pursueth it to his own death." (So ch. 18:32; 10:21; 14:12; 19:16; 1:18,32; 5:5,6,23; 7:22,26,27; 9:18; 11:19; 15:10; 18:21; 21:16 and 23:13,14) In these places he cannot mean temporal death; for he often speaks of it as a punishment of the wicked, wherein the righteous shall certainly be distinguished from 'em: as in Prov. 12:28, "In the way of righteousness is life, and in the pathway thereof is no death." (So in ch. 10:2, 11:4; 13:14; 14:27 and many other places.) But we find, this same wise man observes, that as to temporal death, and temporal events in general, there is no distinction, but that they happen alike to good and bad. (Eccles. 2:14,15,16; 8:14 and 9:2,3) His words are remarkable in Eccles. 7:15: "There is a just man that perisheth in his righteousness; and there is a wicked man that prolongeth his life in his wickedness." So we find David in the book of Psalms uses the word "death" in the same sense, when he speaks of it as the proper wages and issue of sin. (Ps. 34:21), "Evil shall slay the wicked." He speaks of it as a certain thing. (Ps. 139:19), "Surely thou wilt slay the wicked, O God." And he speaks of it as a thing wherein the wicked are distinguished from the righteous. (Ps. 69:28), "Let them be blotted out of the book of the living, and not be written with the righteous." And thus we find the word "death" used in the Pentateuch, or books of Moses: in which part of the Scripture it is, that we have the account of the threatening of death to Adam. When death, in these books, is spoken of as the proper fruit and appointed reward of sin, it is to be understood of eternal death. (So, Deut. 30:15), "See, I have set before thee this day, life and good, and death and evil." (v. 19), "I call heaven and earth to record this day against you, that I have set before you life and death, blessing and cursing." The life that is spoken of here, is doubtless the same that is spoken of in Lev. 18:5, "Ye shall therefore keep my statutes and my judgments, which if a man do, he shall live in them." This the Apostle understands of eternal life; as is plain by Rom. 10:5 and Gal. 3:12—but that the death threatened for sin in the law of Moses meant eternal death, is what Dr. Taylor abundantly declares. (So in his *Note on Rom.* 5:20), "Such a constitution the law of Moses was, subjecting those who were under it to death for every transgression; meaning by death *eternal death.*" These are his words. The like he asserts in many other places. When it is said, in the place now mentioned, "I have set before thee life and death, blessing and cursing," without doubt, the same blessing and cursing is meant which God had already set before them with such solemnity, in the 27th and 28th chapters [Deut.]; where we have the sum of the curses in those last words of the 27th chapter, "Cursed is everyone, which confirmeth not all the words of this law to do them." Which the Apostle speaks of as a threatening of eternal death; and with him Dr. Taylor himself.[3] In this sense also Job and his friends, spake of death, as the wages and end of sin, who lived before any written revelation, and had their religion and their phraseology about the things of religion from the ancients.

If any should insist upon it as an objection against supposing that death was intended to signify eternal death in the threatening to Adam, that this use of the word is figurative: though this should be allowed, yet it is by no means so figurative as many other phrases used in the history contained in these three chapters: as when it is said, "God said, 'Let there be light'; God said, 'Let there be a firmament,' " etc. as though God spake such words with a voice. So when it is said, "God called the light, day: God called the firma-

3. *Note on Rom.* 5:20 in his exposition pp. 371, 373, 374, 376. There on p. 371 he says expressly, the law of Moses subjected those who were under it to death, meaning by "death" eternal death.

ment, heaven, etc., God rested on the seventh day": as though he had been weary, and then rested. And when it is said, "they heard the voice of God walking"; as though the deity had two feet, and took steps on the ground. Dr. Taylor supposes, that when it is said of Adam and Eve, "Their eyes were opened, and they saw that they were naked"; by the word "naked" is meant a state of guilt (p. 12). Which sense of the word "naked" is much further from the common use of the word, than the supposed sense of the word "death." So this author supposes the promise concerning the seed of the woman's bruising the serpent's head, while the serpent should bruise his heel, is to be understood as the "Messiah's destroying the power and sovereignty of the devil, and receiving some slight hurt from him" (pp. 15, 16). Which makes the sentence full of figures, vastly more beside the common use of words. And why might not God deliver threatenings to our first parents in figurative expressions, as well as promises? Many other strong figures are used in these chapters.

But indeed, there is no necessity of supposing the word "death," or the Hebrew word so translated, if used in the manner that has been supposed, to have been figurative at all. It does not appear but that this word, in its true and proper meaning, might signify perfect misery, and sensible destruction; though the word was also applied to signify something more external and visible. There are many words in our language, such as "heart," "sense," "view," "discovery," "conception," "light," and many others, which are applied to signify external things, as that muscular part of the body called "heart"; external feeling called "sense"; the sight of the bodily eye called "view"; the finding of a thing by its being uncovered, called "discovery"; the first beginning of the foetus in the womb, called "conception"; and the rays of the sun, called "light"; yet these words do as truly and properly signify other things of a more spiritual internal nature, as those: such as the disposition, affection, perception and thought of the mind, and manifestation and evidence to the soul. Common use, which governs the propriety of language, makes the latter things to be as much signified by those words, in their proper meaning, as the former. 'Tis especially common in the Hebrew, and I suppose, other Oriental languages, that the same word that signifies something external, does no less properly and usually signify something more spiritual. So the Hebrew words used for "breath," have such a double signification; "Neshama" signifies both "breath" and the "soul"; and the latter as commonly as the former: "ruach" is used for "breath" or "wind," but yet more commonly signifies "spirit." "Nephesh" is used for "breath," but yet more commonly signifies "soul." So the word "lébh," "heart" no less properly signifies the "soul," especially with regard to the will and affections, than that part of the body so called. The word "shalom," which we render "peace," no less properly signifies prosperity and happiness, than mutual agreement. The word translated "life" signifies the natural life of the body, and also the perfect and happy state of sensible active being; and the latter as properly as the former. So the word "death" signifies "destruction," as to outward sensibility, activity and enjoyment: but it has most evidently another signification, which, in the Hebrew tongue, is no less proper, viz. "perfect, sensible, hopeless ruin and misery."

'Tis therefore wholly without reason urged that death properly signifies only the loss of this present life: and that therefore nothing else was meant by that death which was threatened for eating the forbidden fruit. Nor does it at all appear but that Adam, who from what God said concerning the seed of the woman, that was so very figurative, could understand, that relief was promised, as to the death which was threatened (as Dr. Taylor himself supposes, p. 18), understood the death that was threatened, in the more important sense; especially seeing temporal death, as it is originally, and in itself, and is evermore, excepting as changed by divine grace, an introduction or entrance into that gloomy dismal state of misery, which is shadowed forth by the dark and awful circumstances of this death, naturally suggesting to the mind the most dreadful state of hopeless, sensible ruin.

As to that objection which some have made, that the phrase, "dying thou shalt die," is several times used in the books of Moses to signify temporal death, it can be of no force. For it has been shewn already, that the same phrase is sometimes used in Scripture to signify eternal death, in instances much more parallel with this. But indeed nothing can be certainly argued concerning the nature of the thing intended, from its being expressed in such a manner. For 'tis evident, that such repetitions of a word in the Hebrew language, are no more than an emphasis upon a word in the more modern languages, to signify the great degree of a thing, the importance of it, or the certainty of it, etc. When we would signify and impress these, we commonly put an emphasis on our words: instead of this, the Hebrews, when they would express a thing strongly, repeated or doubled the word, the more to impress the mind of the hearer; as may be plain to everyone in the least conversant with the Hebrew Bible. The repetition in the threatening to Adam, therefore only implies the solemnity, and importance of the threatening. But God may denounce either eternal or temporal death with peremptoriness and solemnity, and nothing can certainly be inferred concerning the nature of the thing threatened, because 'tis threatened with emphasis, more than this, that the threatening is much to be regarded. Though it be true, that it might in an especial manner be expected that a threatening of eternal death, would be denounced with great emphasis, such a threatening being infinitely important, and to be regarded above all others.

SECTION 3. WHEREIN IT IS INQUIRED, WHETHER THERE BE ANYTHING IN THE HISTORY OF THE THREE FIRST CHAPTERS OF GENESIS, WHICH SHOULD LEAD US TO SUPPOSE, THAT GOD, IN HIS CONSTITUTION WITH ADAM, DEALT WITH MANKIND IN GENERAL, AS INCLUDED IN THEIR FIRST FATHER, AND THAT THE THREATENING OF DEATH, IN CASE HE SHOULD EAT THE FORBIDDEN FRUIT, HAD RESPECT NOT ONLY TO HIM, BUT HIS POSTERITY?

DR. TAYLOR, rehearsing that threatening to Adam, "Thou shalt surely die," and giving us his paraphrase of it (pp. 7, 8), concludes thus; "Observe, here is not one word relating to Adam's posterity." But it may be observed in opposition to this, that there is scarcely *one word* that we have an account of, which God ever said to Adam or Eve, but what does manifestly include their posterity in the meaning and design of it. There is as much of a word said about Adam's posterity in that threatening, as there is in those words of God to Adam and Eve (Gen. 1:28), "Be fruitful, and multiply, and replenish the earth, and subdue it"; and as much in events, to lead us to suppose Adam's posterity to be included. There is as much of a word of his posterity in that threatening, as in those words (v. 29): "Behold, I have given you every herb bearing seed . . . and every tree in which is the fruit of a tree yielding seed," etc. Even when God was about to create Adam, what he said on that occasion, had not respect only to Adam, but to his posterity (Gen. 1:26), "Let us make man in our image, and let them have dominion over the fish of the sea," etc. And, what is more remarkable, there is as much of a word said about Adam's posterity in the threatening of death, as there is in that sentence (Gen. 3:19), "Unto dust shalt thou return." Which Dr. Taylor himself supposes to be a sentence pronounced for the execution of that very threatening, "Thou shalt surely die": and which sentence he himself also often speaks of as including Adam's posterity. And, what is much more remarkable still, is a sentence which Dr. Taylor himself often speaks of, as including his posterity, as a sentence of condemnation, as a judicial sentence, and a sentence which God pronounced with regard to Adam's *posterity, acting the part of a judge,* and as such condemning them to temporal death. Though he is therein utterly inconsistent with himself, inasmuch as he at the same time abundantly insists, that death is not brought on Adam's posterity, in consequence of his sin, at all as a punishment; but merely by the gracious disposal of a father, bestowing a benefit of the highest nature upon them.[1]

But I shall shew that I don't in any of these things falsely charge, or misrepresent Dr. Taylor. He speaks of the sentence in ch. 3:19 as pronounced in pursuance of the threatening in the former chapter, in these words (pp. 17, 18): "The sentence upon the man, v. 17, 18, 19, first affects the earth, upon which he was to subsist: the ground should be incumbered with many noxious weeds, and the tillage of it more toilsome: which would oblige man to procure a sustenance by hard labour, till he should die, and drop into the ground, from whence he was taken. Thus death entered by sin into the world, and man became mortal, *according to the threatning in the former chapter.*" Now, if mankind becomes mortal, and must die, according to the threatening in the former chapter, then doubtless the threatening in the former chapter, "Thou shalt die," had respect not only to Adam, but to mankind, and included Adam's posterity. Yea, and Dr. Taylor is express in it, and very often so, that the sentence concerning dropping into the ground, or returning to the dust, did include Adam's posterity. So, pp. 19, 20, speaking there of that sentence, "Observe," says he, "that we their posterity are in fact subjected to the same affliction and mortality, here by sentence inflicted upon our first parents" (p. 42). "But yet men, through that long tract, were all subject to death, therefore they must be included in the sentence." The same he affirms in innumerable other places, some of which I shall have occasion to mention presently.

The sentence which is founded on the threatening, and (as Dr. Taylor says), "according to the threatening," extends to as many as were included in the threatening, and to no more. If the sentence be upon a collective subject, infinitely, as it were, the greatest part of which were not included in the threatening, nor were ever threatened at all by any threatening whatsoever, then certainly this sentence is not *according to the threatening,* nor built upon it. If the sentence be according to the threatening, then we may justly explain the threatening by the sentence: and if we find the sentence spoken to the same person, to whom the threatening was spoken, and spo-

1. P. 303.

ken in the second person singular, in like manner with the threatening, and *founded on* the threatening, and *according to* the threatening; and if we find the sentence includes Adam's posterity; then we may certainly infer, that so did the threatening: and hence, that both the threatening and sentence were delivered to Adam as the public head and representative of his posterity.

And we may also further infer from it, in another respect directly contrary to Dr. Taylor's doctrine, that the sentence which included Adam's posterity, was to death as a punishment to that posterity, as well as to Adam himself. For a sentence pronounced in execution of a threatening, is to a punishment. Threatenings are of punishments. Neither God nor man are wont to threaten others with favors and benefits.

But lest any of this author's admirers should stand to it, that it may very properly be said, God *threatened* mankind with bestowing great kindness upon them, I would observe, that Dr. Taylor often speaks of this sentence as pronounced by God on all mankind as condemning them, speaks of it as a sentence of condemnation judicially pronounced, or a sentence which God pronounced on all mankind acting as their judge, and in a judicial proceeding: which he affirms in multitudes of places. In p. 20 speaking of this sentence, which he there says, subjects us, Adam's and Eve's posterity, to affliction and mortality, he calls it a judicial act of condemnation. "The judicial act of condemnation," says he, "clearly implies, a taking him to pieces, and turning him to the ground, from whence he was taken." And pp. 28, 29, "In all the Scripture, from one end to the other, there is recorded but one judgment to condemnation, which came upon all men, and that is, Gen. 3:17,18,19. 'Dust thou art.' " P. 40, speaking of the same, he says, "All men are brought under condemnation." In pp. 27, 28, "By judgment, *judgment of condemnation,* it appeareth evidently to me, he (Paul) means the being adjudged to the forementioned death; he means the sentence of death, of a general mortality, pronounced upon mankind, in consequence of Adam's first transgression. And the condemnation inflicted by the judgment of God, answereth to, and is in effect the same thing with, being dead." (p. 30), "The many, that is mankind, were subject to death by the *judicial act* of God." (p. 31), "Being made sinners, may very well signify, being *adjudged,* or *condemned* to death . . . for the Hebrew word, etc. signifies to make one a sinner by a judicial sentence, or to condemn." (paraphrase on Rom. 5:19 in his Exp. of the epistle), "Upon the account of one man's disobedience, mankind were judicially constituted sinners; that is, subjected to death, by the sentence of God the judge." And there are many other places where he repeats the same thing. And 'tis pretty remarkable, that in pp. 48, 49, immediately after citing Prov. 17:15, "He that justifieth the wicked, and he that condemneth the just, are both an abomination to the Lord"; and when he is careful in citing these words, to put us in mind, that it is meant of a judicial act; yet in the very next words, he supposes that God himself does so, since he constantly supposes that Adam's posterity whom God condemns, are innocent. His words are these, "From all which it followeth, that the judgment, that passed upon all men to condemnation, is death's coming upon all men, by the judicial act of God, upon occasion of Adam's transgression." And 'tis very remarkable, that in pp. 279, 280, and 283 he insists, "That in Scripture no action is said to be imputed, reckon'd or accounted to any person, either for righteousness or condemnation, but the proper act and deed of that person." And yet he thus continually affirms, that all mankind are made sinners by a judicial act of God the judge, even to condemnation, and judicially constituted sinners, and so subjected to a judicial sentence of condemnation, on occasion of Adam's sin; and all according to the threatening denounced to Adam, "Thou shalt surely die." Though he supposes Adam's posterity were not included in the threatening, and are looked upon as perfectly innocent, and treated wholly as such.

I am sensible, Dr. Taylor don't run into all this inconsistence, only through oversight and blundering; but that he is driven to it, to make out his matters in his evasion of that noted paragraph in the fifth chapter of Romans; especially those three sentences (v. 16), "The judgment was by one to condemnation," (v. 18), "By the offense of one, judgment to condemnation came upon all men," and (v. 19), "By one man's disobedience many were made sinners." And I am also sensible of what he offers to salve the inconvenience, viz. "That if the threatening had immediately been executed on Adam, he would have had no posterity; and that so far the possible existence of Adam's posterity fell under the threatening of the law, and into the hands of the judge, to be disposed of as he should think fit: and that this is the ground of the judgment to condemnation, coming upon all men." [2] But this is trifling, to a great degree: For,

1. Suffering death and failing of possible existence, are entirely

2. Pp. 95, 366, 367. [JE's free paraphrase of last clause.]

different things. If there had never been any such thing as sin committed, there would have been infinite numbers of possible beings, which would have failed of existence, by God's appointment. God has appointed not to bring into existence numberless possible worlds, each replenished with innumerable possible inhabitants. But is this equivalent to God's appointing them all to suffer death?

2. Our author represents, that by Adam's sin the possible existence of his posterity fell into the hands of the Judge, to be disposed of as he should think fit. But there was no need of any sin of Adam's or anybody else's, in order to their being brought into God's hands in this respect. The future possible existence of all created beings, is in God's hands, antecedently to the existence of any sin. And therefore by God's sovereign appointment, infinite numbers of possible beings, without any relation to Adam, or any other sinning being, do fail of their possible existence. And if Adam had never sinned, yet it would be unreasonable to suppose, but that innumerable of his possible posterity, would have failed of existence by God's disposal. For will any be so unreasonable as to imagine, that God would and must have brought into existence as many of his posterity as it was possible should be, if he had not sinned? Or that in that case, it would not have been possible, any other persons of his posterity should ever have existed, than those individual persons, who now actually fall under that sentence of suffering death, and returning to the dust?

3. We have many accounts in Scripture, which imply the actual failing of the possible existence of innumerable multitudes of Adam's posterity, yea, of many more than ever come into existence. As, of the possible posterity of Abel, the possible posterity of all them that were destroyed by the flood, and the possible posterity of the innumerable multitudes, which we read of in Scripture, destroyed by sword, pestilence, etc. And if the threatening to Adam reached his posterity, in no other respect than this, that they were liable to be deprived by it of their possible existence, then these instances are much more properly a fulfillment of that threatening, than the suffering of death by such as actually come into existence; and so is that which is most properly the judgment to condemnation, executed by the sentence of the Judge, proceeding on the foot of that threatening. But where do we ever find this so represented in Scripture? We read of multitudes cut off for their personal sins, who thereby failed of their possible posterity. And these are mentioned as

God's judgments on them, and effects of God's condemnation of them: but when are they ever spoken of as God's judicially proceeding against, and condemning their possible posterity?

4. Dr. Taylor, in what he says concerning this matter, speaks of the threatening of the law delivered to Adam, which the possible existence of his posterity fell under, as the ground of the judgment to condemnation coming upon all men. But herein he is exceeding inconsistent with himself: for he affirms in a place forecited, that the Scripture never speaks of any sentence of condemnation coming upon all men, but that sentence in the third of Genesis, concerning man's turning to dust. But according to him, the threatening of the law delivered to Adam, could not be the ground of that sentence; for he greatly insists upon it, that the law was entirely abrogated before that sentence was pronounced, that this law at that time was not in being, had no existence to have any such influence, as might procure a sentence of death; and that therefore this sentence was introduced entirely on another foot, viz. on the foot of a new dispensation of grace. The reader may see this matter strenuously urged, and particularly argued by him, pp. 389–396. So that this sentence could not, according to him, have the threatening of that law for its ground, as he supposes; for it never stood upon that ground. It could not be called a judgment of condemnation, under any such view; for it could not be viewed under circumstances, under which it never existed.

5. If it be as our author supposes, that the sentence of death on all men comes under the notion of a judgment to condemnation by this means, viz. that the threatening to Adam was in some respect the ground of it; then it also comes under the notion of a punishment: for threatenings annexed to breaches of laws, are to punishments; and a judgment of condemnation, to the thing threatened, must be to punishment; and the thing condemned to, must have as much the notion of a punishment, as the sentence has the notion of a judgment to condemnation. But this Dr. Taylor wholly denies: he denies that the death sentenced to, comes as any punishment at all; but insists that it comes only as a favor and benefit, and a fruit of fatherly love to Adam's posterity, respected not as guilty, but wholly innocent. So that his scheme will not admit of its coming under the notion of a sentence to condemnation in any respect whatsoever. Our author's supposition, that the possible existence of Adam's posterity comes under the threatening of the law, and into the hands of

the Judge, and is the ground of the condemnation of all men to death, implies that death by this sentence is appointed to mankind as an evil, at least, negatively so; as it is a privation of good: for he manifestly speaks of a non-existence as a negative evil. But herein he is inconsistent with himself: for he continually insists, that mankind are subjected to death only as a benefit, as has been before shewn. According to him, death is not appointed to mankind as a negative evil, as any cessation of existence, as any cessation or even diminution of good; but on the contrary, as a means of a more happy existence, and a great increase of good.

So that this evasion, or salvo of Dr. Taylor's is so far from helping the matter, or salving the inconsistence, that it increases and multiplies it.

And that the constitution or law, with the threatening of death annexed, which was given to Adam, was to him as the head of mankind, and to his posterity as included in him, not only follows from some of our author's own assertions, and the plain and full declarations of the Apostle in the fifth of Romans (of which more afterwards) which drove Dr. Taylor into such gross inconsistencies. But the account given in the three first chapters of Genesis, directly and inevitably leads us to such a conclusion.

Though the sentence (Gen. 3:19), "Unto dust thou shalt return," be not of equal extent with the threatening in the foregoing chapter, or an execution of the main curse of the law therein denounced; for, that it should have been so, would have been inconsistent with the intimations of mercy just before given: yet 'tis plain, this sentence is in pursuance of that threatening, being to something that was included in it. The words of the sentence were delivered to the same person, with the words of the threatening, and in the same manner, in like singular terms, as much without any express mention of his posterity: and yet it manifestly appears by the consequence, as well as all circumstances, that his posterity were included in the words of the sentence; as is confessed on all hands. And as the words were apparently delivered in the form of the sentence of a judge, condemning for something that he was displeased with, and ought to be condemned, viz. sin; and as the sentence to him and his posterity was but one, dooming to the same suffering, under the same circumstances, both the one and the other sentenced in the same words, spoken but once, and immediately to but one person, we hence justly infer, that it was the same thing to both; and not as Dr. Taylor suggests (p. 67) a sentence to a proper punishment to Adam, but a mere promise of favor to his posterity.

Indeed, sometimes our author seems to suppose, that God meant the thing denounced in this sentence, as a favor both to Adam and his posterity.[3] But to his posterity, or mankind in general, who are the main subject, he ever insists, that it was purely intended as a favor. And therefore, one would have thought, the sentence should have been delivered, with manifestations and appearances of favor, and not of anger. How could Adam understand it as a promise of great favor, considering the manner and circumstances of the denunciation? How could he think that God would go about to delude him, by clothing himself with garments of vengeance, using words of displeasure and rebuke, setting forth the heinousness of his crime, attended with cherubims and the flaming sword; when all that he meant was only higher testimonies of favor than he had before in a state of innocence, and to manifest fatherly love and kindness, in promises of great blessings? If this was the case, God's words to Adam must be understood thus: "Because thou hast done so wickedly, hast hearkened unto the voice of thy wife, and hast eaten of the tree of which I commanded thee, saying, thou shalt not eat of it; therefore I will be more kind to thee than I was in thy state of innocence, and do now appoint for thee the following great favors: cursed be the ground for thy sake, etc." And thus Adam must understand what was said; unless any will say (and God forbid that any should be so blasphemous) that God clothed himself with appearances of displeasure, to deceive Adam, and make him believe the contrary of what he intended, and lead him to expect a dismal train of evils on his posterity, contrary to all reason and justice, implying the most horribly unrighteous treatment of millions of perfectly innocent creatures! 'Tis certain, there is not the least appearance in what God said, or the manner of it, as Moses gives us the account, of any other, than that God was now testifying displeasure, condemning the subject of the sentence he was pronouncing, as justly exposed to punishment for sin, and for that sin which he mentions.

When God was pronouncing this sentence, Adam doubtless understood, that God had respect to his posterity, as well as himself; though God spake wholly in the second person singular, "Because thou hast eaten. . . . In sorrow shalt thou eat. . . . Unto the dust shalt thou return." But he had as much reason to understand God as

3. Pp. 301, 321, 322.

having respect to his posterity, when he directed his speech to him in like manner in the threatening, "Thou shalt surely die." The sentence plainly refers to the threatening, and results from it. The threatening says, "If thou eat, thou shalt die": the sentence says, "Because thou hast eaten, thou shalt die." And Moses, who wrote the account, had no reason to doubt but that the affair would be thus understood by his readers; for such a way of speaking was well understood in those days: the history he gives us of the origin of things, abounds with it. Such a manner of speaking to the first of the kind, or heads of the race, having respect to the progeny, is not only used in almost everything that God said to Adam and Eve, but even in what he said to the very birds and fishes (Gen. 1:22). And also in what he said afterwards to Noah (Gen. 9), and to Shem, Ham, and Japheth, and Canaan (Gen. 9:25,26,27). So in promises made to Abraham, in which God directed his speech to him, and spake in the second person singular, from time to time, but meant chiefly his posterity: "To thee will I give this land. In thee shall all the families of the earth be blessed, etc. etc." And in what is said of Ishmael, as of his person, but meant chiefly of his posterity (Gen. 6:12 and 17:20). And so in what Isaac said to Esau and Jacob, in his blessing; in which he spake to them in the second person singular; but meant chiefly their posterity. And so for the most part in the promises made to Isaac and Jacob; and in Jacob's blessing of Ephraim and Manasseh, and of his twelve sons.

But I shall take notice of one or two things further shewing that Adam's posterity were included in God's establishment with him, and the threatening denounced for his sin; and that the calamities which come upon them in consequence of his sin, are brought on them as punishments.

This is evident from the *curse on the ground;* which if it be any curse at all comes equally on Adam's posterity with himself. And if it be a curse, then against whomsoever it is designed, and on whomsoever it terminates, it comes as a punishment, and not as a blessing, so far as it comes in consequence of that sentence.

Dr. Taylor (p. 19) says, "A curse is pronounced upon the ground, but no curse upon the woman and the man." And in pp. 321, 322 he insists, that the ground only was cursed, and not the man: just as though a curse could terminate on lifeless, senseless earth! To understand this curse otherwise than as terminating upon man, through the ground, would be as senseless as to suppose the meaning to be "The ground shall be punished, and shall be miserable for thy sake." Our author interprets the curse on the ground, of its being encumbered with noxious weeds: but would these weeds have been any curse on the ground, if there had been no inhabitants, or if the inhabitants had been of such a nature, that these weeds should not have been noxious, but useful to 'em? It is said (Deut. 28:17), "Cursed shall be thy basket and thy store": and would he not be thought to talk very ridiculously, who should say, "Here is a curse upon the basket; but not a word of any curse upon the owner": and therefore we have no reason at all to look upon it as any punishment upon him, or any testimony of God's displeasure towards him! How plain is it, that when lifeless things, which are not capable of either benefit or suffering, are said to be cursed or blessed with regard to sensible beings, that use or possess these things, or have connection with them, the meaning must be, that these sensible beings are cursed or blessed in the other, or with respect to them? In Ex. 23:25 'tis said, "He shall bless thy bread and thy water." And I suppose, never anybody yet proceeded to such a degree of subtlety in distinguishing, as to say, "Here is a blessing on the bread and the water, which went into the possessors' mouths, but no blessing on them." To make such a distinction with regard to the curse God pronounced on the ground, would in some respects be more unreasonable, because God is express in explaining the matter, declaring that it was *for man's sake,* expressly referring this curse to *him,* as being with respect to him, and for the sake of his guilt; and as consisting in the sorrow and suffering he should have from it: "In sorrow shalt thou eat of it . . . thorns and thistles shall it bring forth to thee." So that God's own words tell us where the curse terminates. The words are parallel with those in Deut. 28:16, but only more plain and explicit, "Cursed shalt *thou* be in the field" or in the ground.

If this part of the sentence was pronounced under no notion of any curse or punishment at all upon mankind, but on the contrary, as making an alteration in the ground, that should be for the better, as to them; that instead of the sweet, but tempting, pernicious fruits of paradise, it might produce wholesome fruits, more for the health of the soul; that it might bring forth thorns and thistles, as excellent medicines, to prevent or cure mortal distempers, diseases which would issue in eternal death; I say, if what was pronounced was under this notion, then it was a blesssing on the ground, and not a curse; and it might more properly have been said, "*Blessed* shall the ground be for thy sake—I will make a happy change in it, that it may be a habitation more fit for a creature so infirm, and so apt to be overcome with temptation, as thou art."

The event makes it evident, that in pronouncing this curse, God had as much respect to Adam's posterity, as to himself: and so it was understood by his pious posterity, before the flood; as appears by what Lamech, the father of Noah, says (Gen. 5:29), "And he called his name Noah; saying 'This same shall comfort us concerning our work, and the toil of our hands, because of the ground which the Lord hath cursed.' "

Another thing which argues that Adam's posterity were included in the threatening of death, and that our first parents understood, when fallen, that the tempter, in persuading them to eat the forbidden fruit, had aimed at the punishment and ruin of both them and their posterity, and had procured it, is Adam's immediately giving his wife that new name, Eve, or Life, on the promise or intimation of the disappointment and overthrow of the tempter in that matter, by her seed; which Adam understood to be by his procuring life; not only for themselves, but for many of their posterity, and thereby delivering them from that death and ruin which the serpent had brought upon them. Those that should be thus delivered, and obtain life, Adam calls *the living:* and because he observed, by what God had said, that deliverance and life was to be by the seed of the woman, he therefore remarks, that "she is the mother of all living," and thereupon gives her a new name, calls her Chavah, "Life" (Gen. 3:20).

There is a great deal of evidence, that this is the occasion of Adam's giving his wife her new name. This was her new honor, and the greatest honor, at least in her present state, that the Redeemer was to be of her seed. New names were wont to be given for something that was the person's peculiar honor. So it was with regard to the new names of Abraham, Sarah, and Israel. Dr. Taylor himself (*Key* no. 255) observes, that they who are saved by Christ, are called the Livers. οἱ ζῶντες (II Cor. 4:11). The living, or, they that live. So we find in the Old Testament, the righteous are called by the name of the living (Ps. 69:28). "Let them be blotted out of the book of the living, and not be written with the righteous." If what Adam meant by her being the mother of all living, was only her being the mother of mankind, and gave her the name *Life* on that account, it were much the most likely that he would have given her this name at first; when God first united them, under that blessing, "Be fruitful and multiply," and when he had a prospect of her being the mother of mankind *in a state of immortality, living indeed,* living and never dying. But that Adam should at that time give her only the name of *Isha,* and then immediately on that melancholy change, by their coming under the *sentence of death,* with all their posterity, having now a new awful prospect of her being the mother of nothing but a dying race, all from generation to generation turning to dust, through her folly: I say, that immediately on this, he should change her name into *Life,* calling her now the mother of *all living,* is perfectly unaccountable. Besides, it is manifest, that it was not her being the mother of all mankind, or her relation as a mother, which she stood in to her posterity, but the quality of those she was to be the mother of, which was the thing Adam had in view, in giving his wife this new name; as appears by the name itself, which signifies *Life.* And if it had been only a natural and mortal life which he had in view, this was nothing distinguishing of her posterity from the brutes; for the very same name of living ones, or living things, is given from time to time in this book of Genesis to them, as in ch. 1:21,24,28; ch. 2:19; ch. 6:19–7:23; 8:1 and many other places in the Bible. Besides, if by *Life* was not the quality of her posterity meant, there was nothing in it to distinguish her from Adam; for thus she was no more the mother of all living, than he was the father of all living; and she could no more properly be called by the name of *Life* on any such account, than he: but names are given for distinction. Doubtless Adam took notice of something distinguishing concerning her, that occasioned his giving her this new name. And I think, it is exceeding natural to suppose, that as Adam had given her her first name from the manner of her *creation,* so he gave her her new name from *redemption,* and as it were new creation, through a Redeemer, of her seed. And that he should give her this name from that which comforted him, with respect to the curse that God had pronounced on him and the earth, as Lamech named Noah (Gen. 5:29), saying, "This same shall comfort us concerning our work, and toil of our hands, because of the ground which the Lord hath cursed." Accordingly he gave her this new name, not at her first creation, but immediately after the promise of a Redeemer, of her seed (See Gen. 3:15–20).

Now as to the consequence which I infer from Adam's giving his wife this name, on the intimation which God had given, that Satan should by her seed be overthrown and disappointed, as to his malicious design, in that deed of his which God then spake of, viz. his tempting the woman; Adam infers from it, that great numbers of mankind should be saved, whom he calls the *living;* they should be saved from the effects of this malicious design of the old serpent, and from that ruin which he had brought upon them by tempting their first parents to sin; and so the serpent would be, with respect to them disappointed and overthrown in his design. But how is any death or ruin, or indeed any calamity at all brought upon their posterity by Satan's malice in that temptation, if instead of that, all the death and sorrow that was consequent, was the fruit of God's fatherly love, and not Satan's malice, and was an instance of God's free and sovereign favor, such favor as Satan could not possibly foresee? And if multitudes of Eve's posterity are saved, from either spiritual or temporal death, by a Redeemer, of her seed, how is that any disappointment of Satan's design, in tempting our first parents? How came he to have any such thing in view, as the death of Adam's and Eve's posterity, by tempting them to sin, or any expectation that their death would be the consequence, unless he knew that they were included in the threatening?

Some have objected against Adam's posterity's being included in the threatening delivered to Adam, that the threatening itself was inconsistent with his having any posterity: it being that he should die on the day that he sinned.

To this I answer, that the threatening was not inconsistent with his having posterity, on two accounts:

I. Those words, "In the day thou eatest thereof thou shalt surely die," according to the use of such-like expressions among the Hebrews, don't signify immediate death, or that the execution shall be within twenty-four hours from the commission of the fact; nor did God by those words, limit himself as to the time of executing the threatened punishment; but that was still left to God's pleasure. Such a phrase, according to the idiom of the Hebrew tongue, signifies no more than these two things:

1. A *real connection* between the sin and the punishment. So Ezek. 33:12,13, "The righteousness of the righteous shall not deliver him in the day of his transgression. As for the wickedness of the wicked, he shall not fall thereby in the day that he turneth from his wickedness: neither shall the righteous be able to live . . . in the

day that he sinneth: . . . but for his iniquity that he hath committed, he shall die for it." Here 'tis said, that *in the day* he sinneth, he shall not be able to live, but he shall die; not signifying the time when death shall be executed upon him, but the connection between his sin and death; such a connection as in our present common use of language is signified by the adverb of time, "when"; as if one should say, "According to the laws of our nation, so long as a man behaves himself as a good subject, he may live; but *when* he turns rebel, he must die": not signifying the hour, day, or month, in which he must be executed, but only the connection between his crime and death.

2. Another thing which seems to be signified by such an expression is, that Adam should be exposed to death for one transgression, without waiting on him to try him the second time. If he eat of that tree, he should immediately fall under condemnation, though afterwards he might abstain ever so strictly. In this respect, the words are much of the same force with those words of Solomon to Shimei (I Kgs. 2:37), "For it shall be that on the day that thou goest out, and passest over the brook Kidron, thou shalt know for certain, that thou shalt surely die." Not meaning, that he should certainly be executed on that day, but that he should be assuredly liable to death for the first offense, and that he should not have another trial, to see whether he would go over the brook Kidron a second time.

And then besides,

II. If the words had implied, that Adam should die that very day, within 24 or 12 hours, or that moment that he transgressed, yet it will by no means follow, that God obliged himself to execute the punishment *in its utmost extent* on that day. The sentence was in great part executed immediately; he then died spiritually; he lost his innocence and original righteousness, and the favor of God; a dismal alteration was made in his soul, by the loss of that holy divine principle, which was in the highest sense the life of the soul. In this he was truly ruined and undone that very day; becoming corrupt, miserable and helpless. And I think it has been shewn, that such a spiritual death was one great thing implied in the threatening. And the alteration then made in his body and external state, was the beginning of temporal death. Grievous external calamity is called by the name of "death" in Scripture. (Ex. 10:17), "Intreat the Lord that he may take away this death." Not only was Adam's soul ruined that day, but his body was ruined; it lost its beauty and vigor, and became a poor dull, decaying, dying thing. And besides all this, Adam was that day undone in a more dreadful sense: he immediately fell under the curse of the law, and condemnation to eternal perdition. In the language of Scripture, he is *dead,* that is in a state of condemnation to death; even as our author often explains this language in his exposition upon Romans. In Scripture language, he that believes in Christ, immediately receives life. He passes at that time from death to life, and thenceforward (to use the apostle John's phrase) "has eternal life abiding in him." But yet he don't then receive eternal life in its highest completion; he has but the beginnings of it; and receives it in a vastly greater degree at death: but the proper time for the complete fullness is not till the day of judgment. When the angels sinned, their punishment was immediately executed in a degree: but their full punishment is not till the end of the world. And there is nothing in God's threatening to Adam, that bound him to execute his full punishment at once; nor anything which determines, that he should have no posterity. The law or constitution which God established and declared, determined, that if he sinned, and had posterity, he and they should die: but there was no constitution determining concerning the actual being of his posterity in this case; what posterity he should have, how many, or whether any at all. All these things God had reserved in his own power: the law and its sanction intermeddled not with the matter.

It may be proper in this place also to take some notice of that objection of Dr. Taylor's against Adam's being supposed to be a federal head for his posterity, that it gives him greater honor than Christ, as it supposes that all his posterity would have had eternal life by his obedience, if he had stood; and so a greater number would have had the benefit of his obedience, than are saved by Christ.[4] I think, a very little consideration is sufficient to shew, that there is no weight in this objection. For the benefit of Christ's merits may nevertheless be vastly beyond that which would have been by the obedience of Adam. For those that are saved by Christ are not merely advanced to happiness by his merits, but are saved from the infinitely dreadful effects of Adam's sin, and many from immense guilt, pollution and misery by personal sins; also brought to a holy and happy state, as it were through infinite obstacles; and are exalted to a far greater degree of dignity, felicity and glory, than would have been due for Adam's obedience; for aught I know, many

4. Pp. 396 etc.

thousand times so great. And there is enough in the gospel dispensation, clearly to manifest the sufficiency of Christ's merits for such effects in all mankind. And how great the number will be, that shall actually be the subjects of them, or how great a proportion of the whole race, considering the vast success of the gospel, that shall be in that future extraordinary, exempt, and glorious season, often spoken of, none can tell. And the honor of these two federal heads arises not so much from what was proposed to each for his trial, as from their success, and the good actually obtained; and also the manner of obtaining: Christ obtains the benefits men have through him by proper merit of condignity, and a true purchase by an equivalent: which would not have been the case with Adam, if he had obeyed.

I have now particularly considered the account which Moses gives us in the beginning of the Bible, of our first parents, and God's dealings with them, the constitution he established with them, their transgression, and what followed. And on the whole, if we consider the manner in which God apparently speaks to Adam, from time to time; and particularly, if we consider how plainly and undeniably his posterity are included in the sentence of death pronounced on Adam after his fall, founded on the foregoing threatening; and consider the curse denounced on the ground for his sake, and for his and his posterity's sorrow: and also consider what is evidently the occasion of his giving his wife the new name of Eve, and his meaning in it, and withal consider apparent fact in constant and universal events, with relation to the state of our first parents, and their posterity from that time forward, through all ages of the world; I can't but think, it must appear to every impartial person, that Moses' account does, with sufficient evidence, lead all mankind, to whom his account is communicated, to understand that God, in his constitution with Adam, dealt with him as a public person, and as the head of the human species, and had respect to his posterity as included in him: and that this history is given by divine direction, in the beginning of the first-written revelation, to exhibit to our view the origin of the present sinful, miserable state of mankind, that we might see what that was, which first gave occasion for all those consequent wonderful dispensations of divine mercy and grace towards mankind, which are the great subject of the Scriptures, both of the Old and New Testament; and that these things are not obscurely and doubtfully pointed forth, but delivered in a plain account of things, which easily and naturally exhibits them to our understandings.

And by what follows in this discourse, we may have, in some measure, opportunity to see how other things in the holy Scripture agree to what has been now observed from the three first chapters of Genesis.

CHAPTER II

OBSERVATIONS ON OTHER PARTS OF THE HOLY SCRIPTURES, CHIEFLY IN THE OLD TESTAMENT, THAT PROVE THE DOCTRINE OF ORIGINAL SIN

ORIGINAL depravity may well be argued from wickedness being often spoken of in Scripture as a thing *belonging to the race of mankind, and as if it were a property of the species.* So in Ps. 14:2,3, "The Lord looked down from heaven upon the children of men, to see if there were any that did understand, and seek God. They are all gone aside; they are altogether become filthy: there is none that doth good; no, not one." The like we have again (Ps. 53:2,3). Dr. Taylor says, "The holy spirit don't mean this of every individual; because in the very same Psalm, he speaks of some that were righteous. (v. 5), 'God is in the generation of the righteous.' "[1] But how little is this observation to the purpose? For who ever supposed, that no unrighteous men were ever changed by divine grace, and afterwards made righteous? The Psalmist is speaking of what men are as they are the children of men, born of the corrupt human race; and not as born of God, whereby they come to be the children of God, and of the generation of the righteous. The apostle Paul cites this place in Rom. 3:10,11,12, to prove the universal corruption of mankind; but yet in the same chapter he supposes, these same persons here spoken of as wicked, may become righteous, through the righteousness and grace of God.

So wickedness is spoken of in other places in the book of Psalms, as a thing that belongs to men, as of the human race, as sons of men. Thus, in Ps. 4:2, "O ye sons of men, how long will ye turn my glory into shame? How long will ye love vanity? etc." (Ps. 57:4), "I lie among them that are set on fire, even the sons of men, whose teeth are spears and arrows, and their tongue a sharp sword." (Ps. 58:1,2),

1. [JE refers to Ps. 14 not Ps. 53. The "quotation" is a free paraphrase of *Scripture-Doctrine,* pp. 104, 105, and 107.]

"Do ye indeed speak righteousness, O congregation? Do ye judge uprightly, O ye sons of men? Yea, in heart ye work wickedness; ye weigh out the violence of your hands in the earth." Our author mentioning these places, says, "There was a strong party in Israel disaffected to David's person and government, and sometimes he chooseth to denote them by the sons or children of men" (p. 105n). But it would have been worth his while to have inquired, why the Psalmist should choose to denote the wickedest and worst men in Israel by this name? Why he should choose thus to disgrace the human race, as if the compellation of sons of men most properly belonged to such as were of the vilest character, and as if all the sons of men, even every one of them, were of such a character, and none of them did good; no, not one? Is it not strange, that the righteous should not be thought worthy to be called sons of men, and ranked with that noble race of beings, who are born into the world wholly right and innocent! It is a good, easy and natural reason why he chooseth to call the wicked sons of men, as a proper name for 'em, that by being of the sons of men, or of the corrupt ruined race of mankind, they come by their depravity. And the Psalmist himself leads us to this very reason (Ps. 58 at the beginning). "Do ye judge uprightly, O ye sons of men? yea, in heart ye work wickedness, ye weigh out the violence of your hands. The wicked are estranged from the womb etc." Of which I would speak more by and by.

Agreeable to these places is Prov. 21:8. "The way of man is froward and strange; but as for the pure, his work is right." He that is perverse in his walk, is here called by the name of man, as distinguished from the pure: which I think is absolutely unaccountable, if all mankind by nature are pure, and perfectly innocent, and all such as are froward and strange in their ways, therein depart from the native purity of all mankind. The words naturally lead us to suppose the contrary; that depravity and perverseness properly belong to mankind as they are naturally, and that a being made pure, is by an afterwork, by which some are delivered from native pollution, and distinguished from mankind in general: which is perfectly agreeable to the representation in Rev. 14:4, where we have an account of a number that were not defiled, but were pure, and following the Lamb; of whom it is said, "These were redeemed from among men."

To these things agree, Jer. 17:5,9. In the 5th v. it is said, "Cursed is he that trusteth in man." and in the 9th v. this reason is given, "The heart is deceitful above all things, and desperately wicked;

who can know it?" What heart is this, so wicked and deceitful? Why, evidently the heart of him who, it was said before, we must not trust; and that is *man*. It alters not the case as to the present argument, whether the deceitfulness of the heart here spoken of, be its deceitfulness to the man himself, or to others. So that fore-mentioned Eccles. 9:3, "Madness is in the heart of the sons of men, while they live." And those words of Christ to Peter, (Matt. 16:23), "Get thee behind me, Satan—for thou savorest not the things that be of God, but the things that be of men." Signifying plainly, that to be carnal and vain, and opposite to what is spiritual and divine, is what properly belongs to men in their present state. The same thing is supposed in that of the Apostle (I Cor. 3:3), "For ye are yet carnal. For whereas there is among you envying and strife, are ye not carnal, and walk as men?" And that in Hos. 6:7, "But they like men, have transgressed the Covenant." To these places may be added (Matt. 7:11), "If ye being evil, know how to give good gifts," (Jas. 4:5), "Do ye think that the Scripture saith in vain, 'The spirit that dwelleth in us, lusteth to envy'?" (I Pet. 4:2), "That he no longer should live the rest of his time in the lusts of men, but to the will of God." Yet above all, that in Job 15:16, "How much more abominable and filthy is man, who drinketh iniquity like water?" Of which more presently.

Now what account can be given of these things, on Dr. Taylor's scheme? How strange is it, that we should have such descriptions, all over the Bible, of man, and the sons of men! Why should man be so continually spoken of as evil, carnal, perverse, deceitful, and desperately wicked, if all men are by nature as perfectly innocent, and free from any propensity to evil, as Adam was the first moment of his creation, all made right, as our author would have us understand (Eccles. 7:29)? Why, on the contrary, is it not said, at least as often, and with equal reason; that the heart of man is right and pure; that the way of man is innocent and holy; and that he who savors true virtue and wisdom, savors the things that be of men? Yea, and why might it not as well have been said, the Lord looked down from heaven on the sons of men, to see if there were any that did understand, and did seek after God, and they were all right, altogether pure, there was none inclined to do wickedness, no not one!

Of the like import with the texts mentioned, are those which represent wickedness as what properly belongs to the *world;* and that they who are otherwise, are saved from the world, and called out of it. As (John 7:7), "The world cannot hate you; but me it hateth; because I testify of it, that the works thereof are evil." (ch. 8:23), "Ye are of this world: I am not of this world." (ch. 14:17), "The spirit of truth, whom the world cannot receive; because it seeth him not, neither knoweth him: but ye know him." (ch. 15:18,19), "If the world hate you, ye know that it hated me before it hated you. If ye were of the world, the world would love its own: but because ye are not of the world, but I have chosen you out of the world, therefore the world hateth you." (Rev. 14:3,4), "These are they which were redeemed from the earth, redeemed from among men." (John 17:9), "I pray not for the world, but for them which thou hast given me." (v. 14), "I have given them thy word; and the world hath hated them, because they are not of the world, even as I am not of the world." (I John 3:13), "Marvel not, my brethren, if the world hate you." (ch. 4:5), "They are of the world, therefore speak they of the world, and the world heareth them." (ch. 5:19), "We are of God, and the whole world lieth in wickedness." 'Tis evident, that in these places, by "the world" is meant the world of mankind; not the habitation, but the inhabitants. For, 'tis the world spoken of as loving, hating, doing evil works, speaking, hearing, etc.

It shews the same thing, that wickedness is often spoken of as being man's *own,* in contradistinction from virtue and holiness. So men's lusts are often called their own heart's lusts, and their practising wickedness is called walking in their own ways, walking in their own counsels, in the imagination of their own heart, and in the sight of their own eyes, according to their own devices etc. These things denote wickedness to be a quality belonging properly to the character and nature of mankind, in their present state: as, when Christ would represent that lying is remarkably the character and the very nature of the devil in his present state, he expresses it thus (John 8:44): "When he speaketh a lie, he speaketh of his own; for he is a liar, and the father of it."

And that wickedness belongs to the nature of mankind in their present state, may be argued from those places which speak of mankind as being wicked *in their childhood,* or *from their childhood.* So, that in Prov. 22:15, "Foolishness is bound in the heart of a child; but the rod of correction shall drive it far from him." Nothing is more manifest, than that the wise man in this book continually uses the word "folly," or "foolishness," for "wickedness": and that this is what he means in this place, the words themselves do shew: for the rod of correction is proper to drive away no other foolishness, but that which is a moral nature. The word rendered "bound" signifies, as is observed in Poole's *Synopsis,* a close and firm union.[2] The same word is used in ch. 6:21, "Bind them continually upon thine heart." And ch. 7:3, "Bind them upon thy fingers, write them upon the table of thine heart." To the like purpose is ch. 3:3 and Deut. 11:18, where this word is used. The same verb is used (I Sam. 18:1), "The soul of Jonathan was knit (or bound) to the soul of David, and Jonathan loved him as his own soul." But how comes wickedness to be so firmly bound, and strongly fixed, in the hearts of children, if it be not there naturally? They having had no time firmly to fix habits of sin, by long custom in actual wickedness, as those that have lived many years in the world.

The same thing is signified in that noted place (Gen. 8:21), "For the imagination of man's heart is evil *from his youth.*" It alters not the case, whether it be translated "for" or "though" the imagination of man's heart is evil from his youth, as Dr. Taylor would have it; still the words suppose it to be so as is said. The word translated "youth," signifies the whole of the former part of the age of man, which commences from the beginning of life. The word in its derivation, has reference to the birth, or beginning of existence. It comes from "nagnar," which signifies to shake off, as a tree shakes off its ripe fruit, or a plant its seed; the birth of children being commonly represented by a tree's yielding fruit, or a plant's yielding seed. So that the word here translated "youth," comprehends not only what we in English most commonly call the time of youth, but also childhood and infancy, and is very often used to signify these latter. A word of the same root is used to signify a young child, or a little child, in the following places: I Sam. 1:24,25,27; I Kgs. 3:7 and 11:17; II Kgs. 2:23; Job 33:25; Prov. 22:6 and 23:13 and 29:21; Is. 10:19 and 11:6 and 65:29; Jer. 10:6; Hos. 11:1. The same word is used to signify an infant, in Ex. 2:6 and 10:9; Judg. 13:5,7,8 and 12:24; I Sam. 1:22 and 4:21; II Kgs. 5:14; Is. 7:16 and 8:4.

Dr. Taylor says (p. 124) that he "conceives, *from the youth,* is a phrase signifying the greatness, or long duration of a thing." [3] But if by "long duration" he means anything else than what is literally expressed, viz. from the beginning of life, he has no reason to conceive so; neither has what he offers, so much as the shadow of a reason

2. [See above, Intro., Sec. 5.]
3. [JE's free paraphrase.]

for his conception. There is no appearance in the words of the two or three texts he mentions, of their meaning anything else than what is most literally signified. And 'tis certain, that what he suggests, is not the ordinary import of such a phrase among the Hebrews: but thereby is meant, from the beginning, or early time of life, or existence; as may be seen in the places following, where the same word in the Hebrew is used, as in this place in the eighth of Genesis. (I Sam. 12:2), "I am old, and gray-headed . . . and I have walked before you from my childhood, unto this day": where the original word is the same. (Ps. 71:5,6), "Thou art my trust from my youth: by thee have I been holden up from the womb. Thou art he that took me out of my mother's bowels." (vv. 17, 18), "O God, thou hast taught me from my youth; and hitherto have I declared thy wondrous works: now also, when I am old and gray-headed, forsake me not." (Ps. 129:1,2), "Many a time have they afflicted me from my youth, may Israel now say: many a time have they afflicted me from my youth; yet have they not prevailed against me." (Is. 47:12), "Stand now with the multitude of thy sorceries, wherein thou hast laboured from thy youth." (So v. 15 and II Sam. 19:7), "That will be worse unto thee, than all the evil that befell thee from thy youth, until now." (Jer. 3:24, 25), "Shame hath devoured the labor of our fathers, from our youth. We have sinned against the Lord our God, from our youth, even to this day." (So Jer. 32:30 and 48:11; Job 31:18; Gen. 46:34; Ezek. 4:14; Zech. 13:5).

And it is to be observed, that according to the manner of the Hebrew language, when it is said, such a thing has been from youth, or the first part of existence, the phrase is to be understood as including that first time of existence. (So, Josh. 6:21), "They utterly destroyed all, from the young to the old." So it is in the Hebrew, i.e. including both. So Esther 3:13 and Gen. 19:4.

And as mankind are represented in Scripture, as being of a wicked heart *from their youth,* so in other places they are spoken of as being thus *from the womb.* (Ps. 58:3), "The wicked are estranged from the womb: They go astray as soon as they be born, speaking lies." 'Tis observable, that the Psalmist mentions this as what belongs to the wicked, as sons of men: for, these are the preceding words: "Do ye judge uprightly, O ye sons of men? Yea, in heart ye work wickedness." A phrase of the like import with that in Gen. 8:21. "The imagination," or "operation," as it might have been rendered, "of his heart is evil." Then it follows, "the wicked are estranged from the womb, etc." The next verse is, "Their poison is like the poison of a serpent." 'Tis so remarkably, as the very nature of a serpent is poison: serpents are poisonous as soon as they come into the world: they derive a poisonous nature by their generation. Dr. Taylor (pp. 134, 135) says, " 'Tis evident that this is a scriptural figurative way of aggravating wickedness, on the one hand, and virtue on the other, to speak of it as being from the womb." [4] And as an instance of the latter, he cites that in Is. 49:1: "The Lord hath called me from the womb; from the bowels of my mother, he made mention of my name." But I apprehend, that in order to seeing this to be evident, which he asserts, a man must have eyes peculiarly affected. I humbly conceive, that such phrases as that in the 49th of Isaiah, of God's calling the prophet from the womb, are evidently, not of the import which he supposes, but mean truly from the beginning of existence, and are manifestly of like signification with that which is said of the prophet Jeremiah. (Jer. 1:5), "Before I formed thee in the womb, I knew thee: before thou camest out of the womb, I sanctified thee, and ordained thee a prophet of the nations." Which surely means something else besides a high degree of virtue: it plainly signifies that he was, from his first existence, set apart by God for a prophet. And it would be as unreasonable to understand it otherwise, as to suppose, the angel meant any other than that Samson was set apart to be a Nazarite from the beginning of his life, when he says to his mother (Judg. 13:3–4), "Behold, thou shalt conceive and bear a son: and now drink no wine, nor strong drink etc. For the child shall be a Nazarite to God, from the womb, to the day of his death." By these instances it is plain, that the phrase, "from the womb," as the other, "from the youth," as used in Scripture, properly signifies from the beginning of life.

Very remarkable is that place (Job 15:14,15,16), "What is man, that he should be clean? And he that is born of a woman, that he should be righteous? Behold, he putteth no trust in his saints; yea, the heavens are not clean in his sight: How much more abominable and filthy is man, which drinketh iniquity like water?" And no less remarkable is our author's method of managing of it. The 16th v. expresses an exceeding degree of wickedness, in as plain and emphatical terms, almost, as can be invented; every word representing this in the strongest manner: "how much more abominable and filthy is man, that drinketh iniquity like water?" I can't now recol-

4. [JE's free paraphrase.]

lect, where we have a sentence equal to it, in the whole Bible, for an emphatical, lively and strong representation of great wickedness of heart. Any one of the words, as such words are used in Scripture, would represent great wickedness: if it had been only said, "How much more abominable is man?" Or, "How much more filthy is man?" Or, "Man drinketh iniquity." But all these are accumulated, with the addition of "like water," the further to represent the boldness or greediness of men, in wickedness: though iniquity be the most deadly poison, yet men drink it as boldly as they drink water, are as familiar with it as with their common drink, and drink it with like greediness, as he that is thirsty drinks water. That boldness and eagerness in persecuting the saints, by which the great degree of the depravity of man's heart often appears, is represented thus (Ps. 14:4), "Have the workers of iniquity no knowledge, who eat up my people, as they eat bread?" And the greatest eagerness of thirst is represented by thirsting as an animal thirsts after water. (Ps. 42:1).

Now let us see the soft, easy, light manner in which Dr. Taylor treats this place (p. 143). " 'How much more abominable and filthy is man,' *in comparison of the divine purity,* 'who drinketh iniquity like water?' Who is attended with so many sensual appetites, and so apt to indulge them. You see the argument; man in his present weak, and fleshly state, cannot be clean before God. Why so? Because he is conceived and born in sin, by reason of Adam's sin? No such thing. But because the purest creatures are not pure in comparison of God. Much less a being subject to so many infirmities, as a mortal man. Which is a demonstration to me, not only, that Job and his friends did not intend to establish the doctrine we are now examining, but that they were wholly strangers to it." Thus the author endeavors to reconcile this text with his doctrine of the perfect native innocence of mankind: in which we have a notable specimen of his demonstrations, as well as of that great impartiality and fairness in examining and expounding the Scripture, which he makes so often a profession of.

In this place we are not only told, how wicked man's heart is, but also how men come by such wickedness; even by being of the race of mankind, by ordinary generation: "What is man, that he should be clean? and he that is born of a woman, that he should be righteous?" Our author (pp. 141, 142), represents man's being born of a woman, as a periphrasis, to signify man; and that there is no design in the words to give a reason, why man is not clean and righteous.

But the case is most evidently otherwise, if we may interpret the book of Job by itself: 'Tis most plain, that man's being born of a woman is given as a reason of his not being clean (ch. 14:4); "Who can bring a clean thing out of an unclean?" Job is speaking there expressly of man's being born of a woman, as appears in v. 1. And here how plain is it, that this is given as a reason of man's not being clean? Concerning this Dr. Taylor says, "That this has no respect to any moral uncleanness, but only common frailty etc." But how evidently is this also otherwise, when that uncleanness which a man has by being born of a woman, is expressly explained of unrighteousness, in the next chapter at the 14th v.? "What is man, that he should be clean? and he that is born of a woman, that he should be righteous?" and also in ch. 25:4, "How then can man be justified with God? And how can he be clean, that is born of a woman?" 'Tis a moral cleanness Bildad is speaking of, which a man needs in order to being justified—his design is, to convince Job of his moral impurity, and from thence of God's righteousness in his severe judgments upon him; and not of his natural frailty.

And without doubt, David has respect to this same way of derivation of wickedness of heart, when he says (Ps. 51:5), "Behold, I was shapen in iniquity, and in sin did my mother conceive me." It alters not the case as to the argument we are upon, whether the word translated "conceive," signify conceive or nurse; which latter, our author takes so much pains to prove: for when he has done all, he speaks of it as a just translation of the words to render 'em thus, "I was born in iniquity, and in sin did my mother nurse me" (p. 135). If it is owned that man is *born in sin,* 'tis not worth the while to dispute, whether 'tis expressly asserted, that he is *conceived in sin.* But Dr. Taylor after his manner insists, that such expressions, as being "born in sin," "being transgressors from the womb," and the like, are only phrases figuratively to denote aggravation, and high degree of wickedness. But the contrary has been already demonstrated, from many plain Scripture-instances. Nor is one instance produced, in which there is any evidence that such a phrase is used in such a manner. A poetical sentence out of Virgil's *Aeneids,* has here been produced, and made much of by some, as parallel with this, in what Dido says to Aeneas, in these lines:

"Nec tibi diva parens generis, nec Dardanus auctor,
Perfide: sed duris genuit te cautibus horrens
Caucasus, Hyrcanaeque admorunt ubera tigres."

In which she tells Aeneas, that not a goddess was his mother, nor Anchises his father; but that he had been brought forth by a horrid rocky mountain, and nursed at the dugs of tigers, to represent the greatness of his cruelty to her. But how unlike and unparallel is this? Nothing could be more natural, than for a woman overpowered with the passion of love, and distracted with raging jealousy and disappointment, thinking herself treated with brutish perfidy and cruelty, by a lover whose highest fame had been his being the son of a goddess, to aggravate his inhumanity and hard-heartedness with this, that his behavior was not worthy the son of a goddess, nor becoming one whose father was an illustrious prince; and that he acted more as if he had been brought forth by hard unrelenting rocks, and had sucked the dugs of tigers. But what is there in the case of David, parallel, or at all in like manner leading him to speak of himself as born in sin, in any such sense? He is not speaking himself, nor anyone else speaking to him, of any excellent and divine father and mother, that he was born of: nor is there any appearance of his aggravating his sin, by its being unworthy of his high birth. There is nothing else visible in David's case, to lead him to take notice of his being born in sin, but only his having such experience of the continuance and power of indwelling sin, after so long a time, and so many and great means to engage him to holiness; which shewed, that sin was inbred, and in his very nature.

Dr. Taylor very often objects to these and other texts, brought by divines to prove original sin, that there is no mention made in them of Adam, nor of his sin. He cries out, "Here is not the least mention, or intimation of Adam, or any ill effects of his sin upon us. . . . Here's not one word, nor the least hint of Adam, or any consequences of his sin" etc. etc.[5] He says,[6] "If Job and his friends had known and believed the doctrine of a corrupt nature, derived from Adam's sin only, they ought in reason and truth to have given this as the true and only reason of the human imperfection and uncleanness they mention." But these objections and exclamations are made no less impertinently, than they are frequently. 'Tis no more a proof, that corruption of nature did not come by Adam's sin, because many times when it is mentioned, Adam's sin is not expressly mentioned as the cause of it, than that death did not come by Adam's sin (as Dr. Taylor says it did), because though death as inci-

5. Pp. 5, 64, 97, 98, 102, 108, 112, 118, 120, 122, 123, 127, 128, 136, 142, 143, 152, 155, 229, 149.

6. P. 142.

dent to mankind, is mentioned so often in the Old Testament, and by our Savior in his discourses, yet Adam's sin is not once expressly mentioned, after the three first chapters of Genesis, anywhere in all the Old Testament, or the four Evangelists, as the occasion of it.

What Christian has there ever been, that believed the moral corruption of the nature of mankind, who ever doubted that it came that way, which the Apostle speaks of, when he says, "By one man sin entered into the world, and death by sin"? Nor indeed have they any more reason to doubt of it, than to doubt of the whole history of our first parents, because Adam's name is so rarely mentioned, on any occasion in Scripture, after that first account of him, and Eve's never at all; and because we have no more any express mention of the particular manner, in which mankind were first brought into being, either with respect to the creation of Adam, or Eve. 'Tis sufficient, that the abiding, most visible effects of these things remain, in the view of mankind in all ages, and are often spoken of in Scripture; and the particular manner of their being introduced, is once plainly set forth in the beginning of the Bible, in that history which gives us an account of the origin of all things. And doubtless it was expected, by the great Author of the Bible, that the account in the three first chapters of Genesis should be taken as a plain account of the introduction of both natural and moral evil, into the world; as it has been shewn to be so indeed. The history of Adam's sin, with its circumstances, God's threatening, and the sentence pronounced upon him after his transgression, and the immediate consequences, consisting in so vast an alteration in his state, and the state of the world, which abides still, with respect to all his posterity, do most directly and sufficiently lead to an understanding of the rise of calamity, sin and death, in this sinful miserable world.

'Tis fit, we all should know, that it don't become us to tell the Most High, how often he shall particularly explain and give the reason of any doctrine which he teaches, in order to our believing what he says. If he has at all given us evidence that it is a doctrine agreeable to his mind, it becomes us to receive it with full credit and submission; and not sullenly to reject it, because our notions and humors are not suited in the manner, and number of times, of his particularly explaining it to us. How often is pardon of sins promised in the Old Testament to repenting and returning sinners? How many hundred times is God's special favor there promised to the sincerely righteous, without any express mention of these benefits being through Christ? Would it therefore be becoming us to say, that ina- much as our dependence on Christ for these benefits, is a doctrine, which, if true, is of such importance, that God ought expressly to have mentioned Christ's merits as the reason and ground of the benefits, if he knew they were the ground of 'em, and should have plainly declared it sooner, and more frequently, if ever he expected we should believe him, when he did tell us of it? How often is vengeance and misery threatened in the Old Testament to the wicked, without any clear and express signification of any such thing intended, as that everlasting fire, where there is wailing and gnashing of teeth, in another world, which Christ so often speaks of as the punishment appointed for all the wicked? Would it now become a Christian, to object and say, that if God really meant any such thing, he ought *in reason and truth* to have declared it plainly and fully; and not to have been so silent about a matter of such vast importance to all mankind, for four thousand years together?

R III

OBSERVATIONS ON VARIOUS OTHER PLACES OF SCRIPTURE, PRINCIPALLY OF THE NEW TESTAMENT, PROVING THE DOCTRINE OF ORIGINAL SIN

SECTION 1. OBSERVATIONS ON JOHN 3:6 IN CONNECTION WITH SOME OTHER PASSAGES IN THE NEW TESTAMENT

THOSE words of Christ, giving a reason to Nicodemus, why we must be born again (John 3:6), "That which is born of the flesh, is flesh; and that which is born of the spirit, is spirit"; have not without good reason been produced by divines, as a proof of the doctrine of original sin: supposing, that by "flesh" here is meant *the human nature in a debased and corrupt state.* Yet Dr. Taylor (p. 144) thus explains these words, " 'That which is born of the flesh, is flesh'; That which is born by natural descent and propagation, is a man consisting of body and soul, or the mere constitution and powers of a man, in their natural state." But the constant use of these terms, "flesh" and "spirit" in other parts of the New Testament, when thus set in opposition one to another, and the latter said to be produced by the spirit of God, as here; and when speaking of the same thing, which Christ is here speaking of to Nicodemus, viz. the requisite qualifications to salvation, this will fully vindicate the sense of our divines. Thus in the 7th and 8th chapters of Romans, where these terms "flesh" and "spirit" (σὰρξ and πνεῦμα) are abundantly repeated, and set in opposition, as here. (So ch. 7:14), The law is spiritual (πνευματικός) but I am carnal (σαρκικός) sold under sin. He can't only mean, "I am a man, consisting of body and soul, and having the powers of a man" (v. 18), "I know that in me, that is, in my flesh, dwelleth no good thing." He don't mean to condemn his frame as consisting of body and soul; and to assert, that in his human constitution, with the powers of a man, dwells no good thing. And when he says in the last verse of the chapter, "With the mind I myself serve the law of God, but with the flesh the law of sin"; he can't mean, "I myself serve the law of God; but with my innocent human constitution, as having the powers of a man, I serve the law of sin." And when he says in the next words, in the beginning of the 8th chapter, "There is no condemnation to them . . . that walk not after the flesh, but after the spirit"; and v. 4, "The righteousness of the law is fulfilled in us, who walk not after the flesh"; he can't mean, "There is no condemnation to them that walk not according to the powers of a man" etc. And when he says (vv. 5 and 6), "They that are after the flesh, do mind the things of the flesh"; and "to be carnally minded is death"; he don't intend, "They that are according to the human constitution and the powers of a man, do mind the things of the human constitution and powers; and to mind these, is death." And when he says (vv. 7 and 8), "The carnal (or fleshly) mind is enmity against God, and is not subject to the law of God, nor indeed can be; so that they that are in the flesh, cannot please God"; he can't mean, that to mind the things which are agreeable to the powers and constitution of a man (who, as our author says, is constituted or made right) is enmity against God; and that a mind which is agreeable to this right human constitution, as God hath made it, is not subject to the law of God, nor indeed can be; and that they who are according to such a constitution, cannot please God. And when it is said (v. 9), "Ye are not in the flesh, but in the spirit," the Apostle can't mean, "Ye are not in the human nature, as constituted of body and soul, and with the powers of a man." 'Tis most manifest, that by the flesh here the Apostle means some nature that is corrupt, and of an evil tendency, and directly opposite to the law, and holy nature of God; so that to be and walk according to it, and to have a mind conformed to it, is to be an utter enemy to God and his law, in a perfect inconsistence with being subject to God, and pleasing God; and in a sure and infallible tendency to death, and utter destruction. And it is plain, that here by "being" and "walking after," or "according to the flesh," is meant the same thing as being and walking according to a corrupt and sinful nature; and to be and walk according to the spirit, is to be and walk according to a holy and divine nature, or principle: and to be *carnally* minded, is the same as being viciously and corruptly minded; to be *spiritually* minded, is to be of a virtuous and holy disposition.

When Christ says (John 3:6), "That which is born of the flesh, is flesh," he represents the flesh not merely as a quality; for it would be incongruous, to speak of a quality as a thing born: 'tis a person, or man, that is born. Therefore man, as in his whole nature corrupt, is called flesh: which is agreeable to other Scripture-representations, where the corrupt nature is called the "old man," the "body of sin," and the "body of death." Agreeable to this are those representations in the 7th and 8th chapters of Romans: there flesh is figuratively represented as a person, according to the Apostle's manner, observed by Mr. Locke, and after him by Dr. Taylor; who takes notice, that the Apostle, in the 6th and 7th of Romans represents sin as a person; and that he figuratively distinguishes in himself two persons, speaking of flesh as his person. "For I know that in me" (that is, in my flesh), "dwelleth no good thing." [1] And it may be observed, that in the 8th chapter, he still continues this representation, speaking of the flesh as a person; and accordingly in the 6th and 7th verses, speaks of the mind of the flesh (*φρόνημα* [*τῆς*] *σαρκὸς*) [2] and of the mind of the spirit (*φρόνημα* [*τοῦ*] *πνεύματος*) as if the flesh and spirit were two opposite persons, each having a mind contrary to the mind of the other. Dr. Taylor interprets this "mind of the flesh," and "mind of the spirit," as though the flesh and the spirit were here spoken of as the different objects, about which the mind spoken of is conversant; which is plainly beside the Apostle's sense; who speaks of the flesh and spirit as the subjects and agents, in which the mind spoken of is; and not the objects, about which it acts. We have the same phrase again (v. 27), "He that searcheth the hearts, knoweth what is the mind of the spirit" (*φρόνημα πνεύματος*); the mind of the spiritual nature in the saints being the same with the mind of the spirit of God himself, who imparts and actuates that spiritual nature. Here the spirit is the subject and agent, and not the object. The same Apostle in like manner uses the word *νοὸς* in Col. 2:18. "Vainly puffed up by his fleshly mind" (*απο* [*ὑπὸ*] *τοῦ νοὸς τῆς σαρκὸς αὐτοῦ*) by the mind of his flesh. And this agent so often called "flesh," represented by the Apostle, as altogether evil, without any good thing dwelling in it, or belonging to it, yea perfectly contrary to God and his law, and tending wholly to death and ruin, and directly opposite to the spirit, is what Christ speaks of to Nicodemus as born in the first birth, as giving a reason why there is a necessity of a new birth, in order to a better production.

One thing is particularly observable in that discourse of the Apos-

1. [Rom. 7:18.]
2. [Here and elsewhere Greek accents added.]

tle, in the 7th and 8th of Romans, in which he so often uses the term "flesh," as opposite to "spirit," which, as well as many other things in his discourse, makes it plain, that by flesh he means something in itself corrupt and sinful; and that is, that he expressly calls it "sinful flesh" (Rom. 8:3). 'Tis manifest, that by "sinful flesh" he means the same thing with that flesh spoken of in the immediately foregoing and following words, and in all the context: and that when it is said, Christ was made in the likeness of sinful flesh, the expression is equipollent with those that speak of Christ as made sin, and made a curse for us.

Flesh and spirit are opposed one to another in Gal. 5 in the same manner as in the 8th of Romans: and there, by "flesh" cannot be meant only the human nature of body and soul, or the mere constitution and powers of a man, as in its natural state, innocent and right. In the 16th verse the Apostle says, "Walk in the spirit, and ye shall not fulfill the lusts of the flesh," where the flesh is spoken of as a thing of an evil inclination, desire or lust. But this is more strongly signified in the next words, "For the flesh lusteth against the spirit, and the spirit against the flesh; and these are contrary one to another." What could have been said more plainly, to shew that what the Apostle means by flesh, is something very evil in its nature, and an irreconcilable enemy to all goodness? And it may be observed, that in these words, and those that follow, the Apostle still figuratively represents the flesh as a person or agent, desiring, acting, having lusts, and performing works. And by "works of the flesh," and "fruits of the spirit," which are opposed to each other, from v. 19 to the end, are plainly meant the same as "works of a sinful nature," and "fruits of a holy renewed nature." "Now the works of the flesh are manifest, which are these: adultery, fornication, uncleanness, lasciviousness, idolatry, witchcraft, hatred, variance, wrath, strife, seditions, heresies, etc. . . . But the fruit of the spirit is love, joy, peace, long-suffering, gentleness, goodness, etc." The Apostle, by "flesh," don't mean anything that is innocent and good in itself, that only needs to be restrained, and kept in proper bounds; but something altogether evil, which is to be destroyed, and not only restrained. (I Cor. 5:5), "To deliver such an one to Satan, for the destruction of the flesh." We must have no mercy on it; we can't be too cruel to it; it must even be crucified. (Gal. 5:24), "They that are Christ's, have crucified the flesh, with the affections and lusts.

The apostle John, the same apostle that writes the account of what Christ said to Nicodemus, by the spirit means the same thing as a new, divine and holy nature, exerting itself in a principle of divine love, which is that sum of all Christian holiness. (I John 3:23, 24), "And that we should love one another, as he gave us commandment; and he that keepeth his commandments, dwelleth in him, and he in him: and hereby we know that he abideth in us, by the spirit that he hath given us." (With ch. 4:12,13), "If we love one another, God dwelleth in us, and his love is perfected in us: hereby know we, that we dwell in him, because he hath given us of his spirit." The spiritual principle in us being as it were a communication of the spirit of God to us.

And as by *πνεῦμα* is meant a holy nature, by the epithet *πνευματικὸς*, spiritual, is meant the same as truly virtuous and holy. (Gal. 6:1), "Ye that are spiritual, restore such an one in the spirit of meekness." The Apostle refers to what he had just said, in the end of the foregoing chapter, where he had mentioned meekness, as a fruit of the spirit. And so by carnal, or fleshly *σαρκινὸς*, is meant the same as sinful. (Rom. 7:14), "The law is spiritual" (i.e. holy), "but I am carnal, sold under sin."

And 'tis evident, that by "flesh," as the word is used in the New Testament, and opposed to spirit, when speaking of the qualifications for eternal salvation, is not meant only what is now vulgarly called the sins of the flesh, consisting in inordinate appetites of the body, and their indulgences; but the whole body of sin, implying those lusts that are most subtle, and furthest from any relation to the body; such as pride, malice, envy, etc. When the works of the flesh are enumerated (Gal. 5:19,20,21), they are vices of the latter kind chiefly, that are mentioned; idolatry, witchcraft, hatred, variance, emulations, wrath, strife, seditions, heresies, envyings. So, pride of heart is the effect or operation of the flesh. (Col. 2:18), "Vainly puffed up by his fleshly mind"; in the Greek, by the mind of the flesh. So pride, envying, strife and division, are spoken of as works of the flesh. (I Cor. 3:3,4), "For ye are yet carnal (*σαρκικοί*, fleshly). For whereas there is . . . envying, and strife, and divisions, are ye not carnal, and walk as men? For while one saith, I am of Paul; and another, I am of Apollos, are ye not carnal?" Such kind of lusts don't depend on the body, or external senses; for the devil himself has them in the highest degree, who has not, nor ever had, any body or external senses to gratify.

Here, if it should be inquired, how corruption or depravity in general, or the nature of man as corrupt and sinful, came to be called flesh; and not only that corruption which consists in inordinate bodily appetites, I think, what the Apostle says in the last cited place, "Are ye not carnal, and walk as men?" leads us to the true reason. 'Tis because a corrupt and sinful nature is what properly belongs to mankind, or the race of Adam, as they are in themselves, and as they are by nature. The word "flesh" is a word often used in both Old Testament and New to signify mankind in their present state. To enumerate all the places, would be very tedious; I shall therefore only mention a few places in the New Testament. (Matt. 24:22), "Except those days should be shortened, no flesh should be saved." (Luke 3:6), "All flesh shall see the salvation of God." (John 17:2), "Thou hast given him power over all flesh." (See also Acts 2:17; Rom. 3:20; I Cor. 1:29; Gal. 2:16.) Man's nature, being left to itself, forsaken of the spirit of God, as it was when man fell, and consequently forsaken of divine and holy principles, of itself became exceeding corrupt, utterly depraved and ruined. And so the word "flesh," which signifies man, came to be used to signify man as he is in himself, in his natural state, debased, corrupt and ruined. And on the other hand, the word "spirit" came to be used to signify a divine and holy principle, or new nature; because that is not of man, but of God, by the indwelling and vital influence of his spirit. And thus to be corrupt, and to be carnal, or fleshly, and to walk as men, are the same thing with the Apostle. And so in other parts of the Scripture, to savor things that be of man, and to savor things which are corrupt, are the same; and the sons of men, and wicked men, also are the same, as was observed before. And on the other hand, to savor the things that be of God, and to receive the things of the spirit of God, are phrases that signify as much as relishing and embracing true holiness or divine virtue.

All these things confirm what we have supposed to be Christ's meaning, in saying (John 3:6), "That which is born of the flesh, is flesh; and that which is born of the spirit, is spirit." His speech implies, that what is born in the first birth of man, is nothing but man as he is of himself, without anything divine in him; depraved, debased, sinful, ruined man, utterly unfit to enter into the kingdom of God, and incapable of the spiritual divine happiness of that kingdom: but that which is born in the new birth, of the spirit of God, is a spiritual principle, and holy and divine nature, meet for the divine and heavenly kingdom. 'Tis a confirmation that this is the true meaning, that it is not only evidently agreeable to the constant language of the spirit of Christ in the New Testament; but the words understood in this sense, contain the proper and true reason, why a man must be born again, in order to enter into the kingdom of God; the reason that is given everywhere in other parts of the Scripture for the necessity of a renovation, a change of mind, a new heart, etc. in order to salvation: to give a reason of which to Nicodemus, is plainly Christ's design in the words which have been insisted on.

Before I proceed, I would observe one thing as a corollary from what has been said.

Corollary. If by "flesh" and "spirit" when spoken of in the New Testament, and opposed to each other, in discourses on the necessary qualifications for salvation, we are to understand what has been now supposed, it will not only follow, that men by nature are corrupt, but *wholly corrupt,* without any good thing. If by "flesh" is meant man's nature, as he receives it in his first birth, then "therein dwelleth no good thing"; as appears by Rom. 7:18. 'Tis wholly opposite to God, and to subjection to his law, as appears by Rom. 8:7,8. 'Tis directly contrary to true holiness, and wholly opposes it, and holiness is opposite to that; as appears by Gal. 5:17. So long as men are in their natural state, they not only have no good thing, but it is impossible they should have, or do any good thing; as appears by Rom. 8:8. There is nothing in their nature, as they have it by the first birth, whence should arise any true subjection to God; as appears by Rom. 8:7. If there were anything truly good in the flesh, or in man's nature, or natural disposition, under a moral view, then it should only be amended; but the Scripture represents as though we were to be enemies to it, and were to seek nothing short of its entire destruction, as has been observed. And elsewhere the Apostle directs not to the amending of the old man, but putting it off, and putting on the new man; and seeks not to have the body of death made better, but to be delivered from it; and says (II Cor. 5:17), that "if any man be in Christ, he is a new creature" (which doubtless means the same as a man new-born) "old things are (not amended) but passed away, and all things are become new."

But this will be further evident, if we particularly consider the Apostle's discourse in the latter part of the second chapter of I Cor. and the beginning of the third. There the Apostle speaks of the "natural man," and the "spiritual man": where natural and spiritual are opposed just in the same manner, as I have observed carnal and spiritual often are. In ch. 2:14,15, he says, "The natural man receiveth not the things of the spirit of God: for they are foolishness unto him: neither can he know them, because they are spiritually discerned. But he that is spiritual, judgeth all things." And not only does the Apostle here oppose natural and spiritual, just as he elsewhere does carnal and spiritual, but his following discourse evidently shows, that he means the very same distinction, the same two distinct and opposite things. For immediately on his thus speaking of the difference between the natural and spiritual man, he turns to the Corinthians, in the first words of the next chapter, connected with this, and says, "And I, brethren, could not speak unto you as unto spiritual, but as unto carnal." Referring manifestly to what he had been saying, in the immediately preceding discourse, about spiritual and natural men, and evidently using the word "carnal" as synonymous with "natural." By which it is put out of all reasonable dispute, that the Apostle by "natural men" means the same as men in that carnal, sinful state, that they are in by their first birth; notwithstanding all the glosses and criticisms, by which modern writers have endeavored to palm upon us another sense of this phrase, and so to deprive us of the clear instruction the Apostle gives in that 14th verse concerning the sinful miserable state of man by nature. Dr. Taylor says, by ψυχικὸς, is meant the animal man, the man who maketh sense and appetite the law of his action. If he aims to limit the meaning of the word to external sense, and bodily appetite, his meaning is certainly not the Apostle's. For the Apostle in his sense includes the more spiritual vices of envy, strife, etc. as appears by the four first verses of the next chapter; where, as I have observed, he substitutes the word "carnal" in the place of ψυχικὸς. So the apostle Jude uses the word in like manner, opposing it to "spiritual," or "having the spirit." (v. 19), "These are they that separate themselves, sensual" (ψυχικοί) "not having the spirit." The vices he had been just speaking of, were chiefly of the more spiritual kind. (v. 16), "These are murmurers, complainers, walking after their own lusts; and their mouth speaketh great swelling words, having men's persons in admiration because of advantage." The vices mentioned are much of the same kind with those of the Corinthians, for which he calls them carnal; envying, strife, and divisions, and saying "I am of Paul," and "I am of Apollos"; and "being puffed up for one against another." We have the same word again (Jas. 3:14,15), "If ye have bitter envying and strife, glory not, and lie not against the truth: this wisdom descendeth not from above, but is earthly, sensual (ψυχική) and devilish"; where also the vices the Apostle speaks of are of the more spiritual kind.

So that on the whole, there is sufficient reason to understand the Apostle, when he speaks of the natural man in that I Cor. 2:14 as meaning man in his native corrupt state. And his words represent him as totally corrupt, wholly a stranger and enemy to true virtue or holiness, and things appertaining to it, which it appears are commonly intended in the New Testament by things spiritual, and are doubtless here meant by things of the spirit of God. These words also represent, that it is impossible man should be otherwise, while in his natural state. The expressions are very strong: "the natural man receiveth not the things of the spirit of God," is not susceptible of things of that kind, "neither can he know them," can have no true sense or relish of them, or notion of their real nature and true excellency; "because they are spiritually discerned"; they are not discerned by means of any principle in nature, but altogether by a principle that is divine, something introduced by the grace of God's holy spirit, which is above all that is natural. The words are in a considerable degree parallel with those of our savior. (John 14:16, 17), "He shall give you the spirit of truth, whom the world cannot receive, because it seeth him not, neither knoweth him: but ye know him; for he dwelleth with you, and shall be in you."

SECTION 2. OBSERVATIONS ON ROMANS 3:9–24

IF the Scriptures represent all mankind as wicked in their first state, before they are made partakers of the benefits of Christ's redemption, then they are wicked by nature: for doubtless men's first state is their native state, or the state they come into the world in. But the Scriptures do thus represent all mankind.

Before I mention particular texts to this purpose, I would observe, that it alters not the case as to the argument in hand, whether we suppose these texts speak directly of infants, or only of such as are capable of some understanding, so as to understand something of their own duty and state. For if it be so with all mankind, that as soon as ever they are capable of reflecting and knowing their own moral state, they find themselves wicked, this proves that they are wicked by nature, either born wicked, or born with an infallible disposition to be wicked as soon as possible, if there be any difference between these; and either of 'em will prove men to be born exceedingly depraved. I have before proved, that a native propensity to sin certainly follows from many things said in the Scripture, of mankind; but what I intend now, is something more direct, to prove by direct Scripture-testimony, that all mankind in their first state are really of a wicked character.

To this purpose is exceeding full, express and abundant that passage of the Apostle, in Rom. 3 beginning with the 9th verse to the end of the 24th; which I shall set down at large, distinguishing the universal terms which are here so often repeated, by a distinct character. The Apostle having in the first chapter, verses 16, 17, laid down his proposition, that none can be saved in any other way than through the righteousness of God, by faith in Jesus Christ, he proceeds to prove this point, by shewing particularly that all are in themselves wicked, and without any righteousness of their own. First, he insists on the wickedness of the *Gentiles,* in the first chapter; and next, on the wickedness of the *Jews,* in the second chapter. And then in this place, he comes to sum up the matter, and draw the conclusion in the words following: "What then, are we better than they? No, in no wise; for we have before proved both Jews and Gentiles, that they are all under sin; as it is written, there is *none* righteous, no, not one; there is none that understandeth; there is *none* that seeketh after God; they are all gone out of the way; they are *together* become unprofitable; there is none that doth good, no, not one. Their throat is an open sepulchre; with their tongues they have used deceit; the poison of asps is under their lips; whose mouth is full of cursing and bitterness; their feet are swift to shed blood; destruction and misery are in their ways, and the way of peace they have not known; there is no fear of God before their eyes. Now we know, that whatsoever things the law saith, it saith to them that are under the law, that *every* mouth may be stopped, and *all* the world may become guilty before God. Therefore by the deeds of the law, there shall *no flesh* be justified in his sight; for by the law is the knowledge of sin. But now the righteousness of God without the law is manifest, being witnessed by the law and the prophets; even the righteousness of God, which is by faith of Jesus Christ, unto all, and upon all them that believe; for there is no difference. For all have sinned, and come short of the glory of God, being justified freely by his grace, through the redemption which is in Jesus Christ."

Here the thing which I would prove, viz. that mankind in their first state, before they are interested in the benefits of Christ's redemption, are universally wicked, is declared with the utmost possible fullness and precision. So that if here this matter ben't set forth plainly, expressly and fully, it must be because no words can do it, and it is not in the power of language or any manner of terms and phrases, however contrived and heaped up one upon another, determinately to signify any such thing.

Dr. Taylor to take off the force of the whole, would have us to understand (pp.104–107) that these passages, quoted from the Psalms, and other parts of the Old Testament, don't speak of all mankind, nor of all the Jews; but only of them of whom they were true. He observes, there were many that were innocent and righteous; though there were also many, a strong party, that were wicked, corrupt, etc. of whom these texts were to be understood. Concerning which I would observe the following things.

1. According to this, the universality of the terms that are found in these places, which the Apostle cites from the Old Testament, to prove that *all the world, both Jews and Gentiles, are under sin,* is nothing to his purpose. The Apostle uses universal terms in his prop-

osition, and in his conclusion, that all are under sin, that every mouth is stopped, all the world guilty, that by the deeds of the law no flesh can be justified. And he chooses out a number of universal sayings or clauses out of the Old Testament, to confirm this universality; as (Rom. 3:10–11) "There is none righteous; no, not one; They are all gone out of the way; there is none that understandeth, etc." But yet the universality of these expressions is nothing to his purpose; because the universal terms found in 'em have indeed no reference to any such universality as this the Apostle speaks of, nor anything akin to it; they mean no universality, either in the collective sense, or personal sense; no universality of the nations of the world, or of particular persons in those nations, or in any one nation in the world: "But only of those of whom they are true." That is (Rom. 3:10–11) "There is none of them righteous, of whom it is true, that they are not righteous, no, not one: there is none that understand, of whom it is true, that they understand not: they are all gone out of the way, of whom it is true, that they are gone out of the way, etc." Or these expressions are to be understood concerning that strong party in Israel, in David's and Solomon's days and in the prophets' days: they are to be understood of them universally. And what is that to the Apostle's purpose? How does such an universality of wickedness, as this—that all were wicked in Israel, who were wicked, or that there was a particular evil party, all of which were wicked—confirm that universality which the Apostle would prove, viz. that all Jews and Gentiles, and the whole world were wicked, and every mouth stopped, and that no flesh could be justified by their own righteousness.

Here nothing can be said to abate the nonsense, but this, that the Apostle would convince the Jews, that they were capable of being wicked as well as other nations; and to prove it, he mentions some texts, which shew that there was a wicked party in Israel, a thousand years ago: and that as to the universal terms which happened to be in these texts, the Apostle had no respect to these; but his reciting them is as it were accidental, they happened to be in some texts which speak of an evil party in Israel, and the Apostle cites 'em as they are, not because they are any more to his purpose for the universal terms, which happen to be in them. But let the reader look on the words of the Apostle, and observe the violence of such a supposition. Particularly let the words of the 9th and 10th verses, and their connection, be observed. "All are under sin: as it is written, there is none righteous; no, not one." How plain it is, that the Apostle cites that latter universal clause out of the 14th Psalm, to confirm the preceding universal words of his own proposition? And yet it will follow from the things which Dr. Taylor supposes, that the universality of the terms in the last words, "There is none righteous; no, not one," have no relation at all to that universality he speaks of in the preceding clause, to which they are joined, "All are under sin"; and is no more a confirmation of it, than if the words were thus: "There are some, or there are many in Israel, that are not righteous."

2. To suppose, the Apostle's design in citing these passages, was only to prove to the Jews, that of old there was a considerable number of their nation that were wicked men, is to suppose him to have gone about to prove what none of the Jews denied, or made the least doubt of. Even the Pharisees, the most self-righteous sect of them, who went furthest in glorying in the distinction of their nation from other nations, as a holy people, knew it, and owned it: they openly confessed that their "forefathers killed the prophets (Matt. 23:29,-30,31)." And if the Apostle's design had been only to refresh their memories, to put 'em in mind of the ancient wickedness of their nation, to lead to reflection on themselves as guilty of the like wickedness (as Stephen does, Acts 7), what need had the Apostle to go so far about to prove this; gathering up many sentences here and there, which prove that their Scriptures did speak of some as wicked men; and then, in the next place, to prove that the wicked men spoken of must be of the nation of the Jews, by this argument that "What things soever the law saith, it saith to them that are under the law," or that whatsoever the books of the Old Testament said, it must be understood of that people that had the Old Testament? What need had the Apostle of such an ambage or fetch as this,[1] to prove to the Jews, that there had been many of their nation in some of the ancient ages, which were wicked men; when the Old Testament was full of passages that asserted this expressly, not only of a strong party, but of the nation in general? How much more would it have been to such a purpose, to have put 'em in mind of the wickedness of the people in general, in worshipping the golden calf, and the unbelief, murmuring and perverseness of the whole congregation in

1. [JE's plural of "ambage" has been dropped. "Ambage" means circumlocution or ambiguity. Obviously he is charging Taylor with introducing farfetched interpretations of Scripture.]

the wilderness, for forty years, as Stephen does? Which things he had no need to prove to be spoken of their nation, by any such indirect argument as that, "Whatsoever things the law saith, it saith to them that are under the law."

3. It would have been impertinent to the Apostle's purpose, even as our author understands his purpose, for him to have gone about to convince the Jews, that there had been a strong party of bad men in David's and Solomon's and the prophets' times. For Dr. Taylor supposes, the Apostle's aim is to prove the great corruption of both Jews and Gentiles at that day, when Christ came into the world.[2]

In order the more fully to evade the clear and abundant testimonies to the doctrine of original sin, contained in this part of the holy Scripture, our author says, the Apostle is here speaking of bodies of people, of Jews and Gentiles in a collective sense, as two great bodies into which mankind are divided; speaking of them in their collective capacity, and not with respect to particular persons; that the Apostle's design is to prove, neither of these two great collective bodies, in their collective sense, can be justified by law, because both were corrupt; and so, that no more is implied, than that the generality of both were wicked.[3] On this I observe,

(1) That this supposed sense disagrees extremely with the terms and language which the Apostle here makes use of. For according to this, we must understand, either

First, that the Apostle means no universality at all, but only the far greater part. But if the words which the Apostle uses, don't most fully and determinately signify an universality, no words ever used in the Bible are sufficient to do it. I might challenge any man to produce any one paragraph in the Scripture, from the beginning to the end, where there is such a repetition and accumulation of terms, so strongly and emphatically and carefully to express the most perfect and absolute universality; or any place to be compared to it. What instance is there in the Scripture, or indeed [in] any other writing, when the meaning is only the much greater part, where this meaning is signified in such a manner, by repeating such expressions, "They are all . . . they are all . . . they are all . . . together . . . every one . . . all the world" joined to multiplied negative terms, to shew the universality to be without exception; saying "There is no flesh . . . there is none . . . there is none . . . there is none"

2. See *Key* no. 275, 278.

3. Pp. 102, 104, 117, 119, 120 and *Note on Romans* 3:10–19.

four times over; besides the addition of "no, not one . . . no, not one" once and again!

Or secondly, if any universality at all be allowed, it is only of the collective bodies spoken of; and these collective bodies but two, as Dr. Taylor reckons them, viz. the Jewish nation, and the Gentile world; supposing the Apostle is here representing each of these parts of mankind as being wicked. But is this the way of men's using language, when speaking of but two things, to express themselves in universal terms, of such a sort, and in such a manner, and when they mean no more than that the thing affirmed is predicated of both of them? If a man speaking of his two feet as both lame should say, "All my feet are lame. They are all lame. All together are become weak; none of my feet are strong, none of them are sound; no, not one," would not he be thought to be lame in his understanding as well as his feet? When the Apostle says, "That every mouth may be stopped," must we suppose that he speaks only of those two great collective bodies, figuratively ascribing to each of them a mouth, and mean that those two mouths are stopped!

And besides, according to our author's own interpretation, the universal terms used in these texts cited from the Old Testament, have no respect to those two great collective bodies, nor indeed to either of them; but to some in Israel, a particular disaffected party in that one nation, which was made up of wicked men. So that his interpretation is every way absurd and inconsistent.

(2) If the Apostle is speaking only of the wickedness or guilt of great collective bodies, then it will follow, that also the justification he here treats of, is no other than the justification of such collective bodies. For they are the same he speaks of as guilty and wicked, that he argues cannot be justified by the works of the law, by reason of their being wicked. Otherwise his argument is wholly disannulled.[4] If the guilt he speaks of be only of collective bodies, then what he argues from that guilt, must be only, that collective bodies cannot be justified by the works of the law, having no respect to the justification of particular persons. And indeed this is Dr. Taylor's declared opinion. He supposes, the Apostle here, and in other parts of this epistle, is speaking of men's justification considered only as in their collective capacity.[5] But the contrary is most manifest. The

4. [An emphatic form of "annul."]

5. See *Note on Rom.* 3:10–19 and on ch. 5:11 and on ch. 9:30,31 and on ch. 11:31.

26th and 28th verses of this third chapter can't, without the utmost violence, be understood otherwise than of the justification of particular persons. "That he might be just, and the justifier of him that believeth in Jesus. . . . Therefore we conclude that a man is justified by faith, without the deeds of the law." (So ch. 4:5), "But to him that worketh not, but believeth on him that justifieth the ungodly, his faith is counted for righteousness." And what the Apostle cites in the 6, 7, and 8th verses from the book of Psalms, evidently shews, that he is speaking of the justification of particular persons. "Even as David also describeth the blessedness of the man unto whom God imputeth righteousness without works, saying, blessed are they whose iniquities are forgiven and whose sins are covered." David says these things in the 32d Psalm, with a special respect to his own particular case; there expressing the great distress he was in, while under a sense of the guilt of his personal sin, and the great joy he had when God forgave him, as in vv. 3, 4.

And then, it is very plain in that paragraph of the third chapter, which we have been upon, that it is the justification of particular persons that the Apostle speaks of, by that place in the Old Testament, which he refers to in v. 20. "Therefore by the deeds of the law, there shall no flesh be justified in his sight." He refers to that in Ps. 143: "Enter not into judgment with thy servant; for in thy sight shall no man living be justified." Here the Psalmist is not speaking of the justification of a nation, as a collective body, or of one of the two parts of the world, but of a particular man. And 'tis further manifest, that the Apostle is here speaking of personal justification, inasmuch as this place is evidently parallel with that [in] Gal. 3:10,11. "For as many as are of the works of the law, are under the curse: for it is written, cursed is everyone that continueth not in all things that are written in the book of the law to do them. But that no man is justified by the works of the law, is evident; for the just shall live by faith." It is plain, that this place is parallel with that in the 3rd of Romans, not only as the thing asserted is the same, and the argument by which it is proved here, is the same as there, viz. that all are guilty, and exposed to be condemned by the law; but the same saying of the Old Testament is cited here in the beginning of this discourse in Galatians (ch. 1:16). And many other things demonstrate, that the Apostle is speaking of the same justification in both places, which I omit for brevity's sake.

And besides all these things, our author's interpretation makes the

Apostle's argument wholly void another way. The Apostle is speaking of a certain subject, which cannot be justified by the works of the law; and his argument is that, that same subject is guilty, and is condemned by the law. If he means, that one subject, suppose a collective body or bodies, can't be justified by the law, because another subject, another collective body, is condemned by the law, 'tis plain, the argument would be quite vain and impertinent. Yet thus the argument must stand according to Dr. Taylor's interpretation. The collective bodies, which he supposes are spoken of as wicked, and condemned by the law, considered as in their collective capacity, are those two, the Jewish nation, and the heathen world: but the collective body which he supposes the Apostle speaks of as justified without the deeds of the law, is neither of these, but the Christian church, or body of believers; which is a new collective body, a new creature, and a new man (according to our author's understanding of such phrases), which never had any existence before it was justified, and therefore never was wicked or condemned unless it was with regard to the individuals of which it was constituted: and it does not appear, according to our author's scheme, that these individuals had before been generally wicked. For according to him there was a number both among the Jews and Gentiles, that were righteous before. And how does it appear, but that the comparatively few Jews and Gentiles, of which this new-created collective body was constituted, were chiefly of the best of each?

So that in every view this author's way of explaining this passage in the third of Romans, appears vain and absurd. And so clearly and fully has the Apostle expressed himself, that 'tis doubtless impossible to invent any other sense to put upon his words, than that which will imply that all mankind, even every individual of the whole race but their Redeemer himself, are in their first original state corrupt and wicked.

Before I leave this passage of the Apostle, it may be proper to observe, that it not only is a most clear, and full testimony to the native depravity of mankind, but also plainly declares that natural depravity to be total and exceeding great. 'Tis the Apostle's manifest design in these citations from the Old Testament, to shew these three things: 1. That *all mankind* are by nature *corrupt*. 2. That every one is *altogether corrupt*, and as it were, depraved in every part. 3. That they are in every part *corrupt in an exceeding degree*. With respect to the second of these, that everyone is wholly, and as it were in every part corrupt, 'tis plain, the Apostle chooses out, and puts together those particular passages of the Old Testament, wherein most of those members of the body are mentioned, that are the soul's chief instruments or organs of external action. The hands (implicitly) in those expressions, "They are together become unprofitable, there is none that doeth good." The throat, tongue, lips, and mouth, the organs of speech; in those words, "Their throat is an open sepulchre: with their tongues they have used deceit: the poison of asps is under their lips; whose mouth is full of cursing and bitterness." The feet, in those words (v. 15), "Their feet are swift to shed blood." These things together signify, that man is as it were all over corrupt, in every part. And not only is the total corruption thus intimated, by enumerating the several parts, but by denying of all good; any true understanding or spiritual knowledge, any virtuous action, or so much as truly virtuous desire, or seeking after God. "There is none that understandeth; there is none that seeketh after God: there is none that doth good; the way of peace have they not known." And in general, by denying all true piety or religion in men, in their first state. (v. 18), "There is no fear of God before their eyes." The expressions also are evidently chosen to denote a most extreme and desperate wickedness of heart. And exceeding depravity is ascribed to every part: to the throat, the scent of an open sepulchre; to the tongue and lips, deceit and the poison of asps; to the mouth, cursing and bitterness; of their feet it is said, they are swift to shed blood: and with regard to the whole man, 'tis said, destruction and misery are in their ways. The representation is very strong, of each of these things, viz. that all mankind are corrupt; that everyone is wholly, and altogether corrupt; and also extremely and desperately corrupt. And it is plain, 'tis not accidental, that we have here such a collection of such strong expressions, so emphatically signifying these things; but that they are chosen of the Apostle on design, as being directly and fully to his purpose; which purpose appears in all his discourse in the whole of this chapter, and indeed from the beginning of the epistle.

Section 3. OBSERVATIONS ON ROMANS 5:6–10, AND EPHESIANS 2:3 WITH THE CONTEXT, AND ROMANS 7

ANOTHER passage of this Apostle in the same epistle to the Romans, which shews that all that are made partakers of the benefits of Christ's redemption, are in their first state wicked and desperately wicked, is that (ch. 5:6–10), "For when we were yet without strength, in due time Christ died for the ungodly. For scarcely for a righteous man will one die; yet peradventure for a good man, some would even dare to die. But God commendeth his love towards us, in that while we were yet sinners, Christ died for us. Much more then, being now justified by his blood, we shall be saved from wrath through him. For if while we were enemies, we were reconciled to God through the death of his son; much more, being reconciled, we shall be saved by his life."

Here all that Christ died for, and that are saved by him, are spoken of as being in their first state sinners, ungodly, enemies to God, exposed to divine wrath, and without strength, without ability to help themselves, or deliver their souls from this miserable state.

Dr. Taylor says, the Apostle here speaks of the Gentiles only in their heathen state, in contradistinction to the Jews; and that not of particular persons among the heathen Gentiles, or as to the state they were in personally; but only of the Gentiles collectively taken, or of the miserable state of that great collective body, the heathen world: and that these appellations, "sinners," "ungodly," "enemies," etc. were names by which the apostles in their writings were wont to signify and distinguish the heathen world, in opposition to the Jews; and that in this sense these appellations are to be taken in their epistles, and in this place in particular.[1] And 'tis observable, that this way of interpreting these phrases in the apostolic writings, is become fashionable with many late writers; whereby they not only evade several clear testimonies to the doctrine of original sin, but make void great part of the New Testament; on which account it deserves the more particular consideration.

1. Pp. 114–120. See also Dr. Taylor's *Paraphrase and Notes* on the place.

'Tis allowed to have been long common and customary among the Jews, in Christ's and the apostles' days, especially those of the sect of the Pharisees, in their pride and confidence in their privileges as the peculiar people of God, to exalt themselves exceedingly above other nations, and greatly to despise the Gentiles, and call them by such names as "sinners," "enemies," "dogs," etc. as notes of distinction from themselves, whom they accounted in general (excepting the Publicans and the notoriously profligate) as the "friends," "special favorites," and "children of God"; because they were the children of Abraham, were circumcised, and had the law of Moses as their peculiar privilege, and as a wall of partition between them and the Gentiles.

But it is very remarkable, that a Christian divine, who has studied the New Testament, and the epistle to the Romans in particular, so diligently as Dr. Taylor, should be strong in an imagination, that the apostles of Jesus Christ should so far countenance, and do so much to cherish these self-exalting, uncharitable dispositions and notions of the Jews, which gave rise to such a custom, as to fall in with that custom, and adopt that language of their pride and contempt; and especially that the apostle Paul should do it. 'Tis a most unreasonable imagination, on many accounts.

1. The whole gospel-dispensation is calculated entirely to overthrow and abolish everything to which this self-distinguishing, self-exalting language of the Jews was owing. It was calculated wholly to exclude such boasting, and to destroy that pride and self-righteousness, that were the causes of it: it was calculated to abolish the enmity, and break down the partition-wall between Jews and Gentiles, and of twain to make one new man, so making peace; to destroy all dispositions in nations and particular persons to despise one another, or to say one to another, "Stand by thyself, come not near to me, for I am holier than thou," and to establish the contrary principles of humility, mutual esteem, honor and love, and universal union, in the most firm and perfect manner.

2. Christ, when on earth, set himself, through the course of his ministry, to militate against this Pharisaical spirit, practice and language of the Jews; appearing in such representations, names and epithets so customary among them; by which they shewed so much contempt of the Gentiles, Publicans and such as were openly lewd and vicious, and so exalted themselves above them; calling them sinners and enemies, and themselves holy and God's children; not allowing

the Gentile to be their neighbor, etc. He condemned the Pharisees for not esteeming themselves sinners, as well as the Publicans; trusting in themselves that they were righteous, and despising others. He militated against these things in his own treatment of some Gentiles, Publicans and others, whom they called sinners, and in what he said on those occasions.[2] He opposed these notions and manners of the Jews in his parables; [3] and in his instructions to his disciples how to treat the unbelieving Jews; [4] and in what he says to Nicodemus about the necessity of a new birth, even for the Jews, as well as the unclean Gentiles with regard to their proselytism, which some of the Jews looked upon as a new birth; and in opposition to their notions of their being the children of God, because the children of Abraham, but the Gentiles by nature sinners and children of wrath, he tells them that even they were children of the devil.[5]

3. Though we should suppose the apostles not to have been thoroughly brought off from such notions, manners and language of the Jews, till after Christ's ascension; yet after the pouring out of the spirit on the day of Pentecost, or at least, after the calling of the Gentiles, begun in the conversion of Cornelius, they were fully indoctrinated in this matter, and effectually taught no longer to call the Gentiles unclean, as a note of distinction from the Jews (Acts 10:24), which was before any of the apostolic epistles were written.

4. Of all the apostles, none were more perfectly instructed in this matter, and none so abundant in instructing others in it, as Paul, the great Apostle of the Gentiles. He had abundance to do in this matter. None of the apostles had so much occasion to exert themselves against the forementioned notions and language of the Jews,

2. Matt. 8:5–13, 9:9–13, 11:19–24; Luke 7:37 to the end, 17:12–19, 19:1–10; Matt. 15:21–28; John 4:9 etc. v. 39 etc. Compare Luke 10:29 etc.

3. Matt. 21:28–32, 22:1–10; Luke 14:16–24. Compare Luke 13:28,29,30.

4. Matt. 10:14,15.

5. John 8:33–34. It may also be observed, that John the Baptist greatly contradicted the Jews' opinion of themselves, as being a holy people, and accepted of God, because they were the children of Abraham, and on that account better than the heathen, whom they called sinners, enemies, unclean, etc. in baptizing the Jews as a polluted people and sinners, as the Jews used to baptize proselytes from among the heathen; calling them to repentance as sinners, saying, "Think not to say within yourselves, we have Abraham to our father; for I say unto you, that God is able, of these stones, to raise up children unto Abraham"; and teaching the Pharisees, that instead of their being a holy generation and children of God, as they called themselves, they were a generation of vipers.

in opposition of Jewish teachers, and Judaizing Christians, that strove to keep up the separation-wall between Jews and Gentiles, and to exalt the former, and set the latter at naught.

5. This Apostle does especially strive in this matter in this epistle to the Romans, above all his other writings; exerting himself in a most elaborate manner, and with his utmost skill and power to bring the Jewish Christians off from everything of this kind; endeavoring by all means, that there might no longer be in them any remains of these old notions they had been educated in, of such a great distinction between Jews and Gentiles, as were expressed in the names they used to distinguish them by, calling the Jews "holy," "children of Abraham," "friends," and "children of God," but the Gentiles "sinners," "unclean," "enemies," and the like. He makes it almost his whole business, from the beginning of the epistle, to this passage in the 5th chapter which we are upon, to convince them that there was no ground for any such distinction, and to prove that in common, both Jews and Gentiles, all were desperately wicked, and none righteous, no, not one. He tells them (ch. 3:9), that the Jews were by no means better than the Gentiles; and (in what follows in that chapter) that there was no difference between Jews and Gentiles; and represents all as without strength, or any sufficiency of their own in the affair of justification and redemption; and in the continuation of the same discourse, in the 4th chapter, teaches that all that were justified by Christ, were in themselves ungodly; and that being the children of Abraham was not peculiar to the Jews. In this 5th chapter, still in continuation of the same discourse, on the same subject, and argument of justification through Christ, and by faith in him, he speaks of Christ's dying for the ungodly and sinners, and those that were without strength or sufficiency for their own salvation, as he had done all along before. But now, it seems, the Apostle by sinners and ungodly must not be understood according as he used these words before; but must be supposed to mean only the Gentiles, as distinguished from the Jews; adopting the language of those self-righteous, self-exalting, disdainful Judaizing teachers, whom he was with all his might opposing: countenancing the very same thing in them, which he had been from the beginning of the epistle discountenancing, and endeavoring to discourage, and utterly to abolish, with all his art and strength.

One reason, why the Jews looked on themselves better than the Gentiles, and called themselves holy and the Gentiles sinners, was that they had the law of Moses. They made their boast of the law. But the Apostle shews them, that this was so far from making them better, that it condemned them, and was an occasion of their being sinners in a higher degree, and more aggravated manner, and more effectually and dreadfully dead in and by sin (ch. 7:4–13), agreeable to those words of Christ, John 5:45.

It can't be justly objected here, that this Apostle did indeed use this language, and call the Gentiles sinners, in contradistinction to the Jews, in what he said to Peter, which he himself gives an account of in Gal. 2:15,16. "We who are Jews by nature, and not sinners of the Gentiles, knowing that a man is not justified by the works of the law, but by faith in Jesus Christ." 'Tis true, that the Apostle here refers to this distinction, as what was usually made by the self-righteous Jews, between themselves and the Gentiles; but not in such a manner as to adopt, or favor it; but on the contrary, so as plainly to shew his disapprobation of it; q.d. "Though we were born Jews, and by nature are of that people which are wont to make their boast of the law, expecting to be justified by it, and trust in themselves that they are righteous, despising others, calling the Gentiles sinners, in distinction from themselves; yet we being now instructed in the gospel of Christ, know better; we now know, that a man is not justified by the works of the law; that we are all justified only by faith in Christ, in whom there is no difference, no distinction of Greek or Gentile, and Jew, but all are one in Christ Jesus.[6] And this is the very thing, he there speaks of, which he blamed Peter for; that by his withdrawing and separating himself from the Gentiles, refusing to eat with them, etc. he had countenanced this self-exalting, self-distinguishing, separating spirit and custom of the Jews, whereby they treated the Gentiles, as in a distinguishing manner sinners and unclean, and not fit to come near them who were a holy people.

6. The words themselves of the Apostle in this place, shew plainly, that he uses the word "sinners," not as signifying "Gentiles," in opposition to "Jews," but as denoting the *morally evil,* in opposition to such as are *righteous or good:* because this latter opposition or distinction between sinners and righteous is here expressed in plain terms. "Scarcely for a righteous man will one die; yet peradventure for a good man some would even dare to die: but God commended his love towards us, in that while we were yet sinners, Christ died for us." By "righteous men" are doubtless meant the same that

6. [This is a free paraphrase and expansion of Gal. 2:15–16 and 3:28.]

are meant by such a phrase, throughout this Apostle's writings, and throughout the New Testament, and throughout the Bible. Will anyone pretend, that by the "righteous man," whom men would scarcely die for, and by the "good man," that perhaps some might even dare to die for, is meant a Jew? Dr. Taylor himself don't explain it so, in his exposition of this epistle; and therefore is not very consistent with himself, in supposing, that in the other part of the distinction the Apostle means Gentiles, as distinguished from the Jews. The Apostle himself had been laboring abundantly, in the preceding part of the epistle, to prove that the Jews were sinners in this sense, namely in opposition to righteous; that all had sinned, that all were under sin, and therefore could not be justified, could not be accepted as righteous, by their own righteousness.

7. Another thing which makes it evident, that the Apostle when he speaks in this place of the sinners and enemies which Christ died for, don't mean only the Gentiles, is that he includes himself among them, saying, "while we were sinners," and "when we were enemies."

Our author from time to time says, the Apostle, though he speaks only of the Gentiles in their heathen state, yet *puts himself with them, because he was the Apostle of the Gentiles.* But this is very violent and unreasonable. There is no more sense in it, than there would be in a father's ranking himself among his children, when speaking to his children of the benefits they have by being begotten by himself; and saying, "we children," or in a physician's ranking himself with his patients, when talking to them of their diseases and cure, saying, "we sick folks." Paul's being the Apostle of the Gentiles, to save 'em from their heathenism, is so far from being a reason for him to reckon himself among the heathen, that on the contrary, 'tis a very thing that would render it in a peculiar manner unnatural and absurd for him so to do. Because, as the Apostle of the Gentiles, he appears as their healer and deliverer from heathenism; and therefore in that capacity does in a peculiar manner appear in his distinction from the heathen, and in opposition to the state of heathenism. For 'tis by the most opposite qualities only, that he is fitted to be an apostle of the heathen, and recoverer from heathenism. As the clear light of the sun is the thing which makes it a proper restorative from darkness; and therefore, the sun's being spoken of as such a remedy, none would suppose to be a good reason why it should be ranked with darkness, or among dark things. And besides (which makes this supposition of Dr. Taylor's appear more violent) the Apostle, in this epistle, does expressly rank himself with the Jews, when he speaks of them as distinguished from the Gentiles; as in ch. 3:9. "What then? Are we better than they?" That is, are we Jews better than the Gentiles?

It can't justly be alleged in opposition to this, that the apostle Peter puts himself with the heathen. (I Pet. 4:3), "For the time past of our life may suffice us to have wrought the will of the Gentiles; when we walked in lasciviousness, lusts, excess of wine, reviling, banquetings, and abominable idolatries." For the apostle Peter (who by the way was not an apostle of the Gentiles) here don't speak of himself as one of the heathen, but as one of the church of Christ in general, made up of those that had been Jews, proselytes and heathen, who now were all one body, of which body he was a member. 'Tis this society therefore, and not the Gentiles, that he refers to in the pronoun "us." He is speaking of the wickedness that the members of this body or society had lived in before their conversion: not that every member had lived in all those vices here mentioned, but some in one, others in another. Very parallel with that of the apostle Paul to Titus (ch. 3:3), "For we ourselves (i.e. we of the Christian church) sometimes also were foolish, disobedient, deceived, serving divers lusts and pleasures (some one lust and pleasure, others another), living in malice, envy, hateful and hating one another, etc." There is nothing in this, but what is very natural. That the Apostle, speaking *to* the Christian Church and *of* that church, confessing its former sins, should speak of himself as one of that society, and yet mention some sins that he personally had not been guilty of, and among others, heathenish idolatry, is quite a different thing from what it would have been for the Apostle, expressly distinguishing those of the Christians which had been heathen from those which had been Jews, to have ranked himself with the former, though he was truly of the latter.

If a minister in some congregation in England, speaking in a sermon of the sins of the nation, being himself of the nation, should say, "*We* have greatly corrupted ourselves, and provoked God by our Deism, our blasphemy, our profane swearing, our lasciviousness, our venality, etc." speaking in the first person plural, though he himself never had been a Deist, and perhaps none of his hearers, and they might also have been generally free from other sins he mentioned; yet there would be nothing unnatural in his thus expressing himself.

But it would be quite a different thing, if one part of the British dominions, suppose our king's American dominions, had universally apostacized from Christianity to Deism, and had long been in such a state, and if one that had been born and brought up in England among Christians, the country being universally Christian, should be sent among them to shew them the folly and great evil of Deism, and convert them to Christianity; and this missionary, when making a distinction between English Christians, and these Deists, should rank himself with the latter, and say, "*we* American Deists, we foolish blind infidels, etc." This indeed would be very unnatural and absurd.

Another passage of the Apostle, to the like purpose with that which we have been considering in the 5th of Romans, is that in Eph. 2:3, "And were by nature children of wrath, even as others." This remains a plain testimony to the doctrine of original sin, as held by those that used to be called orthodox Christians, after all the pains and art used to torture and pervert it. This doctrine is here not only plainly and fully taught, but abundantly so, if we take the words with the context; where Christians are once and again represented as being, in their first state, dead in sin, and as quickened, and raised up from such a state of death, in a most marvelous display of the free and rich grace and love, and exceeding greatness of the power of God, etc.

With respect to those words ἤμεθα τέκνα φύσει ὀργῆς "We were by nature children of wrath," Dr. Taylor says (pp. 112, 113, 114), "The apostle means no more by this, than truly or really children of wrath; using a metaphorical expression, borrowed from the word that is used to signify a true and genuine child of a family, in distinction from one that is a child only by adoption: to express this we say, he is by nature a child." In which 'tis owned, that the proper sense of the phrase is being a child by nature, in the same sense as a child by birth or natural generation; but only he supposes, that here the word is used metaphorically. The instance he produces as parallel, to confirm his supposed metaphorical sense of the phrase, as meaning only truly, really or properly children of wrath, viz. the apostle Paul's calling Timothy his own son in the faith, γνήσιον τέκνον,[7] is so far from confirming his sense, that it is rather directly against it. For doubtless the Apostle uses the word γνήσιον in its original signification here, meaning his begotten son; γνήσιος being the

7. [I Tim. 1:2.]

adjective from *γὸνη*,[8] "offspring," or the verb *γεννάω*, "to beget"; as much as to say, "Timothy my begotten son in the faith"; only allowing for the two ways of being begotten, spoken of in the New Testament, one natural, and the other spiritual; one being the first generation, the other regeneration; the one a being begotten as to the human nature, the other a being begotten in the faith, begotten in Christ, or as to one's Christianity. The Apostle expressly signifies which of these he means in this place, "Timothy my begotten son in the faith," in the same manner as he says to the Corinthians (I Cor. 4:15), "In Christ Jesus I have begotten you through the gospel." To say, the Apostle uses the word *φύσει* in Eph. 2:3 only as signifying real, true and proper, is a most arbitrary interpretation, having nothing to warrant it in the whole Bible. The word *φύσις* is nowhere used in this sense in the New Testament.[9]

Another thing which our author alleges to evade the force of this is, that the word rendered "nature," sometimes signifies habit contracted by custom, or an acquired nature. But this is not the proper meaning of the word. And it is plain, the word in its common use, in the New Testament, signifies what we properly express in English by the word "nature." There is but one place where there can be the least pretext for supposing it to be used otherwise; and that is I Cor. 11:14, "Doth not even nature itself teach you, that if a man have long hair, it is a shame unto him?" And even here there is, I think, no manner of reason for understanding nature otherwise than in the proper sense. The emphasis used, *αὐτή ἡ φύσις*, "nature itself," shews that the Apostle don't mean "custom," but "nature" in the proper sense. It is true, it was long custom, that made having the head covered a token of subjection, and a feminine habit or appearance; as 'tis custom that makes any outward action or word a sign or signification of anything: but nature itself, nature in its proper sense, "teaches," that it is a shame for a man to appear with the established signs of the female sex, and with significations of inferiority, etc. As nature itself shews it to be a shame for a father to bow down or kneel to his own child or servant, or for men to bow to an idol, because bowing down is by custom an established token or sign of subjection and submission: such a sight therefore would be unnatural,

8. [Probably "*γενος*" is intended.]

9. The following are all the places where the word is used. Rom. 1:26 and 2:14 and 17 and 11:21 and 24, twice in that verse. I Cor. 11:14, Gal. 2:15, and 4:8; Jas. 3:7, twice in that verse, and II Pet. 1:4.

shocking to a man's very nature. So nature would teach, that 'tis a shame for a woman to use such and such lascivious words or gestures: though it be custom, that establishes the unclean signification of those gestures and sounds.

'Tis particularly unnatural and unreasonable, to understand the phrase *τέκνα φύσει* in this place, any otherwise than in the proper sense, on the following accounts. (1) It may be observed, that both the words, *τέκνα* and *φύσις* in their original signification, have reference to the birth of generation. So the word *φύσις*, which comes from *φύω*, which signifies "to beget" or "bring forth young," or "to put forth," or "bud forth," as a plant, that brings forth young buds and branches. And so the word *τέκνον* comes from *τίκτω*, which signifies "to bring forth children." (2) As though the Apostle took care by the word used here, to signify what we are by birth, he changes the word he used before for "children." In the preceding verse he used *υἱοί*, speaking of the children of disobedience; but here *τέκνα*, which is a word derived, as now observed, from *τὶκτω*, "to bring forth a child," and more properly signifies a begotten or born child. (3) 'Tis natural to suppose that the Apostle here speaks in opposition to the pride of some, especially the Jews (for the church in Ephesus was made up partly of Jews, as well as the church in Rome) who exalted themselves in the privileges they had by birth, because they were born the children of Abraham, and were Jews by nature *φύσει Ἰουδαίοι* as the phrase is. (Gal. 2:15) In opposition to this proud conceit, he teaches the Jews, that notwithstanding this, they were by nature children of wrath, even as others, i.e. as well as the Gentiles, which the Jews had been taught to look upon as sinners, and out of favor with God by nature, and born children of wrath. (4) 'Tis more plain, that the Apostle uses the word "nature" in its proper sense here, because he sets what they were by nature, in opposition to what they are by grace. In this verse, the Apostle shews what they are by nature, viz. children of wrath; and in the following verses he shews, how very different their state is by grace; saying (v. 5), "By grace ye are saved"; repeating it again (v. 8), "By grace ye are saved." But if, by being children of wrath by nature, were meant no more than only their being really and truly children of wrath, as Dr. Taylor supposes, there would be no opposition in the signification of these phrases; for in this sense they were by nature in a state of salvation, as much as by nature children of wrath: for they were truly, really and properly in a state of salvation.

If we take these words with the context, the whole abundantly proves, that by nature we are totally corrupt, without any good thing in us. For if we allow the plain scope of the place, without attempting to hide it, by extreme violence used with the Apostle's words and expressions, the design here is strongly to establish this point; that what Christians have that is good in them, or in their state, is in no part of it naturally in themselves, or from themselves, but is wholly from divine grace, all the gift of God, and his workmanship, the effect of his power, and free and wonderful love. None of our good works are primarily from ourselves, but with respect to 'em all, we are God's workmanship, created unto good works, as it were out of nothing: not so much as faith itself, the first principle of good works in Christians, is of themselves, but that is the gift of God. Therefore the Apostle compares the work of God, in forming Christians to true virtue and holiness, not only to a new creation, but a resurrection, or raising from the dead. (v. 1), "You hath he quickened, who were dead in trespasses and sins." (and again v. 5), "Even when we were dead in sins, hath he quickened us together with Christ." In speaking of Christians being quickened with Christ, the Apostle has reference to what he had said before, in the latter part of the foregoing chapter, of God's manifesting the exceeding greatness of his power towards Christian converts, in their conversion, agreeable to the operation of his mighty power, when he raised Christ from the dead. So that it is plain by everything in this discourse, the Apostle would signify, that by nature we have no goodness; but are as destitute of it as a dead corpse is of life: and that all goodness, all good works, and faith the principle of all, are perfectly the gift of God's grace, and the work of his great, almighty and exceeding excellent power. I think there can be need of nothing but reading the chapter, and minding what is read, to convince all who have common understanding, of this; whatever any of the most subtle critics have done, or even can do, to twist, rack, perplex and pervert the words and phrases here used.

Dr. Taylor here again insists, that the Apostle speaks only of the Gentiles in their heathen state, when he speaks of those that were dead in sin, and by nature children of wrath; and that though he seems to include himself among these, saying, "We were by nature children of wrath, we were dead in sins," yet he only puts himself among them because he was the Apostle of the Gentiles. The gross absurdity of which may appear from what was said before. But besides the things which have been already observed, there are some things which make it peculiarly unreasonable to understand it so here. 'Tis true, the greater part of the church of Ephesus had been heathens, and therefore the Apostle often has reference to their heathen state, in this epistle. But the words in this chapter 2:3 plainly shew, that he means himself and other Jews, in distinction from the Gentiles: for the distinction is fully expressed. After he had told the Ephesians, who had been generally heathen, that they had been dead in sin, and had walked according to the course of this world, etc. (vv. 1 and 2), he makes a distinction, and says, "Among whom we also had our conversation etc. and were by nature children of wrath, even as others." Here first he changes the person; whereas, before he had spoken in the second person, "ye were dead . . . ye in time past walked, etc." Now he changes style, and uses the first person, in a most manifest distinction, "Among whom *we also,*" that is, we Jews, as well as ye Gentiles. Not only changing the person, but adding a particle of distinction, "also"; which would be nonsense, if he meant the same without distinction. And besides all this, more fully to express the distinction, the Apostle further adds a pronoun of distinction: "We also, even as others" or, we, as well as others: most evidently having respect to the notions, so generally entertained by the Jews, of their being much better than the Gentiles, in being Jews by nature, children of Abraham, and children of God; when they supposed the Gentiles to be utterly cast off, as born aliens, and by nature children of wrath. In opposition to this, the Apostle says, "We Jews, after all our glorying in our distinction, were by nature children of wrath, as well as the rest of the world." And a yet further evidence, that the Apostle here means to include the Jews, and even himself, is the universal term he uses, "Among whom also we all had our conversation, etc." Though wickedness was supposed by the Jews to be the course of this world, as to the generality of mankind, yet they supposed themselves an exempt people, at least the Pharisees, and the devout observers of the law of Moses, and traditions of the elders; whatever might be thought of Publicans and harlots. But in opposition to this, the Apostle asserts, that they all were no better by nature than others, but were to be reckoned among the children of disobedience, and children of wrath.

And then besides, if the Apostle chooses to put himself among the Gentiles, because he was the Apostle of the Gentiles, I would ask, why he don't do so in the 11th verse of the same chapter, where he speaks of their Gentile state expressly? "Remember that ye being in time past Gentiles in the flesh." Why does he here make a distinction between the Gentiles and himself? Why did he not say, "Let us remember, that *we* being in past time Gentiles?" [1] And why does the same Apostle, even universally, make the same distinction, speaking either in the second or third person, and never in the first, where he expressly speaks of the Gentilism of those that he wrote to; or speaks of 'em with reference to their distinction from the Jews? So everywhere in this same epistle; as in ch. 1:12,13, where the distinction is made just in the same manner as here, by the change of the person, and by the distinguishing particle "also." "That we should be to the praise of his glory who first trusted in Christ (the first believers in Christ being of the Jews, before the Gentiles were called) in whom ye also trusted, after that ye heard the word of truth, the gospel of your salvation." And in all the following part of this second chapter; as vv. 11, 17, 19, and 22. In which last verse the same distinguishing particle again is used, "in whom you also are builded together for an habitation of God through the spirit." (See also in the following chapters: ch. 3:6 and 4:17) And not only in this epistle, but constantly in other epistles: as Rom. 1:12,13; ch. 11:13,14,17,18,19,20,-21,22,23,24,25,28,30,31; ch. 15:15,16; I Cor. 12:2; Gal. 4:8; Col. 1:27; ch. 2:13; I Thess. 1:5,6,9; ch. 2:13,14,15,16.

Though I am far from thinking our author's exposition of the 7th chapter of Romans to be in any wise agreeable to the true sense of the Apostle, yet it is needless here to stand particularly to examine it; because the doctrine of original sin may be argued not the less strongly, though we should allow the thing wherein he mainly differs from such as he opposes in his interpretation, viz. that the Apostle don't speak in his own name, or to represent the state of a true Christian, but as representing the state of the Jews under the law. For even on this supposition, the drift of the place will prove, that every one who is under the law, and with equal reason every one of mankind, is carnal, sold under sin, in his first state, and till delivered by Christ. For, 'tis plain, that the Apostle's design is to shew the insufficiency of the law to give life to anyone whatsoever. This appears by what he says when he comes to draw his conclusion, in the continuation of this discourse (ch. 8:3),[2] "For what the law could not

1. [Emphasis added.]

2. Dr. Taylor himself reckons this a part of the same discourse or paragraph in the division he makes of the epistle, in his *Paraphrase and Notes* upon it.

do, in that it was weak through the flesh; God, sending his own son, etc." Our author supposes, this here spoken of, viz. "That the law can't give life, because it is weak through the flesh," is true with respect to every one of mankind.[3] And when the Apostle gives this reason "in that it is weak through the flesh," 'tis plain, that by the "flesh," which here he opposes to the "spirit," he means the same thing which in the preceding part of the same discourse, in the foregoing chapter, he had called by the name "flesh" (vv. 5, 14, 18) and the law of the members (v. 23) and the body of death (v. 24). Which is the thing that through this chapter he insists on as the grand hindrance and reason why the law could not give life, just as he does in his conclusion (ch. 8:3). Which in this last place, is given as a reason why the law can't give life to any of mankind. And it being the same reason, of the same thing, spoken of in the same discourse, in the former part of it; as appears, because this last place is the conclusion, of which that former part is the premise: and inasmuch as the reason there given is being in the flesh, and a being carnal, sold under sin. Therefore taking the whole of the Apostle's discourse, this is justly understood to be a reason why the law can't give life to any of mankind; and consequently, that all mankind are in the flesh, and are carnal, sold under sin, and so remain till delivered by Christ: and consequently all mankind in their first or original state are very sinful; which was the thing to be proved.

3. See *Note on Rom.* 5:20.

CHAPTER IV

CONTAINING OBSERVATIONS ON ROMANS 5:12 TO THE END

SECTION 1. REMARKS ON DR. TAYLOR'S WAY OF EXPLAINING THIS TEXT

THE following things are worthy to be taken notice of, concerning our author's exposition of this remarkable passage of the apostle Paul.

I. He greatly insists that by death in this place no more is meant, than that death which we all die, when this present life is extinguished, and the body returns to the dust; that no more is meant in the 12, 14, 15, and 17th verses (p. 27). He speaks of it as evidently clearly and infallibly so, because the Apostle is still discoursing on the same subject; plainly implying, that it must most infallibly be so, that the Apostle means no more by death, throughout this paragraph on the subject. But as infallible as this is, if we believe what Dr. Taylor elsewhere says, it must needs be otherwise. He, in p. 396, speaking of those words in the last verse of the next chapter, "The wages of sin is death, but the gift of God is eternal life, through Jesus Christ our Lord," says, "Death in this place is widely different from the death we now die; as it stands there opposed to eternal life, which is the gift of God through Jesus Christ, it manifestly signifies eternal death, the second death, or that death which they shall hereafter die, who live after the flesh." But death, in the conclusion of the paragraph we are upon in the 5th chapter, concerning the death that comes by Adam, and the life that comes by Christ, in the last verse of the chapter, is opposed to eternal life, just in the same manner as it is in the last verse of the next chapter: "That as sin has reigned unto death, even so might grace reign, through righteousness, unto eternal life, by Jesus Christ our Lord." So that by our author's own argument, death in this place also is manifestly widely different from the death we now die, as it stands here opposed to eternal life through Jesus Christ, and signifies eternal death, the second death. And yet this is a part of the same discourse or paragraph with that begun in the 12th verse as reckoned by Dr. Taylor himself in his division of paragraphs, in his *Paraphrase and Notes* on the epistle. So that if we will follow him, and admit his reasonings in the various parts of his book, here is manifest proof, against infallible evidence! So that 'tis true, the Apostle throughout this whole passage on the same subject, by death, evidently, clearly and infallibly means no more, than that death we now die, when this life is extinguished; and yet by death, in some part of this passage, is meant something widely different from the death we now die, and is manifestly intended eternal death, the second death.

But had our author been more consistent with himself in his laying of it down as so certain and infallible, that because the Apostle has a special respect to temporal death, in the 14th verse, "Death reigned from Adam to Moses," therefore he means no more in the several consequent parts of this passage, yet he is doubtless too confident and positive in this matter. This is no more evident, clear and infallible, than that Christ meant no more by perishing in Luke 13:5, when he says, "I tell you, nay, but except ye repent, ye shall all likewise perish," than such a temporal death, as came on those that died by the fall of the tower of Siloam, spoken of in the preceding words of the same speech: and no more infallible, than that by "life," Christ means no more than this temporal life, in each part of that one sentence. (Matt. 10:39), "He that findeth his life, shall lose it; and he that loseth his life for my sake, shall find it"; because in the first part of each clause he has respect especially to temporal life.[1]

1. There are many places parallel with these, as John 11:25,26. "I am the resurrection, and the life: he that believeth in me, though he were dead, yet shall he live: and whosoever liveth, and believeth in me, shall never die." Here both the words "life" and "death" are used with this variation: "I am the resurrection, and the life," meaning spiritual and eternal life: "He that believeth in me, though he were dead," having respect to temporal death, "Yet shall he live," with respect to spiritual life, and the restoration of the life of the body. "And whosoever liveth and believeth in me, shall never die," meaning a spiritual and eternal death. So in John 6:49,50. "Your fathers did eat manna in the wilderness, and are dead," having respect chiefly to temporal death. "This is the bread which cometh down from heaven, that a man may eat thereof, and not die," i.e. by the loss of spiritual life, and by eternal death. See also v. 58. And in the next verse, "If any man eat of this bread, he shall live forever," have eternal life. So v. 54. See another like instance, John 5:24–29.

The truth of the case with respect to what the Apostle intends by the word "death" in this place, is this, viz. that the same thing is meant, as is meant by "death" in the foregoing and following parts of this epistle, and other writings of this Apostle, where he speaks of death as the consequence of sin, namely, the whole of that death, which he, and the Scripture everywhere, speaks of as the proper wages and punishment of sin, including death temporal, spiritual and eternal; though in some parts of this discourse he has a more special respect to one part of this whole, in others to another, as his argument leads him; without any more variation, than is common in the same discourse. That life which the Scripture speaks of as the reward of righteousness, is a whole containing several parts, viz. the life of the body, union of soul and body, and the most perfect sensibility, activity and felicity of both, which is the chief thing. In like manner the death, which the Scripture speaks of as the punishment of sin, is a whole including the death of the body, and the death of the soul, and the eternal, sensible, perfect destruction and misery of both. 'Tis this latter whole, that the Apostle speaks of by the name of death in this discourse, in Rom. 5. Though in some sentences he has a more special respect to one part, in others to another: and this without changing the signification of the word. For an having respect to several things included in the extensive signification of the word, is not the same thing as using the word in several distinct significations. As for instance, the appellative, "man," or the proper name of any particular man, is the name of a whole, including the different parts of soul and body. And if anyone in speaking of James or John, should say, he was a wise man, and a beautiful man; in the former part of the sentence, respect would be had more especially to his soul, in the latter to his body, in the word "man": but yet without any proper change of the signification of the name, to distinct senses. In John 21:7, it is said, "Peter was naked," and in the following part of the same story 'tis said, "Peter was grieved." In the former proposition, respect is had especially to his body, in the latter to his soul: but yet here is no proper change of the meaning of the name, Peter. And as to the Apostle's use of the word "death," in the passage now under consideration, on the supposition that he in the general, means the whole of that death which is the wages of sin, there is nothing but what is perfectly natural in supposing, that he, in order to evince, that death, the proper punishment of sin, comes on all mankind, in consequence of Adam's sin, should take notice of that part of this punishment, which is visible in this world, and which everybody therefore sees does in fact come on all mankind (as in v. 14), and from thence should infer, that all mankind are exposed to the whole of that death which is the proper punishment of sin, whereof that temporal death which is visible, is a part, and a visible image of the whole, and (unless changed by divine grace) an introduction to the principal, and infinitely the most dreadful part.

II. Dr. Taylor's explanation of this passage makes wholly insignificant those first words, "By one man sin entered into the world," and leaves this proposition without any sense of signification at all. The Apostle had been largely and elaborately representing, how the whole world was full of sin, in all parts of it, both among Jews and Gentiles, and all exposed to death and condemnation. 'Tis plain, that in these words he would tell us, how this came to pass, namely, that this sorrowful event came by one man, even the first man. That the world was full of sin, and full of death, were two great and notorious facts, deeply affecting the interests of mankind; and they seemed very wonderful facts, drawing the attention of the more thinking part of mankind everywhere, who often asked this question, *"Whence comes evil,* moral and natural evil?" (The latter chiefly visible in death.) 'Tis manifest, the Apostle here means to tell us, how these came into the world, and came to prevail in it as they do. But all that is meant, according to Dr. Taylor's interpretation, is "He begun transgression." [2] As if all that the Apostle meant, was to tell us who happened to sin first; not how such a malady came upon the world, or how anyone in the world, besides Adam himself, came by such a distemper. The words of the Apostle, "By one man sin entered into the world, and death by sin," shew the design to be, to tell us how these evils came, as affecting the state of the world; and not only as reaching one man in the world. If this were not plain enough in itself, the words immediately following demonstrate it, "And so death passed upon all men, for that all have sinned." By "sin's being in the world," the Apostle don't mean being in the world only in that one instance of Adam's first transgression, but being abroad in the world, among the inhabitants of the earth, in a wide extent and continued series of wickedness; as is plain in the first words of the next verse, "For until the law, sin was in the world."

2. P. 56.

And therefore when he gives us an account how it came to be in the world, or which is the same thing, how it entered into the world, he don't mean only coming in in one instance.

If the case were as Dr. Taylor represents, that the sin of Adam, either in its pollution or punishment, reached none but himself, any more than the sin of any other man, it would be no more proper to say, that by one man sin entered into the world, than if it should be inquired, how mankind came into America, and there had anciently been a ship of Phoenicians wrecked at sea, and a single man of the crew was driven ashore on this continent, and here died as soon as he reached the shore, and it should be said, "By that one man mankind came into America."

And besides, it is not true that by one man, or by Adam, sin entered into the world, in Dr. Taylor's sense: for it was not he, but Eve, that begun transgression. By "one man" Dr. Taylor understands Adam, as the figure of Christ. And it is plain, that it was for his transgression, and not Eve's, that the sentence of death was pronounced on mankind after the fall (Gen. 3:9). It appears unreasonable to suppose the Apostle means to include Eve, when he speaks of Adam: for he lays great stress on it, that it was *by one,* repeating it no less than seven times.

III. In like manner this author brings to nothing the sense of the *causal particles,* in such phrases as these, so often repeated, "Death *by* sin" (v. 12), "If *through* the offense of one, many be dead" (v. 15), "*By* one that sinned, judgment was *by* one to condemnation" (v. 16), "*By* one man's offense, death reigned *by* one" (v. 17), "*By* the offense of one, judgment came upon all etc." (v. 18), "*By* one man's disobedience" (v. 19). These causal particles, so dwelt upon, and so variously repeated, unless we make mere nonsense of the discourse, signify some connection and dependence, by some sort of influence of that sin of one man, or some tendency to that effect which is so often said to come *by* it. But according to Dr. Taylor, there can be no real dependence or influence in the case of any sort whatsoever. There is no connection by any *natural* influence of that one act to make all mankind mortal. Our author don't pretend to account for this effect in any such manner; but in another most diverse, viz. a gracious act of God, laying mankind under affliction, toil and death, from special favor and kindness. Nor can there be any dependence of this effect on that transgression of Adam, by any *moral* influence, as deserving such a consequence, or exposing to it on any moral account: for he supposes, that mankind are not in this way exposed to the least degree of evil. Nor has this effect any *legal* dependence on that sin, or any connection by virtue of any antecedent constitution, which God had established with Adam: for he insists, that in that threatening, "In the day thou eatest thou shalt die," there is not a word said of his posterity: and death on mankind, according to him, can't come by virtue of the legal constitution with Adam; because the sentence by which it came, was after the annulling and abolishing that constitution. And 'tis manifest, that this consequence can't be through any kind of tendency of that sin to such an effect; because the effect comes only as a benefit, and is the fruit of mere favor: but sin has no tendency, either natural or moral, to benefits and divine favors. And that sin of Adam could neither be the *efficient* cause, nor the *procuring* cause, neither the *natural, moral,* nor *legal* cause, nor an *exciting* and *moving* cause, any more than Adam's eating of any other tree of the garden. And the only real relation that the effect can have to that sin, is a relation as to time, viz. that 'tis *after* it. And when the matter is closely examined, the whole amounts to no more than this: that God is pleased, of his mere good will and pleasure, to bestow a greater favor upon us, than he did upon Adam in innocency, *after that sin* of his eating the forbidden fruit; which sin we are no more concerned in, than in the sin of the king of Pegu, or emperor of China.

IV. 'Tis altogether inconsistent with the Apostle's scope, and the import of what he says, to suppose that the death which he here speaks of as coming on mankind by Adam's sin, comes not as a punishment, but only as a favor. It quite makes void the opposition, in which the Apostle sets the consequences of Adam's sin, and the consequences of the grace and righteousness of Christ. They are set in opposition to each other, as opposite effects, arising from opposite causes, throughout the paragraph: one as the *just consequence of an offense,* the other a *free gift* (vv. 15, 16, 17, 18). Whereas, according to this scheme, there is no such opposition in the case; both are benefits, and both are free gifts. A very wholesome medicine, to save from perishing, ordered by a kind father, or a shield to preserve from an enemy, bestowed by a friend, is as much a free gift, as pleasant food. The death that comes by Adam is set in opposition to the life and happiness that comes by Christ, as being the fruit of sin, and judgment for sin; when the latter is the fruit of divine grace (vv. 15, 17, 20, 21). Whereas, according to our author, both come by grace: death comes on mankind by the free kindness and love of God, much more truly and properly than by Adam's sin. Dr. Taylor speaks of it as coming by *occasion* of Adam's sin. (But as I have observed, it is an occasion without any influence.) Yet the proper cause is God's grace: so that the true cause is wholly good. Which, by the way, is directly repugnant to the Apostle's doctrine in Rom. 7:13. "Was then that which is good, made death unto me? God forbid. But sin, that it might appear sin, working death in me by that which is good," where the Apostle utterly rejects any such suggestion, as though that which is good were the proper cause of death; and signifies, that *sin* is the proper *cause,* and that which is *good,* only the *occasion.* But according to this author, the reverse is true: that which is good in the highest sense, even the love of God, and a divine gracious constitution, is the proper *cause* of death; and *sin,* only the *occasion.*

But to return, 'tis plain, that death by Adam, and life and happiness by Christ, are here set in opposition; the latter being spoken of as good, the other as evil; one as the effect of righteousness, the other of an offense; one the fruit of obedience, the other of disobedience; one as the fruit of God's favor, in consequence of what was pleasing and acceptable to him, but the other the fruit of his displeasure, in consequence of what was displeasing and hateful to him: the latter coming by *justification,* the former by the *condemnation* of the subject. But according to the scheme of our author, there can be no opposition in any of these respects: the death here spoken of, neither comes as an evil, nor from an evil cause, either an evil efficient cause, or a procuring cause; nor at all as any testimony of God's displeasure to the subject, but as properly the effect of God's favor, no less than that which is spoken of as coming by Christ; yea, and as much as that, appointed by an act of *justification* of the subject; as he understands and explains the word "justification": for both are by a grant of favor, and are instances of mercy and goodness. And he does abundantly insist upon it, that *"any* grant of favor, *any* instance of mercy and goodness, whereby God delivers and exempts from any kind of danger, suffering, or calamity, or confers *any* favor, blessing or privilege, is called *justification,* in the Scripture-sense and use of the word." [3]

3. *Key* no. 342, where 'tis to be observed, that he himself puts the word "any" in capital letters. The same thing in substance is often asserted elsewhere. And this indeed is his main point in what he calls the "true Gospel-Scheme."

And over and above all these things, our author makes void and destroys the grand and fundamental opposition of all, to illustrate which is the chief scope of this whole passage, viz. that between the *first* and *second Adam,* in the *death* that comes by *one,* and the *life* and happiness by the *other.* For, according to his doctrine, both come by Christ, the second Adam; both by his grace, righteousness and obedience: the death, that God sentenced mankind to in Gen. 3:19 being a great deal more properly and truly by Christ, than by Adam. For, according to him, that sentence was not pronounced on the foot of the covenant with Adam, because that was abrogated, and entirely set aside, as what was to have no more effect, before it was pronounced; as he largely insists for many pages together (pp. 389–395). He says (p. 389), "This covenant with Adam was disannulled immediately after Adam sinned. Even before God passed sentence upon Adam, grace was introduced." And in p. 395 he says, "The death that mankind are the subjects of now, stands under the covenant of grace," and in p. 396, "In the counsel and appointment of God, it stood in this very light, even before the sentence of death was pronounced upon Adam; and consequently death is no proper and legal punishment of sin." And he often insists, that it comes only as a favor and benefit: and standing, as he says, under the Covenant of Grace, which is by Christ, therefore is truly one of the benefits of the new Covenant, which comes by Christ, the second Adam. For he himself is full in it, to use his own words,[4] "That all the grace of the gospel is dispensed to us *in, by* or *through* the Son of God." "Nothing is clearer," says he,[5] "from the whole current of Scripture, than that all the mercy and love of God, and all the blessings of the gospel, from first to last, are *in, by,* and *through* Christ, and particularly by his blood, by the redemption that is in him. . . . This," says he, "can bear no dispute among Christians." What then becomes of all this discourse of the Apostle's about the great difference and opposition between Adam and Christ; as death is by one, and eternal life and happiness by the other? This grand distinction between the two Adams, and all the other instances of opposition and difference, here insisted on, as between the effects of sin and righteousness, the consequences of obedience and disobedience, of the offense and the free gift, judgment and grace, condemnation and justification, they all come to nothing: and this whole

4. *Key* ch. 10, Title.

5. *Key* no. 119.

discourse of the Apostle's wherein he seems to labor much, as if it were to set forth some very grand and most important distinctions and oppositions in the state of things, as derived from the two great heads of mankind, proves nothing but a multitude of words without meaning, or rather an heap of inconsistencies.

V. Our author's own doctrine entirely makes void what he supposes to be the Apostle's argument in the 13th and 14th verses; in these words, "For until the law sin was in the world: but sin is not imputed, where there is no law. Nevertheless death reigned from Adam to Moses, even over them that had not sinned after the similitude of Adam's transgression."

What he supposes the Apostle would prove here, is that death or the mortality of mankind comes only by Adam's sin, and not by men's personal sins; and that it is here proved by this argument, viz. because there was no law, threatening death to Adam's posterity for personal sins, before the law of Moses; but death or mortality of Adam's posterity took place many ages before the law was given; therefore death could not be by any law threatening death for personal sins, and consequently could be by nothing but Adam's sin.[6] On this I would observe,

1. That which he supposes the Apostle to take for truth in this argument, viz. that there was no law of God in being, by which men were exposed to death for personal sin, during the time from Adam to Moses, is neither true, nor agreeable to this Apostle's own doctrine.

First, it is not true. For the law of nature, written in men's hearts, was then in being, and was a law by which men were exposed to death for personal sin. That there was a divine establishment, fixing the death and destruction of the sinner as the consequence of personal sin, which was well known before the giving of Moses' law, is plain by many passages in the book of Job; as fully and clearly implying a connection between such sin and such a punishment, as any passage in the law of Moses: such as that in Job 24:19, "Drought and heat consume the snow-waters; so doth the grave them that have sinned." (cf. vv. 20 and 24, also ch. 36:6), "He preserveth not the life of the wicked." (ch. 21:29–32), "Have ye not asked them that go by the way? and do ye not know their tokens? That the wicked is reserved to the day of destruction; they shall be

6. Pp. 40–42, 57 and often elsewhere.

brought forth to the day of wrath." (v. 31), "He shall be brought to the grave." [7]

Secondly, to suppose that there is no law in being, by which men are exposed to death for personal sins, where or when the revealed law of God in or after Moses' time is not in being, is contrary to this Apostle's own doctrine in this epistle. (Rom. 2:12,14,15), "For as many as have sinned without law" (i.e. revealed law) "shall perish without law." But how they can be exposed to die and perish, who have not the law of Moses, nor any revealed law, the Apostle shews us in the 14th and 15th verses; viz. in that they have the law of nature, by which they fall under sentence to this punishment. "For when the Gentiles which have not the law, do by nature the things contained in the law, these having not the law, are a law to themselves; which shew the work of the law written in their hearts; their conscience also bearing witness." Their conscience not only bore witness to the duty prescribed by this law, but also to the punishment before spoken of, as that which they who sinned without law, were liable to suffer, viz. that they should perish. In which the Apostle is yet more express (ch. 1:32), speaking more especially of the heathen "who knowing the judgment of God, that they which commit such things are worthy of death." [8] Dr. Taylor often calls the law the *rule of right:* and this rule of right sentenced those sinners to death, who were not under the law of Moses, according to this author's own paraphrase of this verse, in these words, "The heathen were not ignorant of the rule of right, which God has implanted in the human nature; and which shews that they which commit such things, are deserving of death." And he himself supposes Abraham, who lived between Adam and Moses, to be under law, by which he would have been exposed to punishment without hope, were it not for the promise of grace, in his *Paraphrase* on Rom. 4:15.

So that in our author's way of explaining the passage before us, the grand argument, which the Apostle insists upon here, to prove his main point, viz. that death don't come by men's personal sins,

7. See also Job 4:7–9; 15:17–35; 18:5–21, and 19:29, and 20:4–8; 23:23–29; 21:16–18,20–26, and 22:13–20; 27:11 to the end; 31:2,3,23; 33:18,22–24,28,30; 34:11,21–26; 37:12,18–20, and 38:13,14.

8. [The MS which parallels approximately the last third of the *Original Sin* begins at this point and continues to the end of the work. For major changes from the first ed., see footnotes following. Yale Collection, Folder 36. See above, Intro., Sec. 5.]

but by Adam's sin, because it came before the law was given, that threatened death for personal sin; I say, this argument which Dr. Taylor supposes so clear and strong,[9] is brought to nothing more than a mere shadow without substance; the very foundation of the argument having no truth. To say, there was no such law actually expressed in any standing revelation would be mere trifling: for it no more appears, that God would not bring temporal death for personal sins, without a standing revealed law threatening it, than that he would not bring eternal death before there was a revealed law threatening that: which yet wicked men that lived in Noah's time, were exposed to, as appears by I Pet. 3:19,20, and which Dr. Taylor supposes all mankind are exposed to by their personal sins; and he himself says,[1] sin in its own unalterable nature leads to death. Yea, it might be argued with as much strength of reason, that God could bring on men no punishment at all for any sin, that was committed from Adam to Moses, because there was no standing revealed law then extant, threatening any punishment. It may here be properly observed, that our author supposes, the shortening of man's days, and hastening of death, entered into the world by the sin of the antediluvians, in the same sense as death and mortality entered into the world by Adam's sin,[2] but where was there any standing revealed law for that, though the event was so universal? If God might bring this on all mankind, on occasion of other men's sins, for which they deserved nothing, without a revealed law, what could there be to hinder God's bringing death on men for their personal sins, for which their own consciences tell 'em they do deserve death, without a revealed law?

2. If it had been so, that from Adam to Moses there had been no law in being, of any kind, revealed or natural by which men could be properly exposed to temporal death for personal sin, yet the mention of Moses' law would have been wholly impertinent, and of no signification in the argument, according to our author's understanding of it. He supposes, what the Apostle would prove, is, that temporal death, or the death we now die, comes by Adam; and not by any law threatening such a punishment for personal sin; because this death prevailed before the law of Moses was in being, which is the only law threatening death for personal sin. And yet he himself

9. P. 393.
1. Pp. 77–78.
2. P. 68. [First ed. begins a new sentence.]

supposes, that the law of Moses, when it was in being, threatened no such death for personal sin. For he abundantly asserts, that the death which the law of Moses threatened for personal sin, was eternal death, as has been already noted: and he says in express terms, that eternal death is of a nature widely different from the death we now die; [3] as was also observed before.

How impertinently therefore does Dr. Taylor make an inspired writer argue, when according to him the Apostle would prove, that this kind of death did not come by any law threatening this kind of death, because it came before the existence of a law threatening another kind of death, of a nature widely different? How is it to the Apostle's purpose, to fix on that period, the time of giving Moses' law, as if that had been the period wherein men began to be threatened with this punishment, for their personal sins, when in truth it was no such thing? And therefore it was no more to his purpose, to fix on that period, from Adam to Moses, than from Adam to David, or any other period whatsoever. Dr. Taylor holds, that even now, since the law of Moses has been given, the mortality of mankind, or the death we now die, don't come by that law; but that it always comes only by Adam.[4] And if it never comes by that law, we may be sure it never was threatened in that law.

3. If we should allow the argument in Dr. Taylor's sense of it, to prove that death don't come by personal sin, yet it will be wholly without force to prove the main point, even that it must come by Adam's sin. For it might come by God's sovereign and gracious pleasure; as innumerable other divine benefits do. If it be ordered, agreeable to our author's supposition, not as a punishment, nor as a calamity, but only a favor, what necessity of any settled constitution, or revealed sentence, in order to the bestowing such a favor, more than other favors; and particularly more than that great benefit, which he says entered into the world by the sin of the antediluvians, the shortening men's lives so much after the flood? Thus the Apostle's arguing, by Dr. Taylor's explanation of it, is turned into mere trifling, and a vain and impertinent use of words, without any real force or significance.

VI. The Apostle here speaks of that great benefit, which we have by Christ as the antitype of Adam, under the notion of a fruit of *grace*. I don't mean only that super-abounding of grace, wherein the

3. P. 396. He says to the like purpose in his *Note on Rom.* 5:17.

4. This is plain by what he says, pp. 38, 40, 53, 393.

benefit we have by Christ goes beyond the damage sustained by Adam; but that benefit, with regard to which *Adam was the figure of him that was to come,* and which is as it were the counterpart of the suffering of Adam, and which repairs the loss we have by him.[5] This is here spoken of as the fruit of the free grace of God; as appears by vv. 15, 16, 17, 18, 20, 21. This, according to our author, is the restoring of mankind to that life which they lost in Adam: and he himself supposes this restoration of life by Christ to be what grace does for us, and calls it the free gift of God, and the grace and favor of the lawgiver.[6] And speaking of this restoration, he breaks out in admiration of the unspeakable riches of this grace.[7]

But it follows from his doctrine, that there is *no grace at all* in this benefit, and it is no more than a mere act of *justice,* being only a removing of what mankind suffer, being innocent. Death, as it commonly comes on mankind, and even on infants (as has been observed) is an extreme positive calamity; to bring which on the perfectly innocent, unremedied, and without anything to countervail it, we are sufficiently taught, is not consistent with the righteousness of the Judge of all the earth. What grace therefore, worthy of being so celebrated, would there be in affording remedy and relief, after there had been brought on innocent mankind that which is (as Dr. Taylor himself represents),[8] the dreadful and universal destruction of their nature; being a striking demonstration how infinitely odious sin is to God! What grace in delivering, from such shocking ruin, them that did not deserve the least calamity! Our author says, "We could not *justly* lose communion with God by Adam's sin." [9] If so, then we could not justly lose our lives, and be annihilated, after a course of extreme pains and agonies of body and mind, without any restoration; which would be an eternal loss of communion with God,[1] and all other good, besides the positive suffering. The Apos-

5. [In one of his strangest typological references, JE had once identified Satan, before the fall, as Christ, rather than as Adam, as here. "Hence learn that Satan before his fall was the Messiah or Christ as anointed." "Miscellanies," No. 980, corol. 1.]

6. Pp. 39, 40, 70, 148, 303. See also contents of this paragraph in Rom. 5 in his *Notes on the Epistle* and his Note on vv. 15, 16, 17.

7. P. 395.

8. P. 69.

9. P. 148.

1. [MS continues: "and therefore there would have been no grace in restoring to life and to communion. Thus Dr. T's scheme is doubly contrary

tle, throughout this passage, represents the death, which is the consequence of Adam's transgression, as coming in a way of judgment and condemnation for sin; but deliverance and life through Christ, as by grace, and the free gift of God. Whereas, on the contrary, by Dr. Taylor's scheme, the death that comes by Adam, comes by grace, great grace; it being a great benefit, ordered in fatherly love and kindness, and on the foot of a Covenant of Grace! But in the deliverance and restoration by Christ, there is no grace at all. So things are turned topsy-turvy, the Apostle's scope and scheme entirely inverted and confounded.

VII. Dr. Taylor explains the words "judgment," "condemnation," "justification," and "righteousness," as used in this place, in a very unreasonable manner.

I will first consider the sense he puts upon the two former, "judgment" and "condemnation." He often calls this condemnation a judicial act, and a sentence of condemnation. But, according to his scheme, 'tis a judicial sentence of condemnation passed upon them that are perfectly innocent, and viewed by the judge, even in his passing the sentence and condemning them, as having no guilt of sin, or fault at all chargeable upon them; and a judicial proceeding, passing sentence arbitrarily, without any law or rule of right, before established: for there was no preceding law or rule threatening death, that he, or anyone else, ever pretended to have been established, but only this, "In the day that thou eatest thereof, thou shalt surely die." And concerning this, he insists, that there is not a word said in it of Adam's posterity. So that the condemnation spoken of, is a sentence of condemnation to death, for, or in consequence of the sin of Adam, without any law, by which that sin could be imputed, to bring any such consequence; contrary to the Apostle's plain scope. And not only so, but over and above all this, 'tis a judicial sentence of condemnation to that which is no calamity, nor is considered as such in the sentence: but 'tis condemnation to a great favor!

The Apostle uses the words "judgment" and "condemnation," in other places; they are no strange and unusual terms with him: but never are they used by him in this sense, or any like it; nor are they ever used thus anywhere else in the New Testament. This Apostle elsewhere in this epistle to the Romans is often speaking of condem-

---

to the apostle's in this place. It being a great benefit ordered in fatherly love and kindness. But if this redemption then is the counterpart which we have by the second Adam there is no grace at all."]

nation; using the same or similar terms and phrases, as here; but never in the abovesaid sense. (ch. 2:1,2,3, six times in these verses; also vv. 12 and 27, and ch. 3:7; ch. 8:1 and 3; ch. 14:3,4, and vv. 10, 13, 22 and 23) This will be plain to everyone that casts his eye on these places. And if we look into the former part of this chapter, the Apostle's discourse here makes it evident, that he is here speaking of a condemnation, that is no testimony of favor to the innocent; but of God's displeasure, towards those that he is not reconciled to, but looks on as offenders, sinners, and enemies, and holds as the objects of his wrath, which we are delivered from by Christ; as may be seen in verses 6, 7, 8, 9, 10, and 11.

And viewing this discourse itself, in the very paragraph we are upon, if we may judge anything by language and manner of speaking, there is everything to lead us to suppose, that the Apostle uses these words here, as he does elsewhere, properly, and as implying a supposition of sin, chargeable on the subject, and exposing to punishment. He speaks of condemnation with reference to sin, as what comes by sin, and as a condemnation to death, which seems to be a most terrible evil, and capital punishment, even in what is temporal and visible; and this in the way of judgment and execution of justice, in opposition to grace or favor, and gift or a benefit coming by favor. And sin and offense, transgression and disobedience are, over and over again, spoken of as the ground of the condemnation and of the capital suffering condemned to, for ten verses successively, that is, in every verse in the whole paragraph, without missing one.

The words "justification" and "righteousness" are explained by Dr. Taylor in a no less unreasonable manner. He understands "justification" in v. 18 and "righteousness" in v. 19 in such a sense, as to suppose 'em to belong to all, and actually to be applied to all mankind,[2] good and bad, believers and unbelievers; to the worst enemies of God, remaining such, as well as his peculiar favorites, and many that never had any sin imputed to 'em; meaning thereby no more than what is fulfilled in an universal resurrection from the dead, at the last day.[3] Now this is a most arbitrary, forced sense. Though these terms are used everywhere, all over the New Testament, yet nothing like such an use of 'em is to be found, in any one

2. [MS continues: "and many that never had been guilty of any sin. So thus all mankind actually became the subjects of the justification and righteousness the apostle speaks of."]

3. So pp. 47, 49, 60–62 and other places.

instance, through all the writings of the apostles and evangelists. The words "justify," "justification," and "righteousness," as from God to men, are never used but to signify a privilege belonging only to some, and that which is peculiar to distinguished favorites. This Apostle in particular, above all the other writers of the New Testament, abounds in the use of these terms; so that we have all imaginable opportunity to understand his language, and know the sense in which he uses these words: but he never elsewhere uses 'em in the sense supposed here, nor is there any pretense that he does. Above all, does this Apostle abound in the use of these terms in this epistle. *Justification* is the subject he had been upon through all the preceding part of the epistle. It was the grand subject of all the foregoing chapters, and the preceding part of this chapter; where these terms are continually repeated. And the word "justification" is constantly used to signify something peculiar to believers, who had been sinners; implying some reconciliation and forgiveness of sin, and special privilege in nearness to God, above the rest of the world. Yea, the word is constantly used thus, according to Dr. Taylor's own explanations, in his *Paraphrase and Notes* on this epistle. And there is not the least reason to suppose but that he is still speaking of the same justification and righteousness, which he had dwelt upon from the beginning, to this place. He speaks of justification and righteousness here, just in the same manner, as he had done in the preceding part of the epistle. He had all along spoken of justification as standing in relation to sin, disobedience to God, and offense against God, and so he does here: he had before been speaking of justification through free grace, and so he does here: he before had been speaking of justification through righteousness, as in Christ Jesus, and so he does here.

And if we look into the former part of this very chapter, there we shall find justification spoken of just in the same sense as in the rest of the epistle; which is also supposed by our author in his exposition: 'Tis still *justification by faith,* justification of them that had been sinners, justification attended with reconciliation, justification peculiar to them that had "the love of God shed abroad in their hearts." The Apostle's foregoing discourse on justification by grace, through faith, and what he had so greatly insisted on as the evidence of the truth of this doctrine, even the universal sinfulness of mankind in their original state, is plainly what introduces this discourse in the latter part of this 5th chapter; where he shews how all mankind came to be sinful and miserable, and so to need this grace of God, and righteousness of Christ. And therefore we can't without the most absurd violence, suppose any other than that he is still speaking of the same justification.

And as to the universal expression used in the 18th verse, "By the righteousness of one, the free gift came upon all men to justification of life," 'tis needless here to go into the controversy between the Remonstrants and anti-Remonstrants,[4] concerning universal redemption, and their different interpretations of this place. If we take the words even as the Arminians do; yet, in their sense of them, the free gift comes on all men to justification only conditionally, i.e. provided they believe, repent, etc. But in our author's sense, it actually comes on all, whether they believe and repent, or not; which certainly can't be inferred from the universal expression, as here used.[5] Dr. Taylor himself supposes, the main design of the Apostle in this universal phrase, "all men," is to signify that the benefits of Christ shall come on Gentiles, as well as Jews.[6] And he supposes, that the *many*, and the *all*, here signify the same: but 'tis quite certain, that all the benefits here spoken of, which the Apostle says are to the many, don't actually come upon all mankind; as particularly the *abounding of grace*, spoken of in v. 15. "The grace of God, and the gift by grace, hath abounded unto the many εἰς τοὺς πολλοὺς."

This abounding of grace our author explains thus: "The rich over-plus of grace, in erecting a new dispensation, furnished with a glorious fund of light, means and motives." But will any pretend, that all mankind have actually been partakers of this new fund of

4. [MS reads: "Calvinists and Arminians."]

5. [MS continues: "mankind, believers and unbelievers, penitent and impenitent. There is no manner of need of signifying from what the apostle says that all men are actually justified by X's righteousness any more than to supposed [sic] this. All men are actually enlightened by X with the light of life, in John v. 9 it is found this is the true light. This light [illeg.] among men then cometh into the ⊙ when nothing more can consistent with [illeg.] and plans. First he understood that light was introduced not to be confined to the Jews or profit of any particular nation, denomination, or kind but to be free for all of any nation and every sort and degree and thus every particular person under heaven that can have true light has it from him."]

6. Pp. 60, 61. See also contents of this paragraph, in his *Notes* on the epistle. [And therefore, as he [Paul] considers both Jews and Gentiles, at the coming of Christ, and Abraham, when the Covenant was made with him, so he considers Adam and all men as standing in the court before the tribunal of God. Taylor, *Notes upon Romans,* p. 285.]

light, etc.? How were the many millions of Indians, on the American side of the globe, partakers of it, before the Europeans came hither? Yea, Dr. Taylor himself supposes, all that is meant, is, that it is *free for all that are willing to accept of it.*[7] The agreement between Adam as the type of figure of him that was to come, and Christ as the antitype, appears as full and clear, if we suppose, *all* which are *in Christ* (to use the common Scripture-phrase) have the benefit of his obedience, as *all* that are *in Adam* have the sorrowful fruit of his disobedience. The Scripture speaks of believers as the seed or posterity of Christ (Gal. 3:29). They are *in Christ by grace,* as *Adam's* posterity are in him *by nature:* the one are in *the first Adam naturally,* as the other are *in the second Adam spiritually:* exactly agreeable to the representation this Apostle makes of the matter (I Cor. 15:45–49). The spiritual seed are those which this Apostle often represents as Christ's body: and the οἱ πολλοὶ here spoken of as made righteous by Christ's obedience, are doubtless the same with the οἱ πολλοὶ which he speaks of in ch. 12:5. "We being many, are one body"; or we, the many ὅι πολλοὶ ἓν σῶμά ἐσμεν. And again (I Cor. 10:17) ἓν σῶμα οἱ πολλοὶ ἐσμεν. And the same which the Apostle had spoken of in the preceding chapter, Rom. 4:18, compared with Gen. 15:5.

Dr. Taylor much insists on that place (I Cor. 15:21,22), "For since by man came death, by man came also the resurrection of the dead: For as in Adam all die, so in Christ shall all be made alive"; to confirm his suppositions, that the Apostle here in the 5th of Romans, speaking of the death and condemnation which come by Adam, has respect only to the death we all die, when this life ends: and that by the justification and life which come by Christ, he has respect only to the general resurrection at the last day. But it is observable, that his argument is wholly built on these two suppositions, viz. first, that the resurrection meant by the Apostle, in that place in the I Cor. 15 is the resurrection of all mankind, both just and unjust. Secondly, that the opposite consequences of Adam's sin, and Christ's obedience, spoken of here in the Rom. 5th, are the very same, neither more nor less, as are spoken of there. But there are no grounds for supposing either of these things to be true.

1. There is no evidence, that the *resurrection* there spoken of, is the resurrection both of the just and unjust; but abundant evidence of the contrary. The resurrection of the wicked is seldom mentioned

7. Id. Ibid.

in the New Testament, and rarely included in the meaning of the word;[8] it being esteemed not worthy to be called a rising to life, being only for a great increase of the misery and darkness of eternal death: and therefore by the resurrection is most commonly meant a rising to life and happiness; as may be observed in Matt. 22:30; Luke 20:35,36; John 6:39,40,54; Phil. 3:11 and other places. The saints are called the children of the resurrection, as Dr. Taylor observes in his *Note on Rom.* 8:11.[9] And 'tis exceeding evident, that 'tis the resurrection to life and happiness, the Apostle is speaking of in this I Cor. 15:21,22. It appears by each of the three foregoing verses. (v. 18), "Then they which are fallen asleep in Christ" (i.e. the saints) "are perished." (v. 19), "If in this life only we" (Christians and apostles) "have hope in Christ" (and have no resurrection and eternal life to hope for) "we are of all men most miserable." (v. 20), "But now is Christ risen from the dead, and is become the first fruits of them that slept." He is the forerunner and first fruits only with respect to them that are his; who are to follow him, and partake with him in the glory and happiness of his resurrection: but he is not the first fruits of them who shall come forth to the resurrection of damnation. It also appears by the verse immediately following. (v. 23), "But every man in his own order; Christ the first fruits, and afterwards, they that are Christ's at his coming." The same is plain by what is said in vv. 29, 30, 31, and 32; and by all that is said from the 35th verse to the end of the chapter, for twenty-three verses together: it there expressly appears, that the Apostle is speaking only of a rising to glory, with a glorious body, as the little grain that is sown, being quickened, rises a beautiful flourishing plant. He there speaks of the different degrees of glory among them that shall rise, and compares it to the different degrees of glory among the celestial

8. [MS continues: "included in the manner of the word resurrection. For in the resurrection they neither marry nor are given in marriage but are like the angels of God in heaven. The saints are spoken of as they only then are accorded worthy to accept the resurrection of the dead, it being affirmed."]

9. [MS omits the following sentence and continues: "As a being raised from the dead or from time to time mentioned as a promise made primarily to true saints as in Gal. 6:39,40,54 and 11:25. And this the resurrection of the dead the apostle speaks of as the great prize of the Xtian calling. Phil. 3:11. If by any man might attain to the resurrection of the dead. But plainly the resurrection to attain life. And so exceeding harken this to the resurrection. Thus 'tis the resurrection thus [sic] the apostle is speaking of in in [sic] this place in I. Cor. 15:21,22."]

luminaries. The resurrection which he treats of, is expressly a being raised in incorruption, in glory, in power, with a spiritual body, having the image of the second man, the spiritual and heavenly Adam; a resurrection, wherein this corruptible shall put on incorruption, and this mortal put on immortality, and death be swallowed up in victory, and the saints shall gloriously triumph over that last enemy. Dr. Taylor himself says that which is in effect owning, the resurrection here spoken of, is only of the righteous: for 'tis expressly a resurrection *ἐν*[*δύσασθαι*] and *ἀθανασίαν ἀφθαρσίαν* (vv. 53 and 42). But Dr. Taylor says, "These are never attributed to the wicked, in Scripture." [1] So that when the Apostle says here, "As in Adam all die, so in Christ shall all be made alive"); 'tis as much as if he had said, "As in Adam we all die, and our bodies are sown in corruption, in dishonor, and in weakness; so in Christ we all (we Christians, whom I have been all along speaking of) shall be raised in power, glory and incorruption, spiritual and heavenly, conformed to the second Adam. For as we have borne the image of the earthy, we shall also bear the image of the heavenly" (v. 49). Which clearly explains and determines his meaning in vv. 21, 22.

2. There is no evidence, that the benefit by the second Adam, spoken of in Rom. 5th, is the very same (containing neither more nor less) as the resurrection spoken of in I Cor. 15. It is no evidence of it, that the benefit is opposed to the death that comes by the first Adam, in like manner in both places. The resurrection to eternal life, though it be not the whole of that salvation and happiness which comes by the second Adam, yet is it that wherein this salvation is principally obtained. The time of the saints' glorious resurrection is often spoken of as the proper time of the saints' salvation, the day of their redemption, the time of their adoption, glory and recompense. (as in Eph. 4:30; Rom. 8:23; Luke 14:14 and 21:38; II Tim. 4:1,9; Col. 3:4; I Thess. 1:7; Heb. 9:23; I Pet. 1:13 and 5:4; I John 3:2 and other places) All that salvation and happiness which is given before, is only a prelibation and earnest of their great reward. Well therefore may that consummate salvation bestowed on them be set in opposition to the death and ruin which comes by the first Adam, in like manner as the whole of their salvation is opposed to the same in Rom. 5. Dr. Taylor himself observes,[2] "That the revival and resurrection of the body, is frequently put for our ad-

1. *Note on Rom.* 8:28.
2. *Note on Rom.* 8:11.

vancement to eternal life." It being the highest part, 'tis often put for the whole.

This notion, as if the justification, righteousness and life spoken of in Rom. 5th, implied the resurrection to damnation, is not only without ground from Scripture, but contrary to *reason.* For those things are there spoken of as great benefits, by the grace and free gift of God; but this is the contrary, in the highest degree possible, being the most consummate and infinite calamity. To obviate this, our author supposes the resurrection of all to be a great benefit in itself, though turned into a calamity by the sin and folly of obstinate sinners, who abuse God's goodness. But the far greater part of mankind since Adam have never had opportunity to abuse this goodness, it having never been made known to them. Men can't abuse a kindness, which they never had either in possession, promise, offer, or some intimation; but a resurrection is made known only by divine revelation; which few comparatively have enjoyed. So that as to such wicked men as die in lands of darkness, if their resurrection comes at all by Christ, it comes, from him and to them, only as a curse, and not as a blessing; for it never comes to them at all by any conveyance, grant, promise, or offer, or anything by which they can claim it, or know anything of it, till it comes as an infinite calamity, past all remedy.

VIII. In a peculiar manner is there an unreasonable violence used in our author's explanation of the words "sinners" and "sinned," in the paragraph before us. He says, "These words, 'by one man's disobedience, many were made sinners,' [. . .] mean neither more nor less, than that by one man's disobedience the many were made subject to death, by the judicial act of God." [3] And he says in the same place, "By death, most certainly, is meant no other than the death and mortality common to all mankind." And those words, v. 12, "For that all have sinned," he thus explains, "All men became sinners, as all mankind are brought into a state of suffering." [4] Here I observe,

1. The main thing, by which he justifies such interpretations, is, that sin, in various instances, is used for suffering, in the Old Testament. To which I reply; though it be true, that the word "chattaah," signifies both sin, and a sin-offering; and this, and some other Hebrew words, which signify sin, iniquity, and wickedness, are some-

3. P. 30.

4. P. 54 and elsewhere. [JE's free paraphrase.]

times put for the effect or punishment of iniquity, by a metonymy of the cause for the effect; yet it does not appear, that these words are ever used for enduring suffering, where the suffering is not spoken of under any notion of a punishment of sin, or a fruit of God's anger for sin, or of any imputation of guilt, or under any notion of sin's being at all laid to the charge of the sufferer, or the suffering's being at all of the nature of any recompense, compensation, or satisfaction for sin. And therefore none of the instances he mentions, come up to his purpose. When Lot is commanded to leave Sodom, that he might not be consumed in the iniquity of the city, meaning, in that fire, which is the effect and punishment of the iniquity of the city; this is quite another thing, than if that fire came on the city in general as no punishment at all, nor as any fruit of a charge of iniquity on the city, or of God's displeasure for their sin, but as a token of God's favor to the inhabitants; which is what is supposed with respect to the death of mankind; it being introduced only as a benefit, on the foot of a Covenant of Grace. And especially is this quite another thing, than if, in the expression used, the iniquity had been ascribed to Lot; and God, instead of saying, "Lest thou be consumed in the iniquity of the city," had said, "Lest thou be consumed in thine iniquity" or "Lest thou sin, or be made a sinner." Whereas, the expression is such as does expressly remove the iniquity, spoken of, from Lot, and fix it on another subject, viz. the city. The place cited by our author, in Jer. 51 is exactly parallel. And as to what Abimelech says to Abraham (Gen. 20:9), "What have I offended thee, that thou hast brought on me, and on my kingdom, a great sin?" 'Tis manifest, Abimelech was afraid that God was angry, for what he had done to Sarah; or would have been angry with him, if he had done what he was about to do, as imputing sin to him for it: which is a quite different thing from calling some calamity, sin, under no notion of its being any punishment of sin, nor in the least degree from God's displeasure. And so with regard to every place our author cites in the margin, 'tis plain, that what is meant in each of them, is the punishment of sin, and not some suffering which is no punishment at all. And as to the instances he mentions in his *Supplement* (p. 284),[5] the two that look most favorable to his design, are those in Gen. 31:39 and II Kgs. 7:9. With respect to the former, where Jacob says, "That which was torn of beasts, anochi achattenah"—which Dr. Taylor is pleased to translate, "I was the sinner": but is properly

5. [I.e. *Scripture-Doctrine of Original Sin.*]

rendered, "I expiated it"; the verb "in pihel" properly signifying "to expiate." And the plain meaning is "I bore the blame of it and was obliged to pay for it" as being supposed to be lost through my fault or neglect. Which is a quite different thing from suffering without any supposition of fault. And as to the latter place, where the lepers say, "This day is a day of good tidings, and we hold our peace: If we tarry till morning some mischief will befall us." In the Hebrew, "umetzaanu gnaon"; "Iniquity will find us," that is, some punishment of our fault will come upon us. Elsewhere such phrases are used, as "your iniquity will find you out," and the like. But certainly this is a different thing from suffering without fault, or supposition of fault. And it does not appear, that the verb in hiphil, "hirshiang," is ever put for condemn, in any other sense than condemning for sin, or guilt, or supposed guilt, belonging to the subject condemned. This word is used, in the participle of "hiphil," to signify "condemning" in Prov. 17:15. "He that justifieth the wicked, and he that condemneth the just, even both are an abomination to the Lord." This Dr. Taylor observes, as if it were to his purpose, when he is endeavoring to shew, that in this place in the 5th of Romans, the Apostle speaks of God himself as condemning the just, or perfectly innocent, in a parallel-signification of terms. Nor is any instance produced, wherein the verb "sin," which is used by the Apostle when he says, "all have sinned," is anywhere used in our author's sense, for being brought into a state of suffering, and that not as a punishment for sin, or as anything arising from God's displeasure; much less for being the subject of what comes only as the fruit of divine love, and as a favor of the highest nature.[6] Nor can anything like this sense of the verb be found in the whole Bible.

2. If there had been anything like such an use of the words "sin" and "sinner," as our author supposes, in the Old Testament, 'tis evident that such an use of them is quite alien from the language of the New Testament. Where can an instance be produced, of anything like it, in any one place, besides what is pretended in this? And particularly, where else shall we find these words and phrases used in such a sense, in any of this Apostle's writings? We have enough of his writings, by which to learn his language and way of speaking about sin, condemnation, punishment, death and suffering. He wrote much more of the New Testament, than any other person.

6. P. 303.

He very often has occasion to speak of condemnation; but where does he express it by "being made sinners"? Especially how far is he elsewhere from using such a phrase, to signify a being condemned without guilt, or any imputation or supposition of guilt, or atonement for guilt? Vastly more still is it remote from his language, so to use the verb "sin," and to say, "man sinneth, or has sinned," though hereby meaning nothing more nor less, than that he, by a judicial act is condemned, on the foot of a dispensation of grace, to receive a great favor! He abundantly uses the words "sin" and "sinner"; his writings are full of such terms: but where else does he use them in such a sense? He has much occasion in his epistles to speak of death, temporal and eternal; he has much occasion to speak of suffering, of all kinds, in this world, and the world to come: but where does he call these things "sin," and denominate innocent men "sinners" or say, "they have sinned," meaning that they are brought into a state of suffering? If the Apostle, because he was a Jew, was so addicted to the Hebrew idiom, as thus in one paragraph to repeat this particular Hebraism, which, at most, is comparatively rare even in the Old Testament, 'tis strange that never anything like it should appear anywhere else in his writings; and especially that he should never fall into such a way of speaking in his epistle to the Hebrews, written to Jews only, who were most used to the Hebrew idiom. And why does Christ never use such language in any of his speeches, though he was born and brought up amongst the Jews, and delivered almost all his speeches only to Jews? And why do none of the rest of the writers of the New Testament ever use it, who were all born and educated Jews (at least all excepting Luke) and some of them wrote especially for the benefit of the Jews?

'Tis worthy to be observed, what liberty is taken, and boldness used with this Apostle; such words as αμαρτολους [?], αμαρτάνω, κρίμα, κατάκρίμα, δικκαιόω, δικαίωσις [7] and words of the same root and signification, are words abundantly used by him elsewhere in this and other epistles, and also when speaking, as he is here, of Christ's redemption and atonement, and of the general sinfulness of mankind, and of the condemnation of sinners, and of justification by Christ, and of death as the consequence of sin, and of life and restoration to life by Christ, as here; yet nowhere are any of these words used, but in a sense very remote from what is supposed here. However,

7. [For "'αμαρτολους" probably read "ἁμαρτωλός."]

in this place these terms must have distinguished singular sense found out for them, and annexed to 'em! [8] A new language must be coined for the Apostle, which he is evidently quite unused to, and put into his mouth on this occasion, for the sake of evading this clear, precise and abundant testimony of his, to the doctrine of original sin.

3. The putting such a sense on the word "sin," in this place, is not only to make the Apostle greatly to disagree with himself in the language he uses everywhere else, but also to disagree with himself no less in the language he uses in this very passage. He often here uses the word "sin," and other words plainly of the same design and import, such as "transgression," "disobedience," "offense." Nothing can be more evident, than that these are here used as several names of the same thing; for they are used interchangeably, and put one for another; as will be manifest only on the cast of an eye on the place. And these words are used no less than seventeen times in this one paragraph. Perhaps we shall find no place in the whole Bible, in which the word "sin," and other words synonymous, are used so often in so little compass: and in all the instances, in the proper sense, as signifying "moral evil," and even so understood by Dr. Taylor himself (as appears by his own exposition) but only in these two places; where in the midst of all, to evade a clear evidence of the doctrine of original sin, another meaning must be found out, and it must be supposed that the Apostle uses the word in a sense entirely different, signifying something that neither *implies* nor *supposes* any moral evil at all in the subject.

Here 'tis very remarkable, the gentleman who so greatly insisted upon it, that the word "death" must needs be understood in the same sense throughout this paragraph; yea, that it is evidently,

8. [MS continues: "Thus the sense used elsewhere much used with a like connection and context. He elsewhere abundantly speaks of sin and sinners when speaking of X's redemption and atonement as he does here and when speaking of the very general sinfulness of mankind and condemnation of sinners of justification by X as here and when speaking of death or the consequences of sin and of life by X as here or for instance the apostle in I Cor. chap. 3 uses the same words, death, condemnation, righteousness and with 'em together here v. 6, 7, 8, 9 and speaks of death and condemnation as coming by law and as approved to the righteousness indicated not by the law but by another dispensation brought in by X as here. And the like might be affirmed. But here those persons must have a distinguished singular sense found once and annexed to 'em a new language."]

clearly, and infallibly so, inasmuch as the Apostle is still discoursing on the same subject; yet can, without the least difficulty, suppose the word "sin," to be used so differently in the very same passage, wherein the Apostle is discoursing on the same thing. Let us take that one instance in v. 12. "Wherefore as by one man sin entered into the world, and death by sin, and so death passed upon all men, for that all have sinned." Here, by "sin," implied in the word, "sinned," in the end of the sentence, our author understands something perfectly and altogether diverse from what is meant by the word "sin," not only in the same discourse, on the same subject, but twice in the former part of the very same sentence, of which this latter part is not only the conclusion, but the explication: and also entirely different from the use of the word twice in the next sentence, wherein the Apostle is still most plainly discoursing on the same subject, as is not denied: and in the next sentence to that (v. 14) the Apostle uses the very same verb, "sinned," and as signifying the committing of moral evil, as our author himself understands it. Afterwards (v. 19) the Apostle uses the word "sinners," which our author supposes to be in somewhat of a different sense still. So that here is the utmost violence, of the kind, that can be conceived of, to make out a scheme, against the plainest evidence, in changing the meaning of a word, backward and forward, in one paragraph, all about one thing, and in different parts of the same sentences, coming over and over in quick repetitions, with a variety of other synonymous words to fix its signification; besides the continued use of the word in the former part of this chapter, and in all the preceding part of the epistle, and the continued use of it in the next chapter, and in the next to that, and the 8th chapter following that, and to the end of the epistle; in none of which places is it pretended, but that the word is used in the proper sense, by our author in his *Paraphrase and Notes* on the whole epistle.[9]

9. [MS continues with section now in JE's footnote:] Agreeable to this manner, our author in explaining the 7th chapter of Romans, understands the pronoun "I" or "me" used by the Apostle in that one continued discourse, in no less than six different senses. He takes it in the 1st verse to signify the apostle Paul himself. In the 8, 9, 10, 11th verses, for the people of the Jews, through all ages, both before and after Moses, especially the carnal ungodly part of 'em. In the 13th verse for an objecting Jew, entering into a dialogue with the Apostle. In the 15, 16, 17, 20th and latter part of the 25th verse it is understood in two different senses, for two "I's" in the same person; one, a man's reason; and the other, his passions and carnal appetites. And in the 7th

But indeed we need go no further than that one v. 12. What the Apostle means by sin, in the latter part of the verse, is evident with the utmost plainness, by comparing it with the former part; one part answering to another, and the last clause exegetical of the former. "Wherefore, as by one man sin entered into the world, and death by sin; and so death passed upon all men, for that" (or, unto which) "all have sinned." Here sin and death are spoken of in the former part, and sin and death are spoken of in the latter part; the two parts of the sentence so answering one another, that the same things are apparently meant by sin and death in both parts.

And besides to interpret sinning, here, of falling under the suffering of death, is yet the more violent and unreasonable, because the Apostle in this very place does once and again distinguish between sin and death; plainly speaking of one as the effect, and the other the cause. So in the 21st verse "That as sin hath reigned unto death" and in the 12th verse "Sin entered into the world, and death by sin." And this plain distinction holds through all the discourse, as between death and the offense (vv. 15 and 17) and between the offense and condemnation (v. 18).

4. Though we should omit the consideration of the manner in which the Apostle uses the words "sin," "sinned," etc. in other places, and in other parts of this discourse, yet Dr. Taylor's interpretation of 'em would be very absurd.

The case stands thus: according to his exposition, we are said to have sinned; by an active verb, as though we had actively sinned, yet this is not spoken truly and properly, but it is put figuratively for our becoming sinners passively, our being made or constituted sinners. Yet again, not that we do truly become sinners passively, or are really made sinners, by anything that God does; this also is only a figurative or tropical representation; and the meaning is only "we are condemned," and treated as if we were sinners. Not indeed that we are properly condemned; for God never truly condemns the innocent: but this also is only a figurative representation of the thing. It is but as it were condemning; because it is appointing to death, a terrible evil, *as if it were* a punishment. But then, in reality, here is no appointment to a terrible evil, or any evil at all; but truly to a benefit, a great benefit: and so, in representing death as a punish-

and former part of the last verse, for us Christians in general; or for all that enjoy the Word of God, the law and the gospel. And these different senses, the most of 'em, strangely intermixed and interchanged, backwards and forwards.

ment or calamity condemned to, another figure or trope is made use of, and an exceeding bold one; for, as we are appointed to it, it is so far from being an evil or punishment, that it is really a favor, and that of the highest nature, appointed by mere grace and love; though it seems to be a calamity. Thus we have tropes and figures multiplied, one upon the back of another; and all in that one word, "sinned"; according to the manner, as it is supposed, the Apostle uses it. We have a *figurative representation,* not of a reality, but of a *figurative representation.* Neither is this a representation of a reality, but of another thing that still is but a figurative representation of something else: yea, even this *something else* is still but a figure, and one that is very harsh and farfetched. So that here we have a figure to represent a figure, even a *figure of a figure* representing some very remote figure, which most obscurely represents the thing intended; if the most terrible evil can indeed be said at all to represent the contrary good, of the highest kind. And now, what cannot be made of any place of Scripture, in such a way of managing it, as this? And is there any hope of ever deciding any controversy by the Scripture, in the way of using such a license with the Scripture, in order to force it to a compliance with our own schemes? If the Apostle indeed uses language after so strange a manner in this place 'tis perhaps such an instance, as not only there is not the like of it in all the Bible besides, but perhaps in no writing whatsoever. And this, not in any parabolical, visionary, or prophetic description, in which difficult and obscure representations are wont to be made use of; nor in a dramatic or poetical representation, in which a great license is often taken, and bold figures are commonly to be expected: but 'tis in a familiar letter, wherein the Apostle is delivering gospel instruction, as a minister of the New Testament; and wherein as he professes, he delivers divine truth without the veil of ancient figures and similitudes, and uses great plainness of speech. And in a discourse that is wholly didactic, narrative and argumentative; evidently setting himself to explain the doctrine he is upon, in the reason and nature of it, with a great variety of expressions, turning it as it were on every side, to make his meaning plain, and to fix in his readers the exact notion of what he intends. Dr. Taylor himself observes,[1] "This apostle takes great care to guard and explain every part of his subject: and I may venture to say, he has left no part of it unexplained, or unguarded. Never was an author more exact and cau-

1. *Pref. to Paraph. on Rom.* [p. 204].

tious in this, than he. Sometimes he writes notes, on a sentence liable to exception, and wanting explanation." Now I think, this care and exactness of the Apostle nowhere appears more than in the place we are upon. Nay, I scarcely know another instance equal to this, of the Apostle's care to be well understood, by being very particular, explicit and precise, setting the matter forth in every light, going over and over again with his doctrine, clearly to exhibit, and fully to settle and determine the thing which he aims at.

SECTION 2. SOME OBSERVATIONS ON THE CONNECTION, SCOPE AND SENSE OF THIS REMARKABLE PARAGRAPH IN ROMANS V—WITH SOME REFLECTIONS ON THE EVIDENCE, WHICH WE HERE HAVE OF THE DOCTRINE OF ORIGINAL SIN

THE connection of this remarkable paragraph with the foregoing discourse in this epistle, is not obscure and difficult; nor to be sought for at a distance. It may be plainly seen, only by a general glance on things which went before, from the beginning of the epistle: and indeed what is said immediately before in the same chapter, leads directly to it. The Apostle in the preceding part of this epistle had largely treated of the sinfulness and misery of all mankind, Jews as well as Gentiles. He had particularly spoken of the depravity and ruin of mankind in their natural state, in the foregoing part of this chapter; representing them as being sinners, ungodly, enemies, exposed to divine wrath, and without strength. No wonder now, this leads him to observe, *how* this so great and deplorable an event came to pass; *how* this universal sin and ruin came into the world. And with regard to the Jews in particular, who, though they might allow the doctrine of original sin in their own profession, yet were strongly prejudiced against what was implied in it, or evidently following from it, with regard to themselves; in this respect they were prejudiced against the doctrine of universal sinfulness, and exposedness to wrath by nature, looking on themselves as by nature holy and favorites of God, because they were the children of Abraham; and with them the Apostle had labored most in the foregoing part of the epistle, to convince them of their being by nature as sinful, and as much the children of wrath, as the Gentiles: I say, with regard to them, it was exceeding proper, and what the Apostle's design most naturally led him to, to take off their eyes from their father Abraham, who was their father in distinction from other nations, and direct them to their father Adam, who was the common father of mankind, and equally of Jews and Gentiles. And when he was entered on this doctrine of the derivation of sin and ruin, or death to all mankind from Adam, no wonder if he thought it needful to be somewhat particular in it, seeing he wrote to Jews and Gentiles; the former of which had been brought up under the prejudices of a proud opinion of themselves, as a holy people by nature, and the latter had been educated in total ignorance of all things of this kind.

Again, the Apostle had from the beginning of the epistle been endeavoring to evince the absolute dependence of all mankind on the free *grace of God* for salvation, and the greatness of this grace; and particularly in the former part of this chapter. The greatness of this grace he shews especially by two things. (1) The universal corruption and misery of mankind; as in all the foregoing chapters, and in the 6, 7, 8, 9, and 10 verses of this chapter. (2) The greatness of the benefits which believers receive, and the greatness of the glory they have hope of. So especially in verses 1, 2, 3, 4, 5 and 11th of this chapter. And here, in this place we are upon, from v. 12 to the end, he is still on the same design of magnifying the grace of God, in the same thing, viz. the favor, life and happiness which believers in Christ receive; speaking here of the *grace of God, the gift by grace, the abounding of grace, and the reign of grace.* And he still sets forth the freedom and riches of grace by the same two arguments, viz. the universal sinfulness and ruin of mankind, all having sinned, all naturally exposed to death, judgment, and condemnation; and the exceeding greatness of the benefit received, being far greater than the misery which comes by the first Adam, and abounding beyond it. And 'tis by no means consistent with the Apostle's scope, to suppose, that the benefit which we have by Christ as the antitype of Adam, here mainly insisted on, is without any grace at all, being only a restoration to life, of such as never deserved death.

Another thing observable in the Apostle's scope from the beginning of the epistle, is, he endeavors to shew the greatness and absoluteness of the dependence of all mankind on the *redemption and righteousness of Christ,* for justification and life, that he might magnify and exalt the Redeemer: which design his whole heart was swallowed up in, and may be looked upon as the main design of the whole epistle. And this is what he had been upon in the preceding part of this chapter; inferring it from the same argument, the utter sinfulness and ruin of all men. And he is evidently still on the same thing in this place, from the 12th verse to the end; speaking of the *same* justification and righteousness, which he had dwelt on before; and not another totally diverse. No wonder, when the Apostle is treating so fully and largely of our restoration, righteousness and life by Christ, that he is led by it to consider our fall, sin, death and ruin by Adam; and to observe wherein these two opposite heads of mankind agree, and wherein they differ, in the manner of conveyance of opposite influences and communications from each.

Thus, if this place be understood, as it used to be understood by orthodox divines, the whole stands in a natural, easy, and clear connection with the preceding part of the chapter, and all the former part of the epistle; and in a plain agreement with the express design of all that the Apostle had been saying; and also in connection with the words last before spoken, as introduced by the two immediately preceding verses, where he is speaking of our justification, reconciliation and salvation by Christ; which leads the Apostle directly to observe, how, on the contrary, we have sin and death by Adam. Taking this discourse of the Apostle in its true and plain sense, there is no need of great extent of learning, or depth of criticism, to find out the connection: but if it be understood in Dr. Taylor's sense, the plain scope and connection are wholly lost, and there was truly need of a skill in criticism, and art of discerning, beyond, or at least different from that of former divines, and a faculty of seeing something afar off, which other men's sight could not reach, in order to find out the connection.[1]

What has been already observed, may suffice to shew the Apostle's general scope in this place. But yet there seem to be some other things, which he has his eye to, in several expressions; some particular things in the then present state, temper and notions of the Jews, which he also had before spoken of, or had reference to, in certain places of the foregoing part of the epistle. As particularly, the Jews had a very superstitious and extravagant notion of their law, delivered by Moses; as if it were the prime, grand, and indeed only rule of God's proceeding with mankind, as their judge, both in men's justification and condemnation, or from whence all, both sin and righteousness, was imputed; and had no consideration of the law of nature, written in the hearts of the Gentiles, and of all mankind. Herein they ascribed infinitely too much to their particular law, beyond the true design of it. They made their boast of the law; as if their being distinguished from all other nations by that great privilege, the giving of the law, sufficiently made 'em a holy people, and God's children. This notion of theirs the Apostle evidently refers to (ch.

1. [The following paragraph was largely rewritten from manuscript by JE, to sentence beginning, "And he has a manifest regard."]

2:13, 17–19) and indeed throughout that whole chapter. They looked on the law of Moses as intended to be the only rule and means of justification; and as such, trusted in the works of the law, especially circumcision: which appears by the 3d chapter. But as for the Gentiles, they looked on them as by nature sinners, and children of wrath; because born of uncircumcised parents, and aliens from their law, and who themselves did not know, profess and submit to the law of Moses, become proselytes, and receive circumcision. What they esteemed the sum of their wickedness and condemnation was, that they did not turn Jews, and act as Jews.[2] This notion of theirs the Apostle has a plain respect to, and endeavors to convince them of the falseness of, in ch. 2:12–16. And he has a manifest regard again to the same thing here, in the 12, 13, and 14th verses of ch. 5th. Which may lead us the more clearly to see the true sense of those verses; about the sense of which is the main controversy, and the meaning of which being determined, it will settle the meaning of every other controverted expression through the whole discourse.

Dr. Taylor misrepresents the Apostle's argument in these verses (which, as has been demonstrated, is in his sense altogether vain and impertinent). He supposes, the thing which the Apostle mainly intends to prove, is that death or mortality don't come on mankind by personal sin; and that he would prove it by this medium, that death reigned when there was no law in being, which threatened personal sin with death. 'Tis acknowledged, that this is implied, even that death came into the world by Adam's sin; yet this is not the main thing the Apostle designs to prove. But his main point evidently is, that sin and guilt and just exposedness to death and ruin came into the world by Adam's sin; as righteousness, justification, and a title to eternal life come by Christ. Which point he confirms by this consideration, that from the very time when Adam sinned, these things, namely, sin, guilt, and desert of ruin, became universal in the world, long before the law given by Moses to the Jewish nation had any being.

The Apostle's remark, that sin entered into the world by one man, who was the father of the whole human race, was an observation which afforded proper instruction for the Jews, who looked on themselves an holy people, because they had the law of Moses, and

2. Here are worthy to be observed the things which Dr. Taylor himself says to the same purpose. *Key* no. 270, 271 and *Preface to Par. on Epist. to Rom.* no. 43.

were the children of Abraham, and holy father; while they looked on other nations as by nature unholy and sinners, because they were not Abraham's children. He leads 'em up to an higher ancestor than this patriarch, even to Adam, who being equally the father of Jews and Gentiles, both alike come from a sinful father; from whom guilt and pollution were derived alike to all mankind. And this the Apostle proves by an argument, which of all that could possibly be invented, tended the most briefly and directly to convince the Jews: even by this reflection, that death had come equally on all mankind from Adam's time, and that the posterity of Abraham were equally subject to it with the rest of the world. This was apparent in fact; a thing they all knew. And the Jews had always been taught, that death (which began in the destruction of the body, and of this present life) was the proper punishment of sin. This they were taught in Moses' history of Adam, and God's first threatening of punishment for sin, and by the constant doctrine of the law and the prophets; as has been already observed.

And the Apostle's observation, that sin was in the world long before the law was given, and was as universal in the world from the times of Adam, as it had been among the heathen since the law of Moses, this shewed plainly, that the Jews were quite mistaken in their notion of their particular law; and that the law which is the original and universal rule of righteousness and judgment for all mankind, was another law, of far more ancient date, even the law of nature; which began as early as the human nature began, and was established with the first father of mankind, and in him with the whole race: the positive precept of abstaining from the forbidden fruit, being given for the trial of his compliance with this law of nature; of which the main rule is supreme regard to God and his will. And the Apostle proves that it must be thus, because, if the law of Moses had been the highest rule of judgment, and if there had not been a superior, prior, divine rule established, mankind in general would not have been judged and condemned as sinners, before that was given (for "sin is not imputed, when there is no law") as it is apparent in fact they were, because death reigned before that time, even from the times of Adam.

It may be observed, the Apostle in this epistle, and that to the Galatians, endeavors to convince the Jews of these two things, in opposition to the notions and prejudices they had entertained concerning their law. (1) That it never was intended to be the *Covenant,* or method by which they would actually be justified. (2) That it was not the *highest* and *universal* rule or law, by which mankind in general, and particularly the heathen world, were condemned. And he proves both by similar arguments. He proves that the law of Moses was not the Covenant, by which any of mankind were to obtain justification, because that Covenant was of older date, being expressly established in the time of Abraham, and Abraham himself was justified by it. This argument the Apostle particularly handles in the third chapter of Galatians, especially in vv. 17, 18, 19. And this argument is also made use of in the Apostle's reasonings in the fourth chapter of this epistle to the Romans, especially vv. 13, 14, 15. He proves also, that the law of Moses was not the prime rule of judgment, by which mankind in general, and particularly the heathen world, were condemned. And this he proves also the same way, viz. by shewing this to be of older date than that law, and that it was established with Adam. Now, these things tended to lead the Jews to right notions of their law, not as the intended method of justification, nor as the original and universal rule of condemnation, but something superadded to both: both being of older date. Superadded to the latter, to illustrate and confirm it, that the *offense might abound;* and superadded to the former, to be as a schoolmaster, to prepare men for the benefits of it, and to magnify divine *grace* in it, that this might *much more abound.*

The chief occasion of the obscurity and difficulty, which seems to attend the scope and connection of the various clauses in the three first verses of this discourse, particularly the 13th and 14th verses, is, that there are *two* things (although things closely connected), which the Apostle has in his eye *at once,* in which he aims to enlighten them he writes to; which will not be thought at all strange, by them that have been conversant with, and have attended to this Apostle's writings. He would illustrate the grand point he had been upon from the beginning, even justification through Christ's righteousness alone, by shewing how we are originally in a sinful miserable state, and how we derive this sin and misery from Adam, and how we are delivered and justified by Christ as a second Adam. At the same time, he would confute those foolish and corrupt notions of the Jews, about their nation and their law, that were very inconsistent with these doctrines. And he here endeavors to establish, at once, these two things in opposition to those Jewish notions:

(1) That 'tis our natural relation to Adam, and not to Abraham,

which determines our native moral state; and that therefore the being natural children of Abraham, will not make us by nature holy in the sight of God, since we are the natural seed of sinful Adam; nor does the Gentiles being not descended from Abraham, denominate them sinners, any more than the Jews, seeing both alike are descended from Adam.

(2) That the law of Moses is not the prime and general law and rule of judgment for mankind, to condemn them, and denominate them sinners; but that the state they are in with regard to a higher, more ancient and universal law, determines mankind in general to be sinners in the sight of God, and liable to be condemned as such. Which observation is, in many respects, to the Apostle's purpose; particularly in this respect, that if the Jews were convinced, that the law which was the prime rule of *condemnation,* was given to *all,* was common to all mankind, and that all fell under condemnation through the violation of that law by the common father of all, both Jews and Gentiles, then they would be led more easily and naturally to believe, that the method of justification, which God had established, also extended equally to all mankind: and that the Messiah, by whom we have this justification, is appointed, as Adam was, for a common head to all, both Jews and Gentiles.

The Apostle's aiming to confute the Jewish notion, is the principal occasion of those words in the 13th verse, "For until the law, sin was in the world; but sin is not imputed, when there is no law."

As to the import of that expression, "Even over them that had not sinned after the similitude of Adam's trangression," not only is the thing signified by it, in Dr. Taylor's sense of it, *not true;* or if it had been true, would have been impertinent, as has been shewn: but his interpretation is, otherwise, very much strained and unnatural. According to him, by "sinning after the similitude of Adam's transgression," is not meant any similitude of the act of sinning, nor of the command sinned against, nor properly any circumstance of the sin; but only the similitude of a circumstance of the *command,* viz. the *threatening* it is attended with. A farfetched thing, to be called a *similitude of sinning!* Besides, this expression, in such a meaning, is only a needless, impertinent, and awkward repeating over again the same thing, which, it is supposed, the Apostle had observed in the foregoing verse, even after he had left it, and had proceeded another step in the series of his discourse, or chain of arguing. As thus, in the foregoing verse, the Apostle had plainly laid down his argument (as our author understands it) by which he would prove, death did not come by personal sin, viz. that death reigned before any law, threatening death for personal sin, was in being; so that the sin then committed was against *no law,* threatening death for personal sin. Having laid this down, the Apostle leaves this part of his argument, and proceeds another step, "nevertheless death reigned from Adam to Moses," and then returns, in a strange, unnatural manner, and *repeats* that argument or assertion again, but only more obscurely than before, in these words, "Even over them that had not sinned after the similitude of Adam's transgression," i.e. over them that had not sinned against a law threatening death for personal sin. Which is just the same thing, as if the Apostle had said, "They that sinned *before the law,* did not sin against a law threatening death for personal sin; for there was *no such law,* for any to sin against, at that time: *nevertheless* death reigned at that time, *even over such as did not sin* against a law threatening death for personal sin." Which latter clause adds nothing to the premises, and tends nothing to illustrate what was said before, but rather to obscure and darken it. The particle (καὶ) "even," when prefixed in this manner, used to signify something additional, some advance in the sense or argument; implying, that the words following express something more, or express the same thing more fully, plainly, or forcibly.[3] But to unite two clauses by such a particle, in such a manner, when there is nothing besides a flat repetition, with no superadded sense or force, but rather a greater uncertainty and obscurity, would be very unusual, and indeed very absurd.[4]

I can see no reason, why we should be dissatisfied with that explanation of this clause, which has more commonly been given, viz. that by "them who have not sinned after the similitude of Adam's transgression," are meant infants; who, though they have indeed sinned in Adam, yet never sinned as Adam did, by actually transgressing in their own persons; unless it be, that this interpretation is too *old,* and too *common.* It was well known by those the Apostle wrote to, that vast numbers had died in infancy, within that period which the Apostle speaks of, particularly in the time of the deluge: and it would be strange, the Apostle should not have the case of

3. [JE's incomplete sentences have here been retained.]

4. [MS reads: "But to unite two clauses with such a particle in such a manner, when there is nothing besides a flat repetition, without additional sense or force, but rather a greater obscurity, would be to speak nonsensically."]

such infants in his mind; even supposing, his scope were what our author supposes, and he had only intended to prove that death did not come on mankind for their personal sin. How directly would it have served the purpose of proving this, to have mentioned so great a part of mankind, that are subject to death, who, all know, never committed any sin in their own persons? How much more plain and easy the proof of the point by that, than to go round about, as Dr. Taylor supposes, and bring in a thing so dark and uncertain, as this, that God never would bring death on all mankind for personal sin (though they had personal sin) without an express revealed constitution; and then to observe, that there was no revealed constitution of this nature from Adam to Moses; which also seems a thing without any plain evidence; and then to infer, that it must needs be so, that it could come only on *occasion* of Adam's sin, though not *for* his sin, or as any punishment of it; which inference also is very dark and unintelligible.

If the Apostle in this place meant those who never sinned by their personal act, it is not strange that he should express this by their "not sinning after the similitude of Adam's transgression." We read of two ways of men's being like Adam, or in which a similitude to him is ascribed to men. One is a being begotten or born in his *image* or *likeness* (Gen. 5:3). Another is a transgressing God's covenant or law, *like him* (Hos. 6:7). "They, like Adam (so, in the Heb[rew] and vulg[ate] Lat[in]) have transgressed the Covenant." Infants have the former similitude; but not the latter. And it was very natural, when the Apostle would infer, that infants become sinners by that one act and offense of Adam, to observe, that they had not renewed the act of sin themselves, by any second instance of a like sort. And such might be the state of language among Jews and Christians at that day, that the Apostle might have no phrase more aptly to express this meaning. The manner in which the epithets, "personal" and "actual," are used and applied now in this case, is probably of later date and more modern use.

And then this supposition of the Apostle's having the case of infants in view, in this expression, makes it more to his purpose, to mention death reigning before the law of Moses was given. For the Jews looked on all nations, besides themselves, as sinners, by virtue of their law; being made so especially by the law of circumcision, given first to Abraham, and completed by Moses, making the want of circumcision a legal pollution, utterly disqualifying for the privileges of the sanctuary. This law, the Jews supposed, made the very infants of the Gentiles sinners, polluted and hateful to God; they being uncircumcised, and born of uncircumcised parents. But the Apostle proves, against these notions of the Jews, that the nations of the world don't become sinners by nature, and sinners from infancy, by virtue of their law, in this manner, but by Adam's sin; inasmuch as infants were treated as sinners long before the law of circumcision was given, as well as before they had committed actual sin.

What has been said, may, as I humbly conceive, lead us to that which is the *true* scope and sense of the Apostle in these three verses; which I will endeavor more briefly to represent in the following paraphrase.

12. "Wherefore, as by one man sin entered into the world, and death by sin; and so death passed upon all men, for that all have sinned."

The things which I have largely insisted on, viz. the evil that is in the world, the general wickedness, guilt and ruin of mankind, and the opposite good, even justification and life, as only by Christ, lead me to observe the *likeness* of the manner, in which they are each of them *introduced*. For it was by one man, that the general corruption and guilt which I have spoken of, came into the world, and condemnation and death by sin: and this dreadful punishment and ruin came on all mankind, by the great *law of works,* originally established with mankind in their first father, and by his *one offense,* or breach of that law; *all* thereby becoming sinners in God's sight, and exposed to final destruction.

13. "For until the law sin was in the world; but sin is not imputed, when there is no law."

It is manifest, that it was in this way the world became sinful and guilty: and not in that way which the Jews suppose, viz. that their law, given by Moses, is the grand universal rule of righteousness and judgment for mankind, and that it is by being Gentiles, uncircumcised and aliens from that law, that the nations of the world are constituted sinners and unclean. For *before* the law of Moses was given, mankind were all looked upon by the great Judge as sinners, by corruption and guilt derived from Adam's violation of the original law of works; which shews, that the original, universal rule of righteousness is not the law of Moses; for if so, there would have been no sin imputed *before* that was given; because sin is not imputed, when there is no law.

14. "Nevertheless, death reigned from Adam to Moses, even over them that had not sinned after the similitude of Adam's transgression."

But, that at that time sin was *imputed,* and men were by their Judge reckoned as sinners, through guilt and corruption derived from Adam, and condemned for sin to death, the proper punishment of sin, we have a plain proof; in that it appears in fact, all mankind, during that whole time which preceded the law of Moses, were subjected to that temporal death, which is the visible introduction and image of that utter destruction which sin deserves; not excepting even infants, who could be sinners no other way than by virtue of Adam's transgression, having never in their own persons actually sinned as Adam did; nor could at that time be made polluted by the law of Moses, as being uncircumcised, or born of uncircumcised parents.

Now, by way of reflection on the whole, I would observe, that though there are two or three expressions in this paragraph (Rom. 5:12, etc.), the design of which is attended with some difficulty and obscurity, as particularly in the 13th and 14th verses; yet the scope and sense of the discourse in general is not obscure, but on the contrary very clear and manifest; and so is the particular doctrine mainly taught in it. The Apostle sets himself with great care and pains to make it plain, and precisely to fix and settle the point he is upon. And the discourse is so framed, that one part of it does greatly clear and fix the meaning of other parts; and the whole is determined by the clear connection it stands in with other parts of the epistle, and by the manifest drift of all the preceding part of it.

The doctrine of original sin is not only here taught, but most plainly, explicitly and abundantly taught. This doctrine is asserted, expressly or implicitly, in almost every verse; and in some of the verses several times. 'Tis fully implied in that first expression in the 12th verse, "By one man sin entered into the world." Which implies, that sin became *universal in the world;* as the Apostle had before largely shewn it was; and not merely (which would be a trifling insignificant observation) that one man, who was made first, sinned first, before other men sinned; or, that it did not so happen that many men began to sin just together at the same moment. The latter part of the verse, "And death by sin, and so death passed upon all men, for that" (or, if you will, unto which) "all have sinned," shews, that in the eye of the Judge of the world, in Adam's first sin, *all* sinned; not only in *some sort,* but all sinned so as to be exposed to that death, and final destruction, which is the proper wages of sin. The same doctrine is taught again twice over in the 14th verse. It is there observed, as a proof of this doctrine, that "death reigned over them which had not sinned after the similitude of Adam's transgression," i.e. by their personal act; and therefore could be exposed to death, only by deriving guilt and pollution from Adam, in consequence of his sin. And 'tis taught again, in those words, "Who is the figure of him that was to come." The resemblance lies very much in this circumstance, viz. our deriving sin, guilt and punishment by Adam's sin, as we do righteousness, justification, and the reward of life by Christ's obedience; for so the Apostle explains himself. The same doctrine is expressly taught again, v. 15th, "Through the offense of one many be dead." And again twice in the 16th verse, "It was by one that sinned," i.e. it was by Adam that guilt and punishment (before spoken of) came on mankind: and in these words, "Judgment was by one to condemnation." It is again plainly and fully laid down in the 17th verse. "By one man's offense, death reigned by one." So again in the 18th verse, "By the offense of one, judgment came upon all men to condemnation." Again, very plainly in the 19th verse, "By one man's disobedience, many were made sinners."

And here is everything to determine and fix the meaning of all important terms, that the Apostle makes use of: as the *abundant use* of 'em in all parts of the New Testament; and especially in this Apostle's writings, which make up a very great part of the New Testament: and his repeated use of 'em in this epistle in particular, especially in the preceding part of the epistle, which leads to and introduces this discourse, and in the former part of this very chapter; and also, the light, that one sentence in this paragraph casts on another; which fully settles their meaning: as, with respect to the words, "justification," "righteousness," and "condemnation"; and above all, in regard of the word, "sin," which is the most important of all, with relation to the doctrine and controversy we are upon. Besides the constant use of this term everywhere else through the New Testament through the epistles of this Apostle, this epistle in particular, and even the former part of this chapter, 'tis often repeated in this very paragraph, and evidently used in the very sense, that is denied to belong to it in the end of v. 12th and v. 19th, though owned everywhere else; and its meaning is fully determined by the Apostle's varying the term; using together with it, to signify the same thing, such a variety of other synonymous words, such as "offense," "transgression," "disobedience." And further, to put the matter out of all controversy, 'tis particularly and expressly, and repeatedly distinguished from that which our opposers would explain it by, viz. "condemnation" and "death." And what is meant by "sin's entering into the world" in v. 12th, is determined by a like phrase of "sin's being in the world," in the next verse. And that by "the offense of one," so often spoken of here, as bringing death and condemnation on all, the Apostle means the sin of one, derived in its guilt and pollution to mankind in general, is a thing which (over and above all that has been already observed) is settled and determined by those words in the conclusion of this discourse (v. 20), "Moreover, the law entered, that the offense might abound: But sin abounded, grace did much more abound." These words plainly shew, that the *offense,* spoken of so often and evidently spoken of still in these words, which was the offense of one man, became the sin of all. For when he says, "The law entered, that the offense might abound," his meaning can't be, that the offense of Adam, merely as his personally, should abound; but, as it exists in its *derived* guilt, corrupt influence, and evil fruits, in the sin of mankind in general, even as a tree in its root and branches.[5]

5. The offense, according to Dr. Taylor's explanation, don't *abound by the law* at all really and truly, in any sense; neither the sin, nor the punishment. For he says, "The meaning is not, that man should be made more wicked; but, that men should be liable to death for every transgression." But after all, they are liable to no more deaths, nor to any worse deaths, if they are not more sinful: for they were to have punishment, according to their deserts *before.* Such as died and went into another world before the law of Moses was given, were punished according to their deserts; and the law, when it came, threatened no more.

'Tis a thing that confirms the certainty of the *proof* of the doctrine of original sin, which this place affords, that the utmost art *cannot* pervert it to *another* sense. What a variety of the most artful methods have been used by the enemies of this doctrine, to wrest and darken this paragraph of Holy Writ, which stands so much in their way, as it were to *force* the Bible to speak a language that is agreeable to their mind! How have expressions been strained, words and phrases racked! What strange figures of speech have been invented and with violent hands thrust into the Apostle's mouth; and then with a bold countenance and magisterial airs obtruded on the world, as from him! But, blessed by God, we have his words as he delivered them, and the rest of the same epistle and his other writings, to compare with them; by which his meaning stands in too strong and glaring a light to be hid by any of the artificial mists, which they labor to throw upon it.

'Tis really no less than *abusing* the Scripture and its readers, to represent this paragraph as the most *obscure* of all the places of Scripture, that speak of the consequences of Adam's sin; and to treat it as if there was need first to consider other places as more plain. Whereas, 'tis most manifestly a place in which these things are declared, beyond all, the most plainly, particularly, precisely and of set purpose, by that great Apostle, who has most fully explained to us those doctrines, in general, which relate to the redemption by Christ, and the sin and misery we are redeemed from. And it must be now left to the reader's judgment, whether the Christian church has not proceeded reasonably, in looking on this as a place of Scripture most clearly and fully treating of these things, and in using its determinate sense as an help to settle the meaning of many other passages of Sacred Writ.

As this place in general is very plain and full, so the doctrine of the corruption of nature, as derived from Adam, and also the imputation of his first sin, are both clearly taught in it. The imputation of Adam's one transgression, is indeed most directly and frequently asserted. We are here assured, that "by one man's sin, death passed on all"; all being adjudged to this punishment, as having sinned (so it is implied) in that one man's sin. And 'tis repeated over and over, that "all are condemned," "many are dead," "many made sinners," etc. "by one man's offense," "by the disobedience of one," and "by one offense." And the doctrine of original depravity is also here taught, when the Apostle says, "By one man sin entered into the world"; having a plain respect (as hath been shewn) to that universal corruption and wickedness, as well as guilt, which he had before largely treated of.

PART THREE.

Observing the Evidence Given Us, Relative to the Doctrine of Original Sin, in what the Scriptures Reveal Concerning the Redemption by Christ

CHAPTER I

THE EVIDENCE OF ORIGINAL SIN FROM THE NATURE OF REDEMPTION, IN THE PROCUREMENT OF IT

ACCORDING to Dr. Taylor's scheme, a very great part of mankind are the subjects of Christ's redemption, who live and die perfectly *innocent;* who never have had, and never will have any sin charged to their account, and never are either the subjects of, or exposed to any punishment whatsoever, viz. all that die in *infancy.* They are the subjects of Christ's redemption, as he redeems 'em from death, or as they by his righteousness have justification, and by his obedience are made righteous, in the resurrection of the body, in the sense of Rom. 5:18,19. And all mankind are thus the subjects of Christ's redemption, while they are perfectly guiltless, and exposed to no punishment, as by Christ they are entitled to a resurrection. Though with respect to such persons as have sinned, he allows it is in *some sort* by Christ and his death, that they are saved from sin and the punishment of it. Now let us see whether such a scheme well consists with the Scripture account of the redemption by Jesus Christ.

I. The representations of the redemption by Christ, everywhere in Scripture, lead us to suppose, that *all* whom he came to redeem, are *sinners;* that his salvation, as to the term from which (or the evil to be redeemed from) in all is sin, and the deserved punishment of sin. 'Tis natural to suppose, that when he had his name Jesus, or Saviour, given him by God's special and immediate appointment, the salvation meant by that name should be his salvation in general; and not only a part of his salvation, and with regard only to some of them that he came to save. But this name was given him to signify his saving his people from their sins (Matt. 1:21). And the great doctrine of Christ's salvation is, that "he came into the world to save sinners" (I Tim. 1:15), and that "Christ hath once suffered, the just for the unjust" (I Pet. 3:18). "In this was manifested the love of God towards us" (towards such in general as have the benefit of God's love in giving Christ) "that God sent his only begotten son into the world, that we might live through him. Herein is love . . . that he sent his son to be the propitiation for our sins" (I John 4:9,10). Many other texts might be mentioned, which seem evidently to suppose, that all who are redeemed by Christ, are saved from sin. We are led by what Christ himself said, to suppose, that if any are not sinners, they have no need of him as a Redeemer, any more than a well man of a physician (Mark 2:17). And that men, in order to being the proper subjects of the mercy of God through Christ, must first be in a state of sin, is implied in Gal. 3:22. "But the scripture hath concluded all under sin, that the promise by faith of Jesus Christ might be given to them that believe." To the same effect is Rom. 11:32.[1]

These things are greatly confirmed by the Scripture doctrine of sacrifices. 'Tis abundantly plain, by both Old and New Testaments, that they were types of Christ's death, and were for sin, and supposed sin in those for whom they were offered. The Apostle supposes, that in order to any having the benefit of the eternal inheritance by Christ, there must of necessity be the death of the testator; and gives that reason for it, that without shedding of blood there is no remission (Heb. 9:15 etc.). And Christ himself, in representing the benefit of his blood, in the institution of the Lord's Supper, under the notion of the blood of a testament, calls it "the blood of the New Testament, shed for the remission of sins" (Matt. 26:28). But according to the scheme of our author, many have the eternal inheritance by the death of the testator, who never had any need of remission.

II. The Scripture represents the redemption by Christ as a redemption from *deserved* destruction; and that, not merely as it respects some particulars, but as the fruit of God's love to mankind. (John 3:16), "God so loved the world, that he gave his only begotten son, that whosoever believeth in him might not perish, but have everlasting life." Implying, that otherwise they must perish, or be destroyed. But what necessity of this, if they did not deserve to be destroyed? Now, that the destruction here spoken of, is deserved destruction, is manifest, because it is there compared to the perishing

1. [This paragraph and parts of the next are a greatly condensed version of a long section found on pp. 180–1 of the MS.]

of such of the children of Israel as died by the bite of the fiery serpents, which God in his wrath, for their rebellion, sent amongst them. And the same thing clearly appears by the last verse of the same chapter, "He that believeth on the son, hath everlasting life; and he that believeth not the son, shall not see life, but the wrath of God abideth on him," or, is left remaining on him: implying, that all in general are found under the wrath of God, and that they only of all mankind, who are interested in Christ, have this wrath removed, and eternal life bestowed; the rest are left, with the wrath of God still remaining on them. The same is clearly illustrated and confirmed by John 5:24. "He that believeth . . . hath everlasting life and shall not come into condemnation, but is passed from death to life." In being passed from death to life is implied, that before they were all in a state of death; and they are spoken of as being so by a sentence of condemnation; and if it be a just condemnation 'tis a deserved condemnation.

III. It will follow on Dr. Taylor's scheme, that Christ's redemption, with regard to a great part of them who are the subjects of it, is not only a redemption from *no sin,* but from *no calamity,* and so from *no evil* of any kind. For as to death, which *infants* are redeemed from, they never were subjected to it as a calamity, but purely as a benefit. It came by no threatening, or curse, denounced upon or through Adam; the Covenant with him being utterly abolished, as to all its force and power on mankind (according to our author) before the pronouncing the sentence of mortality. Therefore trouble and death could be appointed to innocent mankind, no other way than on the foot of another Covenant, the Covenant of Grace; and in this channel they come only as favors, not as evils. Therefore they could need no medicine or remedy; for they had no disease. Even death itself, which it is supposed Christ saves 'em from, is only a medicine; 'tis preventing physic, and one of the greatest of benefits. It's ridiculous, to talk of persons needing a medicine, or a physician, to save 'em from an excellent medicine; or of a remedy from a happy remedy! If it be said, though death be a benefit, yet 'tis so because Christ changes it, and turns it into a benefit, by procuring a resurrection: I would here ask, what can be meant by turning or changing it into a benefit, when it never was otherwise, nor could ever justly be otherwise? Infants could not at all be brought under death as a calamity: for they never deserved it. And it would be only an abuse (be it far from us, to ascribe such a thing to God) in any being, to make the offer, to any poor sufferers, of a redeemer from some calamity, which he had brought upon them without the least desert of it on their part.

But it is plain, that death or mortality was not at first brought on mankind as a blessing, on the foot of the Covenant of Grace through Christ; and that Christ and grace don't *bring* mankind under death, but find 'em under it (II Cor. 5:14), "We thus judge, that if one died for all, then were all dead." (Luke 19:10), "The son of man is come to seek and to save that which was lost." The grace, which appears in providing a deliverer from any state, supposes the subject to be in that state prior to that grace and deliverance; and not that such a state is first introduced by that grace. In our author's scheme, there never could be any sentence of death, or condemnation, that requires a saviour from it; because the very sentence itself, according to the true meaning of it, implies and makes sure all that good, which is requisite to abolish and make void the seeming evil to the innocent subject. So that the sentence itself is in effect the deliverer; and there is no need of another deliverer, to deliver from that sentence. Dr. Taylor insists upon it, that "Nothing comes upon us in consequence of Adam's sin, in any sense, kind, or degree, inconsistent with the original blessing pronounced on Adam, at his creation; and nothing but what is perfectly consistent with God's blessing, love, and goodness, declared to Adam, as soon as he came out of his maker's hands." [2] If the case be so, it is certain there is no evil or calamity at all, for Christ to redeem us from; unless things agreeable to the divine goodness, love and blessing, are things which we need redemption from.

IV. It will follow on our author's principles, not only with respect to infants, but even *adult* persons, that redemption is needless, and Christ is dead in vain. Not only is there no need of Christ's redemption in order to deliverance from any consequences of Adam's sin, but also in order to perfect freedom from personal sin, and all its evil consequences. For God has made other sufficient provision for that, viz. a sufficient power and ability, in all mankind, to do all their duty, and wholly to avoid sin. Yea, this author insists upon it, that "when men have not sufficient power to do their duty, they have no duty to do." [3] We may safely and assuredly conclude, says he, that mankind in all parts of the world have sufficient power to

2. Pp. 364, 365. [JE's free paraphrase.]

3. Pp. 111, 339, 340.

do the duty, which God requires of them; and that he requires of 'em no more than they have sufficient power to do. And in another place,[4] "God has given powers equal to the duty, which he expects." And he expresses a great dislike at R.R.'s supposing,[5] "That our propensities to evil, and temptations, are too strong to be effectually and constantly resisted . . . or that we are unavoidably sinful in a degree, that our appetites and passions will be breaking out, notwithstanding our everlasting watchfulness." [6] These things fully imply, that men have in their own natural ability sufficient means to avoid sin, and to be perfectly free from it; and so, from all the bad consequences of it. And if the means are sufficient, then there is no need of more. And therefore there is no need of Christ's dying in order to it. What Dr. Taylor says in p. 348 fully implies, that it would be unjust in God, to give mankind being in such circumstances, as that they would be more likely to sin, so as to be exposed to final misery, than otherwise. Hence then, without Christ and his redemption, and without any grace at all, *mere justice* makes *sufficient provision* for our being free from sin and misery, by our own power.

If all mankind, in all parts of the world, have such sufficient power to do their whole duty, without being sinful in any degree, then they have sufficient power to obtain righteousness by the law: and then, according to the apostle Paul, "Christ is dead in vain" (Gal. 2:21). "If righteousness comes by the law, Christ is dead in vain." διὰ νόμου without the article, "by law," or the rule of right action, as our author explains the phrase.[7] And according to the sense in which he explains this very place, "It would have frustrated, or rendered useless, the grace of God, if Christ died to accomplish what was or *might* have been effected by law itself, without his death." [8] So that it most clearly follows from his own doctrine, that *Christ is dead in vain,* and the grace of God is *useless.* The same Apostle says, "If there had been a law which *could* have given life, verily righteousness should have been by the law" (Gal. 3:21), i.e. (still according to Dr. Taylor's own sense) if there was a law, that man, in his present state, had sufficient power perfectly to fulfill. For

4. P. 343. [JE's free paraphrase.]
5. [Watts, *Ruin and Recovery of Mankind.*]
6. P. 344.
7. *Pref. to Par. on Rom.* no. 38.
8. *Note on Rom.* 5:20. [P. 379. JE's free paraphrase.]

Dr. Taylor supposes the reason why the law could not give life, to be, "not because it was weak in itself, but through the weakness of our flesh, and the infirmity of the human nature in the present state." [9] But he says, "We are all under a mild dispensation of *grace,* making allowance for our infirmities." [1] By our "infirmities," we may upon good grounds suppose, he means that infirmity of human nature, which he gives as the reason, why the law can't give life. But what grace is there in making that allowance for our infirmities, which justice itself (according to his doctrine) most absolutely requires, as he supposes divine justice exactly proportions our duty to our ability?

Again, if it be said, that although Christ's redemption was not necessary to preserve men from *beginning* to sin, and getting into a course of sin, because they have sufficient power in themselves to avoid it; yet it may be necessary to deliver men, *after* they have by their own folly brought themselves under the dominion of evil appetites and passions.[2] I answer, if it be so, that men need deliverance from those habits and passions, which are become too strong for them, yet that deliverance, on our author's principles, would be no salvation from sin. For, the exercise of passions which are too strong for us, and which we can't overcome, is *necessary;* and he strongly urges, that a necessary evil can be no *moral* evil. It's true, 'tis the effect of evil as 'tis the effect of a bad practice, while the man remained at liberty, and had power to have avoided it. But then, according to Dr. Taylor, that evil *cause* alone is sin; and not so, the necessary *effect:* for he says expressly, "The cause of every effect, *alone,* is chargeable with the effect it produceth, or which proceedeth from it." [3] And as to that sin which was the cause, the man needed no saviour from that, having had sufficient power in himself to have avoided it. So that it follows, by our author's scheme, that none of mankind, neither infants, nor adult persons, neither the more nor less vicious, neither Jews nor Gentiles, neither heathens nor Christians, ever did, or ever could stand in any need of a saviour; and that, with respect to all, the truth is, Christ is dead in vain.

If any should say, although all mankind in all ages have sufficient

9. Ibid.

1. P. 368. [JE's free paraphrase.]

2. See p. 228 and also what he says of the helpless state of the heathen, in *Paraph. and Notes on Rom.* 7 and the beginning of ch. 8.

3. P. 128.

ability to do their whole duty, and so may by their own power enjoy perfect freedom from sin, yet God foresaw that they would sin, and that after they had sinned they would need Christ's death: I answer, it's plain by what the Apostle says, in those places which were just now mentioned. (Gal. 2:21 and 3:21), that God would have esteemed it needless to give his Son to die for men, unless there had been a prior impossibility of their having righteousness by law; and that if there had been a law which could have given life, this other way by the death of Christ would not have been provided. And this appears to be agreeable to our author's own sense of things, by his words which have been cited, wherein he says, "It would have *frustrated* or rendered *useless* the grace of God, if Christ died to accomplish what was or might have been effected by law itself, without his death." [4]

V. It will follow on Dr. Taylor's scheme, not only that Christ's redemption is *needless* for the saving from sin or its consequences, but also that it does *no good* that way, has no tendency to any *diminution* of sin in the world. For as to any infusion of virtue or holiness into the heart, by divine power, through Christ or his redemption, it is altogether inconsistent with this author's notions. With him, *inwrought* virtue, if there were any such thing, would be no virtue; not being the effect of our own will, choice and design, but only of a sovereign act of God's power.[5] And therefore, all that Christ does to increase virtue, is only increasing our talents, our light, advantages, means and motives; as he often explains the matter.[6] But sin is not at all diminished. For he says, "Our duty must be measured by our talents": as, a child that has less talents, has less duty; and therefore must be no more exposed to commit sin, than he that has greater talents; because he that has greater talents, has more duty required, in exact proportion.[7] If so, he that has but one talent, has as much advantage to perform that one degree of duty which is required of him, as he that has five talents, to perform his five degrees of duty, and is no more exposed to fail of it. And that man's guilt, who sins against greater advantages, means and motives, is greater in proportion to his talents.[8] And therefore it will follow, on Dr. Taylor's

4. [The preceding paragraph omitted from MS.]
5. See pp. 245, 250, 180.
6. In pp. 44, 50 and innumerable other places.
7. See pp. 55, 224, 234, 337, 338, 342, 343, 344, 345.
8. See *Paraph. on Rom.* 2:9; also on v. 12.

principles, that men stand no better chance, have no more eligible or valuable probability of freedom from sin and punishment, or of contracting but little guilt, or of performing required duty, with the great advantages and talents implied in Christ's redemption, than without them; when all things are computed, and put into the balances together, the numbers, degrees and aggravations of sin exposed to, degrees of duty required, etc. So that men have no redemption from sin, and no new means of performing duty, that are valuable or worth anything at all. And thus the great redemption by Christ in every respect comes to nothing, with regard both to infants and adult persons.

CHAPTER II

THE EVIDENCE OF THE DOCTRINE OF ORIGINAL SIN FROM WHAT THE SCRIPTURE TEACHES OF THE APPLICATION OF REDEMPTION

THE truth of the doctrine of original sin is very clearly manifest from what the Scripture says of that *change of state,* which it represents as necessary to an actual interest in the spiritual and eternal blessings of the Redeemer's kingdom.

In order to this, it speaks of it as absolutely necessary for everyone, that he be regenerated, or born again. (John 3:3), "Verily, verily I say unto thee, except a man (γεννηθῇ ἄνωθεν) be begotten again," or born again, "he cannot see the kingdom of God." Dr. Taylor, though he will not allow, that this signifies any change from a state of *natural propensity* to sin, yet supposes, that the new birth here spoken of means a man's being brought to a "divine life, in a right use and application of the natural powers in a life of true holiness": [1] and that it is the attainment of "those habits of virtue and religion, gives us the real character of true Christians, and the children of God"; [2] and that it is "putting on the new nature of right action." [3]

But in order to proceed in the most sure and safe manner, in our understanding what is meant in Scripture by "being born again," and so in the inferences we draw from what is said of the necessity of it, let us compare Scripture with Scripture, and consider what other terms or phrases are used in other places, where respect is evidently had to the same change. And here I would observe the following things.

I. If we compare one Scripture with another, it will be sufficiently manifest, that by regeneration, or being begotten or born again, the

1. P. 144. [JE's free paraphrase.]
2. Pp. 246, 248. [JE adds "of true Christians."]
3. P. 251.

same change in the state of the mind is signified, with that which the Scripture speaks of as effected in true repentance and conversion. I put repentance and conversion together, because the Scripture puts them together (Acts 3:19), and because they plainly signify much the same thing. The word μετάνοια (repentance) signifies a change of the mind; as the word "conversion" means a change or turning from sin to God. And that this is the same change with that which is called regeneration (excepting that this latter term especially signifies the change, as the mind is passive in it) the following things do shew.

In the change which the mind passes under in repentance and conversion, is attained that character of true Christians, which is necessary to the eternal privileges of such. (Acts 3:19), "Repent ye therefore, and be converted, that your sins may be blotted out, when the times of refreshing shall come from the presence of the Lord Jesus." And so it is with regeneration; as is evident from what Christ says to Nicodemus, and as is allowed by Dr. Taylor.

The change the mind passes under in repentance and conversion, is that in which saving *faith* is attained. (Mark 1:15), "The kingdom of heaven is at hand, repent ye and believe the gospel"—and so it is with a being born again, or born of God; as appears by John 1:12,13. "But to as many as received him, to them gave he power to become the sons of God, even to them that *believe* on his name, which were born, not of blood, etc. but of God."

Just as Christ says concerning conversion (Matt. 18:3), "Verily, verily I say unto you, except ye be converted and become as little children, ye shall not enter into the kingdom of God": so does he say concerning being born again, in what he spake to Nicodemus.

By the change men pass under in conversion, they become as little children; which appears in the place last cited; and so they do by regeneration (I Pet. 1 at the end, and ch. 2 at the beginning). "Being born again . . . wherefore . . . as newborn babes . . . desire . . . etc." 'Tis no objection, that the disciples, whom Christ spake to in Matt. 18:3 were converted already: this makes it not less proper for Christ to declare the necessity of conversion to them, leaving it with them to try themselves, and to make sure their conversion: in like manner as he declared to 'em the necessity of repentance, in Luke 13:3,5, "Except ye repent, ye shall all likewise perish."

The change that men pass under at their repentance, is expressed and exhibited by baptism. Hence it is called the "baptism of repentance," from time to time (Matt. 3:11; Luke 3:3; Acts 19:4 and 2:38). And so is regeneration or being born again expressed by baptism: as is evident by such representations of regeneration as those (John 3:5), "Except a man be born of water, and of the spirit"; (Titus 3:5), "He saved us by the washing of regeneration." Many other things might be observed, to shew, that the change men pass under in their repentance and conversion, is the same with that which they are the subjects of in regeneration. But these observations may be sufficient.

II. The change which a man passes under when born again, and in his repentance and conversion, is the same that the Scripture calls the *circumcision* of the heart. This may easily appear by considering,

That as regeneration is that in which are attained the habits of true virtue and holiness, as has been shewn, and as is confessed; so is circumcision of heart. (Deut. 30:6), "And the Lord thy God will circumcise thine heart, and the heart of thy seed, to love the Lord thy God with all thine heart, and with all thy soul."

Regeneration is that whereby men come to have the character of true Christians; as is evident, and as is confessed; and so is circumcision of heart: for by this men become Jews inwardly, or Jews in the spiritual and Christian sense (and that is the same as being true Christians), as of old proselytes were made Jews by circumcision of the flesh. (Rom. 2:28,29), "For he is not a Jew, which is one outwardly; neither is that circumcision, which is outward of the flesh: but he is a Jew, which is one inwardly; and circumcision is that of the heart, in the spirit and not in the letter, whose praise is not of men, but of God."

That circumcision of the heart is the same with conversion, or turning from sin to God, is evident by Jer. 4:1–4. "If thou wilt return, O Israel, return" (or, convert) "unto me. . . . Circumcise yourselves to the Lord, and put away the foreskins of your heart." (And Deut. 10:16), "Circumcise therefore the foreskin of thine heart, and be no more stiff-necked."

Circumcision of the heart is the same change of the heart, that men pass under in their repentance; as is evident by Lev. 26:4. "If their uncircumcised heart be humbled, and they accept the punishment of their iniquity."

The change men pass under in regeneration, repentance and conversion is signified by baptism, as has been shewn; and so is circumcision of the heart signified by the same thing. None will deny, that it was this internal circumcision, which of old was signified by external circumcision; nor will any deny, now under the New Testament, that inward and spiritual baptism, or the cleansing of the heart, is signified by external washing, or baptism. But spiritual circumcision and spiritual baptism are the same thing; both being the "putting off the body of the sins of the flesh"; as is very plain by Col. 2:11 12,13. "In whom also ye are circumcised, with the circumcision made without hands, in putting off the body of sins of the flesh, by the circumcision of Christ, buried with him in baptism; wherein also ye are risen with him, etc."

III. This inward change, called regeneration, and circumcision of heart, which is wrought in repentance and conversion, is the same with that spiritual *resurrection,* so often spoken of, and represented as a dying unto sin, and living unto righteousness.

This appears with great plainness in that last cited place, Col. 2. "In whom also ye are circumcised with the circumcision made without hands . . . buried with him in baptism, wherein also ye are risen with him, through the faith of the operation of God. . . And you, being dead in your sins, and the uncircumcision of your flesh, hath he quickened together with him; having forgiven you all trespasses."

The same appears by Rom. 6:3,4,5. "Know ye not that so many of us as were baptized into Jesus Christ, were baptized into his death? Therefore we are buried with him by baptism into death; that like as Christ was raised up from the dead, by the glory of the father, even so we also should walk in newness of life, etc." (v. 11), "Likewise reckon ye so yourselves to be dead unto sin, but alive unto God through Jesus Christ our Lord."

In which place also it is evident, by the words recited, and by the whole context, that this spiritual resurrection is that change, in which persons are brought to habits of holiness and to the divine life, by which Dr. Taylor describes the thing obtained in being born again.

That a spiritual resurrection, to a new divine life, should be called a being born again, is agreeable to the language of Scripture; in which we find, a resurrection is called a being born or begotten. So those words in the second Psalm, "Thou art my son, this day have I begotten thee," are applied to Christ's resurrection (Acts 13:33). So in Col. 1:18, Christ is called the first born from the dead; and in

Rev. 1:5, "The first begotten from the dead." The saints, in their conversion or spiritual resurrection, are risen with Christ, and are begotten and born with him. (I Pet. 1:3), "Which hath begotten us again, to a lively hope, by the resurrection of Jesus Christ from the dead, to an inheritance incorruptible." This inheritance is the same thing with that kingdom of heaven, which men obtain by being born again, according to Christ's words to Nicodemus; and that same inheritance of them that are sanctified, spoken of as what is obtained in true conversion. (Acts 26:18), "To turn them" (or convert them) "from darkness to light, and from the power of Satan unto God, that they may receive forgiveness of sins, and inheritance among them that are sanctified, through faith that is in me." Dr. Taylor's own words, in his *Note on Rom.* 1:4, speaking of that place in the second Psalm, just now mentioned, are very worthy to be here recited. He observes how this is applied to Christ's resurrection and exaltation, in the New Testament, and then has this remark,[4] "Note, begetting is conferring a new and happy state; a son is a person put into it. Agreeably to this, good men are said to be the sons of God, as they are the sons of the resurrection to eternal life, which is represented as *παλιγγενεσία,* a being begotten or born again, regenerated."

So that I think it is abundantly plain, that the spiritual resurrection spoken of in Scripture, by which the saints are brought to a new divine life, is the same with that being born again, which Christ says is necessary for everyone, in order to his seeing the kingdom of God.

IV. This change, which men are the subjects of, when they are born again, and circumcised in heart, when they repent and are converted, and spiritually raised from the dead, is the same change which is meant when the Scripture speaks of making the heart and spirit new, or giving a *new heart and spirit.*

'Tis needless here to stand to observe, how evidently this is spoken of as necessary to salvation, and as the change in which are attained the habits of true virtue and holiness, and the character of a true saint; as has been observed of regeneration, conversion, etc. and how apparent it is from thence, that the change is the same. For it is as it were self-evident; 'tis apparent by the phrases themselves, that they are different expressions of the same thing. Thus repentance (*μετάνοια*) or the change of the mind is the same as being changed to a new mind, or new heart and spirit. Conversion is the turning of

4. [The word "Note" refers to one of Taylor's footnotes, see Taylor, p. 315.]

the heart; which is the same thing as changing it so, that there shall be another heart, or a new heart, or a new spirit. To be born again, is to be born anew; which implies a becoming new, and is represented as a becoming new-born babes: but none supposes, it is the body, that is immediately and properly new, but the mind, heart, or spirit. And so a spiritual resurrection is the resurrection of the spirit, or rising to begin a new existence and life, as to the mind, heart or spirit. So that all these phrases imply an having a new heart, and being renewed in the spirit, according to their plain signification.

When Nicodemus expressed his wonder at Christ's declaring it necessary, that a man should be born again in order to see the kingdom of God, or enjoy the privileges of the kingdom of the Messiah, Christ says to him (John 3:10), "Art thou a master of Israel, and knowest not these things?" i.e. "Art thou one who is set to teach others, the things written in the law and the prophets, and knowest not a doctrine so plainly taught in your Scriptures, that such a change as I speak of, is necessary to a partaking of the blessings of the kingdom of the Messiah?" But what can Christ have respect to in this, unless such prophecies as that in Ezek. 36:25,26,27? Where God by the prophet speaking of the days of the Messiah's kingdom, says, "Then will I sprinkle clean water upon you, and ye shall be clean. . . . A *new heart* also will I give you, and a *new spirit* will I put within you . . . and I will put my spirit within you." [5] Here God speaks of having a new heart and spirit, by being washed with water, and receiving the spirit of God, as the qualification of God's people, that shall enjoy the privileges of the kingdom of the Messiah. How much is this like the doctrine of Christ to Nicodemus, of being born again of water and of the spirit? We have another like prophecy in Ezek. 11:19.

Add to these things, that regeneration or being born again, and the renewing (or making new) by the Holy Ghost, are spoken of as the same thing. (Titus 3:5), "By the washing of regeneration and renewing of the Holy Ghost."

V. 'Tis abundantly manifest, that being born again, a spiritually rising from the dead, to newness of life, receiving a new heart, and being renewed in the spirit of the mind, these are the same thing with that which is called putting off the *old man,* and putting on the *new man.*

The expressions are equivalent; and the representations are

5. [Incomplete sentence retained.]

plainly of the same thing. When Christ speaks of being born again, two births are supposed; a first and a second; an *old* birth and a *new* one: and the thing born is called man, so what is born in the first birth, is the old man: and what is brought forth in the second birth, is the new man. That which is born in the first birth (says Christ) is flesh: it is the carnal man, wherein we have borne the image of the earthly Adam, whom the Apostle calls the first man. That which is born in the new birth, is spirit, or the spiritual and heavenly man: wherein we proceed from Christ the second man, the new man, who is made a quickening spirit, and is the Lord from heaven, and the head of the new creation. In the new birth, men are represented as becoming new-born babes (as was observed before) which is the same thing as becoming new men.

And how apparently is what the Scripture says of the spiritual resurrection of the Christian convert, equivalent and of the very same import with putting off the old man, and putting on the new man? So in the 6th of Romans, the convert is spoken of as dying and being buried with Christ: which is explained in the 6th verse by this, that "the old man is crucified, that the body of sin might be destroyed." And in the 14th verse converts in this change are spoken of as rising to newness of life. Are not these things plain enough? The Apostle does in effect tell us, that when he speaks of that spiritual death and resurrection which is in conversion, he means the same thing as crucifying and *burying the old man,* and rising a *new man.*

And 'tis most apparent, that spiritual circumcision, and spiritual baptism, and the spiritual resurrection, are all the same with putting off the old man, and putting on the new man. This appears by Col. 2:11, 12. "In whom also ye are circumcised with the circumcision made without hands, in putting off the body of the sins of the flesh, by the circumcision of Christ, buried with him by baptism; wherein also ye are risen with him." Here it is manifest, that the spiritual circumcision, baptism, and resurrection, all signify that change, wherein men put off the body of the sins of the flesh: but that is the same thing, in this Apostle's language, as "putting off the old man"; as appears by Rom. 6:6. Our old man is crucified, that the body of sin may be destroyed. And that putting off the old man is the same with putting off the body of sins, appears further by Eph. 4:22,23,24, and Col. 3:8,9,10.

As Dr. Taylor confesses, that a being born again is "that wherein are obtained the habits of virtue, religion and true holiness"; so how evidently is the same thing predicated of that change, which is called "Putting off the old man, and putting on the new man"? (Eph. 4:22,23,24), "That ye put off the old man, which is corrupt . . . and put on the new man, which, after God,[6] is created in righteousness and true holiness."

And 'tis most plain, that this putting off the old man, etc. is the very same thing with making the *heart and spirit new*. 'Tis apparent in itself: the spirit is called the "man" in the language of the Apostle; 'tis called the "inward man," and the "hidden man" (Rom. 7:22; II Cor. 4:16; I Pet. 3:4). And therefore putting off the old man, is the same thing with the removal of the old heart, and the putting on the new man is the receiving a new heart and a new spirit. Yea, putting on the new man is expressly spoken of as the same thing with receiving a new spirit, or being renewed in spirit. (Eph. 4:22,23,24), "That ye put off the old man . . . and be renewed in the spirit of your mind, and that ye put on the new man."

From these things it appears, how unreasonable, and contrary to the utmost degree of scriptural evidence, is Dr. Taylor's way of explaining the old man, and the new man,[7] though thereby were meant nothing personal; but that by the old man were meant the heathen state, and by the new man the Christian dispensation, or state of professing Christians, or the whole collective body of professors of Christianity, made up of Jews and Gentiles: when all the color he has for it, is, that the Apostle once calls the Christian church a new man (Eph. 2:15). 'Tis very true, in the Scripture, often both in the Old Testament and New, collective bodies, nations, people, cities, are figuratively represented by persons: particularly the church of Christ is represented as one holy person, and has the same appellatives as a particular saint or believer; and so is called a "child" and a "son of God" (Ex. 4:22; Gal. 4:1,2), and a "servant of God" (Is. 41:8,9 and 44:1), the "daughter of God" and "spouse of Christ" (Ps. 45:10,13,14; Rev. 19:7). Nevertheless, would it be reasonable, to argue from hence that such appellations, as a servant of God, a child of God, etc. are always or commonly to be taken as signifying only the church of God in general, or great collective bodies; and not to be understood in a personal sense? But certainly, this would not be more unreasonable, than to urge, that by the old and the new man, as the phrases are mostly used in Scripture, is to be

6. [I.e. "according to God."]

7. Pp. 425–429.

understood nothing but the great collective bodies of pagans and of Christians, or the heathen and the Christian world, as to their outward profession and the dispensation they are under. It might have been proper, in this case, to have considered the unreasonableness of that practice which our author charges on others, and finds so much fault with in them,[8] "That they content themselves with a few scraps of Scripture, which though wrong understood they make the test of truth, and the ground of their principles, in contradiction to the whole tenour of revelation."

VI. I observe once more, 'tis very apparent, that a being born again, and spiritually raised from death to a state of new existence and life, having a new heart created in us, being renewed in the spirit of our mind, and being the subjects of that change by which we put off the old man, and put on the new man, is the same thing with that which in Scripture is called a being *created anew,* or made new creatures.

Here, to pass over many other evidences of this, which might be mentioned, I would only observe, that the representations are exactly equivalent. These several phrases naturally and most plainly signify the same effect. In the first birth or generation, we are created, or brought into existence; 'tis then the whole man first receives being: the soul is then formed, and then our bodies are fearfully and wonderfully made, being curiously wrought by our Creator; so that a new-born child is a new creature. So, when a man is born again, he is created again; in that new birth, there is a new creation; and therein he becomes as a new-born babe, or a *new creature.* So, in a resurrection, there is a new creation. When a man is dead, that which was created or made in the first birth or creation, is destroyed: when that which was dead is raised to life, the mighty power of the Creator or Author of life, is exerted the second time, and the subject restored to new existence, and new life, as by a new creation. So, giving a new heart is called "creating a clean heart" (Ps. 51:10). Where the word translated "create" is the same that is used in the first verse in Genesis. And when we read in Scripture of the new creature, the creature that is called new is man; not angel, or beast, or any other sort of creature; and therefore the phrase, "new man," is evidently equipollent with "new creature"; and a putting off the old man, and putting on the new man, is spoken of expressly as brought to pass by a work of creation. (Col. 3:9,10), "Ye

8. P. 224.

have put off the old man . . . and have put on the new man, which is renewed in knowledge, after the image of him that created him." (So Eph. 4:22,23,24), "That ye put off the old man, which is corrupt etc. and be renewed in the spirit of your mind, and that ye put on the new man, which after God is created in righteousness and true holiness." These things absolutely fix the meaning of that in II Cor. 5:17, "If any man be in Christ, he is a new creature: old things are passed away; behold, all things are become new."

On the whole, the following reflections may be made:

1. That it is a truth of the utmost certainty, with respect to *every* man, born of the race of Adam, by ordinary generation, that *unless he be born again, he cannot see the kingdom of God.* This is true, not only of the heathen, but of them that are born of the professing people of God, as Nicodemus, and the Jews, and every man born of the flesh. This is most manifest by Christ's discourse, in John 3:3–11. So 'tis plain by II Cor. 5:17, "that every man who is in Christ, is a new creature."

2. It appears from this, together with what has been proved above, that it is most certain with respect to every one of the human race, that he can never have any interest in Christ, or see the kingdom of God, unless he be the subject of that change in the temper and disposition of his heart, which is made in repentance, and conversion, circumcision of his heart, spiritual baptism, dying to sin and rising to a new and holy life; and unless he has the old heart taken away, and a new heart and spirit given, and puts off the old man, and puts on the new man, and old things are passed away and all things made new.

3. From what is plainly implied in these things, and from what the Scripture most clearly teaches of the nature of 'em, 'tis certain, that *every* man is *born* into the world in a state of *moral pollution.* For *spiritual baptism* is a cleansing from moral filthiness. (Ezek. 36:25 compared with Acts 2:16 and John 3:25.) So the washing of regeneration or the new birth, is a change from a state of wickedness (Titus 3:3,4,5). Men are spoken of as purified in their regeneration (I Pet. 1:22,23. See also I John 2:29 and 3:1,5.) And it appears, that every man in his first or natural state is a sinner; for otherwise they would then need no repentance, no conversion, no turning from sin, to God. And it appears, that every man in his original state has a heart of stone; for thus the Scripture calls that old heart, which is taken away, when a new heart and new spirit is given (Ezek. 11:19

and 36:26). And it appears, that man's nature, as in his native state, is corrupt according to the deceitful lusts, and of its own motion exerts itself in nothing but wicked deeds. For thus the Scripture characterizes the old man, which is put off, when men are renewed in the spirit of their minds, and put on the new man (Eph. 4:22,23,24; Col. 3:8,9,10). In a word, it appears, that man's nature, as in his native state, is a body of sin, which must be destroyed, must die, be buried, and never rise more. For thus the old man is represented, which is crucified, when men are the subjects of a spiritual resurrection (Rom. 6:4,5,6). Such a nature, such a body of sin as this, is put off in the spiritual renovation, wherein we put on the new man, and are the subjects of the spiritual circumcision (Eph. 4:21,22,23).

It must now be left with the reader to judge for himself, whether what the Scripture teaches of the application of Christ's redemption, and the change of state and nature necessary to true and final happiness, don't afford clear and abundant evidence to the truth of the doctrine of original sin.

PART FOUR.

Containing Answers to Objections

CHAPTER I

CONCERNING THAT OBJECTION, THAT TO SUPPOSE MEN'S BEING BORN IN SIN, WITHOUT THEIR CHOICE, OR ANY PREVIOUS ACT OF THEIR OWN, IS TO SUPPOSE WHAT IS INCONSISTENT WITH THE NATURE OF SIN

SOME of the objections, made against the doctrine of original sin, which have reference to particular arguments used in defense of it, have been already considered in the handling of those arguments. What I shall therefore now consider, are such objections as I have not yet had occasion to take any special notice of.

There is no argument Dr. Taylor insists more upon, than that which is taken from the Arminian and Pelagian notion of freedom of will, consisting in the will's self-determination, as necessary to the being of moral good or evil. He often urges, that if we come into the world infected with sinful and depraved dispositions, then sin must be *natural* to us; and if natural, then *necessary;* and if necessary, then *no* sin, nor anything we are blameable for, or that can in any respect be our fault, being what we can't help: and he urges, that sin must proceed from our own choice, etc.[1]

Here I would observe in general, that the forementioned notion of freedom of will, as essential to moral agency, and necessary to the very existence of virtue and sin, seems to be a grand favorite point with Pelagians and Arminians, and all divines of such characters, in their controversies with the orthodox. There is no one thing more fundamental in their schemes of religion: on the determination of this one leading point depends the issue of almost all controversies we have with such divines. Nevertheless, it seems a needless task for me particularly to consider that matter in this place; having already largely discussed it, with all the main grounds of this notion, and the arguments used to defend it, in a late book on this subject, to

1. Pp. 125, 128, 129, 130, 186, 187, 188, 190, 200, 245, 246, 253, 258, 339, 340, 437 and other places.

which I ask leave to refer the reader.[2] 'Tis very necessary, that the modern prevailing doctrine concerning this point, should be well understood, and therefore thoroughly considered and examined: for without it there is no hope of putting an end to the controversy about original sin, and innumerable other controversies that subsist, about many of the main points of religion. I stand ready to confess to the forementioned modern divines, if they can maintain their peculiar notion of *freedom,* consisting in the *self-determining power of the will,* as necessary to *moral agency,* and can thoroughly establish it in opposition to the arguments lying against it, then they have an impregnable castle, to which they may repair, and remain invincible, in all the controversies they have with the reformed divines, concerning *original sin,* the *sovereignty* of grace, *election, redemption, conversion,* the *efficacious operation* of the Holy Spirit, the nature of saving *faith, perseverance* of the saints, and other principles of the like kind. However, at the same time I think, this same thing will be as strong a fortress for the Deists, in common with them; as the great doctrines, subverted by their notion of freedom, are so plainly and abundantly taught in the Scripture. But I am under no apprehensions of any danger, the cause of Christianity or the religion of the reformed is in, from any possibility of that notion's being ever established, or of its being ever evinced, that there is not proper, perfect, and manifold demonstration lying against it. But as I said, it would be needless for me to enter into a particular disquisition of this point here; from which I shall easily be excused by any reader who is willing to give himself the trouble of consulting what I have already written: and as to others, probably they will scarce be at the pains of reading the present discourse; or at least would not, if it should be enlarged by a full consideration of that controversy.

I shall at this time therefore only take notice of some gross *inconsistencies,* that Dr. Taylor has been guilty of, in his handling this objection against the doctrine of original sin.

In places which have been cited, he says, that sin must proceed from our own *choice:* and that if it does not, it being necessary to us, it cannot be sin, it can't be our fault, or what we are to blame for: and therefore all our sin must be chargeable on our choice, which is the cause of sin: for he says, "The cause of every effect is alone chargeable with the effect it produceth, and which proceedeth

2. [His *Freedom of the Will,* 1754.]

from it." [3] Now here are implied several gross contradictions. He greatly insists, that nothing can be sinful, or have the nature of sin, but what proceeds from our choice. Nevertheless, he says, not the *effect,* but the *cause* alone is chargeable with *blame.* Therefore the *choice,* which is the *cause* this *alone* is *blameable,* or has the nature of sin; and not the *effect* of that choice. Thus nothing can be sinful, but the effect of choice: and yet the effect of choice never can be sinful, but only the cause, which alone is chargeable with all the blame.

Again, the choice, which chooses and produces sin, or from which sin proceeds is itself sinful. Not only is this implied in his saying, "The cause alone is chargeable with all the blame"; but he expressly speaks of the choice as *faulty;* [4] and calls that choice *wicked,* from which depravity and *corruption proceeds.*[5] Now, if the choice itself be sin, and there be no sin but what proceeds from a sinful choice, then the sinful choice must proceed from another *antecedent* choice; it must be chosen by a foregoing act of will, determining itself to that sinful choice, that so it may have that which he speaks of as absolutely essential to the nature of sin, namely, *that it proceed from our choice,* and don't happen to us necessarily. But if the sinful choice itself proceeds from a foregoing choice, then also that foregoing choice must be sinful; it being the cause of sin, and so alone chargeable with the blame. Yet if that foregoing choice be sinful, then, neither must that happen to us necessarily, but must likewise proceed from choice, another act of choice preceding that: for we must remember, that "nothing is sinful, but what proceeds from our *choice.*" And then, for the same reason, even this prior choice, last mentioned, must also be sinful, being chargeable with all the blame of that consequent evil choice, which was its effect. And so we must go back till we come to the very *first* volition, the prime or original act of choice, in the whole chain. And this, to be sure, must be a sinful choice, because this is the origin or primitive cause of all the train of evils which follow: and according to our author, must therefore be "alone chargeable with all the blame." And yet so it is, according to him, this "cannot be sinful," because it don't "proceed from our own choice," or any foregoing act of our will; it being by

3. P. 128.
4. P. 190.
5. P. 200. See also p. 210.

the supposition, the very *first* act of will in the case. And therefore it must be *necessary,* as to us, having no choice of ours to be the cause of it.

In page 232, he says, "Adam's sin was from his own disobedient will; and so must every man's sin, and all the sin in the world, as well as his." By this, it seems, he must have a "disobedient will" *before* he sins; for the cause must be before the effect: and yet that disobedient will itself is sinful; otherwise it could not be called disobedient. But the question is, how do men come by the disobedient will, this cause of all the sin in the world? It must not come *necessarily,* without men's choice: for if so, 'tis *not* sin, nor is there any *disobedience* in it. Therefore that disobedient will must also come from a disobedient will; and so on, ad infinitum. Otherwise, it must be supposed, that there is some sin in the world, which don't come from a disobedient will; contrary to our author's dogmatical assertions.

In page 442, he says, "Adam could not sin without a sinful inclination." Here he calls that inclination itself sinful, which is the principle from whence sinful acts proceed; as elsewhere he speaks of the disobedient will, from whence all sin comes: and he allows,[6] that "the law reaches to all the latent principles of sin"; meaning plainly, that it forbids, and threatens punishment for those latent principles. Now these latent principles of sin, these sinful inclinations, without which, according to our author, there can be no sinful act, can't all proceed from a sinful choice; because that would imply great contradiction. For, by the supposition, they are the principles from whence a sinful choice comes, and whence all sinful acts of will proceed; and there can be no sinful act without 'em. So that the *first* latent principles, and inclinations, from whence all sinful acts proceed, are *sinful;* and yet they are *not* sinful, because they don't proceed from a *wicked choice,* without which, according to him, "Nothing can be sinful."

Dr. Taylor, speaking of that proposition of the Assembly of Divines, wherein they assert, that "man is by nature utterly corrupt, etc." [7] thinks himself well warranted by the supposed great evidence of these his contradictory notions, to say, "Therefore sin is not natural to us; and therefore I shall not scruple to say, this proposition in the Assembly of Divines is *false.*" But it may be worthy to be consid-

6. Contents of Rom. ch. 7 in *Notes* on that epistle. [P. 388.]

7. P. 125. [Read below "Assembly's Catechism" for "Assembly of Divines," so Taylor.]

ered whether it would not have greatly become him, before he had clothed himself with so much assurance, and proceeded, on the foundation of these his notions, so magisterially to charge the Assembly's proposition with falsehood, to have taken care, that his own propositions, which he has set in opposition to them should be a little more consistent; that he might not have contradicted himself, while contradicting them; lest some impartial judges, observing his inconsistency, should think they had warrant to declare with equal assurance, that "they shall not scruple to say, Dr. Taylor's doctrine is *false!*"

CHAPTER II

CONCERNING THAT OBJECTION AGAINST THE DOCTRINE OF NATIVE CORRUPTION, THAT TO SUPPOSE MEN RECEIVE THEIR FIRST EXISTENCE IN SIN, IS TO MAKE HIM WHO IS THE AUTHOR OF THEIR BEING, THE AUTHOR OF THEIR DEPRAVITY

ONE argument against men's being supposed to be born with sinful depravity, which Dr. Taylor greatly insists upon, is, "That this does in effect charge him who is the *Author* of our nature, who formed us in the womb, with being the *author* of a sinful corruption of nature; and that it is highly injurious to the *God* of our nature, whose hands have formed and fashioned us, to believe our nature to be originally corrupted, and that in the worst sense of corruption." [1]

With respect to this, I would observe in the first place, that this writer, in his handling this grand objection, supposes something to belong to the doctrine objected against, as maintained by the divines whom he is opposing, which does not belong to it, nor does follow from it: as particularly, he supposes the doctrine of original sin to imply, that nature must be corrupted by some *positive influence;* "something, by some means or other, *infused* into the human nature; some quality or other, not from the choice of our minds, but like a *taint, tincture,* or *infection,* altering the natural constitution, faculties and dispositions of our souls.[2] That sin and evil dispositions are implanted in the foetus in the womb." [3] Whereas truly our doctrine neither implies nor infers any such thing. In order to account for a sinful corruption of nature, yea, a total native depravity of the heart of man, there is not the least need of supposing any evil quality *infused, implanted,* or *wrought* into the nature of man, by any

1. Pp. 137, 187, 188, 189, 256, 258, 360, 419, 424, and other places. [JE's free paraphrase.]

2. P. 187. [JE supplies "by some means or other."]

3. Pp. 146, 424, 425, and the like in many other places. [JE's free paraphrase.]

positive cause, or influence whatsoever, either from God, or the creature; or of supposing, that man is conceived and born with a *fountain of evil* in his heart, such as is anything properly positive. I think, a little attention to the nature of things will be sufficient to satisfy any impartial considerate inquirer, that the absence of positive good principles, and so the withholding of a special divine influence to impart and maintain those good principles, leaving the common natural principles of self-love, natural appetite, etc. (which were in man in innocence) leaving these, I say, to themselves, without the government of superior divine principles, will certainly be followed with corruption, yea, the total corruption of the heart, without occasion for any positive influence at all: and that it was thus indeed that corruption of nature came on Adam, immediately on his fall, and comes on all his posterity, as sinning in him and falling with him.[4]

The case with man was plainly this: when God made man at first, he implanted in him two kinds of principles. There was an *inferior* kind, which may be called *natural,* being the principles of mere human nature; such as self-love, with those natural appetites and passions, which belong to the nature of man, in which his love to his own liberty, honor and pleasure, were exercised: these when alone, and left to themselves, are what the Scriptures sometimes call *flesh.* Besides these, there were *superior* principles, that were spiritual, holy and divine, summarily comprehended in divine love; wherein consisted the spiritual image of God, and man's righteousness and true holiness; which are called in Scripture the *divine nature.* These principles may, in some sense, be called *supernatural,*[5] being (however concreated or connate, yet) such as are above those principles that are essentially implied in, or necessarily resulting from, and in-

4. [See above, Intro., Sec. 3, The Cause and Transmission of Sin.]

5. To prevent all cavils, the reader is desired particularly to observe, in what sense I here use the words, "natural" and "supernatural": not as epithets of distinction between that which is concreated or connate, and that which is extraordinarily introduced afterwards, besides the first state of things, or the order established originally, beginning when man's nature began; but as distinguishing between what belongs *to,* or flows *from,* that nature which man has, merely *as* man, and those things which are *above* this, by which one is denominated, not only a *man,* but a truly *virtuous, holy,* and *spiritual* man; which, though they began, in Adam, as soon as humanity began, and are necessary to the perfection and well being of the human nature, yet are not essential to the constitution of it, or necessary to its being: inasmuch as one may

separably connected with, *mere human nature;* and being such as immediately depend on man's union and communion with God, or divine communications and influences of God's spirit: which though withdrawn, and man's nature forsaken of these principles, human nature would be human nature still; man's nature as such, being entire without those divine principles, which the Scripture sometimes calls *spirit,* in contradistinction to *flesh.* These superior principles were given to possess the throne, and maintain an absolute dominion in the heart: the other, to be wholly subordinate and subservient. And while things continued thus, all things were in excellent order, peace and beautiful harmony, and in their proper and perfect state. These divine principles thus reigning, were the dignity, life, happiness, and glory of man's nature. When man sinned, and broke God's Covenant, and fell under his curse, these superior principles left his heart: for indeed God then left him; that communion with God, on which these principles depended, entirely ceased; the Holy Spirit, that divine inhabitant, forsook the house. Because it would have been utterly improper in itself, and inconsistent with the covenant and constitution God had established, that God should still maintain communion with man, and continue, by his friendly, gracious vital influences, to dwell with him and in him, after he was become a rebel, and had incurred God's wrath and curse. Therefore immediately the superior divine principles wholly ceased; so light ceases in a room, when the candle is withdrawn: and thus man was left in a state of darkness, woeful corruption and ruin; nothing but flesh, without spirit. The inferior principles of self-love and natural appetite, which were given only to serve, being alone, and left to themselves, of course became reigning principles; having no superior principles to regulate or control them, they became absolute masters of the heart. The immediate consequence of which was a *fatal catastrophe,* a turning of all things upside down, and the succession of a state of the most odious and dreadful confusion.[6] Man did immediately set up himself, and the objects of his private affections and appetites, as supreme; and so they took the place of God. These inferior principles are like fire in an house; which, we say, is a good serv-

---

have everything needful to his being *man* exclusively of them. If in thus using the words, "natural" and "supernatural," I use them in an uncommon sense, 'tis not from any affectation of singularity, but for want of other terms, more aptly to express my meaning. [This footnote is omitted from the MS.]

6. [See above, Intro., Sec. 3, The Cause and Transmission of Sin.]

ant, but a bad master; very useful while kept in its place, but if left to take possession of the whole house, soon brings all to destruction. Man's love to his own honor, separate interest, and private pleasure, which before was wholly subordinate unto love to God and regard to his authority and glory, now dispose and impel man to pursue those objects, without regard to God's honor, or law; because there is no true regard to these divine things left in him. In consequence of which, he seeks those objects as much when against God's honor and law, as when agreeable to 'em. And God still continuing strictly to require supreme regard to himself, and forbidding all gratifications of these inferior passions, but only in perfect subordination to the ends, and agreeableness to the rules and limits, which his holiness, honor and law prescribe, hence immediately arises enmity in the heart, now wholly under the power of self-love; and nothing but war ensues, in a constant course, against God. As, when a subject has once renounced his lawful sovereign, and set up a pretender in his stead, a state of enmity and war against his rightful king necessarily ensues. It were easy to shew, how every lust and depraved disposition of man's heart would naturally arise from this *privative* original, if here were room for it. Thus 'tis easy to give an account, how total corruption of heart should follow on man's eating the forbidden fruit, though that was but one act of sin, *without God's putting* any evil into his heart, or *implanting* any bad principle, or *infusing* any corrupt taint, and so becoming the *author* of depravity. Only God's *withdrawing,* as it was highly proper and necessary that he should, from rebel-man, being as it were driven away by his abominable wickedness, and men's *natural* principles being *left to themselves,* this is sufficient to account for his becoming entirely corrupt, and bent on sinning against God.

And as Adam's nature became corrupt, without God's implanting or infusing any evil thing into his nature; so does the nature of his *posterity.* God dealing with Adam as the head of his posterity (as has been shewn) and treating them as one, he deals with his posterity as having *all sinned in him.* And therefore, as God withdrew spiritual communion and his vital gracious influence from the common head, so he withholds the same from all the members, as they come into existence; whereby they come into the world mere flesh, and entirely under the government of natural and inferior principles; and so become wholly corrupt, as Adam did.

Now, for God so far to have the disposal of this affair, as to withhold those influences, without which nature will be corrupt, is not to be the *author of sin.*[7] But, concerning this, I must refer the reader to what I have said of it in my discourse on the *Freedom of the Will.*[8] Though, besides what I have there said, I may here observe; that if for God so far to order and dispose the being of sin, as to *permit* it, by withholding the gracious influences necessary to prevent it, is for him to be the author of sin, then some things which Dr. Taylor himself lays down, will equally be attended with this very consequence. For, from time to time, he speaks of God's giving men up to the vilest lusts and affections, by permitting, or leaving them.[9] Now, if the *continuance* of *sin,* and its increase and prevalence, may be in consequence of God's disposal, by withholding his grace, that is needful, under such circumstances, to prevent it, without God's being the author of that continuance and prevalence of sin; then, by parity of reason, may the *being of sin,* in the race of Adam, be in consequence of God's disposal, by withholding his grace, needful to prevent it, without his being the author of that being of sin.

If here it should be said, that God is not the author of sin, in giving men up to sin, who have already made themselves sinful, because when men have once made themselves sinful, their continuing so, and sin's prevailing in them, and becoming more and more habitual, will follow in a *course of nature*—I answer, let that be remembered, which this writer so greatly urges, in opposition to them that suppose original corruption comes in a course of nature, viz. that the course of nature is nothing without God. He utterly rejects the notion of the "course of nature's being a proper active cause, which will work and go on by itself, without God, if he lets or permits it." But affirms, "That the course of nature, separate from the agency of God, is no cause, or nothing; [. . .] and that the course of nature should continue itself, or go on to operate by itself, any more than at first produce itself, is absolutely impossible." [1] These strong expressions are his. Therefore, to explain the continuance of the habits of sin in the same person, when once introduced, yea, to explain the very being of any such habits, in consequence of repeated acts, our author must have recourse to those same principles,

7. [See above, Intro., Sec. 3, God the Author of Sin.]

8. Part IV. Sec. 9, p. 252 etc. [Yale ed., *1,* 397 ff.]

9. *Key* no. 356 and *Par. on Rom.* 1:24, 26.

1. P. 410. See also with what vehemence this is urged in p. 413. [See above, Intro., Sec. 3, The Cause and Transmission of Sin.]

which he rejects as absurd to the utmost degree, when alleged to explain the corruption of nature in the posterity of Adam. For, that habits, either good or bad, should continue after being once established, or that habits should be settled and have existence, in consequence of repeated acts, can be owing only to a *course of nature,* and those *laws of nature* which God has established.[2]

That the posterity of Adam should be born without holiness, and so with a depraved nature, comes to pass as much by the *established course of nature,* as the continuance of a corrupt disposition in a particular person, after he once has it; or as much as Adam's continuing unholy and corrupt, after he had once lost his holiness. For Adam's posterity are from him, and as it were in him, and belonging to him, according to an established course of nature, as much as the branches of a tree are, according to a course of nature, from the tree, in the tree, and belonging to the tree; or (to make use of the comparison which Dr. Taylor himself chooses and makes use of from time to time, as proper to illustrate the matter) [3] "just as the acorn is derived from the oak." And I think, the acorn is as much derived from the oak, according to the course of nature, as the buds and branches. 'Tis true, that God, by his own almighty power, creates the soul of the infant; and 'tis also true, as Dr. Taylor often insists, that God, by his immediate power, forms and fashions the body of the infant in the womb; yet he does both according to that course of nature, which he has been pleased to establish. The course of nature is demonstrated, by late improvements in philosophy, to be indeed what our author himself says it is, viz. nothing but the established order of the agency and operation of the Author of nature. And though there be the immediate agency of God in bringing the soul into existence in generation, yet 'tis done according to the method and order established by the Author of nature, as much as his producing the bud, or the acorn of the oak; and as much as his continuing a particular person in being, after he once has existence. God's immediate agency in bringing the soul of a child into being, is as much according to an established order, as his immediate agency in

2. [In the MS JE had apparently been in the process of developing an argument to the effect that the course of nature, if understood as independent of God, would be "superior to the power of God." However, the notation is too incoherent to be worthy of citation. See p. 198 of MS. A Latin quotation, gleaned from Stapfer, was inserted between pp. 198 and 199 of the MS but was not used in the first edition.]

3. Pp. 146, 187.

any of the works of nature whatsoever. 'Tis agreeable to the established order of nature, that the good qualities wanting in the tree, should also be wanting in the branches and fruit. 'Tis agreeable to the order of nature, that when a particular person is without good moral qualities in his heart, he should continue without 'em, till some new cause or efficiency produces them: and 'tis as much agreeable to an established course and order of nature, that since Adam, the head of the race of mankind, the root of that great tree with many branches springing from it, was deprived of original righteousness, the branches should come forth without it. Or, if any dislike the word "nature" as used in this last case, and instead of it choose to call it a "constitution," or established order of successive events, the alteration of the name won't in the least alter the state of the present argument. Where the name "nature" is allowed without dispute, no more is meant than an established method and order of events, settled and limited by divine wisdom.

If any should object to this, that if the want of original righteousness be thus according to an established course of nature, then why are not principles of holiness, when restored by divine grace, also communicated to posterity? I answer, the divine laws and establishments of the Author of nature are precisely settled by him, as he pleaseth, and limited by his wisdom. Grace is introduced among the race of mankind by a *new establishment;* not on the foot of the original establishment of God, as the Head of the natural world, and Author of the first creation; but by a constitution of a vastly higher kind; wherein Christ is made the root of the tree, whose branches are his spiritual seed and he is the head of the new creation; of which I need not stand now to speak particularly.

But here I desire it may be noted, that I don't suppose, the natural depravity of the posterity of Adam is owing to the course of nature only; 'tis also owing to the just judgment of God. But yet I think, it is as truly, and in the same manner, owing to the course of nature, that Adam's posterity come into the world without original righteousness, as that Adam continued without it, after he had once lost it. That Adam continued destitute of holiness, when he had lost it, and would always have so continued, had it not been restored by a Redeemer, was not only a natural consequence, according to the course of things established by God, as the Author of nature; but it was also a penal consequence, or a punishment of his sin. God, in righteous judgment, continued to absent himself from Adam, after he became a rebel; and withheld from him now those influences of the Holy Spirit, which he before had. And just thus, I suppose it to be with every natural branch of mankind: all are looked upon as sinning in and with their common root; and God righteously withholds special influences and spiritual communications from all, for this sin. But of the manner and order of these things, more may be said in the next chapter.

On the whole, this grand objection against the doctrine of men's being born corrupt, that it makes him who gave us our being, to be the cause of the being of corruption, can have no more force in it, than a like argument has to prove, that if men by a course of nature continue wicked, or remain without goodness, after they have by vicious acts contracted vicious habits, and so made themselves wicked, it makes him who is the *cause of their continuance in being,* and the *cause of the continuance of the course of nature,* to be the *cause of their continued wickedness.* Dr. Taylor says,[4] "God would not make anything that is hateful to him; because, by the very terms, he would hate to make such a thing." But if this be good arguing in the case to which it is applied, may I not as well say, "God would not continue a thing in being that is hateful to him; because, by the very terms, he would hate to continue such a thing in being"? I think, the very terms do as much (and no more) infer one of these propositions, as the other. In like manner, the rest that he says on that head, may be shewn to be unreasonable, by only substituting the word "continue" in the place of "make and propagate." I may fairly imitate his way of reasoning, thus: "To say, God *continues* us according to his own original decree, or law of *continuation,* which obliges him to *continue* us in a manner he abhors, is really to make bad worse: for it is supposing him to be defective in wisdom, or by his own decree or law to lay such a constraint upon his own actions, that he cannot do what he would; but is continually doing what he would not, what he hates to do, and what he condemns in us; viz. *continuing* us sinful, when he condemns us for *continuing* ourselves sinful." If the reasoning be weak in the one case, it's no less so in the other.

If any shall still insist, that there is a difference, between God's so disposing things as that depravity of heart shall be continued, according to the settled course of nature, in the same person, who has by his own fault intoduced it, and his so disposing as that men, ac-

4. P. 412.

cording to a course of nature, should be born with depravity, in consequence of Adam's introducing sin, by his act, which we had no concern in, and cannot be justly charged with: on this I would observe, that it is quite going off the objection, which we have been upon, from God's agency, and flying to another. It is then no longer insisted on, that simply for him, from whose agency the course of nature and our existence derive, so to dispose things, as that we should have existence in a corrupt state, is for him to be the author of sin: but the plea now advanced is, that it is not proper and just for such an agent so to dispose in this case, and only in consequence of Adam's sin; it not being just to charge Adam's sin to his posterity. And this matter shall be particularly considered, in answer to the next objection; to which I now proceed.

CHAPTER III

THAT GREAT OBJECTION AGAINST THE IMPUTATION OF ADAM'S SIN TO HIS POSTERITY CONSIDERED, THAT SUCH IMPUTATION IS UNJUST AND UNREASONABLE, INASMUCH AS ADAM AND HIS POSTERITY ARE NOT ONE AND THE SAME. WITH A BRIEF REFLECTION SUBJOINED, ON WHAT SOME HAVE SUPPOSED, OF GOD'S IMPUTING THE GUILT OF ADAM'S SIN TO HIS POSTERITY, BUT IN AN INFINITELY LESS DEGREE, THAN TO ADAM HIMSELF

THAT we may proceed with the greater clearness in considering the main objections against supposing the guilt of Adam's sin to be imputed to his posterity, I would premise some observations with a view to the right stating of the doctrine of the imputation of Adam's first sin; and then shew the *reasonableness* of this doctrine, in opposition to the great clamor raised against it on this head.

I think, it would go far towards directing us to the more clear and distinct conceiving and right stating of this affair, if we steadily bear this in mind; that God, in each step of his proceeding with Adam, in relation to the covenant or constitution established with him, looked on his posterity as being one with him. (The propriety of his looking upon them so, I shall speak to afterwards.) And though he dealt more immediately with Adam, yet it was as the head of the whole body, and the root of the whole tree; and in his proceedings with him, he dealt with all the branches, as if they had been then existing in their root.

From which it will follow, that both guilt, or exposedness to punishment, and also depravity of heart, came upon Adam's posterity just as they came upon him, as much as if he and they had all coexisted, like a tree with many branches; allowing only for the difference necessarily resulting from the place Adam stood in, as head or root of the whole, and being first and most immediately dealt with, and most immediately acting and suffering. Otherwise, it is as if, in every step of proceeding, every alteration in the root had been attended, at the same instant, with the same steps and alterations throughout the whole tree, in each individual branch. I think, this will naturally follow on the supposition of there being a constituted *oneness* or *identity* of Adam and his posterity in this affair.

Therefore I am humbly of opinion, that if any have supposed the children of Adam to come into the world with a *double guilt,* one the guilt of Adam's sin, another the guilt arising from their having a corrupt heart, they have not so well conceived of the matter. The guilt a man has upon his soul at his first existence, is one and simple: viz. the guilt of the original apostacy, the guilt of the sin by which the species first rebelled against God. This, and the guilt arising from the first corruption or depraved disposition of the heart, are not to be looked upon as two things, distinctly imputed and charged upon men in the sight of God. Indeed the guilt, that arises from the corruption of the heart, as it remains a confirmed principle, and appears in its consequent operations, is a distinct and additional guilt: but the guilt arising from the first existing of a depraved disposition in Adam's posterity, I apprehend, is not distinct from their guilt of Adam's first sin. For so it was not in Adam himself. The first evil disposition or inclination of the heart of Adam to sin, was not properly distinct from his first act of sin, but was included in it. The external act he committed was no otherwise his, than as his heart was in it, or as that action proceeded from the wicked inclination of his heart. Nor was the guilt he had, double, as for two distinct sins: one, the wickedness of his heart and will in that affair; another, the wickedness of the external act, caused by his heart. His guilt was all truly from the act of his inward man; exclusive of which the motions of his body were no more than the motions of any lifeless instrument. His sin consisted in wickedness of heart, fully sufficient *for,* and entirely amounting *to,* all that appeared in the act he committed.

The depraved disposition of Adam's heart is to be considered two ways. (1) As the first rising of an evil inclination in his heart, exerted in his first act of sin, and the ground of the complete transgression. (2) An evil disposition of heart continuing afterwards, as a confirmed principle, that came by God's forsaking him; which was a *punishment* of his first transgression. This confirmed corruption, by its remaining and continued operation, brought additional guilt on his soul.

And in like manner, depravity of heart is to be considered two ways in Adam's posterity. The first existing of a corrupt disposition in their hearts is not to be looked upon as sin belonging to them, distinct from their participation of Adam's first sin: it is as it were the *extended pollution* of that sin, through the whole tree, by virtue of the constituted union of the branches with the root; or the inherence of the sin of that head of the species in the members, in the consent and concurrence of the hearts of the members with the head in that first act. (Which may be, without God's being the author of sin; about which I have spoken in a former chapter.) But the depravity of nature, remaining an *established principle* in the heart of a child of Adam, and as exhibited in after-operations, is a consequence and punishment of the first apostacy thus participated, and brings new guilt. The first being of an evil disposition in the heart of a child of Adam, whereby he is disposed to *approve* of the sin of his first father, as fully as he himself approved of it when he committed it, or so far as to imply a full and perfect consent of heart to it, I think, is not to be looked upon as a consequence of the imputation of that first sin, any more than the full consent of Adam's own heart in the act of sinning; which was not consequent on the imputation of his sin to himself, but rather *prior* to it in the order of nature. Indeed the derivation of the evil disposition to the hearts of Adam's posterity, or rather the *coexistence* of the evil disposition, implied in Adam's first rebellion, in the root and branches, is a consequence of the union, that the wise Author of the world has established between Adam and his posterity: but not properly a consequence of the imputation of his sin; nay, rather *antecedent* to it, as it was in Adam himself. The first depravity of heart, and the imputation of that sin, are both the consequences of that established union: but yet in such order, that the evil disposition is *first,* and the charge of guilt *consequent;* as it was in the case of Adam himself.[1]

1. My meaning, in the whole of what has been here said, may be illustrated thus: let us suppose, that Adam and all his posterity had *coexisted,* and that his posterity had been, through a law of nature established by the Creator, *united* to him, something as the branches of a tree are united to the root, or the members of the body to the head; so as to constitute as it were *one* complex person, or *one* moral whole: so that by the law of union there should have been a *communion* and *coexistence* in acts and affections; all jointly participating, and all concurring, as *one whole,* in the disposition and action of the head: as we see in the body natural, the whole body is affected as the head is affected; and the whole body concurs when the head acts. Now, in this case, the hearts

The first existence of an evil disposition of heart, amounting to a full consent to Adam's sin, no more infers God's being the author of

---

of all the branches of mankind, by the constitution of nature and the law of union, would have been affected just as the heart of Adam, their common root, was affected. When the heart of the root, by a full disposition committed the first sin, the hearts of all the branches would have concurred; and when the root, in consequence of this, became guilty, so would all the branches; and when the heart of the root, as a punishment of the sin committed, was forsaken of God, in like manner would it have fared with all the branches; and when the heart of the root, in consequence of this, was confirmed in permanent depravity, the case would have been the same with all the branches; and as new guilt on the soul of Adam would have been consequent on this, so also would it have been with his moral branches. And thus all things, with relation to evil disposition, guilt, pollution and depravity, would exist, in the same order and dependence, in each branch, as in the root. Now, difference of the *time* of existence don't at all hinder things succeeding in the same order, any more than difference of *place* in a coexistence of time.

Here may be worthy to be observed, as in several respects to the present purpose, some things that are said by Stapferus, an eminent divine of Zurich in Switzerland, in his *Theologia Polemica,* published about fourteen years ago; in English as follows. "Seeing all Adam's posterity are derived from their first parent, as their root, the whole of the human kind, with its root, may be considered as constituting but one whole, or one mass; so as not to be properly a thing distinct from its root; the posterity not differing from it, any otherwise than the branches from the tree. From which it easily appears, how that when the root sinned, all that which is derived from it, and with it constitutes but one whole, may be looked upon as also sinning; seeing it is not distinct from the root, but is one with it." Tome 1, Ch. 3, no. 856–7.

" 'Tis objected, against the imputation of Adam's sin, that we never committed the same sin with Adam, neither in number nor in kind. I answer, we should distinguish here between the *physical* act itself, which Adam committed, and the *morality* of the action, and *consent* to it. If we have respect only to the external act, to be sure it must be confessed, that Adam's posterity did not put forth their hands to the forbidden fruit: in which sense, that act of transgression, and that fall of Adam cannot be *physically* one with the sin of his posterity. But if we consider the *morality* of the action, and what *consent* there is to it, it is altogether to be maintained, that his posterity committed the *same* sin, both in number and in kind, inasmuch as they are to be looked upon as consenting to it. For where there is consent to a sin, there the same sin is committed. Seeing therefore that Adam with all his posterity constitute but *one moral person,* and are united in the same Covenant, and are transgressors of the same law, they are also to be looked upon as having, in a moral estimation, committed the same transgression of the law, both in number and in kind. Therefore this reasoning avails nothing against the righteous imputation of the sin of Adam to all mankind, or to the whole moral person that is consenting to it. And for the reason mentioned, we may rather argue thus; the sin of the

that evil disposition in the child, than in the father.[2] The first arising or existing of that evil disposition in the heart of Adam, was by God's *permission;* who could have prevented it, if he had pleased, by giving such influences of his spirit, as would have been absolutely effectual to hinder it; which, it is plain in fact, he did withhold: and

---

posterity, on account of their consent, and the moral view in which they are to be taken, is the same with the sin of Adam, not only in kind, but in number; therefore the sin of Adam is rightfully imputed to his posterity." Ibid. Tome IV, Ch. 16, no. 60, 61.

"The imputation of Adam's first sin consists in nothing else than this, that his posterity are viewed as in the same place with their father, and are like him. But seeing, agreeable to what we have already proved, God might, according to his own righteous judgment, which was founded on his most righteous law, give Adam a posterity that were *like himself;* and indeed it could not be otherwise, according to the very laws of nature: therefore he might also in righteous judgment impute Adam's sin to them: inasmuch as to give Adam a posterity like himself, and to impute his sin to them, is one and the same thing. And therefore if the former be not contrary to the divine perfections, so neither is the latter. Our adversaries contend with us chiefly on this account, that according to our doctrine of original sin, such an imputation of the first sin is maintained, whereby God, without any regard to universal native corruption, esteems all Adam's posterity as guilty, and holds them as liable to condemnation, purely on account of that sinful act of their first parent; so that they, without any respect had to their own sin, and so, as innocent in themselves, are destined to eternal punishment. . . . I have therefore ever been careful to shew, that they do *injuriously suppose* those things to be *separated,* in our doctrine, which are by no means to be separated. The whole of the controversy they have with us about this matter, evidently arises from this, that they suppose the *mediate* and the *immediate* imputation are distinguished one from the other, not only in the manner of conception, but in reality. And so indeed they consider imputation only as *immediate,* and abstractly from the *mediate;* when yet our divines suppose, that neither ought to be considered *separately* from the other. Therefore I chose not to use any such distinction, or to suppose any such thing, in what I've said on the subject; but only have endeavored to explain the thing itself, and to reconcile it with the divine attributes. And therefore I have everywhere conjoined both these conceptions concerning the imputation of the first sin, as inseparable; and judged, that one ought never to be considered without the other. . . . While I have been writing this note, I consulted all the systems of divinity, which I have by me, that I might see what was the true and genuine opinion of our chief divines in this affair; and I found that they were of the same mind with me; namely, that these two kinds of imputation are by no means to be separated, or to be considered abstractly one from the other, but that one does involve the other." He there particularly cites those two famous reformed divines, Vitringa and Lampius. Tome IV, Ch. 17, no. 78. [This footnote is omitted from the MS.]

2. [See above, Intro., Sec. 3, The Cause and Transmission of Sin.]

whatever mystery may be supposed in the affair, yet no Christian will presume to say, it was not in perfect consistence with God's holiness and righteousness, notwithstanding Adam had been guilty of no offense before. So root and branches being one, according to God's wise constitution, the case in fact is, that by virtue of this oneness, answerable changes of effects through all the branches coexist with the changes in the root: consequently an evil disposition exists in the hearts of Adam's posterity, equivalent to that which was exerted in his own heart, when he eat the forbidden fruit. Which God has no hand in, any otherwise, than in *not* exerting such an influence, as might be effectual to prevent it; as appears by what was observed in the former chapter.

But now the grand objection is against the *reasonableness,* of such a constitution, by which Adam and his posterity should be looked upon as one, and dealt with accordingly, in an affair of such infinite consequence; so that if Adam sinned, they must necessarily be made sinners by his disobedience, and come into existence with the same depravity of disposition, and be looked upon and treated as though they were partakers with Adam in his act of sin. I have not room here to rehearse all Dr. Taylor's vehement exclamations against the reasonableness and justice of this. The reader may at his leisure consult his book, and see them in places referred to in the margin.[3] Whatever black colors and frightful representations are employed on this occasion, all may be summed up in this, that Adam and his posterity are *not one,* but entirely *distinct agents.* But with respect to this mighty outcry made against the reasonableness of any such constitution, by which God is supposed to treat Adam and his posterity as one, I would make the following observations.

I. It signifies nothing, to exclaim against plain fact. Such is the fact, most evident and acknowledged fact, with respect to the state of all mankind, without exception of one individual among all the natural descendants of Adam, as makes it apparent, that God actually deals with Adam and his posterity as one, in the affair of his apostacy, and its infinitely terrible consequences. It has been demonstrated, and shewn to be in effect plainly acknowledged, that every individual of mankind comes into the world in such circumstances, as that there is no hope or possibility of any other than their violating God's holy law (if they ever live to act at all, as moral agents), and being thereby justly exposed to eternal ruin.[4] And it is thus by

3. Pp. 13, 150, 151, 156, 261, 384, 387.

4. Part I, ch. 1, the three first sections.

God's ordering and disposing of things. And God either thus deals with mankind, because he looks upon them as one with their first father, and so treats them as sinful and guilty by his apostacy; or (which won't mend the matter) he, without viewing them as at all concerned in that affair, but as in every respect perfectly innocent, does nevertheless subject them to this infinitely dreadful calamity. Adam by his sin was exposed to the calamities and sorrows of this life, to temporal death, and eternal ruin; as is confessed. And 'tis also in effect confessed, that all his posterity come into the world in such a state, as that the certain consequence is their being exposed, and justly so, to the sorrows of this life, to temporal death, and eternal ruin, unless saved by grace. So that we see, God in fact deals with them together, or as one. If God orders the consequences of Adam's sin, with regard to his posterity's welfare, even in those things which are most important, and which do in the highest degree concern their eternal interest, to be the same with the consequences to Adam himself, then he treats Adam and his posterity as in that affair one. Hence, however the matter be attended with difficulty, fact obliges us to get over the difficulty, either by finding out some solution, or by shutting our mouths, and acknowledging the weakness and scantiness of our understandings; as we must in innumerable other cases, where apparent and undeniable fact, in God's works of creation and providence, is attended with events and circumstances, the manner and reason of which are difficult to our understandings. But to proceed,

II. We will consider the difficulties themselves, insisted on in the objections of our opposers. They may be reduced to these two: first, that such a constitution is *injurious* to Adam's posterity. Secondly, that it is altogether *improper,* as it implies *falsehood;* viewing and treating those as one, which indeed are not one, but entirely distinct.

First difficulty, that the appointing Adam to stand in this great affair, as the moral head of his posterity, and so treating them as one with him, as standing or falling with him, is *injurious* to them, and tends to their hurt.[5] To which I answer, it is demonstrably otherwise; that such a constitution was so far from being injurious and hurtful to Adam's posterity, or tending to their calamity, any more than if every one had been appointed to stand for himself personally, that it was, in itself considered, very much of a contrary tendency, and was attended with a more eligible probability of an happy

5. [Incomplete sentence retained.]

issue, than the latter would have been: and so is a constitution truly expressing the goodness of its author. For here the following things are to be considered.

1. 'Tis reasonable to suppose, that Adam was *as likely,* on account of his capacity and natural talents, to *persevere* in obedience, as his posterity (taking one with another), if they had all been put on the trial singly for themselves. And supposing, that there was a constituted union or oneness of him and his posterity, and that he stood as a public person, or common head, all by this constitution would have been as sure to partake of the benefit of his obedience, as of the ill consequence of his disobedience, in case of his fall.

2. There was a *greater tendency* to a happy issue, in such an appointment, than if every one had been appointed to stand for himself; especially on two accounts. (1) That Adam had *stronger motives* to watchfulness, than his posterity would have had; in that not only his own eternal welfare lay at stake, but also that of all his posterity. (2) Adam was in a state of complete *manhood,* when his trial began. It was a constitution very agreeable to the goodness of God, considering the state of mankind, which was to be propagated in the way of generation, that their first father should be appointed to stand for all. For by reason of the manner of their coming into existence in a state of infancy, and their coming so gradually to mature state, and so remaining for a great while in a state of childhood and comparative imperfection, after they were become moral agents, they would be less fit to stand for themselves, than their first father to stand for them.

If any man, notwithstanding these things, shall say, that for his own part, if the affair had been proposed to him, he should have chosen to have his eternal interest trusted in *his own hands:* 'tis sufficient to answer, that no man's vain opinion of himself, as more fit to be trusted than others, alters the true nature and tendency of things, as they demonstrably are in themselves. Nor is it a just objection, that this constitution has in event proved for the hurt of mankind. For it don't follow, that no advantage was given for a happy event, in such an establishment, because it was not such as to make it utterly impossible there should be any other event.

3. The goodness of God in such a constitution with Adam appears in this: that if there had been no *sovereign gracious* establishment at all, but God had proceeded only on the foot of mere justice, and had gone no further than this required, he might have de-

manded of Adam and all his posterity, that they should perform *perfect perpetual* obedience, without ever failing in the least instance, on pain of eternal death; and might have made this demand without the promise of any positive reward for their obedience. For perfect obedience is a debt, that every one owes to his Creator; and therefore is what his Creator was not obliged to pay him for. None is obliged to pay his debtor, only for discharging his just debt. But such was evidently the constitution with Adam, that an eternal happy life was to be the consequence of his persevering fidelity, to all such as were included within that constitution (of which the Tree of Life was a sign), as well as eternal death to be the consequence of his disobedience. I come now to consider the

Second difficulty. It being thus manifest, that this constitution, by which Adam and his posterity are dealt with as one, is not unreasonable upon account of its being injurious and hurtful to the interest of mankind, the only thing remaining in the objection against such a constitution, is the *impropriety* of it, as implying *falsehood*, and contradiction to the true nature of things; as hereby they are viewed and treated as one, who are not one, but wholly distinct; and no arbitrary constitution can ever make that to be true, which in itself considered is not true.

The objection, however specious, is really founded on a false hypothesis, and wrong notion of what we call *sameness* or *oneness*, among created things; and the seeming force of the objection arises from ignorance or inconsideration of the degree, in which created identity or oneness with past existence, in general, depends on the sovereign constitution and law of the Supreme Author and Disposer of the universe.[6]

Some things, being most simply considered, are entirely distinct, and very diverse; which yet are so united by the established law of the Creator, in some respects and with regard to some purposes and effects, that by virtue of that establishment it is with them as if they were one. Thus a tree, grown great, and an hundred years old, is one plant with the little sprout, that first came out of the ground, from whence it grew, and has been continued in constant succession; though it's now so exceeding diverse, many thousand times bigger, and of a very different form, and perhaps not one atom the very same: yet God, according to an established law of nature, has in a constant succession communicated to it many of the same qualities,

6. [See above, Intro., Sec. 3, The Cause and Transmission of Sin.]

and most important properties, as if it were one. It has been his pleasure, to constitute an union in these respects, and for these purposes, naturally leading us to look upon all as one. So the body of man at forty years of age, is one with the infant body which first came into the world, from whence it grew; though now constituted of different substance, and the greater part of the substance probably changed scores (if not hundreds) of times; and though it be now in so many respects exceeding diverse, yet God, according to the course of nature, which he has been pleased to establish, has caused, that in a certain method it should communicate with that infantile body, in the same life, the same senses, the same features, and many the same qualities, and in union with the same soul; and so, with regard to these purposes, 'tis dealt with by him as one body. Again, the body and soul of a man are one, in a very different manner, and for different purposes. Considered in themselves, they are exceeding different beings, of a nature as diverse as can be conceived; and yet, by a very peculiar divine constitution or law of nature, which God has been pleased to establish, they are strongly united, and become one, in most important respects; a wonderful mutual communication is established; so that both become different parts of the same man. But the union and mutual communication they have, has existence, and is entirely regulated and limited, according to the sovereign pleasure of God, and the constitution he has been pleased to establish.

And if we come even to the *personal identity* of created intelligent beings, though this be not allowed to consist wholly in that which Mr. Locke places it in, i.e. *same consciousness;* yet I think it can't be denied, that this is one thing essential to it. But 'tis evident, that the communication or continuance of the same consciousness and memory to any subject, through successive parts of duration, depends wholly on a divine establishment.[7] There would be no necessity,

7. " 'Tis true that a man has the same consciousness that he had in his youth but that very consciousness itself depends on sovereign, arbitrary constitution. . . . If it be said that the same man has naturally a sense of guilt from what he has done in time past I answer that don't depend wholly on nature but much on principle . . . that man should be guilty for the sin of ancestors is not so far from nature as many would represent. . . . It seemed to be natural among the Jews to be conscious of the guilt of the Jews of ancestors of their people and their being justly exposed to punishment for it and the same is observable among other nations that have refined their notions by metaphysical principles." "Book of Controversies," p. 251.

that the remembrance and ideas of what is past should continue to exist, but by an arbitrary constitution of the Creator. If any should here insist, that there is no need of having recourse to any such constitution, in order to account for the continuance of the *same consciousness;* and should say, that the very nature of the soul is such as will sufficiently account for it; and that the soul will retain the ideas and consciousness it once had, according to the course of nature: then let it be remembered, who it is, gives the soul this nature; and let that be remembered, which Dr. Taylor says of the course of nature, before observed; denying, that "the course of nature is a proper active cause, which will work and go on by itself without God, if he lets and permits it"; saying, that "the course of nature, separate from the agency of God, is no cause, or nothing," and affirming, that "it's absolutely impossible, the course of nature should continue itself, or go on to operate by itself, any more than produce itself" [8] and that "God, the original of all being, is the *only cause* of all natural effects." [9] Here is worthy also to be observed, what Dr. Turnbull says of the laws of nature, in words which he cites from Sir Isaac Newton.[1] "It is the will of the mind that is the first cause, that gives a subsistence and efficacy to all those laws, who is the efficient cause that produces the phenomena, which appear in analogy, harmony and agreement, according to these laws." And he says, "The same principles must take place in things pertaining to moral, as well as natural philosophy." [2]

From these things it will clearly follow, that identity of consciousness depends wholly on a law of nature; and so, on the sovereign will and agency of God; and therefore, that personal identity, and so the derivation of the pollution and guilt of past sins in the same person, depends on an arbitrary divine constitution: and this, even though we should allow the same consciousness not to be the only thing which constitutes oneness of person, but should, besides that, suppose sameness of substance requisite. For if same consciousness be one thing necessary to personal identity, and this depends on God's sovereign constitution, it will still follow, that personal identity depends on God's sovereign constitution.

And with respect to the identity of created substance itself, in the

8. P. 410.
9. P. 416.
1. *Mor*[*al*] *Phil*[*osophy*] p. 7.
2. Ibid., p. 9.

different moments of its duration, I think, we shall greatly mistake, if we imagine it to be like that absolute independent identity of the first being, whereby "he is the same yesterday, today, and forever." Nay, on the contrary, it may be demonstrated, that even this oneness of created substance, existing at different times, is a merely *dependent* identity; dependent on the pleasure and sovereign constitution of him who worketh all in all. This will follow from what is generally allowed, and is certainly true, that God not only created all things, and gave them being at first, but continually preserves them, and upholds them in being. This being a matter of considerable importance, it may be worthy here to be considered with a little attention. Let us inquire therefore, in the first place, whether it ben't evident, that God does continually, by his immediate power, uphold every created substance in being; and then let us see the consequence.[3]

That God does, by his immediate power, *uphold* every created substance in being, will be manifest, if we consider, that their present existence is a *dependent* existence, and therefore is an *effect,* and must have some *cause:* and the cause must be one of these two: either the *antecedent existence* of the same substance, or else the *power of the Creator.* But it can't be the antecedent existence of the same substance. For instance, the existence of the body of the moon at this present moment, can't be the effect of its existence at the last foregoing moment. For not only was what existed the last moment, no active cause, but wholly a passive thing; but this also is to be considered, that no cause can produce effects in a *time* and *place* on which itself is *not.* 'Tis plain, nothing can exert itself, or operate, when and where it is not existing. But the moon's past existence was neither *where* nor *when* its present existence is. In point of time, what is *past* entirely ceases, when *present* existence begins; otherwise it would not be *past.* The past moment is ceased and gone, when the present moment takes place; and does no more coexist with it, than does any other moment that had ceased twenty years ago. Nor could the past existence of the particles of this moving body produce effects in any other place, than where it then was. But its existence at the present moment, in every point of it, is in a different place, from where its existence was at the last preceding moment. From these things, I suppose, it will certainly follow, that the present existence, either of this, or any other created substance, cannot be an effect of

3. [Extensive divergence from the MS occurs here, MS pp. 204 ff.]

its past existence. The existences (so to speak) of an effect, or thing dependent, in different parts of space or duration, though ever so *near* one to another, don't at all coexist one with the other; and therefore are as truly different effects, as if those parts of space and duration were ever so far asunder: and the prior existence can no more be the proper cause of the new existence, in the next moment, or next part of space, than if it had been in an age before, or at a thousand miles distance, without any existence to fill up the intermediate time or space. Therefore the existence of created substances, in each successive moment, must be the effect of the *immediate* agency, will, and power of God.

If any shall say, this reasoning is not good, and shall insist upon it, that there is no need of any immediate divine power, to produce the present existence of created substances, but that their present existence is the effect or consequence of past existence, according to the nature of things; that the established course of nature is sufficient to continue existence, where existence is once given; I allow it: but then it should be remembered, what nature is, in created things: and what the established course of nature is; that, as has been observed already, it is nothing, separate from the agency of God; and that, as Dr. Taylor says, "God, the Original of all being, is the only cause of all natural effects." A father, according to the course of nature, begets a child; an oak, according to the course of nature, produces an acorn, or a bud; so according to the course of nature, the former existence of the trunk of the tree is followed by its new or present existence. In the one case, and the other, the new effect is consequent on the former, only by the established laws, and settled course of nature; which is allowed to be nothing but the continued immediate efficiency of God, according to a constitution that he has been pleased to establish. Therefore, as our author greatly urges, that the child and the acorn, which come into existence according to the course of nature, in consequence of the prior existence and state of the parent and the oak, are truly *immediately* created or made by God; so must the existence of each created person and thing, at each moment of it, be from the immediate *continued* creation of God. It will certainly follow from these things, that God's *preserving* created things in being is perfectly equivalent to a *continued creation,* or to his creating those things out of nothing at *each moment* of their existence. If the continued existence of created things be wholly dependent on God's preservation, then those things would drop into nothing, upon the ceasing of the present moment, without a new exertion of the divine power to cause them to exist in the following moment. If there be any who own, that God preserves things in being, and yet hold that they would continue in being without any further help from him, after they once have existence; I think, it is hard to know what they mean. To what purpose can it be, to talk of God's preserving things in being, when there is no need of his preserving them? Or to talk of their being dependent on God for continued existence, when they would of themselves continue to exist, without his help; nay, though he should wholly withdraw his sustaining power and influence?

It will follow from what has been observed, that God's upholding created substance, or causing its existence in each successive moment, is altogether equivalent to an *immediate production out of nothing,* at each moment,[4] because its existence at this moment is not merely in part from God, but wholly from him; and not in any part, or degree, from its antecedent existence. For the supposing, that its antecedent existence *concurs* with God in *efficiency,* to produce some part of the effect, is attended with all the very same absurdities, which have been shown to attend the supposition of its producing it wholly. Therefore the antecedent existence is nothing, as to any proper influence or assistance in the affair: and consequently God produces the effect as much from *nothing,* as if there had been nothing *before.* So that this effect differs not at all from the first creation, but only *circumstantially;* as in first creation there had been no such act and effect of God's power before; whereas, his giving existence afterwards, *follows* preceding acts and effects of the same kind, in an established order.

Now, in the next place, let us see how the consequence of these things is to my present purpose. If the existence of created substance, in each successive moment, be wholly the effect of God's immediate power, in that moment, without any dependence on prior existence, as much as the first creation out of nothing, then what exists at this moment, by this power, is a *new effect;* and simply and absolutely considered, not the same with any past existence, though it be like it, and follows it according to a certain established method.[5] And

4. [First ed. begins a new sentence.]

5. When I suppose, that an effect which is produced, every moment, by a new action or exertion of power, must be a *new* effect in each moment, and not absolutely and numerically the same with that which existed in preceding

there is no identity or oneness in the case, but what depends on the *arbitrary* constitution of the Creator; who by his wise sovereign establishment so unites these successive new effects, that he *treats them as one,* by communicating to them like properties, relations, and circumstances; and so, leads us to regard and treat them as one. When I call this an arbitrary constitution, I mean, that it is a constitution which depends on nothing but the divine will; which *divine will* depends on nothing but the *divine wisdom.* In this sense, the whole course of nature, with all that belongs to it, all its laws and methods, and constancy and regularity, continuance and proceeding, is an

moments, the thing that I intend, may be illustrated by this example. The lucid color or brightness of the moon, as we look steadfastly upon it, seems to be a *permanent* thing, as though it were perfectly the same brightness continued. But indeed it is an effect produced every moment. It ceases, and is renewed, in each successive point of time; and so becomes altogether a new effect at each instant; and no one thing that belongs to it, is numerically the same that existed in the preceding moment. The rays of the sun, impressed on that body, and reflected from it, which cause the effect, are none of them the same: the impression, made in each moment on our sensory, is by the stroke of new rays: and the sensation, excited by the stroke, is a new effect, an effect of a new impulse. Therefore the brightness or lucid whiteness of this body is no more numerically the same thing with that which existed in the preceding moment, than the sound of the wind that blows now, is individually the same with the sound of the wind that blew just before, which, though it be like it, is not the same, any more than the agitated air, that makes the sound, is the same; or than the water, flowing in a river, that now passes by, is individually the same with that which passed a little before. And if it be thus with the brightness or color of the moon, so it must be with its solidity, and everything else belonging to its substance, if all be, each moment, as much the immediate effect of a new exertion or application of power.

The matter may perhaps be in some respects still more clearly illustrated by this. The images of things in a glass, as we keep our eye upon them, seem to remain precisely the same, with a continuing perfect identity. But it is known to be otherwise. Philosophers well know, that these images are constantly renewed, by the impression and reflection of new rays of light; so that the image impressed by the former rays is constantly vanishing, and a new image impressed by new rays every moment, both on the glass and on the eye. The image constantly renewed, by new successive rays, is no more numerically the same, than if it were by some artist put on anew with a pencil, and the colors constantly vanishing as fast as put on. And the new images being put on *immediately* or instantly, don't make 'em the same, any more than if it were done with the intermission of an hour or a day. The image that exists this moment, is not at all derived from the image which existed the last preceding moment: as may be seen, because, if the succession of new rays be intercepted, by something interposed between the object and the glass, the image immediately ceases; the

arbitrary constitution. In this sense, the continuance of the very being of the world and all its parts, as well as the manner of continued being, depends entirely on an arbitrary constitution: for it don't all *necessarily* follow, that because there was sound, or light, or color, or resistance, or gravity, or thought, or consciousness, or any other dependent thing the last moment, that therefore there shall be the like at the next. All dependent existence whatsoever is in a constant flux, ever passing and returning; renewed every moment, as the colors of bodies are every moment renewed by the light that shines upon them; and all is constantly proceeding from God, as light from the sun. "In him we live, and move, and have our being."

Thus it appears, if we consider matters strictly, there is no such thing as any identity or oneness in created objects, existing at different times, but what depends on *God's sovereign constitution.* And so it appears, that the objection we are upon, made against a supposed divine constitution, whereby Adam and his posterity are viewed and treated as one, in the manner and for the purposes supposed, as if it were not consistent with truth, because no constitution can make those to be one, which are not one; I say, it appears that this objection is built on a false hypothesis: for it appears, that a *divine constitution* is the thing which *makes truth,* in affairs of this nature. The objection supposes, there is a oneness in created beings, whence qualities and relations are derived down from past existence, distinct from, and prior to any oneness that can be supposed to be founded on divine constitution. Which is demonstrably false; and sufficiently appears so from things conceded by the adversaries themselves: and therefore the objection wholly falls to the ground.

There are *various kinds* of identity and oneness, found among created things, by which they become one in different manners, respects

---

past existence of the image has no influence to uphold it, so much as for one moment. Which shews, that the image is altogether new-made every moment; and strictly speaking, is in no part numerically the same with that which existed the moment preceding. And truly so the matter must be with the bodies themselves, as well as their images: they also cannot be the same, with an absolute identity, but must be wholly renewed every moment, if the case be as has been proved, that their present existence is not, strictly speaking, at all the effect of their past existence; but is wholly, every instant, the effect of a new agency, or exertion of the power, of the cause of their existence. If so, the existence caused is every instant a new effect, whether the cause be light, or immediate divine power, or whatever it be.
[This footnote is omitted from the MS.]

and degrees, and to various purposes; several of which differences have been observed; and every kind is ordered, regulated and limited, in every respect, by divine constitution. Some things, existing in different times and places, are treated by their Creator as one in *one respect,* and others in *another;* some are united for this communication, and others for that; but all according to the sovereign pleasure of the Fountain of all being and operation.

It appears, particularly, from what has been said, that all oneness, by virtue whereof pollution and guilt from past wickedness are derived, depends entirely on a divine establishment. 'Tis this, and this only, that must account for guilt and an evil taint on any individual soul, in consequence of a crime committed twenty or forty years ago, remaining still, and even to the end of the world and forever. 'Tis this, that must account for the continuance of any such thing, anywhere, as *consciousness* of acts that are past; and for the continuance of all *habits,* either good or bad: and on this depends everything that can belong to *personal identity.* And all communications, derivations, or continuation of qualities, properties, or relations, natural or moral, from what is past, as if the subject were one, depends on no other foundation.

And I am persuaded, no solid reason can be given, why God, who constitutes all other created union or oneness, according to his pleasure, and for what purposes, communications, and effects he pleases, may not establish a constitution whereby the natural posterity of Adam, proceeding from him, much as the buds and branches from the stock or root of a tree, should be treated as one with him, for the derivation, either of righteousness and communion in rewards, or of the loss of righteousness and consequent corruption and guilt.[6]

6. I appeal to such as are not wont to content themselves with judging by a superficial appearance and view of things, but are habituated to examine things strictly and closely, that they may judge righteous judgment, whether on supposition that all mankind had *coexisted,* in the manner mentioned before, any good reason can be given, why their Creator might not, if he had pleased, have established such an union between Adam and the rest of mankind, as was in that case supposed. Particularly, if it had been the case, that Adam's posterity had actually, according to a law of nature, somehow grown out of him, and yet remained continuous and literally united to him, as the branches to a tree, or the members of the body to the head; and had all, before the fall, existed together at the same time, though in different places, as the head and members are in different places; in this case, who can determine, that the Author of nature might not, if it had pleased him, have established such an union between the root and branches of this complex being, as that all should constitute one

As I said before, all oneness in created things, whence qualities and relations are derived, depends on a divine constitution that is arbitrary, in every other respect, excepting that it is regulated by divine wisdom. The wisdom, which is exercised in these constitutions, appears in these two things. First, in a beautiful *analogy* and *harmony* with *other* laws or constitutions, especially relating to the same subject: and secondly, in the good *ends* obtained, or useful *consequences* of such a constitution. If therefore there be any objection still lying against this constitution with Adam and his posterity, it must be, that it is not sufficiently wise in these respects. But what extreme arrogance would it be in us, to take upon us to act as judges of the beauty and wisdom of the laws and established constitutions of the supreme Lord and Creator of the universe? And not only so, but if this constitution, in particular, be well considered, its wisdom, in the two forementioned respects, may easily be made evident. There is an apparent manifold analogy to other constitutions and laws, established and maintained through the whole system of vital nature in this lower world; all parts of which, in all successions, are derived from the *first of the kind,* as from their root, or fountain; each deriving from thence all properties and qualities, that are proper to the nature and capacity of the kind, or species: no derivative having any one perfection (unless it be what is merely circumstantial) but what was in its primitive. And that Adam's posterity should be without that original righteousness, which Adam had lost, is also analogous to other laws and establishments, relating to the

---

moral whole; so that by the law of union, there should be a communion in each moral alteration, and that the heart of every branch should at the same moment participate with the heart of the root, be conformed to it and concurring with it in all its affections and acts, and so jointly partaking in its state, as a part of the same thing? Why might not God, if he had pleased, have fixed such a kind of union as this, an union of the various parts of such a moral whole, as well as many other unions, which he has actually fixed, according to his sovereign pleasure? And if he might, by his sovereign constitution, have established such an union of the various branches of mankind, when existing in different places, I don't see why he might not also do the same, though they exist in different times. I know not why succession, or diversity of time, should make any such constituted union more unreasonable, than diversity of place. The only reason, why diversity of time can seem to make it unreasonable, is, that difference of time shews, there is no absolute identity of the things existing in those different times: but it shews this, I think, not at all more than the difference of the place of existence.

[This footnote is omitted from the MS.]

nature of mankind; according to which, Adam's posterity have no one perfection of nature, in any kind, superior to what was in him, when the human race began to be propagated from him.

And as such a constitution was *fit* and *wise* in other respects, so it was in this that follows. Seeing the divine constitution concerning the manner of mankind's coming into existence in their propagation, was such as did so naturally unite them, and made 'em in so many respects one, naturally leading them to a close union in society, and manifold intercourse, and mutual dependence, things were wisely so established, that all should naturally be in one and the same *moral state;* and not in such exceeding different states, as that some should be perfectly innocent and holy, but others corrupt and wicked; some needing a saviour, but others needing none; some in a confirmed state of perfect *happiness,* but others in a state of public condemnation to perfect and eternal *misery;* some justly exposed to great calamities in this world, but others by their innocence raised above all suffering. Such a vast diversity of state would by no means have agreed with the natural and necessary constitution and unavoidable situation and circumstances of the world of mankind; "all made of one blood, to dwell on all the face of the earth," to be united and blended in society, and to partake together in the natural and common goods and evils of this lower world.

Dr. Taylor urges,[7] that *sorrow* and *shame* are only for *personal* sin: and it has often been urged, that *repentance* can be for no other sin. To which I would say, that the use of words is very arbitrary: but that men's hearts should be deeply affected with grief and humiliation before God, for the pollution and guilt which they bring into the world with them, I think, is not in the least *unreasonable.* Nor is it a thing strange and unheard of, that men should be ashamed of things done by others, whom they are nearly concerned in. I am sure, it is not unscriptural; especially when they are justly looked upon in the sight of God, who sees the disposition of their hearts, as fully consenting and concurring.

From what has been observed it may appear, there is no sure ground to conclude, that it must be an absurd and impossible thing, for the race of mankind truly to partake of the sin of the first apostacy, so as that this, in reality and propriety, shall become *their* sin; by virtue of a real union between the root and branches of the world of mankind (truly and properly availing to such a conse-

7. P. 13.

quence) established by the Author of the whole system of the universe; to whose establishment is owing all propriety and reality of union, in any part of that system; and by virtue of the full consent of the hearts of Adam's posterity to that first apostacy. And therefore the sin of the apostacy is not theirs, merely because God *imputes* it to them; but it is *truly* and *properly* theirs, and on that ground, God imputes it to them.

By reason of the established union between Adam and his posterity, the case is far otherwise between him and them, than it is between distinct parts or individuals of Adam's race; betwixt whom is no such constituted union: as between children and other ancestors. Concerning whom is apparently to be understood that place (Ezek. 18:1–20),[8] where God reproves the Jews for the use they made of that proverb, "The fathers have eaten sour grapes, and the children's teeth are set on edge"; and tells them, that hereafter they shall no more have occasion to use this proverb; and that if a son sees the wickedness of his father, and sincerely disapproves it and avoids it, and he himself is righteous, "he shall not die for the iniquity of his father; that all souls, both the soul of the father and the son, are his; and that therefore the son shall not bear the iniquity of his father, nor the father bear the iniquity of the son; but the soul that sinneth, it shall die; that the righteousness of the righteous shall be upon him, and the wickedness of the wicked shall be upon him." The thing denied, is communion in the guilt and punishment of the sins of others, that are distinct parts of Adam's race; and expressly, in that case, where there is no consent and concurrence, but a sincere disapprobation of the wickedness of ancestors. It is declared, that children who are adult and come to act for themselves, who are righteous, and don't approve of, but sincerely condemn the wickedness of their fathers, shall not be punished for their disapproved and avoided iniquities. The occasion of what is here said, as well as the design and plain sense, shews, that nothing is here intended in the least degree inconsistent with what has been supposed concerning Adam's posterity's sinning and falling in his apostacy. The occasion is, the people's murmuring at God's methods under the Mosaic dispensation; agreeable to that in Lev. 26:29, "And they that are left of you, shall pine away in their iniquity in their enemies' land, and also in the iniquities of their fathers shall they pine away with them." And other parallel places, respecting external judgments,

8. Which Dr. Taylor alleges, pp. 286, 287.

which were the punishments most plainly threatened, and chiefly insisted on, under that dispensation (which was, as it were, an *external* and *carnal* covenant) and particularly the people's suffering such terrible judgments at that day, even in Ezekiel's time, for the sins of Manasseh; according to what God says by Jeremiah (Jer. 15:4), and agreeable to what is said in that confession (Lam. 5:7), "Our fathers have sinned and are not, and we have borne their iniquities."

In what is said here, there is a special respect to the introducing the gospel-dispensation; as is greatly confirmed by comparing this place with Jer. 31:29,30,31. Under which dispensation, the righteousness of God's dealings with mankind would be more fully manifested, in the clear revelation then to be made of the method of the judgment of God, by which the final state of wicked men is determined; which is not according to the behavior of their particular ancestors; but every one is dealt with according to the sin of his own wicked heart, or sinful nature and practice. The affair of derivation of the natural corruption of mankind in general and of their consent to, and participation of, the primitive and common apostacy, is not in the least intermeddled with, or touched, by anything meant or aimed at in the true scope and design of this place in Ezekiel.

On the whole, if any don't like the philosophy, or the metaphysics (as some perhaps may choose to call it) made use of in the foregoing reasonings; yet I cannot doubt, but that a proper consideration of what is apparent and undeniable in fact, with respect to the dependence of the state and course of things in this universe on the sovereign constitutions of the supreme Author and Lord of all, "who gives none account of any of his matters, and whose ways are past finding out," will be sufficient, with persons of common modesty and sobriety, to stop their mouths from making peremptory decisions against the justice of God, respecting what is so plainly and fully taught in his Holy Word, concerning the derivation of a depravity and guilt from Adam to his posterity; a thing so abundantly confirmed by what is found in the experience of all mankind in all ages.

This is enough, one would think, forever to silence such bold expressions as these—"If this be just," "if the Scriptures teach such doctrine etc., then the Scriptures are of no use," "understanding is no understanding," and "what a God must he be, that can thus curse innocent creatures!" "Is this thy God, O Christian?" etc. etc.

It may not be improper here to add something (by way of supplement to this chapter, in which we have had occasion to say so much about the imputation of Adam's sin), concerning the opinions of two divines, of no inconsiderable note among the dissenters in England, relating to a partial imputation of Adam's first sin.[9]

One of them supposes, that this sin, though truly imputed to infants, so that thereby they are exposed to a proper punishment, yet is not imputed to them in such a degree, as that upon this account they should be liable to eternal punishment, as Adam himself was, but only to temporal death, or annihilation; Adam himself, the immediate actor, being made infinitely more guilty by it, than his posterity. On which I would observe: that to suppose, God imputes not *all* the guilt of Adam's sin, but only some *little* part of it, this relieves nothing but one's *imagination.* To think of poor little infants bearing such torments for Adam's sin, as they sometimes do in this world, and these torments ending in death and annihilation, may sit easier on the imagination, than to conceive of their suffering eternal misery for it. But it does not at all relieve one's *reason.* There is no rule of reason, that can be supposed to lie against imputing a sin in the whole of it, which was committed by one, to another who did not personally commit it, but what will also lie against its being so imputed and punished in part. For all the reasons (if there are any) lie against the imputation; not the *quantity* or *degree of what is imputed.* If there be any rule of reason, that is strong and good, lying against a proper derivation or communication of guilt, from one that acted, to another that did not act; then it lies against *all* that is of this nature. The force of the reasons brought against imputing Adam's sin to his posterity (if there be any force in them) lies in this, that Adam and his posterity are not one. But this lies as properly against charging a part of the guilt, as the whole. For Adam's posterity, by not being the same with him, had no more hand in a *little* of what was done, than in the whole. They were as absolutely free from being concerned in that act partly, as they were wholly. And there is no reason can be brought, why one man's sin can't be justly reckoned to another's account, who was not then in being, in the whole of it; but what will as properly lie against its being reckoned to him in any part, so as that he should be subject to any condemnation or punishment on that account. If those reasons are

9. [Undoubtedly JE has in mind I. Watts and T. Ridgely, to whom he refers in the "Book of Controversies" in connection with the problem of partial imputation. Pp. 69 ff., 72 ff., 76.]

good, all the *difference* there can be, is this; that to bring a great punishment on infants for Adam's sin, is a great act of injustice, and to bring a comparatively *small* punishment, is a *smaller* act of injustice; but not, that this is not as *truly* and *demonstrably* an act of injustice, as the other.

To illustrate this by an instance something parallel. 'Tis used as an argument why I may not exact from one of my neighbors, what was due to me from another, that he and my debtor are not the same; and that their concerns, interests and properties are entirely distinct. Now if this argument be good, it lies as truly against my demanding from him a part of the debt, as the whole. Indeed it is a *greater* act of injustice, for me to take from him the whole of it, than a part; but not more truly and certainly an act of injustice.

The other divine [1] thinks, there is truly an imputation of Adam's sin, so that infants can't be looked upon as *innocent* creatures; yet seems to think it not agreeable to the perfections of God, to make the state of infants in another world *worse* than a state of *nonexistence*. But this to me appears plainly a *giving up* that grand point of the imputation of Adam's sin, both in whole and in part. For it supposes it to be not right, for God to bring any evil on a child of Adam, which is innocent as to personal sin, without *paying for it,* or balancing it with good; so that still the state of the child shall be as good, as could be demanded in justice, in case of mere innocence. Which plainly supposes, that the child is not exposed to any proper punishment at all, or is not at all in debt to divine justice, on the account of Adam's sin. For if the child were truly in *debt;* then surely *justice* might *take* something from him, *without paying for it,* or without giving that which makes its state as good, as mere innocence could in justice require.[2] If he owes the suffering of some punishment, then there is no need that justice should requite the infant for suffering that punishment; or make up for it, by conferring some good, that shall countervail it, and in effect remove and disannul it; so that, on the whole, good and evil shall be at an even balance, yea, so that the scale of good shall *preponderate.* If it is unjust in a judge, to order any quantity of money to be taken from another, without paying him again, and fully making it up to him, it must be because he had justly *forfeited none* at all.

It seems to me pretty manifest, that none can, in good consistence

1. [T. Ridgely.]
2. P. 359 etc.

with themselves, own a real imputation of the guilt of Adam's first sin to his posterity, without owning that they are justly viewed and treated as sinners, truly guilty, and children of wrath, on that account; nor unless they allow a just imputation of the whole of the evil of that transgression; at least, all that pertains to the essence of that act, as a full and complete violation of the covenant, which God had established; even as much as if each one of mankind had the like covenant established with him singly, and had by the like direct and full act of rebellion, violated it for himself.

CHAPTER IV

WHEREIN SEVERAL OTHER OBJECTIONS ARE CONSIDERED

DR. TAYLOR objects against Adam's posterity's being supposed to come into the world under a *forfeiture* of God's *blessing,* and subject to his *curse* through his sin, that at the restoration of the world after the flood, God pronounced equivalent or greater blessings on Noah and his sons, than he did on Adam at his creation, when he said, "Be fruitful and multiply, and replenish the earth, and have dominion over the fish of the sea, etc." [1]

To this I answer in the following remarks.

1. As it has been already shewn, that in the threatening, denounced for Adam's sin, there was nothing which appears inconsistent with the continuance of this present life for a season, or with the propagating his kind; so for the like reason, there appears nothing in that threatening, upon the supposition that it reached Adam's posterity, inconsistent with their enjoying the *temporal blessings* of the present life, as long as this is continued: even those temporal blessings which God pronounced on Adam at his first creation. For it must be observed, that the blessings which God pronounced on Adam, when he first created him, and before the trial of his obedience, were not the same with the blessings which were *suspended on his obedience.* The blessings thus suspended, were the blessings of eternal life; which, if he had maintained his integrity through his trial, would have been pronounced upon him afterwards; when God, as his Judge, should have given him his reward. God might indeed, if he had pleased, immediately have deprived him of life, and of all temporal blessings, given him before. But those blessings pronounced on him beforehand, were not the things, for the obtaining of which his trial was appointed. These were reserved, till the issue of

1. Part II, Ch. 1, sec. 3.

his trial should be seen, and then to be pronounced, in the blessed sentence, which would have been passed upon him by his Judge, when God came to decree to him his reward for his approved fidelity. The pronouncing these latter blessings on a degenerate race, that had fallen under the threatening denounced, would indeed (without a redemption) have been inconsistent with the constitution which had been established. But the giving them the former kind of blessings, which were not the things suspended on the trial, or dependent on his fidelity (and these to be continued for a season) was not at all inconsistent therewith.

2. 'Tis no more an evidence of Adam's posterity's being not included in the threatening, denounced for his eating the forbidden fruit, that they still have the temporal blessings of fruitfulness and a dominion over the creatures continued to them, than it is an evidence of Adam's being not included in that threatening himself, that he had these blessings continued to him, was fruitful, and had dominion over the creatures after his fall, equally with his posterity.

3. There is good evidence, that there were blessings implied in the benedictions God pronounced on Noah and his posterity, which were granted on a *new foundation:* on the foot of a dispensation diverse from any grant, promise, or revelation, which God gave to Adam, antecedently to his fall; even on the foundation of the Covenant of Grace, established in Christ Jesus; a dispensation, the design of which is to deliver men from the curse, that came upon them by Adam's sin, and to bring them to greater blessings than ever he had. These blessings were pronounced on Noah and his seed, on the same foundation, whereon afterwards the blessing was pronounced on Abraham and his seed, which included both spiritual and temporal benefits. Noah had his name prophetically given him by his father Lamech, because by him and his seed deliverance should be obtained from the curse, which came by Adam's fall. (Gen. 5:29), "And he called his name Noah (i.e. rest), saying, this same shall comfort us concerning our work, and toil of our hands, because of the ground which the Lord hath cursed." Pursuant to the scope and intent of this prophecy (which indeed seems to respect the same thing with the prophecy in Gen. 3:15) are the blessings pronounced on Noah after the flood. There is this evidence of these blessings being conveyed through the channel of the Covenant of Grace, and by the redemption through Jesus Christ, that they were obtained by

sacrifice; or were bestowed as the effect of God's favor to mankind, which was in consequence of God's smelling a sweet savor in the sacrifice which Noah offered. And 'tis very evident by the epistle to the Hebrews, that the ancient sacrifices never obtained the favor of God, but only by virtue of the relation they had to the sacrifice of Christ. That now Noah and his family had been so wonderfully saved from the wrath of God, which had destroyed the rest of the world, and that the world was as it were restored from a ruined state, this was a proper occasion to point to the great salvation to come by Christ: as it was a common thing, for God, on occasion of some great temporal salvation of his people, or restoration from a low and miserable state, to renew the intimations of the great spiritual restoration of the world by Christ's redemption.[2] God deals with the generality of mankind, in their present state, far differently, on occasion of the redemption by Jesus Christ, from what he otherwise would do: for, being capable subjects of saving mercy, they have a day of patience and grace, and innumerable temporal blessings bestowed on them; which, as the Apostle signifies (Acts 14:17), are testimonies of God's reconcilableness to sinful men, to put 'em upon seeking after God.

But besides the sense in which the posterity of Noah in general partake of these blessings of dominion over the creatures etc., Noah himself, and all such of his posterity as have obtained like precious faith with that exercised by him in offering his sacrifice, which made it a sweet savor, and by which it procured these blessings, have dominion over the creatures, through Christ, in a more excellent sense than Adam in innocency; as they are made kings and priests unto God and reign with Christ, and all things are theirs, by a Covenant of Grace. They partake with Christ in that dominion over the beasts of the earth, the fowls of the air, and fishes of the sea, spoken of in the 8th Psalm; which is by the Apostle interpreted of Christ's dominion over the world (I Cor. 15:27 and Heb. 2:7). And the time is coming, when the greater part of the posterity of Noah and each of his sons, shall partake of this more honorable and excellent dominion over the creatures, through him in whom all the families of the earth shall be blessed. Neither is there any need of supposing, that these blessings must have their most complete accomplishment until

2. It may be noted that Dr. Taylor himself signifies it as his mind, that these blessings on Noah were on the foot of the Covenant of Grace. Pp. 360, 366, 367, 368.

many ages after they were granted, any more than the blessing on Japhet, expressed in those words, "God shall enlarge Japhet, and he shall dwell in the tents of Shem."

But that Noah's posterity have such blessings given them through the great Redeemer, who suspends and removes the curse which came through Adam's sin, surely is no argument, that they originally, and as they be in their natural state are not under the curse. That men have blessings *through grace,* is no evidence of their being not justly exposed to the curse *by nature;* but it rather argues the contrary: for if they did not deserve the curse, they would not depend on grace and redemption for the removal of it, and for bringing them into a state of favor with God.

Another objection, which our author strenuously urges against the doctrine of original sin, is that it *disparages* the divine *goodness* in giving us our being; which we ought to receive with thankfulness, as a great gift of God's beneficence, and look upon as the first, original and fundamental fruit of the divine liberality.[3]

To this I answer, in the following observations.

1. This argument is built on the supposed truth of a thing in dispute; and so is a *begging the question.* It is built on this supposition, that we are not properly looked upon as one with our first father, in the state wherein God at first created him, and in his fall from that state. If we are so, it becomes the whole race to acknowledge God's great goodness to them, in the state wherein mankind was made at first; in the happy state they were then in, and the fair opportunity they then had of obtaining confirmed and eternal happiness; and to acknowledge it as an aggravation of their apostacy; and to humble themselves, that they were so ungrateful as to rebel against their good Creator. Certainly, we may all do this with as much (yea, much more) reason, as the people of Israel in Daniel's and Nehemiah's times, did with thankfulness acknowledge God's great goodness to their fathers, many ages before, and in their confessions bewailed, and took shame to themselves for, the sins committed by their fathers, notwithstanding such great goodness. (See the 9th chapter of Daniel, and 9th of Nehemiah.)

2. If Dr. Taylor would imply in his objection, that it don't consist with the goodness of God, to give mankind being in a state of misery, whatever was done before by Adam, whether he sinned, or did not sin: I reply, if it be justly so ordered, that there should be a

3. Pp. 256, 257, 260, 347–50.

posterity of Adam, which must be looked upon as one with him, then 'tis no more contrary to God's attribute of goodness to give being to his posterity in a state of punishment, than to continue the being of the same wicked and guilty person, who has made himself guilty, in a state of punishment. The giving being, and the continuing being are both alike the work of God's power and will, and both are alike fundamental to all blessings of man's present and future existence. And if it be said, it cannot be justly so ordered, that there should be a posterity of Adam, which should be looked upon one with him, this is *begging the question.*

3. If our author would have us suppose, that it is contrary to the attribute of goodness, for God, in any case, by an immediate act of his power, to cause existence, and to cause new existence, which shall be an exceeding miserable existence, by reason of exposedness to eternal ruin; then his own scheme must be supposed contrary to the attribute of God's goodness: for he supposes, that God will raise multitudes from the dead at the last day (which will be giving new existence to their bodies, and to bodily life and sense) in order only to their suffering eternal destruction.

4. Notwithstanding we are so sinful and miserable, as we are by nature, yet we may have great reason to bless God, that he has given us our being under so glorious a dispensation of *grace* through Jesus Christ; by which we have a happy opportunity to be *delivered* from this sin and misery, and to obtain unspeakable eternal *happiness.* And because, through our own wicked inclinations, we are disposed so to neglect and abuse this mercy, as to fail of final benefit by it, this is no reason why we ought not to be thankful for it, even according to our author's own sentiments. "What," says he,[4] "if the whole world lies in wickedness, and few therefore shall be saved? Have men no reason to be thankful, because they are wicked and ungrateful, and abuse their being and God's bounty. . . . Suppose, our own evil inclinations do withhold us" (viz. from seeking after happiness, which under the light of the gospel we are placed within the nearer and easier reach of). "Suppose, . . . the whole Christian world should lie in wickedness, and but few Christians should be saved; is it therefore certainly true, that we cannot reasonably thank God for the gospel?" Well, and though the evil inclinations, which hinder our seeking and obtaining happiness by so glorious an advantage, are what we are born with, yet if those inclinations are our

4. P. 349.

fault or sin, that alters not the case, and to say, they are not our sin, is still begging the question. Yea, it will follow from several things asserted by our author, put together, that notwithstanding men are born in such circumstances, as that they are under a very great improbability of ever becoming righteous, yet they may have reason to be thankful for their being. Thus, particularly, those that were born and lived among the heathen, before Christ came. For Dr. Taylor asserts, that all men have reason of thankfulness for their being; and yet he supposes, that the heathen world, taken as a collective body, were dead in sin, and could not deliver or help themselves, and therefore stood in necessity of the Christian dispensation. And not only so, but he supposes, that the Christian world is now at length brought to the like deplorable and helpless circumstances, and needs a new dispensation for its relief; as I observed before. According to these things, the world in general, not only formerly, but even at this day, are dead in sin, and helpless as to their salvation; and therefore the generality of them that are born into it, are much more likely to perish, than otherwise, till the new dispensation comes: and yet he supposes, we all have reason to be thankful for our being. Yea, further still, I think, according to our author's doctrine, men may have great reason to be thankful to God for bringing them into a state, which yet, as the case is, is attended with misery, as its certain consequence. As, with respect to God's raising the wicked to life, at the last day; which, he supposes, is in itself a great benefit, procured by Christ, and the wonderful grace of God through him: and if it be the fruit of God's wonderful grace, surely men ought to be thankful for that grace, and praise God for it. Our doctrine of original sin, therefore, no more disparages God's goodness in man's formation in the womb, than his doctrine disparages God's goodness in their resurrection from the grave.[5]

Another argument, which Dr. Taylor makes use of, against the doctrine of original sin, is what the Scripture reveals of the process of the day of *judgment;* which represents the Judge as dealing with men *singly* and *separately,* rendering to *every* man according to his deeds, and according to the improvement he has made of the particular powers and talents God has given him personally.[6]

But this objection will vanish, if we consider what is the *end* or *design* of that public judgment. Now this will not be, that God may

5. [Much of this paragraph is omitted from the MS.]
6. Pp. 341–343 and 387.

find out what men are, or what punishment or reward is proper for them, or in order to the passing a right judgment of these things within himself, which is the end of human trials; but it is to *manifest* what men are, to their own consciences, and to the world. As the day of judgment is called the day of the revelation of the righteous judgment of God; in order to this, God will make use of evidences, or proofs. But the proper evidences of the wickedness of men's hearts (the true seat of all wickedness) both as to corruption of nature, and additional pollution and guilt, are men's works.

The special end of God's public judgment will be, to make a proper, perfect, open distinction among men, rightly to state and manifest their difference one from another, in order to that separation and difference in the eternal retribution, that is to follow: and this difference will be made to appear, by their personal works.[7]

There are two things, with regard to which men will be tried, and openly distinguished, by the perfect judgment of God at the last day; according to the twofold real distinction subsisting among mankind: viz. (1) The *difference of state;* that primary and grand distinction, whereby all mankind are divided into two sorts, the righteous and the wicked. (2) That *secondary distinction,* whereby both sorts differ from others in the same general state, in degrees of additional fruits of righteousness and wickedness. Now the Judge, in order to manifest both these, will judge men according to their personal works. But to inquire at the day of judgment, whether Adam sinned or no, or whether men are to be looked upon as one with him, and so partakers in his sin, is what in no respect tends to manifest either of these distinctions.

1. The first thing to be manifested, will be the state, that each man is in, with respect to the *grand distinction* of the whole world of mankind into *righteous and wicked;* or, in metaphorical language, wheat and tares; or, the children of the kingdom of Christ, and the children of the wicked one; the latter, the head of the apostacy; but the former, the head of the restoration and recovery. The Judge, in manifesting this, will prove men's hearts by their works, in such as have had opportunity to perform any works in the body. The evil works of the children of the wicked one will be the proper manifestation and evidence or proof of whatever belongs to the general state of such; and particularly they will prove, that they belong to the kingdom of the great deceiver, and head of the apostacy, as

7. [This paragraph is omitted from the MS.]

they will demonstrate the exceeding corruption of their nature, and full consent of their hearts to the common apostacy, and also that their hearts never relinquished the apostacy, by a cordial adherence to Christ, the great Restorer. The Judge will also make use of the good works of the righteous to shew their interest in the redemption of Christ; as thereby will be manifested the sincerity of their hearts in their acceptance of, and adherence to the Redeemer and his righteousness. And in thus proving the state of men's hearts by their actions, the circumstances of those actions must necessarily come into consideration, to manifest the true quality of their actions; as each one's talents, opportunities, advantages, light, motives, etc.[8]

2. The other thing to be manifested, will be that *secondary distinction,* wherein particular persons, both righteous and wicked, differ from one another, in the *degree* of secondary good or evil, that is something beside what is common to all in the same general state: the degree of evil fruit, which is additional to the guilt and corruption of the whole body of apostates and enemies; and the degree of personal goodness and good fruit, which is a secondary goodness, with respect to the righteousness and merits of Christ, which belong to all by that sincere faith manifested in all. Of this also each one's works, with their circumstances, opportunities, talents, etc. will be the proper evidence.

As to the nature and aggravations of the general apostacy by Adam's sin, and also the nature and sufficiency of the redemption by Jesus Christ, the great Restorer, though both these will have vast influence on the eternal state, which men shall be adjudged to, yet neither of them will properly belong to the trial men will be the subjects of at that day, in order to the *manifestation* of their *state,* wherein they are *distinguished one from another.* They will belong to the business of that day no otherwise, than the manifestation of the great truths of religion in general; as the nature and perfections of God, the dependence of mankind on God, as their Creator and Preserver, etc. Such truths as these will also have great influence on the eternal state, which men will then be adjudged to, as they aggravate the guilt of man's wickedness, and must be considered in order

8. [In the MS, p. 216, Edwards was tempted to identify Arminianism as a result of the fall! "God will make use of the wicked works of the wicked to manifest the wickedness of their hearts and nature as true and real enemies, rebels and apostates and to shew the full consent of their hearts to the Arminian apostacy by the first Adam."]

to a due estimate of Christ's righteousness, and men's personal virtue; yet being of general and equal concernment, will not properly belong to the trial of particular persons.

Another thing urged by our author particularly against the imputation of Adam's sin, is this: "Though, in Scripture, action is frequently said to be imputed, reckoned, accounted to a person, it is no other than his own act and deed."[9] In the same place he cites a number of places in Scripture, where these words are used, which he says are all that he can find in the Bible.[1]

But we are no way concerned with this argument at present, any further than it relates to *imputation of sin,* or sinful action. Therefore all that is in the argument, which relates to the present purpose, is this; that the word is so often applied in Scripture to signify God's imputing personal sin, but never once to his imputing Adam's sin. *So often!* How often? But *twice.* There are but two of all those places which he reckons up, that speak of, or so much as have any reference to, God's imputing sin to any person, where there is any evidence that only personal sin is meant; and they are Lev. 17:3,4, and II Tim. 4:16. All therefore the argument comes to, is this; that the word "impute" is applied in Scripture, *two* times, to the case of God's imputing sin, and neither of those times to signify the imputing of Adam's sin, but both times it has reference to personal sin; therefore Adam's sin is not imputed to his posterity. And this is to be noted, that one of these two places, even that in Lev. 17:3,4, don't speak of imputing the act committed, but another not committed. The words are, "What man soever there be of the house of Israel, that killeth an ox or lamb or goat in the camp, or that killeth it out of the camp, and bringeth it not unto the door of the tabernacle of the congregation, to offer an offering unto the Lord, before the tabernacle of the Lord, blood shall be imputed unto that man; he hath shed blood; that man shall be cut off from among his people." I.e. plainly, murder shall be imputed to him: he shall be put to death for it, and therein punished with the same severity as if he had slain a man. 'Tis plain by Is. 66:3 that in some cases, a shedding the blood of beasts, in an unlawful manner, was imputed to them, as if they slew a man.

But whether it be so or not, although in both these places the

9. Pp. 279 etc. and 381.

1. [This paragraph and the following five paragraphs are omitted from the MS.]

word "impute" be applied to personal sin, and to the very act done by the person spoken of, and in ten more places; or although this could be said of all the places, which our author reckons up; yet that the word "impute" is never expressly applied to Adam's sin, does no more argue, that it is not imputed to his posterity, than it argues, that pride, unbelief, lying, theft, oppression, persecution, fornication, adultery, sodomy, perjury, idolatry, and innumerable other particular moral evils, are never imputed to the persons that commit them, or in whom they are; because the word "impute," though so often used in Scripture, is never applied to any of these kinds of wickedness.

I know not what can be said here, except one of these two things; that though these sins are not expressly said to be *imputed,* yet other words are used that do as plainly and certainly *imply* that they are imputed, as if it were said so expressly. Very well, and so I say with respect to the imputation of Adam's sin. The thing meant by the word "impute" may be as plainly and certainly expressed by using other words, as if that word were expressly used; and more certainly, because the words used instead of it, may amount to an explanation of this word. And this, I think, is the very case here. Though the word "impute" is not used with respect to Adam's sin, yet 'tis said, "all have sinned"; which, respecting infants, can be true only of their sinning by his sin. And 'tis said, "By his disobedience many were made sinners"; and "judgment and condemnation came upon all by that sin"; and that by this means "death (the wages of sin) passed on all men" etc. Which phrases amount to full and precise explanations of the word "impute"; and therefore do more certainly determine the point really insisted on.

Or, perhaps it will be said, with respect to those personal sins aforementioned, pride, unbelief, etc., it is no argument, they are not imputed to those who are guilty of 'em, that the very word "impute" is not applied to 'em; for the word itself is rarely used; not one time in a hundred, and perhaps five hundred, of those wherein the thing meant is plainly implied, or may be certainly inferred. Well, and the same also may be replied likewise, with respect to Adam's sin.

'Tis probable, Dr. Taylor intends an argument against original sin, by that which he says in opposition to what R.R. suggests of "Children's discovering the principles of iniquity, and seeds of sin, before they are capable of moral action" [2] viz. "That little children

2. Pp. 353, 354. [JE's free paraphrase.]

are made patterns of humility, meekness and innocence" (in Matt. 18:3; I Cor. 14:20, and Ps. 131:2).

But when the utmost is made of this, there can be no shadow of reason to understand more by these texts, than that little children are recommended as patterns in regard of a *negative* virtue, *innocence* with respect to the exercises and fruits of sin, *harmlessness* as to the hurtful effects of it, and that image of meekness and humility arising from this, in conjunction with a natural tenderness of mind, fear, self-diffidence, yieldableness, and confidence in parents and others older than themselves. And so, they are recommended as patterns of virtue no more than doves, which are an harmless sort of creature, and have an image of the virtues of meekness and love. Even according to Dr. Taylor's own doctrine, no more can be made of it than this: for his scheme will not admit of any such thing as *positive* virtue, or virtuous disposition, in infants; he insisting (as was observed before) that virtue must be the fruit of thought and reflection. But there can be no thought and reflection, that produces positive virtue, in children, not yet capable of moral action; and it is such children he speaks of. And that little children have a *negative* virtue or innocence, in relation to the *positive* acts and hurtful effects of vice, is no argument that they have not corrupt nature within them; for let their nature be ever so corrupt, yet surely 'tis no wonder that they ben't guilty of positive wicked action, before they are capable of any moral action at all. A young viper has a malignant nature, though incapable of doing a malignant action, and at present appearing a harmless creature.

Another objection, which Dr. Taylor and some others offer against this doctrine, is, that it *pours contempt upon the human nature.*[3]

But their declaiming on this topic is like addressing the affections and conceits of *children,* rather than rational arguing with *men.* It seems, this doctrine is not complaisant enough. I am sensible, it is not suited to the taste of some, who are so very *delicate* (to say no worse) that they can bear nothing but compliment and flattery. No contempt is by this doctrine cast upon the noble faculties and capacities of man's nature, or the exalted business, and divine and immortal happiness he is made capable of. And as to speaking ill of man's present moral state, I presume, it will not be denied, that shame be-

3. Pp. 350, 351. [See above, Intro., Sec. 3, Miscellaneous Arguments Answered.]

longs to them that are truly sinful; and to suppose, that this is not the native character of mankind, is still but meanly begging the question. If we, as we come into the world, are truly sinful, and consequently miserable, he acts but a *friendly* part to us, who endeavors fully to discover and manifest our disease. Whereas, on the contrary, he acts an *unfriendly* part, who to his utmost hides it from us; and so, in effect does what in him lies to prevent our seeking a remedy from that, which, if not remedied in time, must bring us finally to shame and *everlasting contempt,* and end in perfect and remedyless destruction hereafter.

Another objection, which some have made against this doctrine, much like the former, is that it tends to *beget in us an ill opinion of our fellow-creatures,* and so to promote ill-nature and mutual hatred.

To which I would say, if it be truly so, that we all come sinful into the world, then our heartily *acknowledging* it, tends to promote *humility:* but our *disowning* that sin and guilt, which truly belongs to us, and endeavoring to persuade ourselves that we are vastly better than in truth we are, tends to a foolish *self-exaltation* and *pride.* And 'tis manifest, by reason, experience, and the Word of God, that pride is the chief source of all the contention, mutual hatred, and ill-will, which are so prevalent in the world; and that nothing so effectually promotes the contrary tempers and deportments, as humility. This doctrine teaches us to think no worse of others, than of ourselves: it teaches us, that we are *all,* as we are by nature, *companions* in a miserable helpless condition; which, under a revelation of the divine mercy, tends to promote mutual *compassion.* And nothing has a greater tendency to promote those amiable dispositions of mercy, forbearance, long-suffering, gentleness and forgiveness, than a sense of our own extreme unworthiness and misery, and the infinite need we have of the divine pity, forbearance and forgiveness, together with a hope of obtaining mercy. If the doctrine, which teaches that mankind are corrupt by nature, tends to promote *ill-will,* why should not Dr. Tayor's doctrine tend to it as much? For he teaches us, that the generality of mankind are very wicked, having made themselves so by their own free choice, without any necessity: which is a way of becoming wicked, that renders men truly *worthy of resentment;* but the other, not at all, even according to his own doctrine.

Another exclamation against the doctrine is, that it tends to *hinder comfort* and *joy,* and to *promote melancholy* and *gloominess* of mind.[4]

To which I shall briefly say, doubtless, supposing men are really become sinful, and so exposed to the displeasure of God, by whatever means, if they once come to have their eyes opened, and are not very stupid, the reflection on their case will tend to make them *sorrowful;* and 'tis fit, it should. Men, with whom this is the case, may well be filled with sorrow, till they are sincerely willing to forsake their sins, and turn to God. But there is nothing in this doctrine, that in the least stands in the way of comfort and exceeding joy, to such as find in their hearts a sincere willingness, wholly to forsake all sin, and give their hearts and whole selves to Christ, and comply with the gospel-method of salvation by him.

Another thing objected, is, that to make men believe that wickedness belongs to their very nature, tends to *encourage* them in *sin,* and plainly to *lead* them to all manner of iniquity; because they are taught, that sin is *natural,* and therefore *necessary* and *unavoidable.*[5]

But if this doctrine, which teaches that sin is natural to us, does also at the same time teach us, that it is *never the better,* or *less to be condemned,* for its being natural, then it don't at all encourage sin, any more than Dr. Taylor's doctrine encourages wickedness that is become *inveterate;* who teaches, that such as by custom have contracted strong habits of sin, are unable to help themselves.[6] And is it reasonable, to represent it as encouraging a man's boldly neglecting and willfully continuing in his disease, without seeking a cure, to tell him of his disease, to shew him that his disease is real and very fatal, and what he can never cure himself of; yet withal directing him to a great Physician, who is sufficient for his restoration? But for a more particular answer to what is objected against the doctrine of our natural impotence and inability, as being an encouragement to go on in sin, and a discouragement to the use of all means for our help, I must for brevity refer the reader to what has been largely written on this head in my discourse on the *Freedom of the Will.*[7]

Our author is pleased to advance another notion, among others, by way of objection against the doctrine of original sin; that if this

4. P. 231 and some other places.

5. Pp. 139 and 259.

6. See his exposition of Rom. 7, pp. 205–220. But especially in his *Paraphrase and Notes* on the epistle.

7. [See Yale ed., *1,* Pt. IV, Sec. 5 and 12.]

doctrine be true, *it would be unlawful to beget children.* He says,[8] "If natural generation be the means of unavoidably conveying all sin and wickedness into the world, it must itself be a sinful, and unlawful thing." Now, if there be any force of argument here, it lies in this proposition, whatsoever is a means or occasion of the certain infallible existence of sin and wickedness, must itself be sinful. But I imagine Dr. Taylor had not thoroughly weighed this proposition, nor considered where it could carry him. For, God's continuing in being the devil, and others that are finally given up to wickedness, will be attended, most certainly and infallibly, with an eternal series of the most hateful and horrid wickedness. But will any be guilty of such vile blasphemy, as to say, therefore God's upholding them in being is itself a sinful thing? In the same place our author says, "So far as we are generated in sin, it is a sin to be generated." (Probably he intended the active voice.) But there is no appearance of evidence in that position, any more than in this; "So far as any is upheld in existence in sin, 'tis a sin to uphold them in existence." Yea, if there were any reason in the case, it would be strongest in the latter position: for parents, as Dr. Taylor himself observes, are not the authors of the beginning of existence: whereas, God is truly the author of the continuance of existence. As 'tis the known will of God, to continue Satan and millions of others in being, though the most sure consequence is the continuance of a vast infernal world, full of everlasting hellish wickedness: so 'tis a part of the revealed will of God, that this world of mankind should be continued, and the species propagated, for his own wise and holy purposes: which will is complied with by the parents joined in lawful marriage. Whose children, though they come into the world in sin, yet are capable subjects of eternal holiness and happiness: which infinite benefits for their children, parents have great reason to encourage a hope of, in the way of giving up their children to God in faith, through a Redeemer, and bringing them up in the nurture and admonition of the Lord. I think, this may be answer enough to such a cavil.

Another objection is, that the doctrine of original sin, is *no oftener,* and *no more plainly spoken of in Scripture;* it being, if true, a very important doctrine. Dr. Taylor in many parts of his book, suggests to his readers, that there are very few texts in the whole Bible, wherein there is the least appearance of their teaching any such doctrine.

Of this I took notice before, but would here say further: that the

8. P. 145.

reader who has perused the preceding defense of this doctrine, must now be left to judge for himself, whether there be any ground for such an allegation; whether there be not texts in *sufficient* number, both in the Old Testament and New, that exhibit undeniable evidence of this great article of Christian divinity; and whether it be not a doctrine taught in the Scripture with great plainness. I think, there are few, if any, doctrines of revelation, taught more plainly and expressly. Indeed it is taught in a more and explicit manner in the New Testament, than the Old: which is not to be wondered at; it being thus with respect to all the most important doctrines of revealed religion.

But if it had been so, that this doctrine were rarely taught in Scripture; yet if we find that it is indeed a thing declared to us by God, if there be good evidence of its being held forth to us by *any* word of his, then what belongs to us, is, to *believe* his word, and *receive* the doctrine which he teaches us; and not, instead of this, to prescribe to him how often he shall speak of it, and to insist upon knowing what reasons he has for speaking of it no oftener, before we will receive what he teaches us; or that he should give us an account, why he did not speak of it so plainly as we think he ought to have done, sooner than he did. In this way of proceeding, if it be reasonable, the Sadducees of old, who denied any resurrection or future state, might have maintained their cause against Christ, when he blamed 'em for not knowing the Scriptures, nor the power of God; and for not understanding by the Scripture, that there would be a resurrection to spiritual enjoyment, and not to animal life, and sensual gratifications; and they might have insisted, that these doctrines, if true, were very important, and therefore ought to have been spoken of in the Scriptures oftener and more explicitly, and not that the church of God should be left, till that time, with only a few obscure intimations of that which so infinitely concerned them. And they might with disdain have rejected Christ's argument, by way of inference, from God's calling himself, in the books of Moses, the God of Abraham, Isaac and Jacob. For answer, they might have said, that Moses was sent on purpose to teach the people the mind and will of God; and therefore, if these doctrines were true, he ought in reason and in truth to have taught them plainly and frequently, and not have left the people to spell out so important a doctrine, only from God's saying, that he was the God of Abraham, etc.

One great *end* of the *Scripture* is, to teach the world *what manner of being* God is; about which the world, without revelation, has been so woefully in the dark: and that God is an *infinite* being, is a doctrine of great importance, and a doctrine sufficiently taught in the Scripture. But yet, it appears to me, this doctrine is not taught there, in any measure, with such explicitness and precision, as the doctrine of original sin; and the Socinians, who deny God's omnipresence and omniscience, have left 'em as much room for cavil, as the Pelagians, who deny original sin.

Dr. Taylor particularly urges, that Christ says not one word of this doctrine throughout the four gospels; which doctrine, if true, being so important, and what so nearly concerned the great work of redemption, which he came to work out (as is supposed) one would think, it should have been emphatically spoken of in every page of the gospels.[9]

In reply to this, it may be observed, that by the account given in the four gospels, Christ was continually saying *those things* which plainly implied, that all men in their original state are sinful and miserable. As, when he declared, that "they which are whole, need not a physician, but they which are sick";[1] that "he came to seek and to save that which was lost";[2] that it was necessary for all to be "born again, and to be converted, and that otherwise they could not enter into the kingdom of heaven";[3] and that all were sinners, as well as those whose blood Pilate mingled with their sacrifices, etc. and that "every one who did not repent, should perish";[4] withal directing everyone to pray to God for forgiveness of sin,[5] using our necessity of forgiveness from God, as an argument with all to forgive the injuries of their neighbors;[6] teaching, that earthly parents, though kind to their children, are in themselves evil;[7] and signifying, that things carnal and corrupt are properly the things of men;[8] warning his disciples rather to beware of men, than of wild beasts;[9] often representing the world as evil, as wicked in its works, at en-

9. Pp. 242, 243.
1. Matt. 9:12.
2. Matt. 18:11; Luke 19:10.
3. Matt. 18:3.
4. Luke 13:1–5.
5. Matt. 6:12; Luke 11:4.
6. Matt. 6:14,15 and 18:35.
7. Matt. 7:11.
8. Matt. 16:23.
9. Matt. 10:16,17.

mity with truth and holiness, and hating him;[1] yea, and teaching plainly, that all men are extremely and inexpressibly sinful, owing ten thousand talents to their divine Creditor.[2]

And whether Christ did not plainly teach Nicodemus the doctrine of original total depravity, when he came to him to know what his doctrine was, must be left to the reader to judge, from what has been already observed on John 3:1–11. And besides, Christ in the course of his preaching took the most proper method to convince men of the corruption of their nature, and to give them an effectual and practical knowledge of it, in application to themselves, in particular, by teaching and urging the holy and strict law of God, in its extent and spirituality and dreadful threatenings: which above all things, tends to search the hearts of men, and to teach them their inbred exceeding depravity: not merely as a matter of speculation, but by proper conviction of conscience; which is the only knowledge of original sin, that can avail to prepare the mind for receiving Christ's redemption; as a man's sense of his own sickness prepares him to apply in good earnest to the physician.

And as to Christ's being no more frequent and particular in mentioning and inculcating this point in a doctrinal manner, 'tis probable, one reason to be given for it, is the same that is to be given for his speaking no oftener of God's creating the world: which, though so important a doctrine, is scarce ever spoken of in any of Christ's discourses: and no wonder, seeing this was a matter which the Jews, to whom he confined his personal ministry, had all been instructed in from their forefathers, and never was called in question among them. And there is a great deal of reason, from the ancient Jewish writers, to suppose, that the doctrine of original sin had ever been allowed in the open profession of that people:[3] though they were gen-

1. John 7:7 and 8:23 and 14:17 and 15:18,19.

2. Matt. 18:21 to the end. [This major expansion of citation of texts was omitted in MS.]

3. What is found in the more ancient of the Jewish rabbis, who have wrote since the coming of Christ, is an argument of this. Many things of this sort are taken notice of by Stapferus, in his *Theologia Polemica* before mentioned. Some of these things which are there cited by him in Latin, I shall here faithfully give in English, for the sake of the English reader.

"So Menasseh, concerning human frailty (p. 129. Gen. 8:21) 'I will not any more curse the earth for man's sake; for the appetite of man is evil from his youth'; that is, from the time when he comes forth from his mother's womb. For at the same time that he sucks the breasts, he follows his lust; and while he is yet an

erally, in that corrupt time, very far from a practical conviction of it; and many notions were then prevalent, especially among the

---

infant, he is under the dominion of anger, envy, hatred and other vices to which that tender age is obnoxious. (Prov. 22:15) Solomon says, 'Foolishness is bound to the mind of a child.' Concerning which place R. Levi Ben Gersom observes thus, 'Foolishness as it were grows to him in his very beginning.' Concerning this sin, which is common and original to all men, David said (Ps. 51:7), 'Behold, I was begotten in iniquity, and in sin did my mother warm me.' Upon which place Eben-Ezra says thus: 'Behold, because of the concupiscence which is innate in the heart of man, it is said, "I am begotten in iniquity." ' And the sense is, that there is implanted in the heart of man *jetzer harang,* an evil figment, from his nativity.

"And Menasseh Ben Israel (*de Fragil.* p. 2), 'Behold, I was formed in iniquity, and in sin hath my mother warmed me.' But whether this be understood concerning the common mother, which was Eve, or whether David spake only of his own mother, he would signify, that sin is as it were natural, and inseparable in this life. For it is to be observed, that Eve conceived after the transgression was committed; and as many as were begotten afterwards, were not brought forth in a conformity to the rule of right reason, but in conformity to disorderly and lustful affections. He adds, 'One of the wise men of the Jews, namely, R. Aha, rightly observed, "David would signify, that it is impossible, even for pious men, who excel in virtue, never to commit any sin." ' Job also asserts the same thing with David (ch. 14:4) saying, 'Who will give a clean thing from an unclean? Truly not one.' Concerning which words Eben-Ezra says thus: 'The sense is the same with that, I was begotten in iniquity, because man is made out of an unclean thing.' " Stapferus, *Theolog. Polem.* Tom. 3, pp. 36, 37.

Id. Ibid. p. 132 etc. "So sal Jarchi ad gemaram, cod. schabbath (fol. 142, p. 2), 'And this is not only to be referred to sinners; because all the posterity of the first man are in like manner subjected to all the curses pronounced on him.' And Menasseh Ben Israel, in his *Preface to Human Frailty,* says, 'I had a mind to shew by what means it came to pass, that when the first father of all had lost his righteousness, his posterity are begotten liable to the same punishment with him.' And Munsterus on the gospel of Matthew cites the following words, from the book called *The Bundle of Myrrh:* 'The blessed Lord said to the first man, when he cursed him, "Thorns and thistles shall it bring forth to thee; and thou shalt eat the herb of the field." ' The thing which he means, is, that because of his sin all who should descend from him, should be wicked and perverse, like thorns and thistles; according to that word of the Lord, speaking to the prophet; 'thorns and irritators are with thee, and thou dwellest among scorpions.' And all this is from the serpent, who was the devil, Sam-mael, who emitted a mortiferous and corruptive poison into Eve, and became the cause of death to Adam himself, when he eat the fruit. Remarkable is the place quoted in *Joseph de Voisin,* against Martin Raymund, p. 471, of Master Menachem Rakanatensis, Sect. Bereschit, from Midrasch Tehillim; which is cited by Hoornbekius, against the Jews, in these words: ' 'Tis no wonder, that the sin of Adam is written and sealed with the King's ring, and to be propagated to all the following generations; because on the day that Adam was created, all things

Pharisees, which were indeed inconsistent with it. And though on account of these prejudices they might need to have this doctrine explained and applied to them, yet 'tis well known, by all acquainted

were finished; so that he stood forth the perfection and completion of the whole workmanship of the world: so when he sinned, the whole world sinned; whose sin we bear and suffer. But the matter is not thus with respect to the sins of his posterity.' " Thus far Stapferus.

Besides these, as Ainsworth on Gen. 8:2 observes, "In *Bereshith Rabba* (a Hebrew commentary on this place) a rabbi is said to be asked, 'When is the evil imagination put into man?' and he answered, 'From the hour that he is formed.' " And in Poole's *Synopsis* it is added, from Grotius, "So Rabbi Salomon interprets Gen. 8:21, 'The imagination of man's heart is evil from his youth, of its being evil from the time that he is taken out of his mother's bowels.' Eben-Ezra thus interprets Ps. 51:5. 'I was shapen in iniquity, and in sin did my mother conceive me'; that evil concupiscence is implanted in the heart from childhood, as if he were formed in it; and by 'my mother' he understands Eve, who did not bear children till she had sinned. And so Kafvenaki says, 'How shall I avoid sinning? My original is corrupt, and from thence are those sins.' So Menasseh Ben Israel, from this place (Ps. 51:5) concludes, that not only David, but all mankind, ever since sin was introduced into the world, do sin from their original. To this purpose is the answer of Rabbi Hakkadosch, which there is an account of in the Talmud. 'From what time does concupiscence rule over man? From the very moment of his first formation, or from his nativity?' Ans. 'From his formation.' " Poole's *Synopsis* in loc.

On these things I observe, there is the greatest reason to suppose, that these old rabbis of the Jewish nation, who gave such heed to the tradition of the elders, would never have received this doctrine of original sin, had it not been delivered down to 'em from their forefathers. For it is a doctrine very disagreeable to those practical principles and notions, wherein the religion of the unbelieving Jews most fundamentally differs from the religion maintained among Christians: particularly their notion of justification by their own righteousness, and privileges as the children of Abraham, etc. without standing in need of any satisfaction, by the sufferings of the Messiah. On which account the modern Jews do now universally reject the doctrine of original sin, and corruption of nature; as Stapferus observes. And it is not likely, that the ancient Jews, if no such doctrine had been received by tradition from the fathers, would have taken it up from the Christians, whom they had in such great contempt and enmity; especially as it is a doctrine so peculiarly agreeable to the Christian notion of the spiritual salvation of Jesus, and so contrary to their carnal notions of the Messiah, and of his salvation and kingdom, and so contrary to their opinion of themselves; and a doctrine, which men in general are so apt to be prejudiced against. And besides, these rabbis do expressly refer to the opinion of their forefathers; as R. Menasseh says, "According to the opinion of the ancients, none are subject to death, but those which have sinned: for where there is no sin, there is no death." Stapferus, Tome III, pp. 37, 38.

But we have more direct evidence, that the doctrine of original sin was truly a received doctrine amongst the ancient Jews, even before the coming of Christ.

with their Bibles, that Christ, for wise reasons, spake more sparingly and obscurely of several of the most important doctrines of revealed religion, relating to the necessity, grounds, nature and way of his redemption, and the method of the justification of sinners, while he lived here in the flesh; and left these doctrines to be more plainly and fully opened and inculcated by the Holy Spirit, after his ascension.

But if after all, Christ did not speak of this doctrine often enough to suit Dr. Taylor, he might be asked, why he supposes Christ did no oftener, and no more plainly teach some of his (Dr. Taylor's) doctrines, which he so much insists on? As, that temporal death comes

---

This appears by ancient Jewish writings, which were written before Christ; as in the Apocrypha (II Esdras 3:21), "For the first Adam, having a wicked heart, transgressed, and was overcome: and so be all they that be born of him. Thus infirmity was made permanent; and the law also in the heart of the people, with the malignity of the root; so that the good departed away, and the evil abode still." (II Esdras 4:30), "For the grain of evil seed hath been sown in the heart of Adam, from the beginning; and how much ungodliness hath it brought forth unto this time? And how much shall it yet bring forth, till the time of threshing shall come?" (and ch. 7:46), "It had been better, not to have given the earth to Adam; or else, when it was given, to have restrained him from sinning: for what profit is it, for man now in this present time, to live in heaviness, and after death, to look for punishment? O thou Adam, what hast thou done! For though it was thou that sinned, thou art not fallen alone, but we all that come of thee." And we read (Ecclus. 25:24), "Of the woman came the beginning of sin, and through her we all die."

As this doctrine of original corruption was constantly maintained in the church of God from the beginning; so from thence, in all probability, as well as from the evidence of it in universal experience, it was, that the wiser heathen maintained the like doctrine. Particularly Plato, that great philosopher, so distinguished for his veneration of ancient traditions, and diligent inquiries after them. Gale, in his *Court of the Gentiles,* observes as follows: "Plato says (Gorg. Fol. 493), 'I have heard from the wise men, that we are now dead, and that the body is but our sepulchre.' And in his *Timaeus Locrus* (Fol. 103) he says, 'The cause of vitiosity is from our parents, and first principles, rather than from ourselves. So that we never relinquish those actions, which lead us to follow these primitive blemishes of our first parents.' . . . Plato mentions the corruption of the will, and seems to disown any free-will to true good; albeit he allows some *εὐφυ'ία*, or natural dispositions, to civil good, in some great heroes. . . . Socrates asserted the corruption of human nature, or *κακὸν 'ἐμφυτον*. . . . Grotius affirms, that the philosophers acknowledged, it was connatural to men, to sin."

Seneca (*Benef.* 5:14) says, "Wickedness has not its first beginning in wicked practice; though by that it is first exercised and made manifest." And Plutarch (*de Sera Vindicta*) says, "Man does not first become wicked, when he first manion all mankind by Adam; and that it comes on them by him, not as a punishment or calamity, but as a great favor, being made a rich benefit, and a fruit of God's abundant grace, by Christ's redemption, who came into the world as a second Adam for this end. Surely, if this were so, it was of vast importance, that it should be known to the church of God in all ages, who saw death reigning over infants, as well as others. If infants were indeed perfectly innocent, was it not needful, that the design of that which was such a melancholy and awful dispensation towards so many millions of innocent creatures, should be known, in order to prevent the worst thoughts of God from arising in the minds of the constant spectators of so mysterious and gloomy a dispensation? But why then such a total silence about it, for four thousand years together, and not one word of it in all the Old Testament; nor one word of it in all the four Gospels; and indeed not one word of it in the whole Bible, but only as forced and wrung out by Dr. Taylor's arts of criticism and deduction, against the plainest and strongest evidence!

As to the arguments made use of by many late writers, from the universal moral sense, and the reasons they offer from experience, and observation of the nature of mankind, to shew that we are born into the world with principles of virtue; with a natural prevailing relish, approbation, and love of righteousness, truth, and goodness, and of whatever tends to the public welfare; with a prevailing natural disposition to dislike, to resent and condemn what is selfish, unjust, and immoral; a native bent in mankind to mutual benevolence, tender compassion, etc. those who have had such objections against the doctrine of original sin, thrown in their way, and desire to see them particularly considered, I ask leave to refer them to a *Treatise on the Nature of True Virtue,* lying by me prepared for the press, which may ere long be exhibited to public view.[4]

---

fests himself so: but he hath wickedness from the beginning; and he shews it as soon as he finds opportunity and ability. As men rightly judge, that the sting is not first engendered in scorpions when they strike, or the poison in vipers when they bite" (Poole's *Synopsis* on Gen. 8:21). To which may be subjoined what Juvenal says,

> . . . Ad mores natura recurrit
> damnatus, fixa et mutari necsia.

Englished, thus, in prose: Nature, a thing fixed and not knowing how to change, returns to its wicked manners. (Watts, *Ruin and Recovery*)
[This footnote is omitted from the MS.]

4. [See above, Intro., Sec. 2, p. 22, n. 2.]

CONCLUSION

On the whole, I observe, there are some *other* things, besides arguments, in Dr. Taylor's book, which are calculated to influence the minds, and bias the judgments of some sorts of readers. Here, not to insist on the taking profession he makes, in many places, of sincerity, humility, meekness, modesty, charity, etc. in his searching after truth; and freely proposing his thoughts, with the reasons of them, to others; [1] nor on his magisterial assurance, appearing on many occasions, and the high contempt he sometimes expresses of the opinions and arguments of very excellent divines and fathers in the church of God, who have thought differently from him,[2] both of which things, it's not unlikely, may have a degree of influence on some of his readers. (However, that they may have only their just influence, these things might properly be compared together, and set in contrast, one with the other) [3]—I say, not to dwell on these matters, I would take some notice of another thing, observable in the writings of Dr. Taylor and many of the late opposers of the more peculiar doctrines of Christianity, tending (especially with juvenile and unwary readers) not a little to abate the force, and prevent the due effect, of the clearest Scripture evidences, in favor of those important doctrines; and particularly to make void the arguments taken from the writings of the apostle Paul, in which those doctrines are more plainly and fully revealed, than in any other part of the Bible. What I mean, is this: these gentlemen express a high opinion of this Apostle, and that very justly, for his eminent genius, his admirable sagacity, strong powers of reasoning, acquired learning, etc. They speak of him as a writer—of masterly address, of extensive reach, and deep design, everywhere in his epistles, almost in every word he says. This looks exceeding *specious:* it carries a plausible appearance of Christian zeal, and attachment to the holy Scriptures,

1. See his *Preface* and pp. 6, 237, 265, 267, 451.
2. Pp. 110, 125, 150, 151, 159, 161, 183, 188, 353.
3. [See above, Intro., Sec. 5, pp. 23.]

in such a testimony of high veneration for that great Apostle, who was not only the principal instrument of propagating Christianity, but with his own hand wrote so considerable a part of the New Testament. And I am far from determining, with respect at least to some of these writers, that they are not sincere in their declarations, or that all is mere artifice, only to make way for the reception of their own peculiar sentiments. However, it tends greatly to subserve such a purpose; as much as if it were designedly contrived, with the utmost sublety, for that end. Hereby their incautious readers are prepared the more easily to be drawn into a belief, that they, and others in their way of thinking, have not rightly understood many of those things in this Apostle's writings, which before seemed very plain to them; and they are also prepared, by a prepossession in favor of these *new writers,* to entertain a favorable thought of the *interpretations* put by them upon the words and phrases of this Apostle; and to admit in many passages a meaning which before lay entirely out of sight; quite foreign to all that in the view of a common reader seems to be their obvious sense; and most remote from the expositions agreed in by those which used to be esteemed the greatest divines, and best commentators. For they must know, that this Apostle being a man of no vulgar understanding, it's nothing strange if his meaning lies very deep; and no wonder then, if the superficial discerning and observation of vulgar Christians, or indeed of the herd of common divines, such as the Westminster Assembly etc. falls vastly short of the Apostle's reach, and frequently don't enter into the true spirit and design of Paul's epistles. They must understand, that the first reformers, and preachers and expositors in general, both before and since the Reformation, for fifteen or sixteen hundred years past, were too *unlearned* and *shortsighted,* to be capable of penetrating into the sense, or fit to undertake the making comments on the writings of so great a man as this Apostle; or else had dwelt in a cave of *bigotry* and *superstition,* too gloomy to allow 'em to use their own understandings with freedom, in reading the Scripture. But at the same time, it must be understood, that there is risen up, now at length in this happy age of light and liberty, a set of men, of a more free and generous turn of mind, a more inquisitive genius, and better discernment. By such insinuations, they seek advantage to their cause; and thus the most unreasonable and extravagant interpretations of Scripture are palliated and recommended: so that, if the simple reader is not very much on his guard, if he don't clearly see with his own eyes, or has too much indolence, or too little leisure, thoroughly to examine for himself (as few, alas, are willing to be at the pains of acquainting themselves so thoroughly with the Apostle's writings, and of comparing one part of them with another, so as to be fully able to judge of these gentlemen's glosses and pretenses) in this case, he is in danger of being imposed on with delusive appearances; as he is prepared by this fair pretext of exalting the sagacity of the Apostle, and by a parade of learning, criticism, exact version, penetration into the true scope, and discerning of wonderful connections, together with the airs these writers assume of dictatorial peremptoriness, and contempt of old opinions and old expositions, I say, such an one is by these things prepared to swallow strange doctrine, as trusting to the superior abilities of these modern interpreters.[4]

But I humbly conceive, their interpretations, particularly of the apostle Paul's writings, though in some things ingenious, yet in many things concerning these great articles of religion, are extremely absurd, and demonstrably disagreeable, in the highest degree, to his real design, to the language he commonly uses, and to the doctrines currently taught in his epistles. Their criticisms, when examined, appear far more subtle, than solid; and it seems as if nothing can possibly be strong enough, nothing perspicuous enough, in any composure whatever, to stand before such liberties as these writers indulge. The plainest and most nervous discourse is analysed and criticized, till it dissolves into nothing, or till it becomes a thing of little significance; the holy Scripture is subtilized into a mere mist;

4. [MS continues: "I would not be understood in this as tho I suppose this is in all those writers is [sic] nothing but design'd artifice in them to deceive their readers and to make others believe what they don't believe themselves. I doubt not but that many of them sincerely believe their opinions to be true and that the interpretation of the apostle's writings are agreeable to the real design of the apostle and also that they sincerely believe that the generality of doctrine have been mistaken and had not sense enough to discern the true meaning of the apostle or too much bigotry to enquire and that they sincerely believe that they themselves are men of vastly superior discerning and of [sic] more free and generous in their reasonings and enquiries. But nevertheless 'tis possible that there may be that which may be called artifice in what has been observed in them. It is undoubtedly true that men often under great prejudices are exceeding artful and cunning to deceive themselves as well as others. But however that be this is beyond doubt that the things which have been spoken of have the same effect on many of their readers to decoy and deceive them as much as if more artfully contrived to that end" (p. 224).]

or made to evaporate into a thin cloud, that easily puts on any shape, and is moved in any direction, with a puff of wind, just as the manager pleases. 'Tis not in the nature and power of language, to afford sufficient defense against such an art, so abused; as I imagine, a due consideration of some things I have had occasion in the preceding discourse to observe, may abundantly convince us.

But this, with the rest of what I have offered on this subject of original sin, must be left to every candid reader to judge of, for himself; and the success of the whole must now be left with God, who knows what is agreeable to his own mind, and is able to make his own truths prevail; however mysterious they may seem to the poor, partial, narrow and extremely imperfect views of mortals, while looking through a cloudy and delusory medium; and however disagreeable they may be to the innumerable prejudices of men's hearts: and who has promised, that the Gospel of Christ, such as is really his, shall finally be victorious; and has assured us, that the Word which goeth out of this mouth, "shall not return to him void, but shall accomplish that which he pleaseth and shall prosper in the thing whereto he sends it." Let God arise, and plead his own cause, and glorify his own great name. AMEN [5]

5. [This paragraph is omitted from the MS.]

INDEX